ETHNOGRAPHIC ATLAS OF INDIAN TRIBES

Editor
Dr. Prakash Chandra Mehta

D P H

DISCOVERY PUBLISHING HOUSE
NEW DELHI-110002

First Published-2004

ISBN 81-7141-852-X

© Editor

Published by
DISCOVERY PUBLISHING HOUSE
4831/24, Ansari Road, Prahlad Street,
Darya Ganj, New Delhi-110002 (India)
Phone: 23279245 • Fax: 91-11-23253475
E-mail:dphtemp@indiatimes.com

Printed at:

DEDICATED
TO
FATHER
Late Sh. K.L. Mehta

(8 January 1924 to 23 March 2002)

Preface

The tribals are an intrinsic part of our national life with their rich-cultural heritage. They have been contributing a lot to the complex amalgam. The tribals, mostly reside in the sparsely populated parts of hills and forests of sub-himalayas and North-eastern regions in the mountain belt of Central India between Narmada and Godavari rivers and in the Southern parts of the western Ghats extending fom Wynad to Kanyakumari. They are primitive and till today, prefer isolation. So they have limited contacts with other societies. The habit of isolation helps them to preserve their age old traditional traits and beliefs to a large extent.

Tribals in India are classified into four racial groups viz. Negrito, Proto-Australoid, Mongoloid and Nordic. Gonds, Bhils, Orons, Mundas and Santhals belong to Proto-Australoid group. The tribaes of North East viz. Garo, Khasi, Mizo, Naga, etc. having Mongoloid feature, while Todas of Nilgiri Hills are of Nordic racical group.

Tribals can be seen throughout the earth. In each part they are, called by the person by different names viz, Jippsy, Aboriginals, Adivasi's and other synonymous names. Every tribal group or race have their own identity & cultural traits. In this way each tribal group can be distinguished with their own existance or identity. The heighest concentration of tribals can be seen in Africa and India stands second. In India, tribals lives on 1/5 part (19 per cent) of the country and having more than 500 different groups. They speak over 150 languages and about 225 subsidiary languages.

Keeping in view the importance of ethnograpgy of every tribal group, there is a gap in the literature. This work was a challanging task for me to collect ethongraphy of every tribal group. This was a voluminious work, so I have decided to work on major tribal groups residing in different parts of the country.

In this volume in introductory chapter, I have tried to explore all essential information regarding every tribal group of the country along with population and special features. In other chapters, the ethnography of all major tribal groups have been discussed by the learned scholars.

I hope this volume would be mile-stone for the well wishers of tribals and learned scholars. I am greatful to friends who have encourged me in this onerous task. I am indebted to Sh. Dinesh Taldar M/s Shiva Publishers' Distributors, Udaipur (Rajasthan) for inspiration, Sh. Tilak Vasan of M/s Discovery Publishing House, New Delhi for efficient publication. I am also thankful to Dr. S.R. Bhakar, Associate Professor, MPUAT, Udaipur for association regarding the publication. I am also thanful to members of my family for their inspiration and association.

Udaipur (Rajasthan)   **Dr. Prakash Chandra Mehta**

List of Contributors

1. **Dr. A. Chandrasekar**
   Anthropoloical Survey of India
   2963, V.V. Mohalla, Mysore (Karnataka)-570002

2. **Dr. Alok Chantia**, Lecturer
   Depatment of Anthropology, Tehri Campus,
   H.N.B. Univesity, Srinagar - Garhwal,
   Srinagar - 246174, 124, Shekheiya Pura
   Bahraich (U.P.) - 271801

3. **Dr. Atul Chandra Bhowmick**, Professor
   Department of Museology, University of Calcutta,
   I, Reformatory Street, Kolkata (W.B.) - 700027

4. **Dr. A.K. Kapoor**, Professor
   Department of Anthropology, University of Delhi,
   Delhi - 110007

5. **Dr. A.K. Sinha**, Reader
   Department of Anthopology, Punjab Univesity,
   Chandigarh (Punjab) - 160014

6. **Dr. B.G. Banerjee,** Professor
   Department of Anthropology, Punjab University,
   Chandigarh (Punjab) - 160014

7. **Dr. (Mrs.) Bindu Ramchandran**
   Department of Anthropology, Kumau University, Thalassery
   Campus, P.O. Palayad - 670661,
   Kunnur District - Kerala

8. **Dr. D.B. Giri**, Research Associate (cul.)
   Anthropological Survey of India, Western Circle,
   16, Madhuban, Udaipur (Rajasthan) - 313001

9. **Dr. D.B. Mandal**, Superintending Anthropologist,
   Anthropoloical Survey of India, Western Circle,
   16, Madhuban, Udaipur (Rajasthan) - 313001

10. **D.K. Dutta**, D.R.O.
    West Siang District, Along (Arunachal Pradessh)

11. **Dr. H.M. Maralusiddaiah Patel**
    Anthropoloiccal Survey of India (Karnataka)
    2963, V.B. Mohalla, Mysore (Kanataka) - 570002
12. **Dr. Mohmed Ajeej Mohidden**
    Anthropological Survey of India, CRC, Nagpur
13. **Dr. Nilanjan Khatua**
    Indira Gandhi Rashtriya Manav Sangrahalaya,
    Shamla Hills, Bhopal (M.P.) - 462013
14. **Dr. Prakash Chandra Mehta**
    45, Ravindranagar, Udaipur (Rajasthan), 313003
15. **Pramod Mishra**, ICSSR Doctoral Fellow,
    1151, Shora Kothi, Sabji Mandi, Delhi - 110007
    (Departent of Anthropology, University of Delhi,
    Delhi - 110007)
16. **Dr. Pratibha Kumari**, Research Associate (cul)
    Anthropological Survey of India,
    Ranchi (Jharkhand)
17. **Dr. P.K. Bhowmick**, Retd. Professor of Anthropology,
    University of Calcutta, 727 - lake town,
    Calcutta (Kolkata - W.B.) - 700809
18. **P.K. Patra**
    Department of Anthropology, University of Delhi,
    Delhi - 110007
19. **Dr. Rajesh Kumar Chaudhary**, Lecturer
    Department of Anthropology,
    Godda College, Godda (Bihar) - 814134
20. **Rajesh Khanna**
    Department of Anthropology,
    University of Delhi, Delhi - 110007
21. **Ramesh Prasad Mohanty**
    Nabakrushna Choudhary Centre for Development Studies,
    Orissa, Bhubaneswar - 751013
22. **Mrs. Sonu Mehta**, Guest faculty
    19, Mahaveer Colony, Hiran Magri, Sector - 4,
    Udaipur (Rajasthan) - 313002
    Department of Clothing and Textile, College of Home
    Science, MPUAT, Udaipur (Rajasthan) - 313001

Contents

Prologue	Dr. Prakash Chandra Mehta	9
ADIYAN	Dr. Bindu Ramchandran	159
AGARIA	Dr. Prakash Chandra Mehta	168
AKA	Dr. Prakash Chandra Mehta	171
BHILS - I	Mrs Sonu Mehta	174
BHILS - II	Dr. D.B. Mandal	199
BIRHOR - I	Dr. Pratibha Kumari	209
BIRHOR - II	A.K. Sinha & B.G. Banerjee	220
BHOTIA	Dr. Alok Chantia	235
BOKAR	Dr. Prakash Chandra Mehta	240
BOMDO	Dr. Prakash Chandra Mehta	240
BORI	Dr. Prakash Chandra Mehta	240
BONDA	Ramesh Chandra Mohanty	241
BOT	Dr. Prakash Chandra Mehta	249
BUGUN	Dr. Prakash Chandra Mehta	255
DAMOR	Dr. Prakash Chandra Mehta	256
JUANGAS - I	Ramesh Prasad Mohanty	260
JUANGAS - II	B.D. Giri	267
KADU KURUBA	Dr. H.M. Maralusiddaiah Patel & Dr. A. Chandrasekar	279
KOYA	Dr. A.K. Kapoor, R. Khanna, P. Mishra & P.K. Patra	285
KAMARS	Dr. Nilanjan Khatua	296
KINNAURI	Rajesh Khanna and A.K. Kapoor	307
KORA	Rajesh Kumar Chaudhary	316
KORAGA	Dr. H.M. Maralusiddaiah Patel	321
MALE KUDIA	Dr. H.M. Maralusiddaiah Patel	327

SUDUGADU SIDDHA	Dr. H.M. Maralusiddaiah Patel	331
LODHA	Dr. P.K. Bhowmick	335
MEMBAS	Dr. D.K. Dutta	346
NAIKAS	Dr. Md. Ajeej Mohideen	355
SAHARIA	Promod Mishra & Dr. A.K. Kapoor	362
SANTHAL	Dr. Atul Chandra Bhowmick	371

PROLOGUE

Dr. Prakash Chandra Mehta

The tribals are an intrinsic part of our national life and with their rich cultural heritage. They have been contributing a lot to the complex amalgam. The tribals settled down in India in pre-historic times, inhabiting mostly in the sparsely populated parts of hills and forests of sub-Himalayan and North-eastern regions in the mountain belt of central India between, Narmada and Godavari rivers, and in the southern parts of the Western Ghats extending from wynad to Kanyakumari.

The tribals are primitive and prefer living in isolation i.e. in dense forests or remote areas which are generally cut-off from civilised area. Hence, tribals have limited contact with other societies. The habit of isolation helps them to preserve their social customs, traditions and beliefs to a large extent. The territorial distribution of tribes overlaps the political boundaries of the state and territory.

Tribals in India are classified into four racial groups viz. Negrito, Proto-Australoid, Mongoloid and Nordic. Gonds, Bhils, oraons, Mundas and Santhals belong to Proto-Austroloid group. The tribes of North-East viz. Garo, Khasi, Mizo, Naga etc. having mongoloid feature. Todas of Nilgiri Hills are of Nordic racial group. Their very existence has dependend during centuries on forest and mountains. The tigrours of climate do not compel them from their nests i.e. home lands nor obliged their way of life.

The tribal majority areas in the country are broadly divided in three categories, viz. (i) Predominantly tribal states/union territories (ii) scheduled area, and (iii) Non-scheduled areas in the states. All the tribal-majority states and union territories are placed in a special category for the allocation of funds. The development and administration of tribal areas is accepted as a special responsibility of the Central Government even though they are integral parts of the concerned states.

According to 1951 census, the scheduled tribes population in India was 19,147,054 which constituted 5.3% of the total population of the country. After the scheduled tribes lists modification order, 1956 tribal population rose to 22,511,845 or 6.23%. This increase of 34 lakhs in population of tribals was due to inclusion of certain groups. According to

1961 census, the tribal population was 29,879,249 i.e. 6.86% of the total population of the country. As per 1971 census the scheduled tribe population was 3.64 millions, while the total population was 54.8 million. This constitute 6.94% of the total population. The above census figures indicate the regular progressive increase in tribal population. The scheduled tribe list was again amended in 1976 vide GOI order No. 108 of 18th Sept.,1976.

According to 1981 census 51,628,638 persons were enumerated in the country excluding Assam where the census was not held due to unavoidable conditions. Out of the total population scheduled tribes constitute 26,038,535 males and 25,590,103 females. The scheduled tribe population constitute only 7.76% of the total population of the country.

According to 1991 census the tribal population of India constitute 67,758,380 persons (62,751,026 rural and 50,007,354) i.e. 8.01 per cent of the total population is given in appendix, which reveals that the tribals were enumerated throughout the country, except in the state of Haryana, Jammu & Kashmir, Punjab, Chandigarh, Delhi and Pondicherry where the tribals are not scheduled, the North eastern region is highly concentrated with tribals.

Tribals can be seen throughout the earth. In each part they are called by the persons by different names viz. Jippsy, Aboriginals, Adivasi's and other synonymous names. The tribals have their own identity, cultural traits even than every tribal group have their own identity. In this way each tribal group can be distinguished their own existence or identity. The isolation problem have deprived them by the developed part of the nations. The isolation problem is not in India, but it can been seen throughout the world. The highest concentration of tribals can be seen in Africa and second stands India. In India on 1/5 part (19 per cent) of the country and having more than 500 different groups. They speak over 150 languages and about 225 subsidiary languages.

Definition

The so called "Tribals" of India are the indigenous people of the land, in the sense that they have been long settled in different parts of the country before the Aryan speaking people penetrated India to settle down first in Kabul and Indus valleys and then within a millennium and a half, to spread out over large parts of the country along the plains and river

Prologue

valleys. At a much later stage of history they here came to this land as civilized foreigners in small numbers like the Achaemenians, the Hellenistic, Greeks, the Parthans and the Romans, nomadic-pastoral tribes in very large numbers and a wave after wave from the steppes of central Asia and this over a period of more than a millennium and a half, beginning with the sakas and closing with the trunks and Mongols and finally, again in several waves, rural and semi-agricultural. Tibeto-Burmano from across the north and north-eastern borders of the country. In between the later, there were small influxes from time to time of the Arabs, Iranians and Abysinians from East Africa and Tibeto-Burmans from Burma and Arkan region.

There is linguistic and archaeological evidence to suggest that pro-Aryan indigenous 'Janas' were settled originally on the plains and rivers and velleys of the land. But they were not all in the same stage of development. Many of there are still in the food gathering economy, not knowing, the use of metal; and perhaps on the thresh-hold of a real food producing economy. They seem to have lived in isolated settlements, in shelters and various levels of constructional activities, some are even in natural or dug-out shelters. They spoke a variety of languages. Their religion consisted in the belief in and practices called 'Primitive religion' and they seem to have lived in closed, well-xnit social units presided over a headman or chief and controlled by a group of elders. In a word, these indigenous so called "tribes" were just slowly but certainly obliged to move bit by bit, to farther and farther areas until they came to find their refuge in relatively more inaccessible regions of forests and hills, large mountain slopes. The process went on centuries and millennia, in a very slow and steady, but in a very relentless manner very slow and steady, but very relentless manner, until very recent times since when state legislation has been trying to put a brake to it because of a rising consciousness among the people themselves.[1]

The term "tribe" refers to cultural and historical concept. It is used in terms of the folk urban continuum along which different groups are classified, given a certain order of material culture and a stage of technological growth and classified as tribes.

The defination of "tribe" as it has emerged that "a social group usually with a definite area, dialect, cultural homogeneity and unifying social organisation having several subgroups, such as clams or sibs".

The term 'tribe' have been defined by various writers in their own specific views. Anthropologists, sociologists, economists and administrators have different approach to the problem of defining the term.

According to oxford Dictionary "tribe is a group of people in primitive or barbarous stage of development acknowledging the authority of a chief and usually regarding themselves as having a common ancestor".

The tribe is "a social group of simple kind, the members of which speak a common dilect, have a single government, act together for common purposes, and have a common name, a contiguous territory, a relatively uniform culture or way of life and a tradition of common descent"[2]

A.B. Bardhan defines the tribe as a "course of socio-cultural entity at a definate historical stage of development. It is a single, endogamous community, with a cultural and psychological make up going back into a distinct historical past"[3]

D.N. Majumbar defines the tribe as "a collection of families or common groups bearing a common name, the members of which occupy the same territory, speak the same language and observe certain taboos, regarding marriage, profession, or occupation and have developed a well assured system of reciprocity and mutuality of obligations"[4]

Kamaladevi Chatopadhyaya[5] explained the term tribe as " a tribe ordinarily has an ancestor or a patron deity. The families or groups composing the larger units are linked through religious, social and socio-economic functions.

Verrier Elwin[6] further explained this term as" but let me turn to the history of the term and concept 'tribe'. Derived from a Latin root, the middle English term ."tribuz' meaning the three divisions into which the early Romans were grouped, came to evolve into the modern English 'tribe'. With the Romans, the 'tribe' was a political division which Greeks seem to have equated it some what with their 'fraternities' at times, with the geographical divisions at others. In Irish history, however, the term meant families or communities of persons having the same surname. In certain other areas of western world and certain period of history, it stood for a division of territory allotted to a family or community.

Similarly various authors have described the tribes by different

Prologue

nomenclature. Dr. Ghurye named them Backward Hindus', Dr. Das and Das rename them as 'Submerged humanity', few named them Aborigionals, Primitive tribe, Adivasi, Vanyajati, Vanabasi, Adimjati, Pahari etc. In the ancient literature of India the veds, the Puranas, the Ramayana, the Mahabharta the tribals appeared as Nishad, Sabarars, Kiratas and Dasyns. They are believed to be the earlier among the present inhabitants of the country.

In constitution the term 'Tribe' have not been defined clearly any where. Only the term 'scheduled tribe' explained as "the tribe or the tribal communities or parts of or groups within tribes or tribal communities" which the president may specify by public notification (article, 342). As these groups are presumed to form the oldest ethonological sector of the people.

The term 'Adivasi' (Adi=original and 'vasi'= inhabitant) has become current among certain people. The International Labour Organisation has classified such people as "indigenous". According to I.L.O. Convention 107 (1957) the aboriginals or tribals have been defined as the tribals or semi-tribals groups of the Independent countries deprived socially or economically and having their own customs, traditions and traits or they have their own special customary laws/conventions".

Hence in this way the term "tribe" have been clearly defined by various social scientists and eminent Anthropologists and identified as a separate group of the persons having their own identity and cultural traits. The tribals have their own mode of management to control their group or society. The customary laws of tribals are still unwritten, but they obey them strictly.

The difficulty in setting out formal criteria for defining the tribe arises from the fact that tribes in India are and have been for some decades in transition. All of them live in various stages of cultural and economic conditions. Because of this transitory process of evolution no scientific and standard defination has so far been evolved.

The concept of 'scheduled tribe' has now become an objective one. The term 'scheduled tribe' as conceived by administrators is different from that of anthropologists and sociologists. Today they recognize a tribe by the list of scheduled tribes declared by the Govt. For the non-tribes a tribe does not exist as a single cultural entity.

The idea behind defining the term tribe is to evolve ways and means of gradual adjustment of the tribal population with the changing conditions and slow integration in the national mainstream. They have suffered from social injustice and economical constraints too long.

Tribal Development

The term development has been used in a wider sense, it is a slow process of civilization. The purpose of development is to provide increasing opportunities to all the people for a better life. It is essential to bring about more equitable distribution of income and wealth for promoting social justice and efficiency of production, to provide a greater variety of facilities like education, health services, nutrition, housing etc.

The aims of development were spelled out in 1970's in the Preamble of the International Development Strategy for the second United Nations Development Decade.

According to I.L.O. development involves 'humans' as distinct form material product. It is defined as a process which involves improvement in the quality of life of the weaker sections and a greater participation and involvement of the masses in the process of decision making in the economic, social, political and cultural life of a society. In his book Cruel choice, Denis Goulet[7] has said, "Development is not a cluster of benefits given to the people in need; it is rather a process by which a populace acquires a greater mastery over its own destiny" Schumpeter[8] defined development as only such changes in economic life as are not forced upon it from without, but arise by its own initiative from within".

According to Dedley seers[9] "development means creating conditions for the realisation of human potential".

Development is an elusive concept and involves mobilization of natural resources, augmentation of trained manpower, capital and technical know-how and their utilisation for attainment of constantly multiplying national goals, higher living standards and the change over from a traditional to a modern society. The essence of development is generally perceived as industrialisation and modernisation. Development is a multi-dimensional and multilinear process."

"Development is usually conceived as an aspect of change that is desirable, broadly predicated or planned and administered or at least influenced by governmental action. Thus the concept of development consists of (a) an aspect of change (b) a plan or prediction, and (c) involvement of the government for the achievements of that planned or predicted goal. The term development is also used for the process of allowing and encouraging people to meet their own aspirations[10].

Development and modernization are not interchangeable terms as development results in a community where as modernization is a particular case of development[11].

The main aim of development is to increase national as well as per capita income and to raise the standard of living of the people and secure justice, freedom, equality and security for them in society. The focus of development is now increasingly on (a) equitable distribution of wealth and income (b) full utilization of manpower; (c) better utilization of natural resources; and (d) protection of human environment, etc.[12]

Hence, development means change plus growth, i.e. it includes growth, modernization, increase in social facilities, etc.

Concepts of Economic Development

Economic development is the process of securing a higher level of productivity in all the sectors as the economy which primarily depends upon the technological advances the community is able to make[13].

Economic growth with social justice is one of the most important goal of developing economy like ours. Harmonious growth of intersectoral income, trade and income distribution are some of the pre-requisites of accelerated economic development. In the process of growth, agriculture and industry depend on each other for raw materials and market, besides, it is often argued that declining output ratio of agriculture and industry increases the net domestic product and affects the income distribution pattern in the economy[14]. Several writers have commended the importance of an "agricultural surplus" for the economic growth or economic development. The tribals have poor-agricultural surplus, in this way they suffer economically.

Conceptually "development is the faithful limitation of the developed" holds John Kenneth Galbraith (and others) recognises three types of economic development[15].
1. Symbolic modernization
2. Maximized economic growth and
3. Selective growth.

1. Symbolic Modernization

Symbolic modernization is a deceptive expression of economic development because the well being of the people is not much advanced by symbolic modernization and it may be retarded for those who must pay the bill. In the past, moreover, much symbolic modernization has been a strategy for making the people into believe that some thing was being done. A poor country like India where more than three fourth of the population lives below the poverty line Symbolic modernization by constructing Asia's best "Ashoka Hotel" as public undertaking is certainly meaningless to a commoner in the street.

2. Maximized Economic Growth

Test of increased income and product (i.e. through obtaining maximized economic growth) obviously has much to commend it and stands up to objective test of performance.

3. Selective Growth

At back of much development planning has been the belief that benefits must accure as a matter of priority to the more needy sector of population. Resources so painfully conscripted from the people, must return benefit to the same people. This politically salutary principle of Selective Growth has, however, led to diverse and even contradictory conclusions as its application. Planned proportionate development of the economy is an objective economic low of socialism.

The common factor in all these three types of economic development is a change from a given situation to attain a better situation. There are a number of norms to measure these changes. Also there are a number of perspectives to look at these changes, for example, the social change, the economic change, the political change, the technological change etc. Thus, the change factor is a basic component of development, Improvement in one situation is normative of desirable change.

The democratic approach to economic planning and implementation leads to equitable distribution of economic resources. One of the directive principles of economic planning in India has its in Socialistic economic mode, which perhaps is more meaningful to achieving the political goal of making it impossible. This is possible by Striving to attain the ideal of democratic socialism. The chances of attaining the orderly process of development are closely related to the effectiveness of measures to distribute the gains of development equitably or at least reasonably equitably among the income groups, regions and sectors.

George Dalton[16] has vividly analysed the different dimensions of the problem of development. What economists call development, political scientists call "Modernization", Sociologists, role differentiation; and anthropologists "Cultural change". These accompanying political and social changes make economic development processes even more complicated. In tribal regions, mostly comprising non-market economy, it is difficult to apply the tools of measurement of economic development as most of them are not relevant.

Characteristics of Tribals Economy

The socio-economic structure in tribal communities is markedly different from that of the non-tribals or advanced groups of people. They have a very simple technology which fits well with their ecological surroundings and conservative outlook. Moreover, their economy can be said to be subsistence type, they practice different types of occupations to sustain themselves and live on "Marginal economy". We find the tribals of India belonging to different economic stages, from food gathering to industrial labour, which present their overlapping economic stages in the border frame work of the stage economy. And the last important point to be emphasized is that a tribe is usually considered an economically independent group of people having their own specific economy and thus having a living pattern of labour, division of labour and specialization, gift and ceremonial exchange, trade and barter, credit and value, wealth, consumption norms, capital formation, land tenure and good tangible and intangible economic status, all these have their own specially which identified the tribal economy in the border set-up of Indian economy[17].

The first and foremost characteristics of the tribal economy is the close relationship between their economic life and the natural environment or habitat, which is, in general, the forest. Exception to this are the tribals inhabiting their own islands. The Bhils of western India depend on Forest for Mahua and biri (Tendu) leaves (Tandu Patta) to a great extent[18]

Tribal - A Concept of Forest Ecosystem

The linkage between the tribal and forests is traditional. Tribals are economically and ecologically inseparable from forests. Be it food, fodder or fuel needs, the tribal inescapably and assuredly depended on his surrounding forests for sustenance even during troubled time of droughts.

Their dependance on forests is such, that they constitute the integral components of forest ecosystem. Forests have been the pivot on which tribal habitat and life revolves and has evolved so far; their religion-cultural artifacts, beliefs and practices, technologies and tools have been nurtured and cultivated under perennial plant associations and benign environment[19].

The tribals are usually surrounded by thick forests or they live in hilly regions away from the modern world. The forests are an integral part of the tribal economy. The object is to focus attention on the integration of forest policy with that of economic development of tribals. The forest and the tribals are inseparable; very rightly, the tribals consider the forest as their nourishing mother. The use of forests and their produce is traditional to tribal economy as food-gatherers and agriculturists. In drought situations the forests are the only source of subsistence for the tribals[20].

Goals of Tribal Development

The goals of Tribal Development in India were best summarised in Nehru's foreword to Varrier Elwin's book on NEFA as follows[21].

1. People should develop along the lines of their own genius and we should avoid imposing anything on term. We should try to encourage in every way their own traditional arts and culture.

2. Tribal rights in land and forest should be respected.

3. We should try to train and build up a team of their own people to do the work of administration and development. Some technical people from outside will no doubt be needed, especially in the beginning, but we should avoid introducing too many outsiders into tribal territory.

4. We should not over administer these areas or overwhelm them with multiplicity of schemes. We should rather work through and not in rivalry to their own social and cultural institutions; and

5. We should guide results not by statistics or the amount of money spent, but by the quality of human character that is involved.

This five point formula enunciated by Nehru (optimises) as the corner stone the government policy. This was further elaborated by

Elwin, who emphasized the need for the tribal people to come to terms with their own past, avoiding danger of pauperism and without creating a sense of interiority. Elwin stressed on recognising the contribution of the tribal people in helping the Indian society as a whole so that they may feel as part and parcel of India as any other citizen.[22]

Dr. B.S. Guha explained the tribal welfare goals in such a manner that "schemes for tribal welfare must fulfil two essential conditions namely, conformity to the social values and patterns of the people for whom they are intended and the psychological receptivity and ability of the tribal population to absorb them. Theoretical perfection of a scheme or its suitability to people in general must not be regarded as the criterion for tribal people. Ignorance of these basic facts and inability to appreciate them are responsible for the failure of many development which by themselves are unexceptionable[23].

Dr. Guha further commented about the tribal development[24] that isolation and absence of intercourse with other communities are injurious to a people. The views put forward here are motivated by these consideration only and not framed with the purpose, conscious or unconscious, of attempting to keep the tribal people as "Museum specimens" as is so often wrongly attributed to the anthropologists. To allow a tribe to retain its traditional value and mode of life in its natural setting and give it the chance to develop along its own genius is the very reverse of the museum specimen idea."

In the context of tribal development, it aims at increasing the incomes and strengthening the material aspects of tribal culture through better utilization of the environmental resources i.e. forests, minerals, flora and fauna, agriculture, horticulture, animal husbandry, industrial potential as was as skill of the tribal people.

The goals of tribal development can be summarised into
(i) long term objectives, and
(ii) short term objectives

The long term objectives are (a) To narrow the gap of development between tribals and non-tribals (b) To improve the quality of life without disturbing their ethnicity. The short term objectives are (a) elimination of exploitation by all means, by rapid Socio economic development (b) improving organisational capabilities and (c) Building up inner strength of the tribal people.

Tribal development is often taken as synonymous with rural

Development. The tribal situation in the country presents a varied picture. Some areas have high tribal concentration, while some have no tribals. There are about 250 tribal communities speaking about 105 languages and 225 subsidiary languages. The developmental parameters of each tribe is different and it depends on the inhabitants and their settling conditions. The tribal development scene was critically reviewed on the eve of fifth plan. The problem of tribal development was categorised in two parts. (i) areas of tribal concentration, and (ii) dispersed tribals. The review of first tribal plan 1974-79 was also discussed in the Report of the Working Group on Tribal Development. During sixth plan 1980-85 under the Chairmanship of B.G. Deshmukh. In respect of tribal concentrated areas" it was decided to accept in area development approach with focus on tribals and for dispersed tribals, family oriented programmes were decided for being taken up"[25].

Approaches for Tribal Development

There are mainly five approaches which have been employed so far in the welfare of tribals in India[26]. These are:

1. Political Approach
2. Administration Approach
3. Religious Approach-with special reference to missionary approach.
4. Voluntary Agencies Approach, and
5. Anthropological Approach

The details of the above approaches are given below:

(i) Political Approach

The Political Approach for the tribal welfare may be understood in the context of the pre and post Independence period. The colonial rule created "excluded" and "Partly excluded" areas and gave separate political representation to the tribes. Nationalists opposed these measures as part of a diabolic conspiracy to a new separatism.

After independence the constitution has given the tribes a number of safeguards considering them to be the weaker section of the population. In the first instance a period of ten years was given to achieve the goal, but as the problem was too complicated to be solved in a single decade, it has persisted through decades. We are to continue to guard the tribal interests. A number of articles of the Indian constitution provide proper safeguards for the tribal people.

(2) Administrative Approach

The Administrative Approach is closely followed by the political approach. The Government of India has constituted a vast administrative machinery for tribal welfare.

At state level, the Governor has been made responsible and on his behalf the Chief Minister and Welfare Minister are incharge of the special schemes to be implemented in the tribal areas. In some major concentrated tribal areas, the state has an independent Tribal Welfare Ministry. The Welfare Ministry is advised by two bodies. The Tribes Advisory Council and the Tribal Research Institute in farming the policies and programmes for tribal welfare.

(3) Religious Approach

The Religious Approach has been attempted by different religious agencies like Christian missionaries, the Ramkrishna mission, the Arya Samaj and other local religious institutions which are engaged in the welfare work for the tribals. At the same time conversion of tribes to a new faith, viz. Christianity, has also taken place. This conversion activity has formed groups among the tribals.

The Christian Missionaries have been active in tribal India. Though they have been primarily interested in evangelization, the welfare works educational, economic, hygienic and social called "work of mercy", have invariably followed it. For both types of work spiritual and material, the missionaries did realize the importance of understanding the tribal culture and language. These they considered essential for communicating with them effectively. Missionary welfare activities have been viewed by different persons in different ways. But if it detribalizes and disintegrates these communities without offering the many alternative satisfaction, the approach can be said to be a problem for the tribals.

(4) Voluntary Agencies Approach

Under the Voluntary Agencies Approach, social workers, social welfare agencies, social movement agencies, social reformers, etc. are working to uplift the weaker section of our society in their own ways.

Voluntary social service organisations have done considerable humanitarian work in the tribal areas; but their idealism and spirit of service have not been matched by their understanding of tribal organization, values and problems.

(5) Anthropological Approach

The fact of the matter is that there is not an anthropological approach; there are anthropological approaches, which instead of offering an omnibus solution to tribal problems, have led to thinking of specific solutions to specific problems.

Anthropological knowledge in the changed situation of the country as a Welfare State is again of great importance. By and large anthropologists believe in the ultimate integration of the tribes into the mainstream of Indian life. After Independence, some anthropologists came out with several papers and addresses, dealing with the importance of applied anthropology in tribal welfare programmes. They made a re-valuation of anthropological position and came out with the theory of "planned acculturation". A vast organization of anthropological researches is available with us to help and guide the welfare work. The various tribal Research Institutes are engaged in conducting researches on scheduled castes and scheduled Tribes. Besides, many University department in the country undertake research on them.

If the welfare projects are implemented with understanding and caution the first effective step against primitiveness will have been taken.

To identify the various approaches which have been in operation in respect of tribal development. The tribal development will have to be examined in the overall context of development planning in India. Prof. B.K. Roy Burman[27] explained their views that "Four phases in the Foci of development planning in India can be identified. In the first phase, the emphasis was on providing immediate relief to the general mass of population. In the second phase, the emphasis was on resource mobilisation and provision of social service infra-structure in the country side, in the third phase the emphasis at the educational level shifted to reduction of disparity and growth with justice. Simultaneously, the commercialisation of resources was stepped up". In each phase, plans and programmes have been drawn up for the tribals keeping in view the National Objectives.

Prof. Roy Burmun further stressed on the Gandhian approach to tribal development. The inner dynamics in the organisation of some of the tribal communities almost reflecting Gandhi's concept of trusteeship in human relations and in approach to nature should also be kept in view while planning tribal development[28].

Further S.L. Sharma[29] suggested three approaches for tribal development; Missionary, Statutory and radical.

The tribal policy of the British rule was at best of indifference and at worst of oppression. They left the field of tribal welfare wide open for the Christian missions to launch their humanitarian activities. The main thrust of the missionary activity among the tribals was on evangelical services. After independence the government of India paid some attention to tribal problems. The Govt. initiated three important measures; provision of special constitutional concessions, programmes of tribal development and the protectionist policy. The focus of constitutional concessions has been on reservations for tribals in educational institutions, jobs and parliament and state assembly seats. This radical approach to tribal development manifested itself in the form of tribal movement.

In the 8th Five Year Plan Tribal Sub-plan area, M.A.D.A. (Modified Area Development Approach) and Scattered development Plans and Primitive tribe Development plans for the tribal development approach have been stressed. In this plan family oriented schemes have been also stressed to uplift the tribal families. The community development programmes are given importance on second priority.

Planning in Tribal Areas

Micro-plans generally adopt area approach as the technique of planning which makes the following specific presumptions[30]

(i) The growth stimuli have an even geographical spread efforts.

(ii) The benefits of development percolate evenly to the lower strata of society.

(iii) The socio-economic topography of the region is even, which, by implication, means that are "Spread-effect" and "percolation effect" will automatically set in and it is only a mater of time for the benefits to spread out both socially and geographically, and

(iv) Man-power is like any other fact or production demand for different skills can be satisfied over a larger region with no implications for the local community.

The situation in the developing countries is extremely complex inhibiting both the "spread effect" and the "percolation effect". The additional stipulation of "full employment" will provide the necessary corrective. In this context, manpower cannot be treated as any other factor of production, "Micro Planning for full employment" appears as a distinct methodology of planning. The micro-world of each area will present it own matrix of natural resources, socio-economic structure, institutional frame of manpower.

Planning for tribal development in our country is based on the actual experience in these areas for the last four decades. Dr. B.D. Sharma, explained his views regarding planning for tribal development that "Much of this experience has relevance even for Planning for general areas in the country." The National Committee on the Development of Backward Areas under the Chairmanship of Shri Sivaraman (Sivaraman Committee) has recommended the "sub-plan approach" with suitable adaptation for other backward areas[31]. For the better planning and development of tribals some committees were formed by Govt. of India under the Chairmanship of prominent politicians/Govt. officials. These committees are detailed in the working group report[32] of VI Plan 1980-85. The scheduled Areas and Scheduled Tribes Commission setup under the Chairmanship of Shri U.N. Dhebar in 1961 referred to this policy approvingly and observed that "the problem of problems is not to disturb the harmony of tribal life and simultaneously work for its advance; not to impose anything upon the tribals and simultaneously work for their integration as member and part of the Indian Family". A study team appointed by the Planning Commission headed by P. Shilu AO opined that" the aim of tribal-welfare policy should be defined as the progressive advancement, social and economic, of the tribals with a view to their integration with the rest of the community on a footing of equality within a reasonable distance of time. The period has necessarily to vary from tribe to tribe and it may be five or ten years in the case of certain tribes".

Another important committee[33] - Renuka Ray (1959) report emphasised that while each aspect of development was important in its own place, while Dhebar Commission (1961) stressed integrated approach,"According to them, problem of economic development for the bulk of the tribals cannot be solved unless that resources of land, forests, cattle wealth, cottage and village industries are all mobilised in an integrated basis". In 1972 under the Chairmanship of S.C. Dube an Expert Committee was set up for advising on formulation of a new strategy during the fifth five year plan defined the task of tribal development.

Selection Criteria of Tribal Areas for Tribal Development

The selection criteria of the tribal development area are discussed in the Report of the working Group on Tribal Development During Sixth Plan 1980-85 in detail. According to the report[34]. "The Tribal sub-plan was initially expected to include all the Scheduled Areas and Tehsils/Block with more than 50 per cent tribal population. As per this approach tribal Majority states namely Arunachal Pradesh, Mehghalaya, Mizoram, Nagaland, Lakshadeep and Dadra and Natgar Heavali were not included since development plans of these states/ U.T's. were primarily meant for the scheduled tribes themselves. However, according to the formulation, substantial tribal population was covered by the tribal sub-plans in Madhya Pradesh, Orissa, Bihar, Rajasthan, Gujarat, Manipur, Himachal Pradesh, A & N Island and Goa, Daman and Diu. In other States where the tribal population was of lower concentration these norms were relaxed with a view to cover a reasonable proportion of the states tribal population, a minimum scheduled tribe population threshold of about 20 thousand was adapted in delineating the tribal sub-plan areas in Maharashtra, Andhra Pradesh and Assam. In the case of Tamil Nadu and Kerala, the norms were further reduced to a S.T. population of about 10 thousand. In Tripura and West Bengal, groups of villages with more than 50% tribal concentration were included. In Karnataka and Uttar Pradesh, where the tribal population is small and dispersed, family based approach was adopted. The tribal sub-plan area was further divided into 180 Integrated Tribal Development Projects for operational purposes".

In constituting the tribal sub-plan areas[35] in the Fifth Plan period, the development Blocks were taken as the smallest unit, when the Blocks were carved out. Originally, the norm for a Community Development Block was 60 thousand population and for a Tribal Development Block 25,000 thousand population. However, in actual practice, the average would be about 40 thousand and one lakh respectively. Those Blocks which had more than two third tribal population were converted into T.D.Blocks, mostly in the Third Plan Period. Many Blocks having S.T. population between 50% and 66% continued as C.D. Blocks. When the tribal sub-plans areas, C.D. Blocks which had more than 50% of the tribal population were included, by the end of sixth plan 181 ITDP's, 248 MADA pockets and 72 primitive tribal projects were in operation in the country and covered 75% of the tribal population.

Regional Classification

The tribals are an intrinsic part of our national life and through their rich cultural heritage they have been contributing a lot to the complex amalgam. The tribals settled down in India in pre-historic times, inhabiting mostly the sparsely populated parts of hills and forests of sub-Himalayan and North-eastern regions in the mountain belt of Central India between, Narmada and Godavari rivers, and in the southern parts of the western Ghats extending from Wynad to Kanyakumari.

The territorial distribution of many tribes overlaps the political boundaries of the state and territory. For a better understanding of the demographic situation of the tribals, the states and territories have been classified into seven regions[36] as mentioned below:

1. North-eastern Region: This region comprises the states of Arunachal Pradesh, Assam, Manipur, Meghalya, Mizoram, Nagaland and Tripura.
2. Eastern Region: This region includes the states of Bihar, Orissa, Sikkim and West Bengal.
3. Northern Region: This region belongs to states of Himachal Pradesh and Uttar Pradesh.
4. Central Region: This region consists of only one i.e. Madhya Pradesh.
5. Western Region: This region is the part of the states of Rajasthan, Maharastra, Gujarat, Dadar and Nagar Haveli, Goa, Daman and Diu.
6. Southern Region: This region comprises the states of Andhra Pradesh, Karnataka, Tamil Nadu and Kerala
7. Island Region: This region constitutes Andaman and Nicobar Island, and Lakshadweep.

Financial Allocations for Tribal Development

The tribal majority areas in the country are broadly divided in the three categories, viz (i) predominantly tribal states/union territories (ii) Scheduled area, and (iii) Non-scheduled areas in the states. All the tribal-majority states and Union Territories are placed in a special category for allocation of funds. The development and administration of tribal areas is accepted as a special responsibility of the Central Government even though they are integral parts of the concerned states. The question of making financial provisions for their development were considered in detail by the constituent Assembly itself.

The schemes have been divided into two categories, viz (i) Central Sector programmes which are fully financed by the central Govt. (ii) the Centrally sponsored programmes which are partly financed by the Central Govt., and rest of the expenditure is met out by the concerned state govt.

Dr. B.D. Sharma explained the elements for state programmes[37] as "the financial resources for developmental programmes in a state may comprise the following elements.

i) Investment in the Central and Centrally sponsored schemes;
ii) State revenues;
iii) Share from certain central revenues;
iv) Plan assistance from the Central Government under the Gadgil Formula; and
v) Grants under Article 275(1) on the basis of the recommendations of the Finance Commission.

The utilisation of State funds is broadly classified under two categories. Plan and Non-plan. The plan technically covers all those items which are included in the state or the Central Plan. The Non-plan includes expenditure on general administration as also on the maintenance of development schemes".

The special Central Assistance for tribal sub-plans is allocated between different states on the basis of three criteria as under:

i) the tribal population of sub-plan area;
ii) the geographical area of the sub-plan; and
iii) the per capita gross output of the state.

The weightage for these three elements has been fixed in a certain proportion. While the first two criteria are simple, the quantum of assistance on the basis of the third criterion is determined with reference to the difference between the inverse of the States per capita gross product and the inverse of the per capita gross national product. Thus, the sub-plan, besides having a share from the state plan, also gets benefit of Special Central Assistance, the assistance under 'Gadgil Formula' as also the devaluation on the basis of recommendations of the Finance Commission are the block grants to states. These can be used by team according to their needs, subject to the guidelines of the Finance Commission and Planning Commission.

Broadly the financing agencies rendering their services in the tribal areas are Central Government, State Governments, Institutions viz. Commercial Banks. Co-operative banks, NABARD and voluntary organisation.

Fundamental Rights

The tribal scene in India presents a very complex picture. Different regions have had different administrative history and, therefore, they are having different administrative structures. Since personnel policies are complementary to the administrative structure they present an equally varied picture. Pre-independence tribals living in forests, hills and even on the plains were isolated from the mainstream. The status of tribals were unsatisfactory during princely and colonial regime. It was a policy of neglect and saga of exploitation. Due to this, their land and forest were slowly and gradually grabbed by the rich people like landlords and money landers. They were turned into bonded labourers, leading a life of extreme poverty and misery. The excessive encroachment on their rights in land and forest let to be expression of anger in the form of risings. Thus independent India inherited from the British colonial system 'a complex tribal problem', in view of our commitment to the objectives of justice, social, economic and political equality of status and opportunity as enshrined in the preamble to the constitution. The result was that makers of the constitution had to pay special attention towards the 'complex tribal problem' and came out with solutions in order to eradicate it for ever. The dire need of day was to engulf the gap between tribals and non-tribals.

The concern of the constituent members of the constitution for protection and promotion of the interests of the deprived sections is amply reflected in the preamble of the constitution, which is amended in 1976, succinctly proclaims the aims and objects of the constitution, i.e. to constitute India into a Sovereign, Socialist, Secular, Democratic Republic and to secure to all its citizens.

The scheduled areas and scheduled tribes commission (1961, Chairman Shri U.N. Dhebar) in the context of tribal welfare and development observed that "the constitution arranged for the provisions of resources and provided the required institutional apparatus. We feel that so far as the basic framework of the constitution is concerned it cannot be considered inadequate. Some of the safeguards for the tribals in the constitution were originally only for ten years. In fixing this period, the constitution had envisaged an effective follow-up programmes which would have obviated the need for their continuance. This hope has not materailiased and the period has been extended, but we are of the opinion that this has not been due to any deficiency in the constitution itself. It is the result of deficiency in performance".

The rights of the scheduled tribes are sought to be preserved first, through the fundamental right. These rights apply generally to all citizens as well as the scheduled tribes. A number of specific provisions haven made in the constitution to protect the rights of the tribals. In constitution both protective and development aspects have been considered. The protective aspects relate to the protection of the rights of the tribals in land and forests alongwith the safeguards against usurious or exploitive elements. The 'developmental' aspects related to the welfare measures.

The constitution deliberately laid emphasis on both aspects protective as well as development. The constituent members of the constitution were keen that the tribals join the mainstream of the national life, while retaining their traits and cultural heritage. Keeping in view the tribal status in constitution, therefore, made special provisions for their social and economic development. The provisions are contained in Articles 46,244, 330,332, 334,335, 338,339, 342 and schedules V and VI to the constitution of India. The constitution also permits for change in laws, according to the tribal situation of concerned area.

Constitutional Safeguards

Development is a slow process of civilization. The purpose of development is to provide minimum basic needs as well as increasing opportunities to all the persons for better life. To meet out the needs, it is essential to bring about more equitable distribution of income and wealth for promoting social justice and efficiency of production. Development also involves constant improvement in the quality of life. In wider sense development means creating environment for the realization of human potential, mobilization of resources and creation of economic potentialities.

Apart from this, basic approach there is the problem of integration and development. The most difficult part of integration is emotional integration and that of developmental activity is its psychological aspect. Despite a lack of clarity about the basic approach, the difficulties of distance, both physical and mental and the inadequacy of resources, it can be said that an impact has been produced upon the tribal mind, side by side with dissatisfaction one can easily perceive statisfication. There are other aspects of this problem. They can be summed up as 'protective' aspects and 'developmental' aspects. The protective aspects are related to the protection of the rights of the tribals and rights to be safeguarded from usurious or exploitative elements. The developmental aspects related to the welfare of the tribals.

The constitution deliberately laid emphasis on both the aspects i.e. protective as well as development. Keeping in view the isolation and socio-economic backwardness of the tribals, the framers of the constitution have given proper weight to the deprived classes of the society. There is a clear commitment in the preamble to the constitution to the effect that it assures to each individual liberty of thought and expression, belief, faith of worship, equality of status and opportunity, promoting through such liberty, equality and fraternity among all, leading ultimately to the unity of all of them.

The rights of the Scheduled Tribes are sought to be preserved, first, through the fundamental rights. But this is not all. A number of specific provisions have also been made in the constitution safeguarding specifically the social, economic, educational and political rights of the tribals i.e. scheduled tribes.

The safeguards provided to the scheduled tribes under the constitution of India are covered in part XVI of the constitution, relating special provisions to the scheduled tribes and other backward classes of the State.

In tribal societies various traditional institutions, law and customs have evolved over the years regarding their personal and social disputes. These disputes or conflicts may however, arise because many customs prevalent among different tribal are in contrivance to the established laws, rules and regulations, tribal follows these conventional laws and they have blind faith on them. In tribal society the chief of the clan is the head of the traditional panchayat and they obey his discission on priority whether they have been punished by the court of law. Hence in this way tribal strictly obey their customary laws. The customary laws are still unwritten. It is necessary to codify these laws, because it leaves a lot of scope for manipulation. No guide lines are available for the traditional institutions and the respective role of police. Their customs, which form the centre of their life and are mixed with their day to day life, have been strongly protected under the constitution.The customs and usage have been safeguarded by Article 13(3) (a) in the territory of India by the force of law.Further the Fifth and Sixth Schedule of constitution have provided right to the state for codification of "customary law's" of the scheduled tribes. Hence by inserting these schedules the customary law rights of the tribals have been given proper protection by the constitution of India. The customary law is difficult to be compiled as it is entwined in various usages, practices followed by various tribal groups.

The constitutional safeguards provided in part XVI of the constitution are detailed as under:

Article-330.
Reservation of seats for Scheduled Castes and Scheduled Tribes in the House of the People-

(1) Seats shall be reserved in the House of the People for -

(a) the Scheduled Castes;

(b) the Scheduled Tribes except the Scheduled Tribes in the autonomous districts of Assam; and

(c) the Scheduled tribes in the autonomous districts of Assam.

(2) The number of seats reserved in any State [or Union territory] for the Scheduled Castes or the Scheduled Tribes under clause (1) shall bear, as nearly as may be, the same proportion to the total number of seats allotted to that State [or Union territory] in the House of the People as the population of the Scheduled Castes in the State [or Union territory] or of the Scheduled Tribes in the State [or Union territory] or part of the State [or Union territory] as the case may be, in respect of which seats are so reserved,bears to the total population of the State [or Union territory].

(3) Notwithstanding anything contained in clause (2), the number of seats reserved in the House of the People for the Scheduled Tribes in the autonomous districts of Assam shall bear to the total number of seats allotted to that State a proportion not less than the population of the Scheduled Tribes in the said autonomous districts bears to the total population of the state.

Explanation- In this article and in article 332, the expression"population" means the population as ascertained at the last receding census of which the relevant figures have been published.

Provided that the reference in this Explanation to the last preceding census of which the relevant figures have been published shall, until the relevant figures for the first census taken after the year 2000 have been published, be construed as a reference to the 1971 census.

In accordance with the provisions envisaged in article 330, the details of reserved seats for the Scheduled Tribes in the Parliament (Lok Sabha), the election-wise details are as under:

Reservation of Lok Sabha

S.No.	General Election	Year	Total seats (No.)	Seats reserved for S.T. (No.)
1.	First	1951-52	481	32
2.	Second	1957	490	33
3.	Third	1962	490	33
4.	Fourth	1967	500	34
5.	Fifth	1971	521	37
6.	Sixth	1977	542	38
7.	Seventh	1980	542	40
8.	Eighth	1984	542	40
9.	Ninth	1989	543	40
10.	Tenth	1991	543	40

According to the provisions of the Delimination of parliamentary and Assembly constituencies order, 1976, 38 seats were reserved out of 542 seats in Lok Sabha. The membership of Scheduled Tribes was increased from 38 to 40 in the Seventh General Election by one seat each from Maharashtra and Assam States.

The State-wise distribution of the reserved seats in states/union territories in Lok Sabha are detailed below:

Prologue

State-wise Reservation in Lok Sabha

S.No.	Name of State/Union Territory	Total seats (No.)	Seats reserved for S.T. (No.)
1	2	3	4
1.	Andhra Pradesh	42	2
2.	Assam	14	2
3.	Bihar	54	5
4.	Gujarat	26	4
5.	Haryana	10	-
6.	Himachal Pradesh	4	-
7.	Jammu and Kashmir	6	-
8.	Karnataka	28	-
9.	Kerala	20	-
10.	Madhya Pradesh	40	9
11.	Maharashtra	48	4
12.	Manipur	2	1
13.	Meghalaya	2	-
14.	Nagaland	1	-
15.	Orissa	21	5
16.	Punjab	13	-
17.	Rajasthan	25	-
18.	Sikkim	1	-
19.	Tamil Nadu	39	-
20.	Tripura	2	-
21.	Uttar Pradesh	85	-
22.	West Bengal	42	2
23.	Andaman & Nicobar Islands	1	-
24.	Arunachal Pradesh	2	-
25.	Chandigarh	1	-
26.	Dadra & Nagar Haveli	1	-
27.	Delhi	7	-
28.	Goa, Daman and Diu	2	-
29.	Lakshadweep	1	1
30.	Mizoram	1	-
31.	Pondichery	1	-

Article-332.
Reservation of seats for Scheduled Castes and Scheduled Tribes in the Legislative Assemblies of the States-

(1) Seats shall be reserved for the Scheduled Castes and the Scheduled Tribes. [[except the Scheduled Tribes in the autonomous districts of Assam],] in the Legislative Assembly of every State.

(2) Seats shall be reserved also for the autonomous districts in the Legislative Assembly of the State of Assam.

(3) The number of seats reserved for the Scheduled Castes or the Scheduled Tribes in the Legislative Assembly of any State under clause (1) shall bear, as nearly as may be, the same proportion to the total number of seats in the Assembly as the population of the Scheduled Castes in the state or of the Scheduled Tribes in the State or part of the State, as the case may be, in respect of which seats are so reserved, bears to the total population of the State.

[(3A) Notwithstanding any thing contained in clause (3) until the taking effect, under article 170, of the re-adjustment, on the basis of the first census after the year 2000, of the number of seats in the Legislative Assemblies of the States of Arunachal Pradesh, Meghalaya, Mizoram and Nagaland, the seats which shall be reserved for the Scheduled Tribes in the Legislative Assembly of any such state shall be-

(a) if all the seats in the Legislative Assembly of such State in existence of the date of coming into force of the Constitution (Fifty-seventh Amendment) Act, 1987 (hereafter in this clause referred to as the existing Assembly) are held by members of the Scheduled Tribes, all the seats except one:

(b) in any other case, such number of seats as bears to the total number of seats, a proportion not less than the number (as on the said date) of members belonging to the Scheduled Tribes in the existing Assembly bears to the total number of seats in the existing Assembly.]

(4) The number of seats reserved for an autonomous district in the Legislative Assembly of the State of Assam shall bear to the total number of seats in that Assembly a proportion not less than the population of the district bears to the total population of the State.

(5) The constituencies for the seats reserved for any autonomous district of Assam shall not comprise any area outside that district.

(6) No person who is not a member of a Scheduled Tribe of any

autonomous district of the State of Assam shall be eligible for election to the Legislative Assembly of the State from any constituency of that district.

Constitution has further provided reservation of seats to the scheduled tribe in the Legislative Assembly of every state by introducing Article 332. The number of reservation in single member constituencies for Scheduled Tribes in the state where the concentration of Scheduled Tribe was small, two members constituencies were formed, out of these two seats one being reserved for the S.T. Hence by this way the Scheduled Tribes have been given adequate representation in the State Legislatures.

According to Article 332 of the constitution and delimination order 1976, and the Representation of People's (Amendment) Act, 1980, 294 seats were reserved for the Scheduled Tribes out of 3,977 seats in state Assemblies.

❑ ❑ ❑

REFERENCES

1. Niharranjan Ray (1972) : "Introductory Address" in S.C. Dube (Ed.) Tribal Situation in India, p.8
2. P.G. Krishnan (1985) : "Constituion and Tribal Welfare": Cochin University Law Review, Vol. IX No.1 and 2, March & June, 1985, pp 45-66.
3. A.B. Bardhan (1973) : The Tribal Problem in India, Communist Party of India Publications, New Delhi, pp 16-17
4. D.N. Majumdar (1961) : Races and Cultures of India, Asia Publishing House, Bombay, p. 367
5. Kamaladevi Chatopadhyaya (1978) : Tribalism in India, p-1.
6. Verrier Elwin (1963) : A new Deal for Tribal India, p. 17
7. Mishra, R.P. (Ed. 1983) : Local Level Planning and Development, Sterling Publishers Pvt. Ltd., New Delhi-16.
8. Sharma, Soumitra (1983) : Development Strategy and the Developing Countries, South Asian Publishers Pvt. Ltd., New Delhi-2
9. Seers, Dudley (1972) : "What are we Trying to mesure", Journal of Development Studies, April 1972, p.21.
10. Basu, (Dr.) Ashok Ranjan (1985) : The Tribal Development Programmes and Administration in India, National Book Organisation, New Delhi, p.27.
11. Alfred Diamant (1967) : "European Models of Bureaucracy and Development." International Review of Administrative Sciences, Vol. 8, No.3, p. 310.
12. The United Nations, Development Administration: Current Approaches and Trends in Public Administration for National Development (New York, No. E7IIH-I), p.8
13. G.S. Kainth and R.S. bawa (1984) : Economic Development and Structural Changes; An emprical Investigation, Inter-India Publication, New Delhi, pp. 1-2.
14. Ibid, pp.3-4
15. Patel, M.L. (1984) : Planning Strategy for Development, Inter-India Publication, New Delhi 1984, pp. 1-2 and Galbraith, John Kenneth: Economic Development, Harward University Press, London, p.57.
16. Ibid, p.2
17. Vidyarthi, L.P. & Rai, Binay Kumar (1977) : The tribal culture of India, Concept Publishing Company, pp. 96-97.
18. Ibid, p.99
19. Desh Bandhu and GArg, R.K. (1986) : Social Forestry and Tribal Development, Indian Environmental Society, New Delhi, pp., 38-50.
20. Deegaonkar, S.G. (1980) : Problems of Development of Tribal Areas, Leela Devi Publications, Delhi, p.65
21. Basu,(Dr.) Ashok Ranjan (1985) : The Tribal Development Programmes and Administration in India, National Book Organisation, New Delhi, pp. 38-39.
22. Mathur, J.S. (1975) : "Tribal Development Administration," Perspective on Tribal Development and Administration (Hyderabad), p. 164.
23. Social Welfare in India, issued on behalf of the Planning Commission, Govt. of India, New Delhi (1960), p. 229
24. Ibid, pp. 229-230.
25. Report of the working group of Tribal Development. During Sixth Plan 1980-85, Ministry of Home Affairs, Govt. of India, New Delhi, 1989, pp. 1-2.
26. Vidyarthi, L.P. and Rai, Binay Kumar: The Tribal Culture of India, Concept

Publishing Company, Delhi, pp. 421-431.
27. Singh, J.P. and Vyas, N.N. (Ed.) (1986) : Tribal Development- Past Efforts and New Challanges, Tribal Research Institue, Rajasthan, Udaipur, TRIBE Vol. XVIII, No. 1-4 January 1986 to December 1986 pp. 5-6.
28. Roy Burman, b.K. (1987) : "Issue of Development in Gandhian Conceptual Frame work and Perspective of Nation Building for World Peace."
29. Singh, J.P. and Vyas, N.N (Ed.) (1986) : Tribal Development Post Efforts and New Challanges, Tribal Research Institute, Rajasthan, Udaipur TRIBE Vol. XVIII. No. 1-4 January 1986 to December 1986, p.29.
30. Chaudhary, Buddhadeb (1982) : Tribal Development in India Problems and Prospects, Inter-India Publications, delhi, 1982, pp.321-322.
31. Sharma (Dr.), B.D. (1984) : Planning for Tribal Development, Prachi Prakash, New Delhi, 1984, p. XIV
32. Ibid, p.8
33. Ibid, pp.10-11
34. Report of the working Group on Tribal development during VIth Plan 1980-85, Ministry of Home Affairs, Govt. of India, New Delhi, 1980, pp. 1-2.
35. Ibid, p.32
36. Mehta, Prakash Chandra (1991) : Demographic Profile of Tribals, Tribe Vol. XXI-XXIII, January 1989 to December 1991, Tribal Research Institute, Rajasthan, udaipur, pp 54-55.
37. Sharma, (Dr.) B.D. (1984) : Planning for Tribal Developments, Prachi Prakashan, New Delhi, 1984, p.85.

ETHNOGRAPHIC MAP OF INDIAN TRIBES

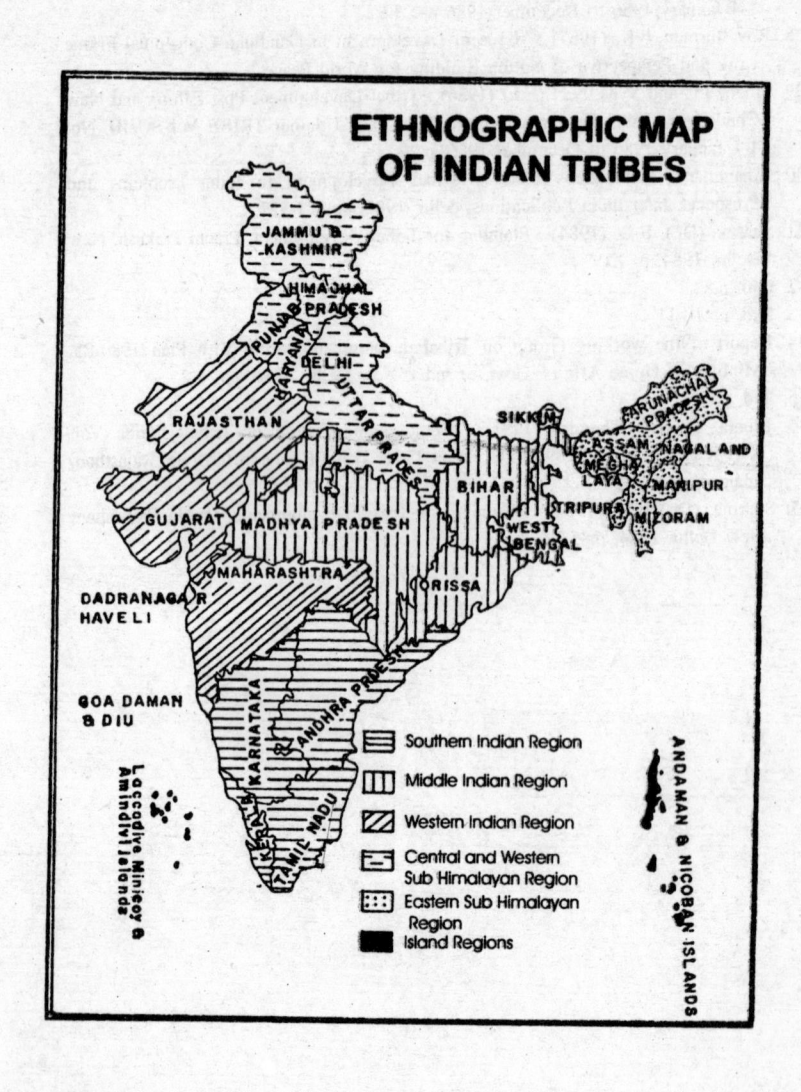

- Southern Indian Region
- Middle Indian Region
- Western Indian Region
- Central and Western Sub Himalayan Region
- Eastern Sub Himalayan Region
- Island Regions

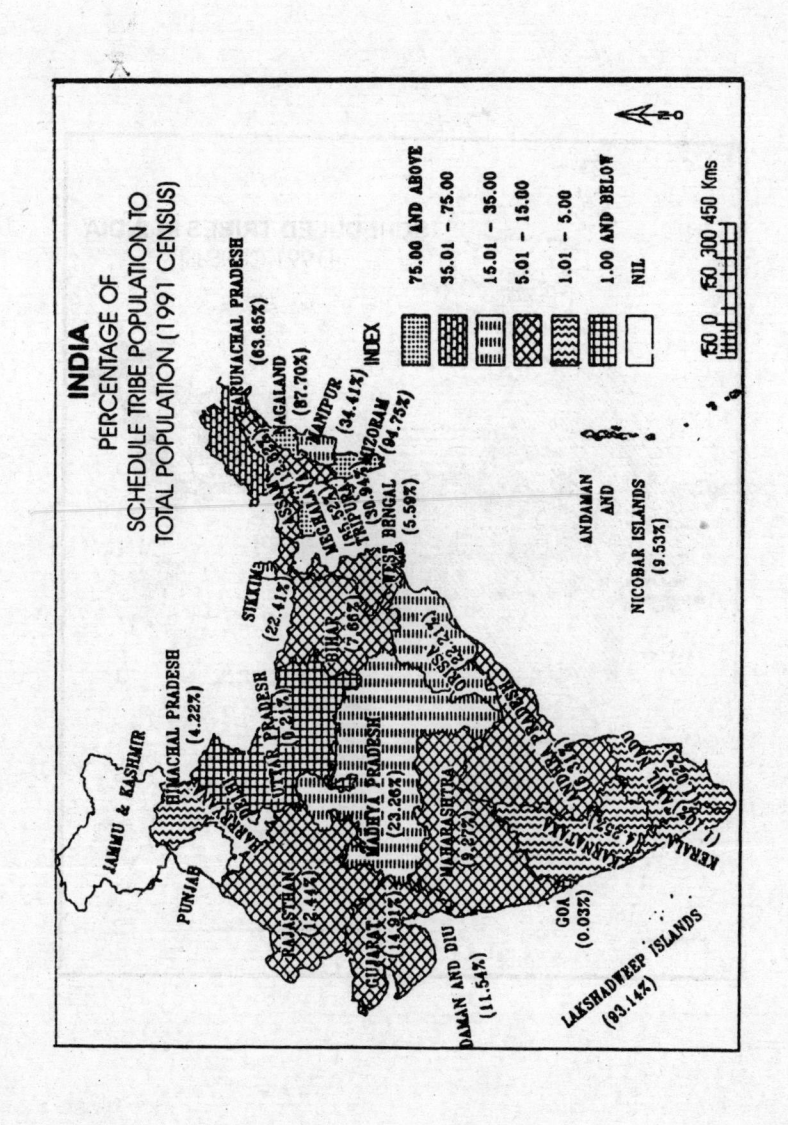

Prologue

INDIA
PERCENTAGE OF
SCHEDULE TRIBE POPULATION TO
TOTAL POPULATION (1991 CENSUS)

INDEX

- 75.00 AND ABOVE
- 35.01 – 75.00
- 15.01 – 35.00
- 5.01 – 15.00
- 1.01 – 5.00
- 1.00 AND BELOW
- NIL

State percentages:
- JAMMU & KASHMIR
- HIMACHAL PRADESH (4.22%)
- PUNJAB
- RAJASTHAN (12.44%)
- GUJARAT (14.91%)
- DAMAN AND DIU (11.54%)
- GOA (0.03%)
- LAKSHADWEEP ISLANDS (93.14%)
- KERALA
- KARNATAKA
- MAHARASHTRA (9.27%)
- MADHYA PRADESH (23.26%)
- UTTAR PRADESH (0.21%)
- BIHAR (7.65%)
- SIKKIM (22.41%)
- ARUNACHAL PRADESH (63.65%)
- NAGALAND (87.70%)
- MANIPUR (34.41%)
- MEGHALAYA (85.53%)
- ASSAM
- TRIPURA (30.94%)
- MIZORAM (94.75%)
- WEST BENGAL (5.59%)
- ANDAMAN AND NICOBAR ISLANDS (9.53%)

Ethnographic Atlas of Indian Tribes

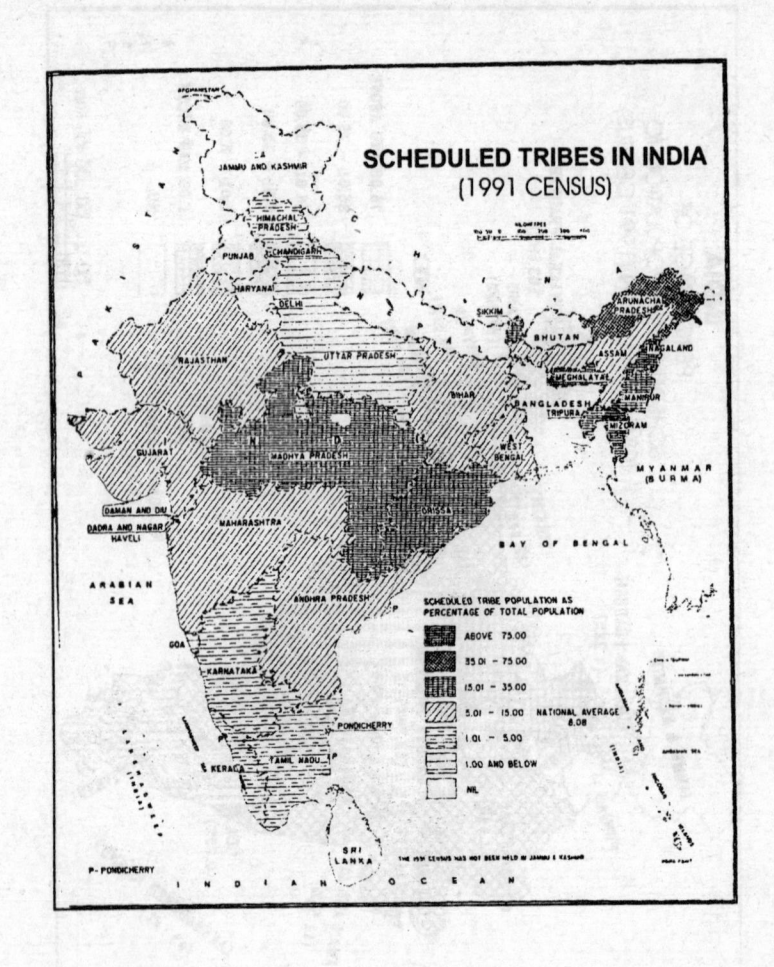

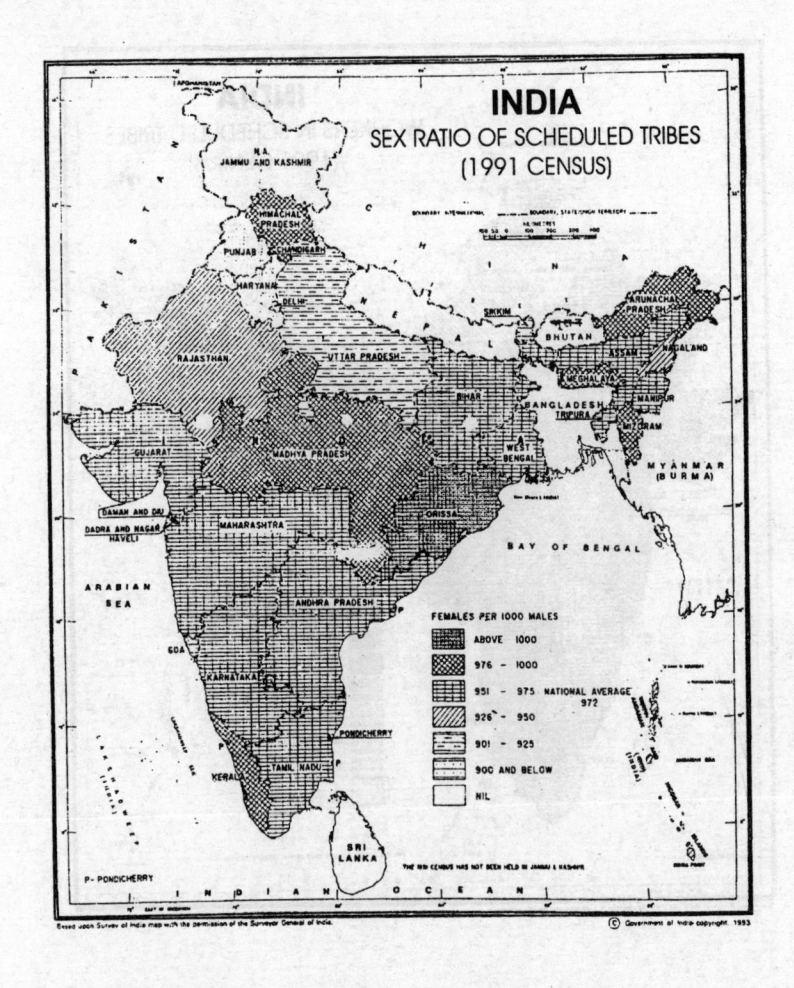

Prologue

INDIA
SEX RATIO OF SCHEDULED TRIBES
(1991 CENSUS)

Ethnographic Atlas of Indian Tribes

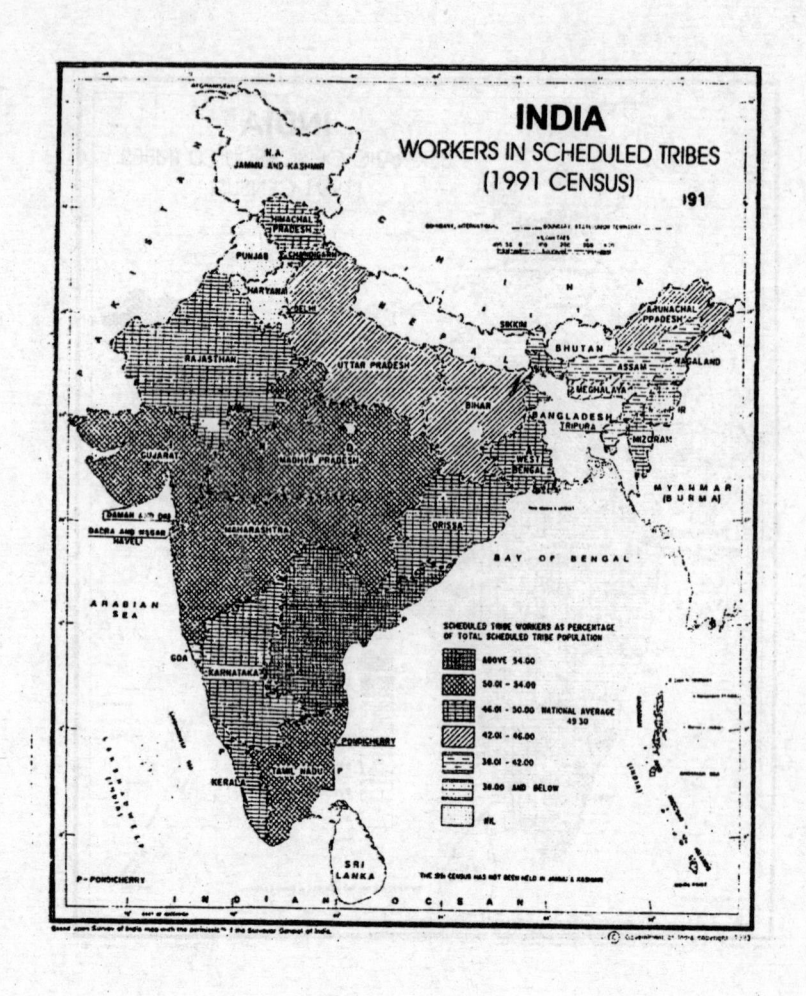

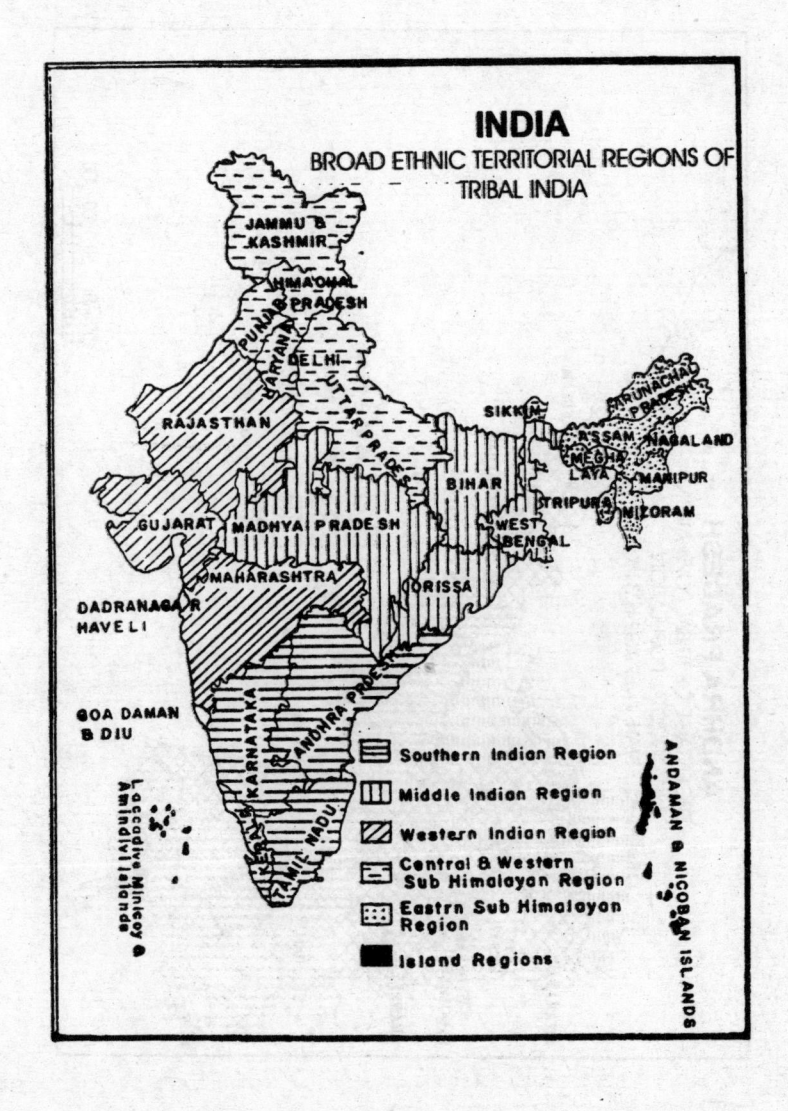

Prologue

INDIA
BROAD ETHNIC TERRITORIAL REGIONS OF TRIBAL INDIA

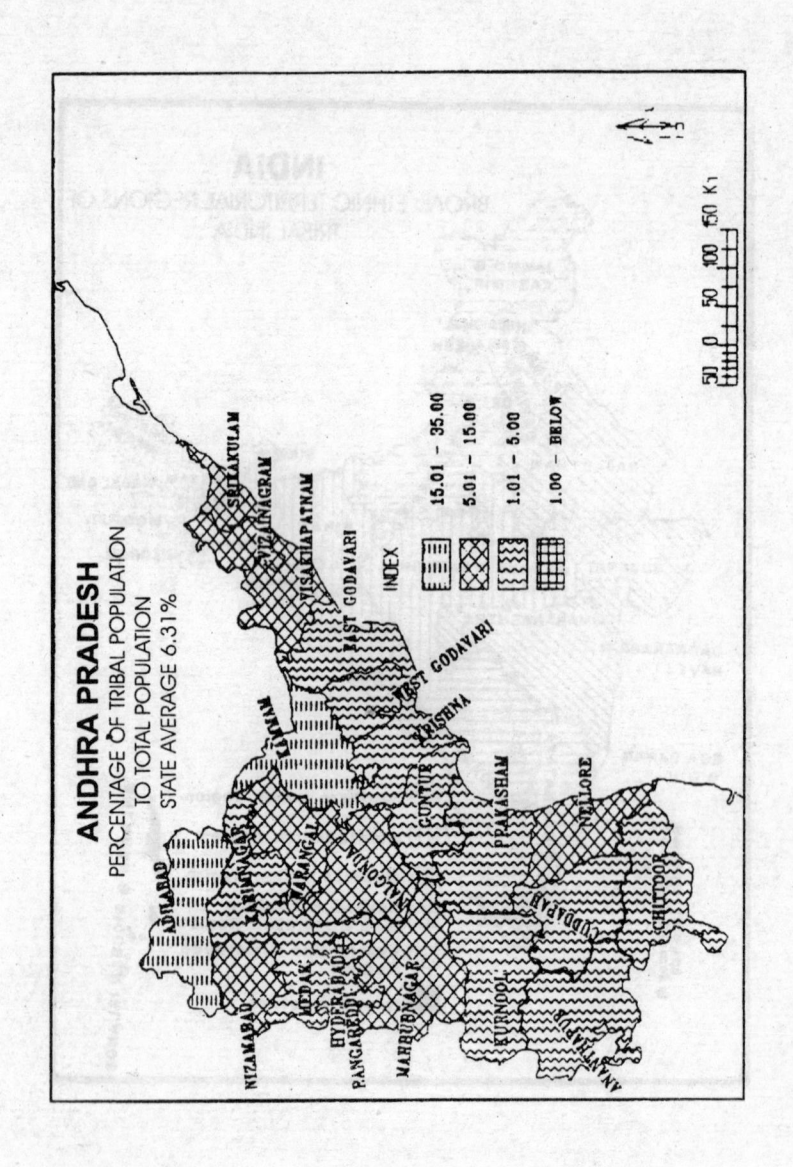

ANDHRA PRADESH
PERCENTAGE OF TRIBAL POPULATION TO TOTAL POPULATION
STATE AVERAGE 6.31%

INDEX:
- 15.01 – 35.00
- 5.01 – 15.00
- 1.01 – 5.00
- 1.00 – BELOW

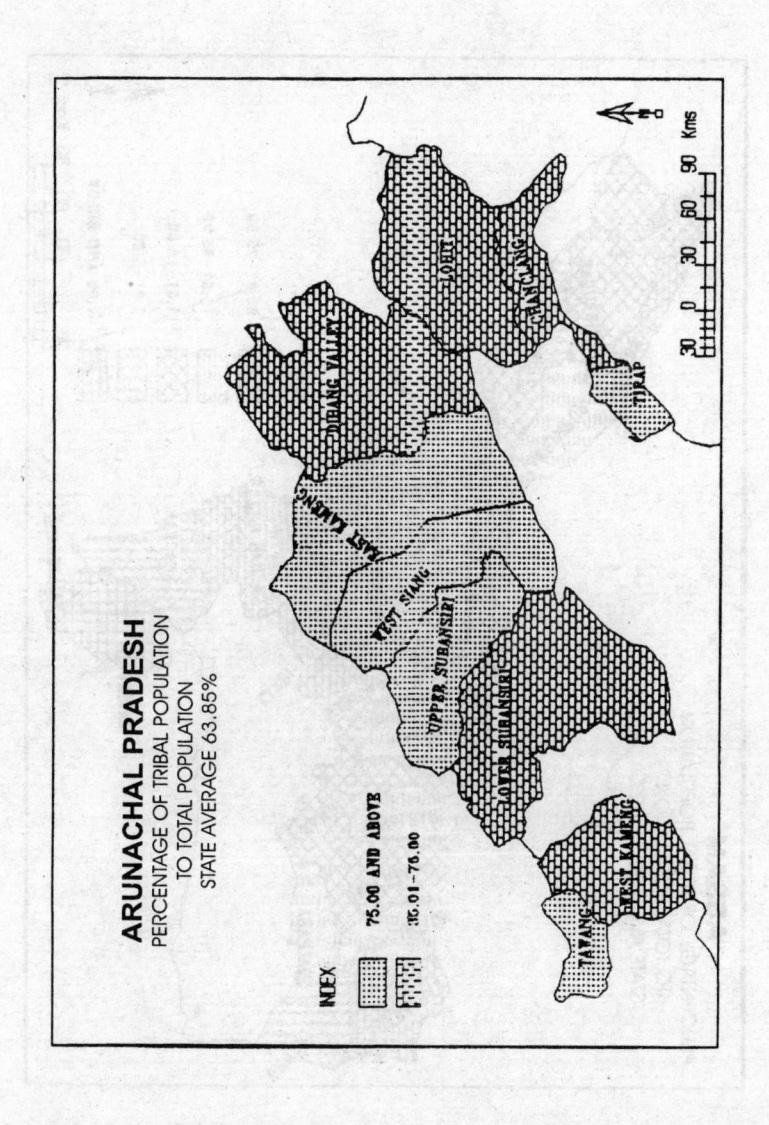

Prologue

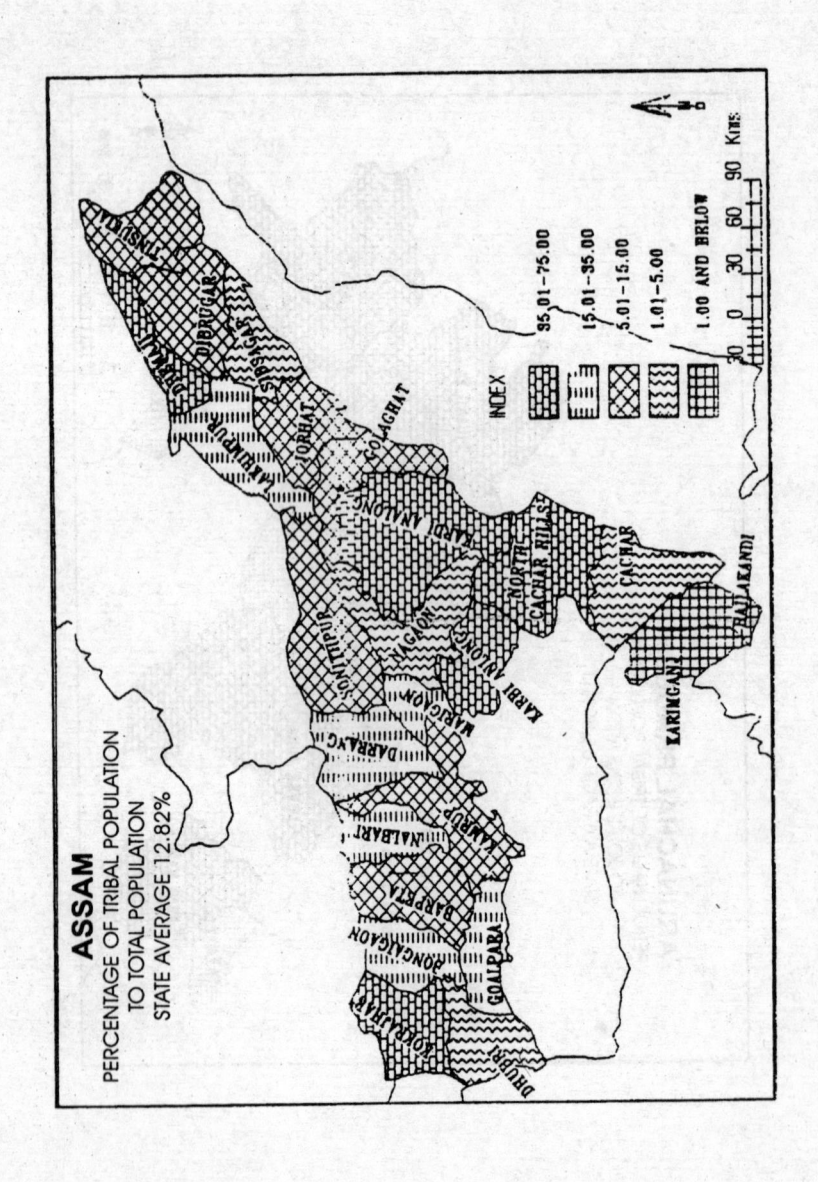

ASSAM
PERCENTAGE OF TRIBAL POPULATION TO TOTAL POPULATION
STATE AVERAGE 12.82%

INDEX

Pattern	Range
	35.01–75.00
	15.01–35.00
	5.01–15.00
	1.01–5.00
	1.00 AND BELOW

Prologue 47

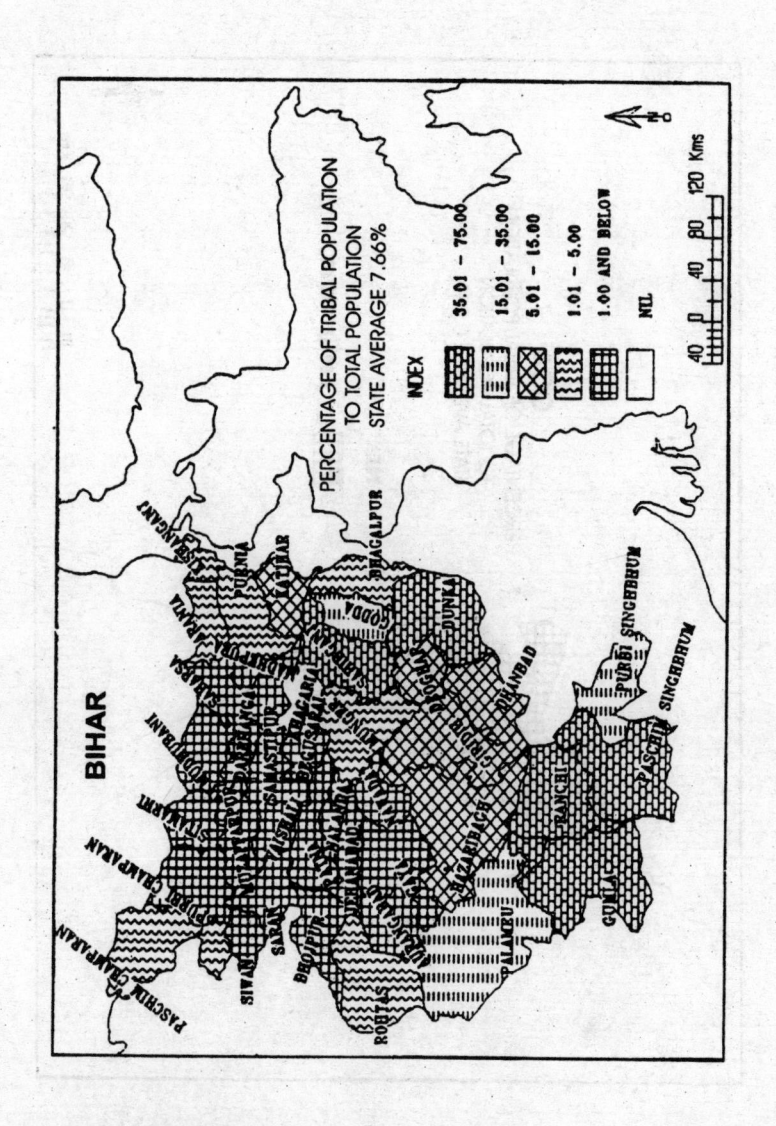

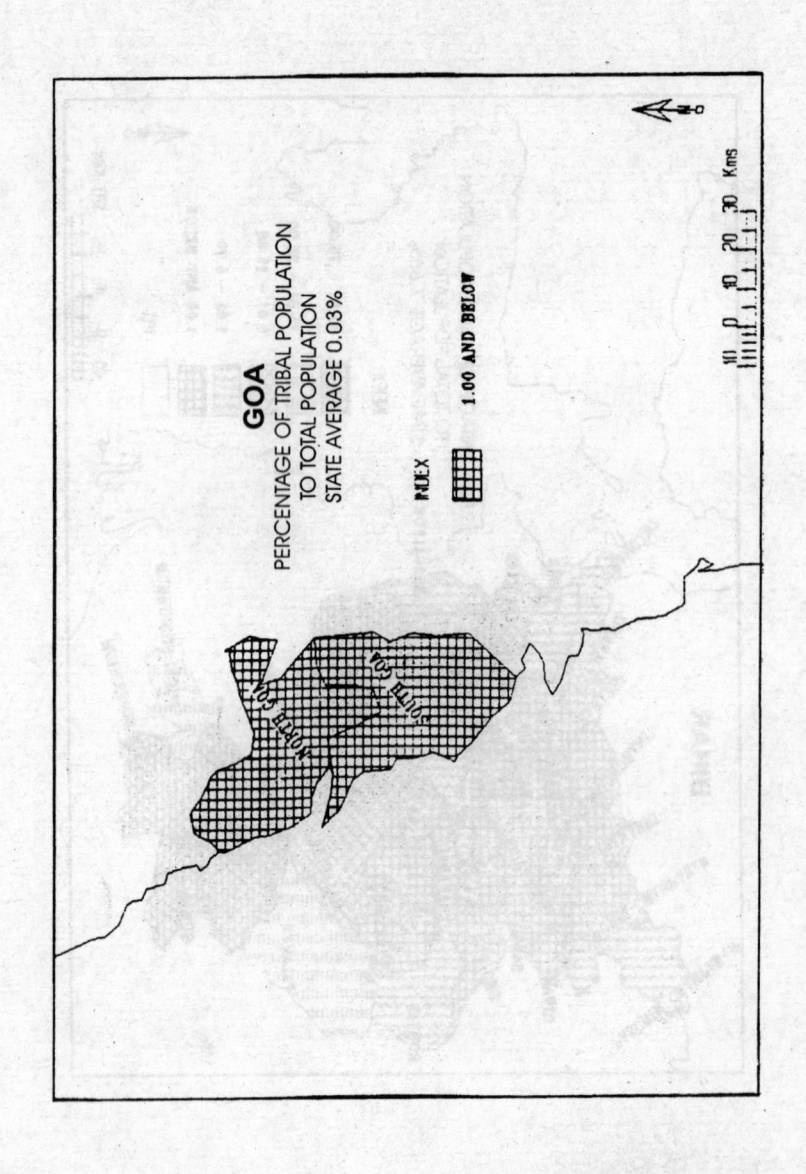

GOA
PERCENTAGE OF TRIBAL POPULATION TO TOTAL POPULATION
STATE AVERAGE 0.03%

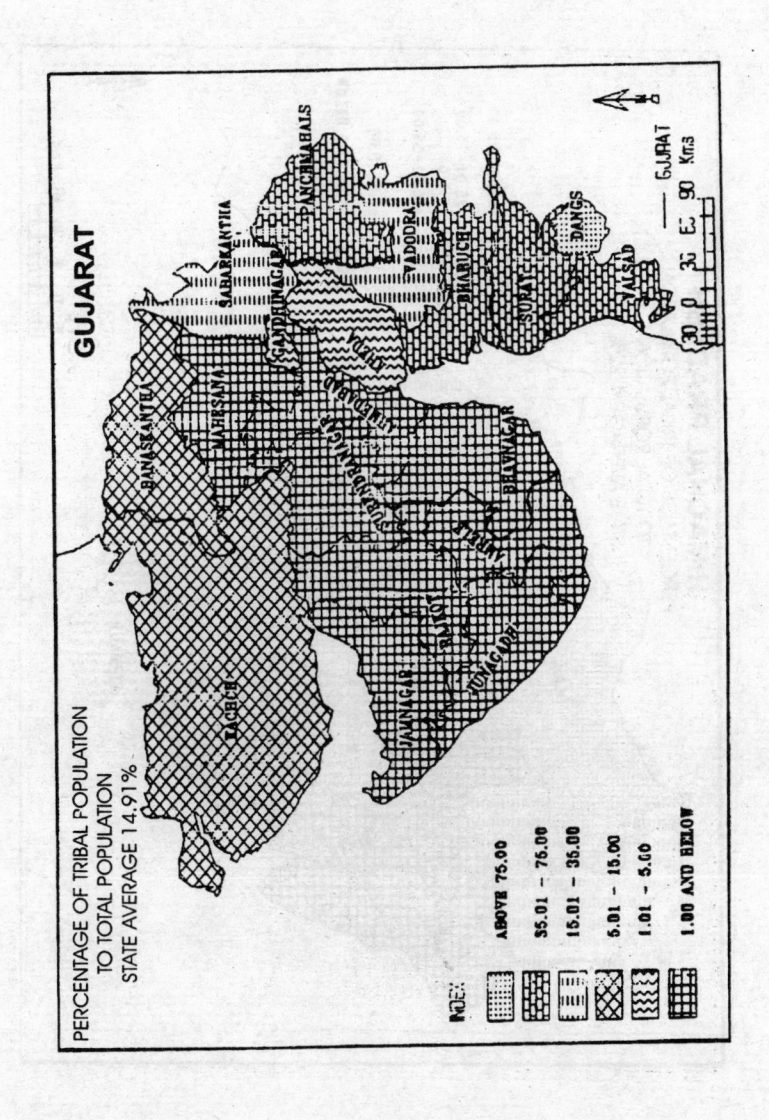

Prologue

GUJARAT

PERCENTAGE OF TRIBAL POPULATION
TO TOTAL POPULATION
STATE AVERAGE 14.91%

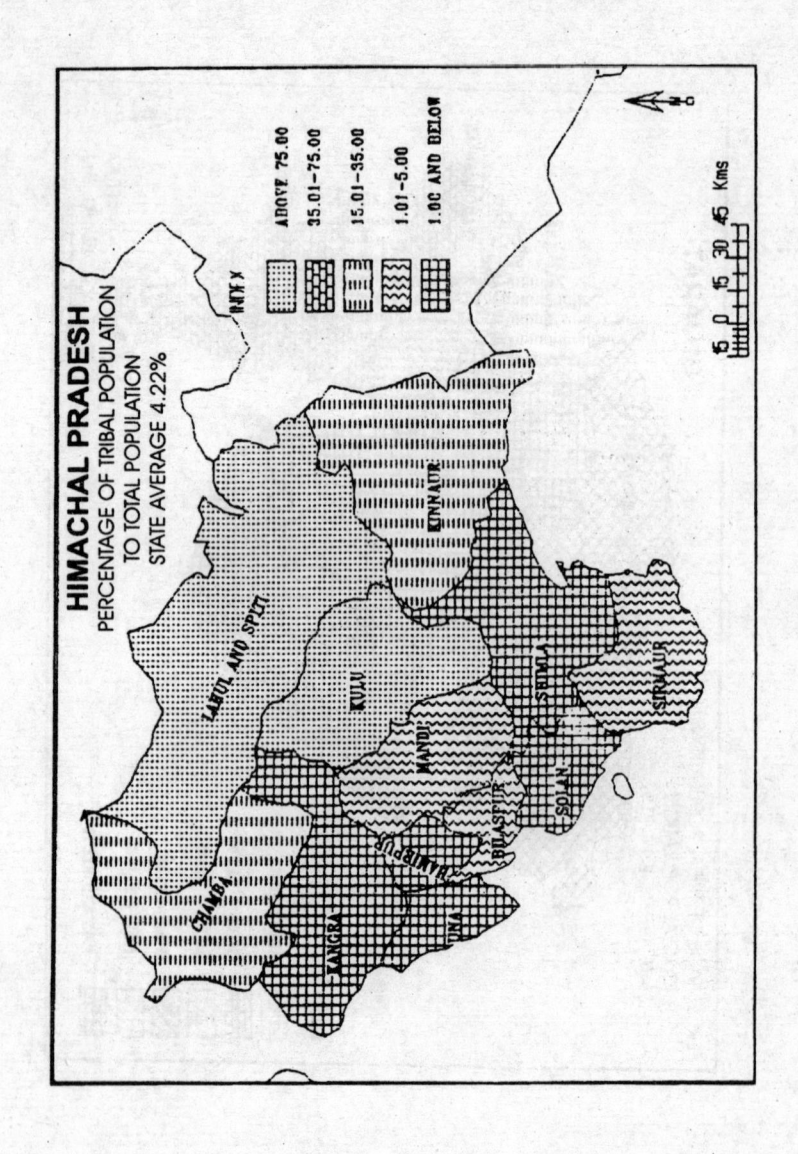

HIMACHAL PRADESH
PERCENTAGE OF TRIBAL POPULATION TO TOTAL POPULATION
STATE AVERAGE 4.22%

- ABOVE 75.00
- 35.01–75.00
- 15.01–35.00
- 1.01–5.00
- 1.00 AND BELOW

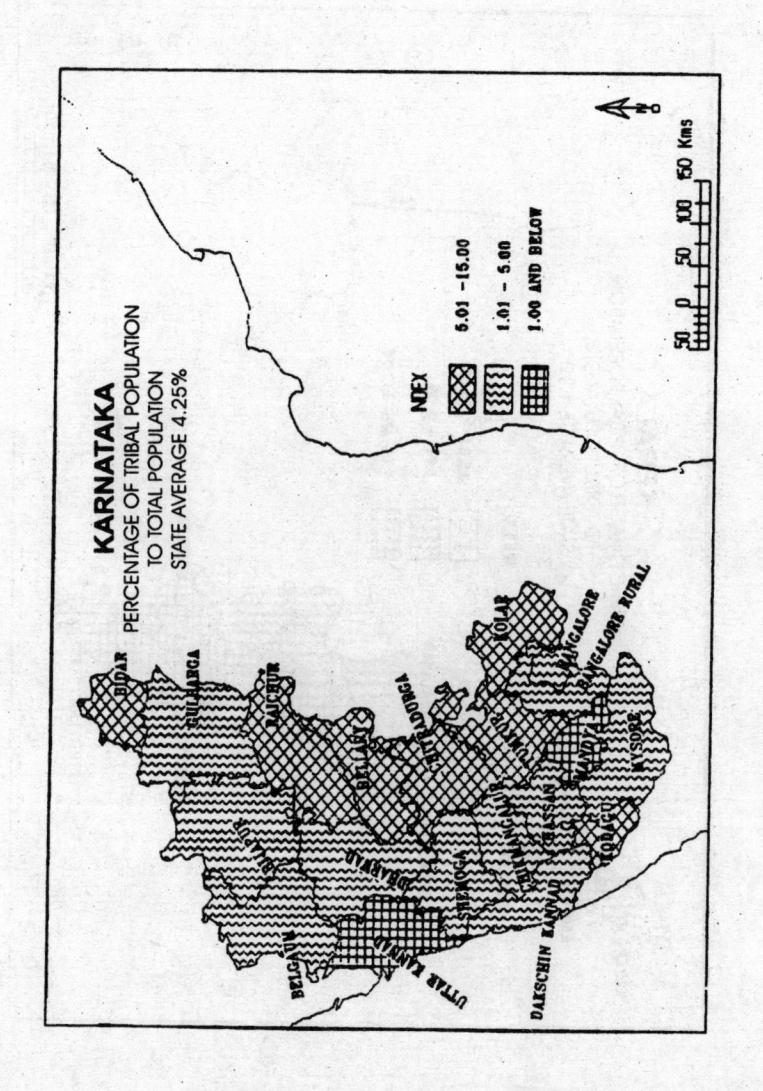

KARNATAKA
PERCENTAGE OF TRIBAL POPULATION TO TOTAL POPULATION
STATE AVERAGE 4.25%

INDEX
- 5.01 – 15.00
- 1.01 – 5.00
- 1.00 AND BELOW

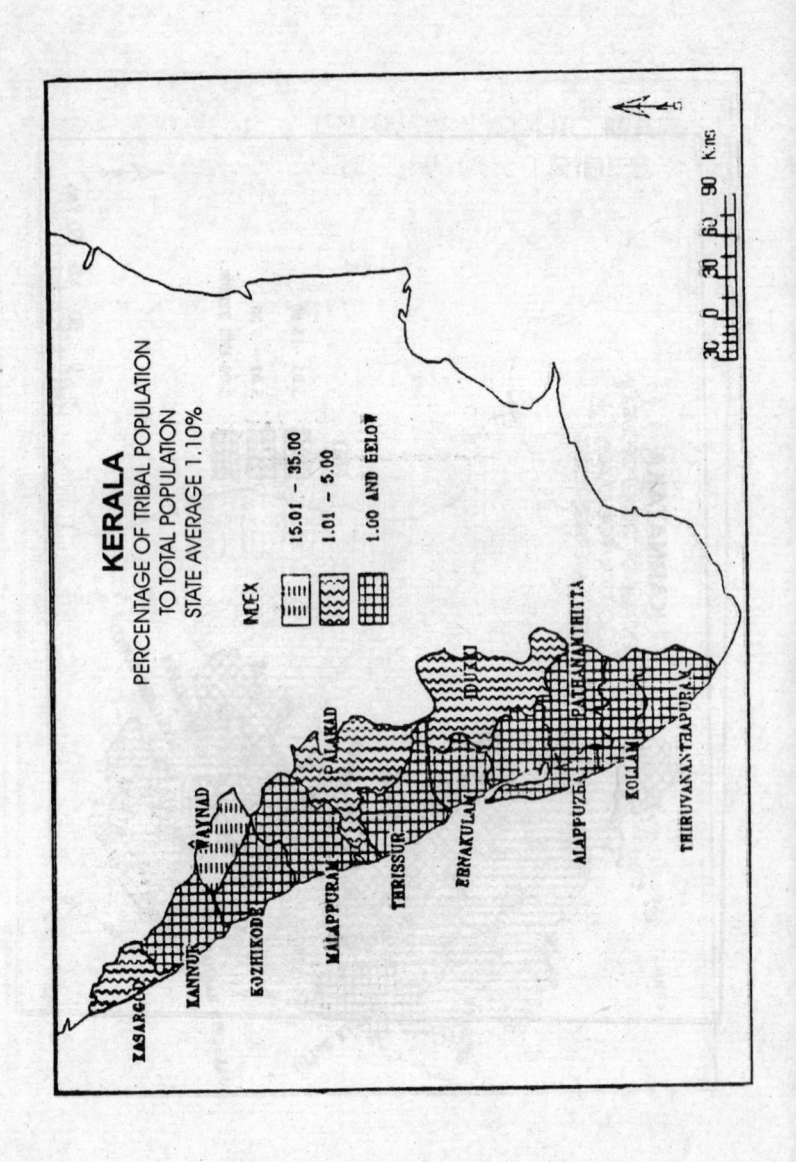

KERALA

PERCENTAGE OF TRIBAL POPULATION TO TOTAL POPULATION
STATE AVERAGE 1.10%

INDEX
- 15.01 – 35.00
- 1.01 – 5.00
- 1.00 AND BELOW

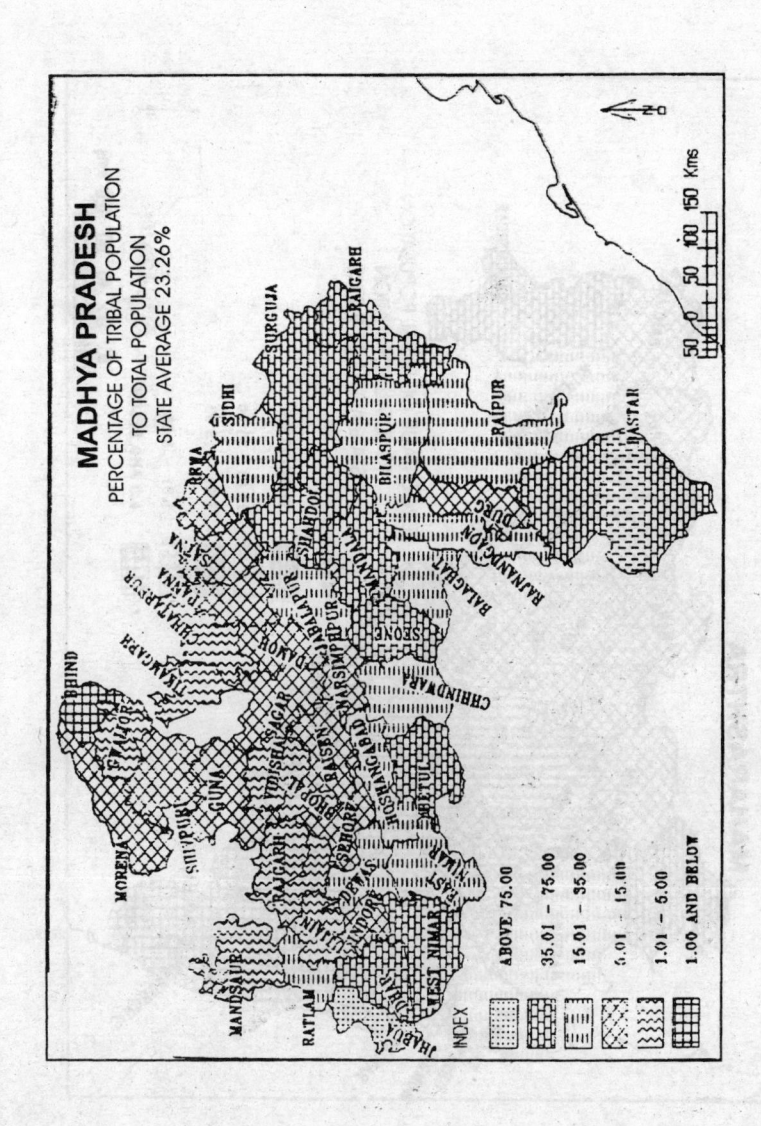

Prologue

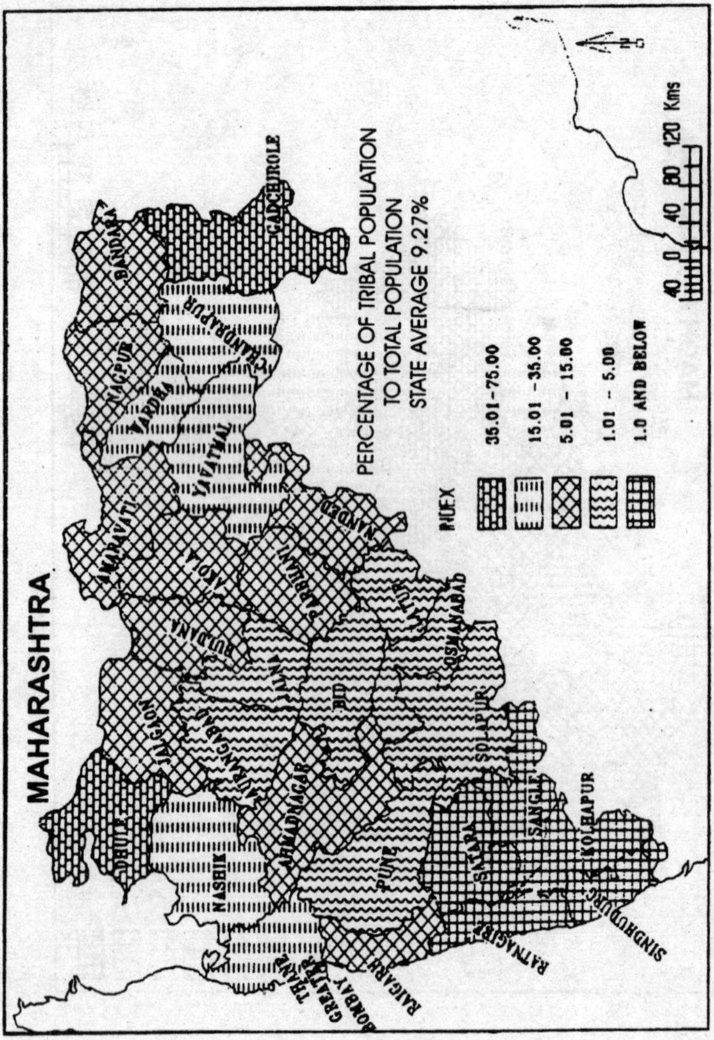
MAHARASHTRA
PERCENTAGE OF TRIBAL POPULATION
TO TOTAL POPULATION
STATE AVERAGE 9.27%
INDEX
35.01-75.00
15.01 -35.00
5.01 - 15.00
1.01 - 5.00
1.0 AND BELOW
40 0 40 80 120 Kms
DHULE
JALGAON
BULDANA
AKOLA
AMARAVATI
NAGPUR
BANDARA
WARDHA
YAVATMAL
CHANDRAPUR
GADCHIROLE
NASHIK
THANE
GREATER BOMBAY
RAIGARH
PUNE
AHMADNAGAR
AURANGABAD
JALNA
PARBHANI
NANDED
BID
LATUR
OSMANABAD
SOLAPUR
SATARA
SANGLI
RATNAGIRI
KOLHAPUR
SINDHUDURG

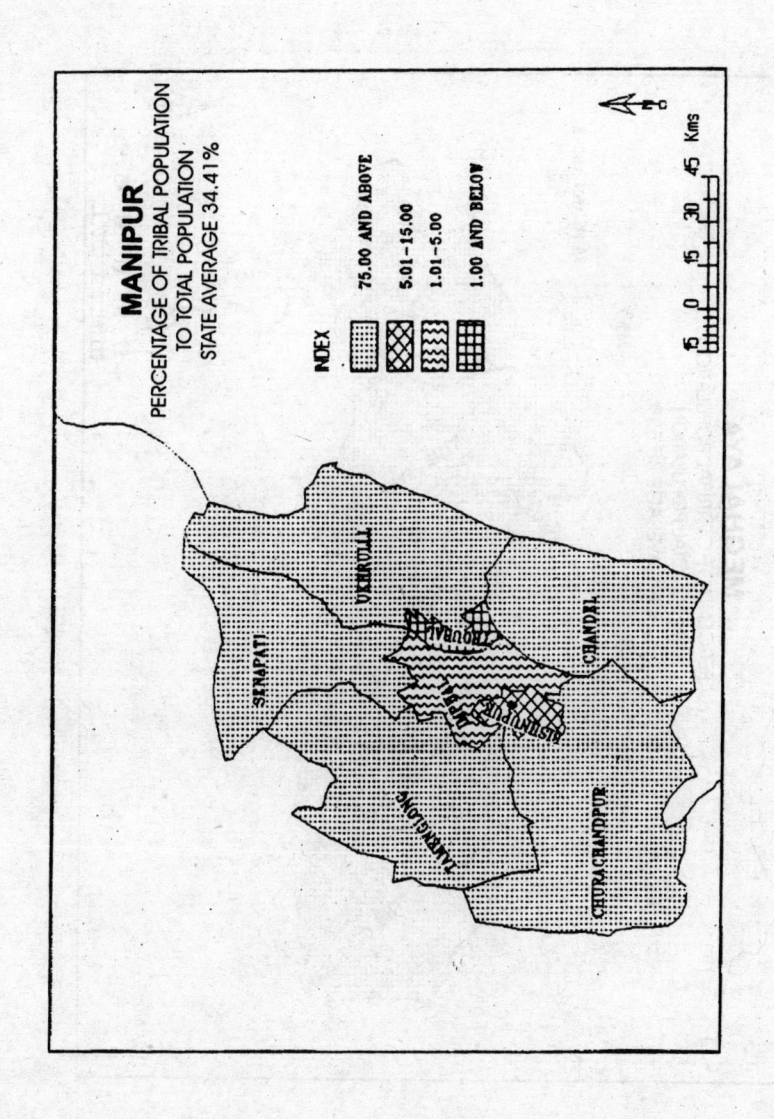

MANIPUR
PERCENTAGE OF TRIBAL POPULATION TO TOTAL POPULATION
STATE AVERAGE 34.41%

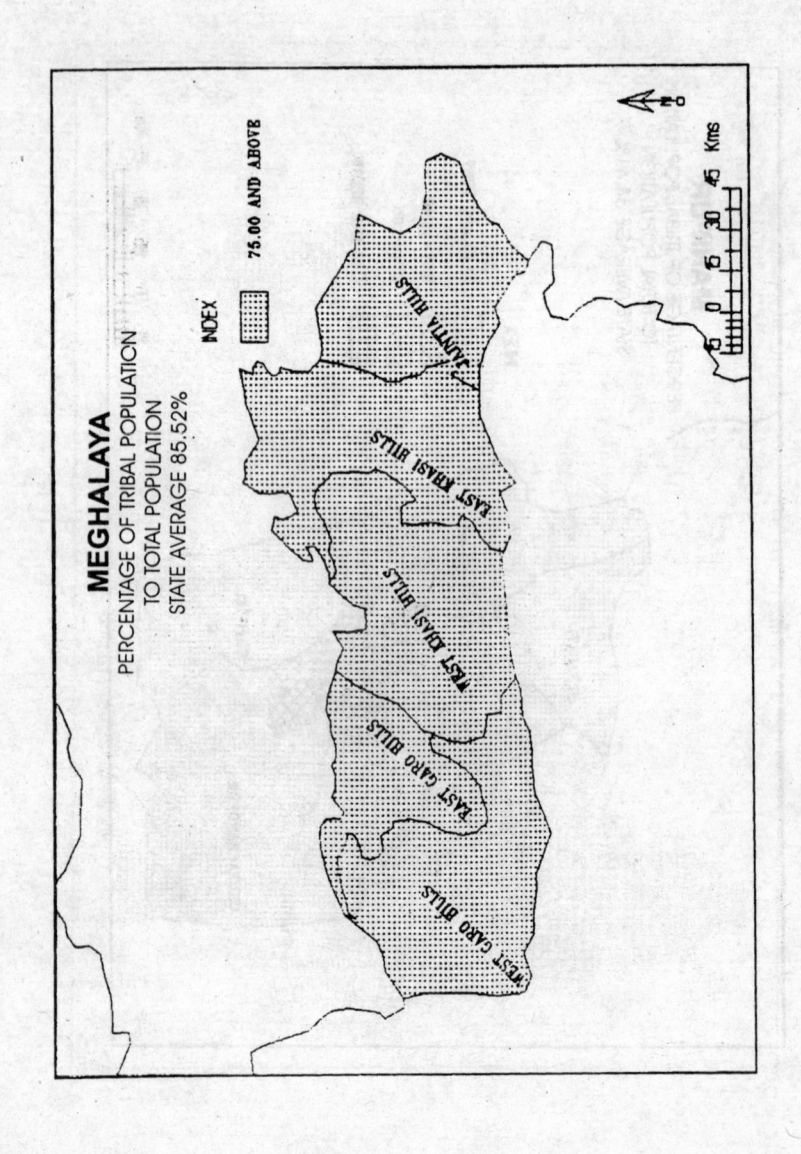

MEGHALAYA

PERCENTAGE OF TRIBAL POPULATION
TO TOTAL POPULATION
STATE AVERAGE 85.52%

INDEX

75.00 AND ABOVE

MIZORAM

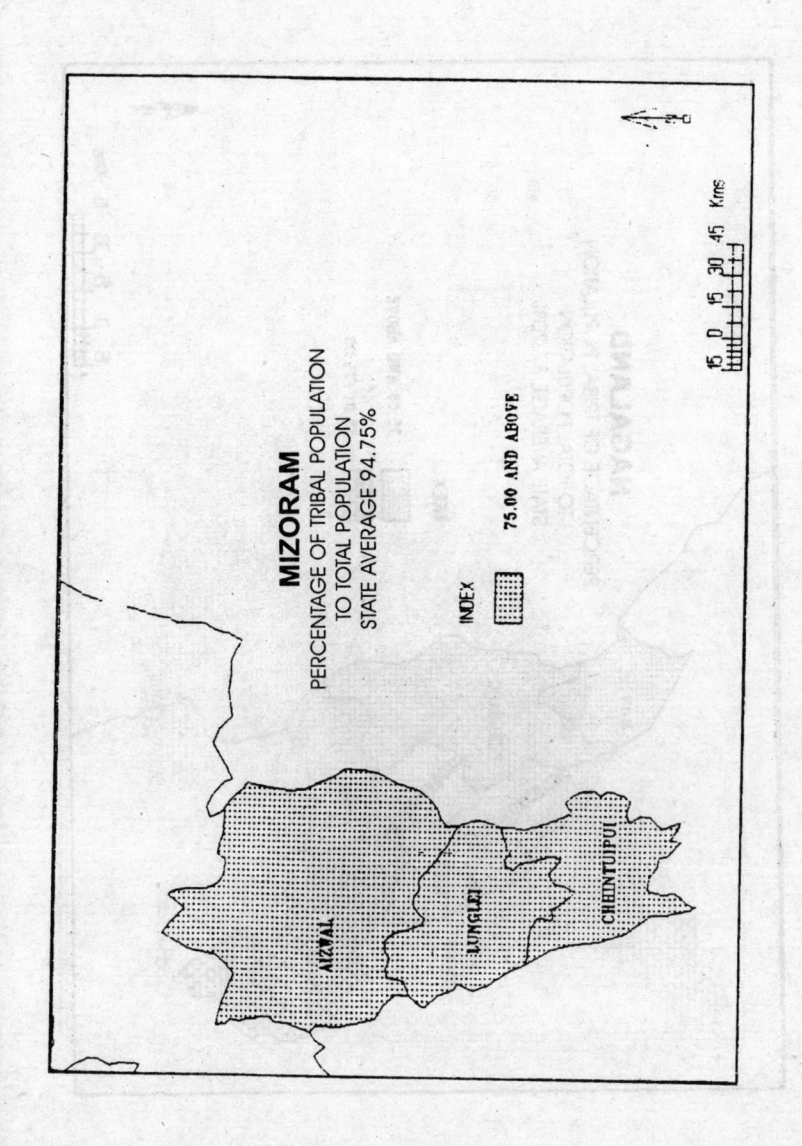

PERCENTAGE OF TRIBAL POPULATION
TO TOTAL POPULATION
STATE AVERAGE 94.75%

INDEX

75.00 AND ABOVE

AIZWAL

LUNGLEI

CHHIMTUIPUI

15 0 15 30 45 Kms

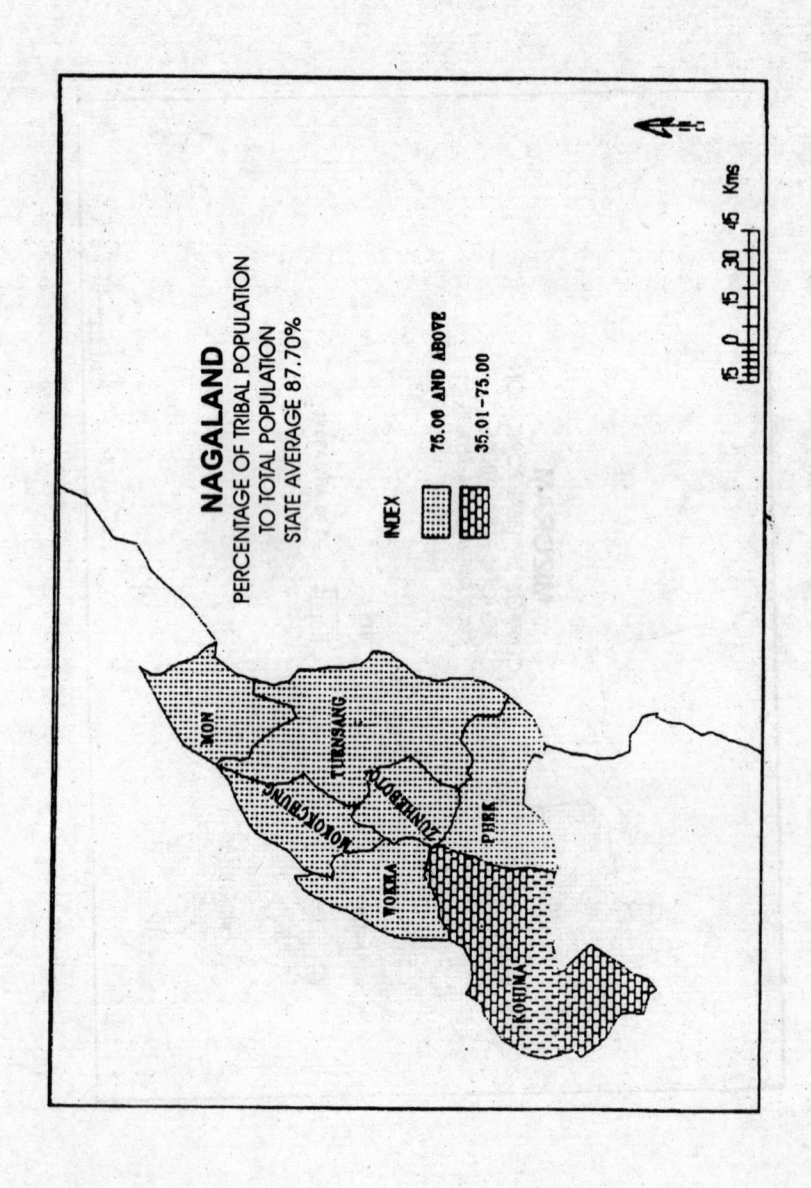

NAGALAND
PERCENTAGE OF TRIBAL POPULATION TO TOTAL POPULATION
STATE AVERAGE 87.70%

INDEX
- 75.00 AND ABOVE
- 35.01–75.00

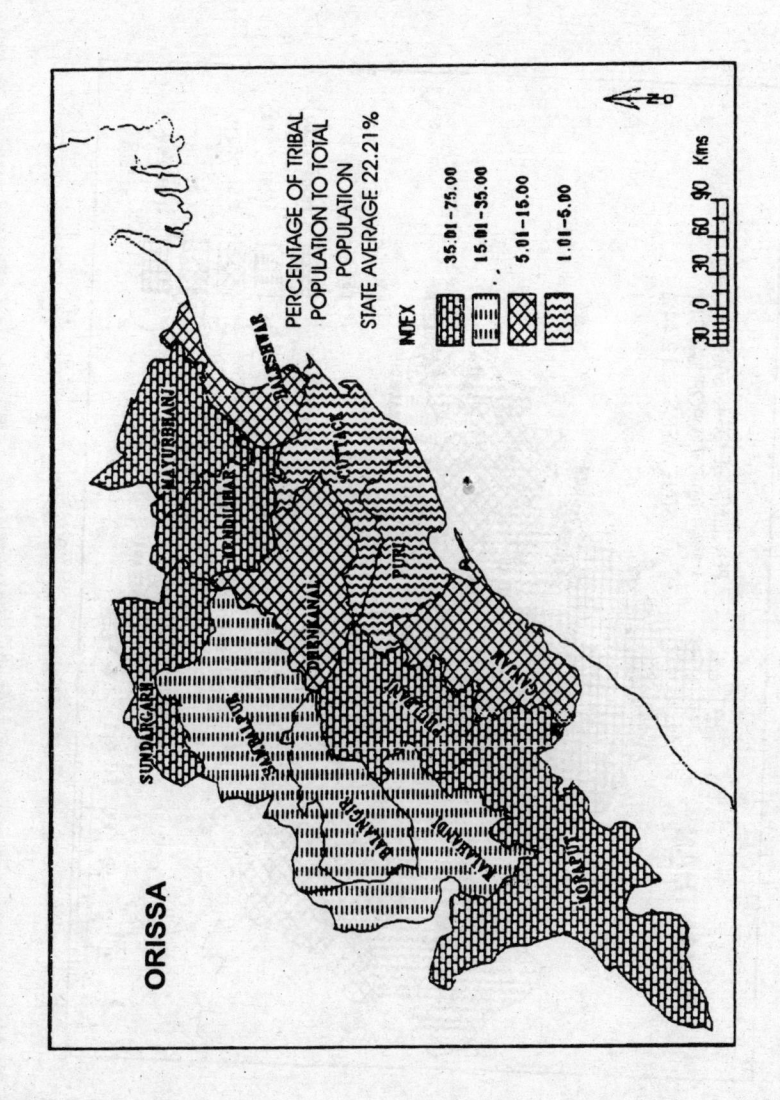

Prologue

60   Ethnographic Atlas of Indian Tribes

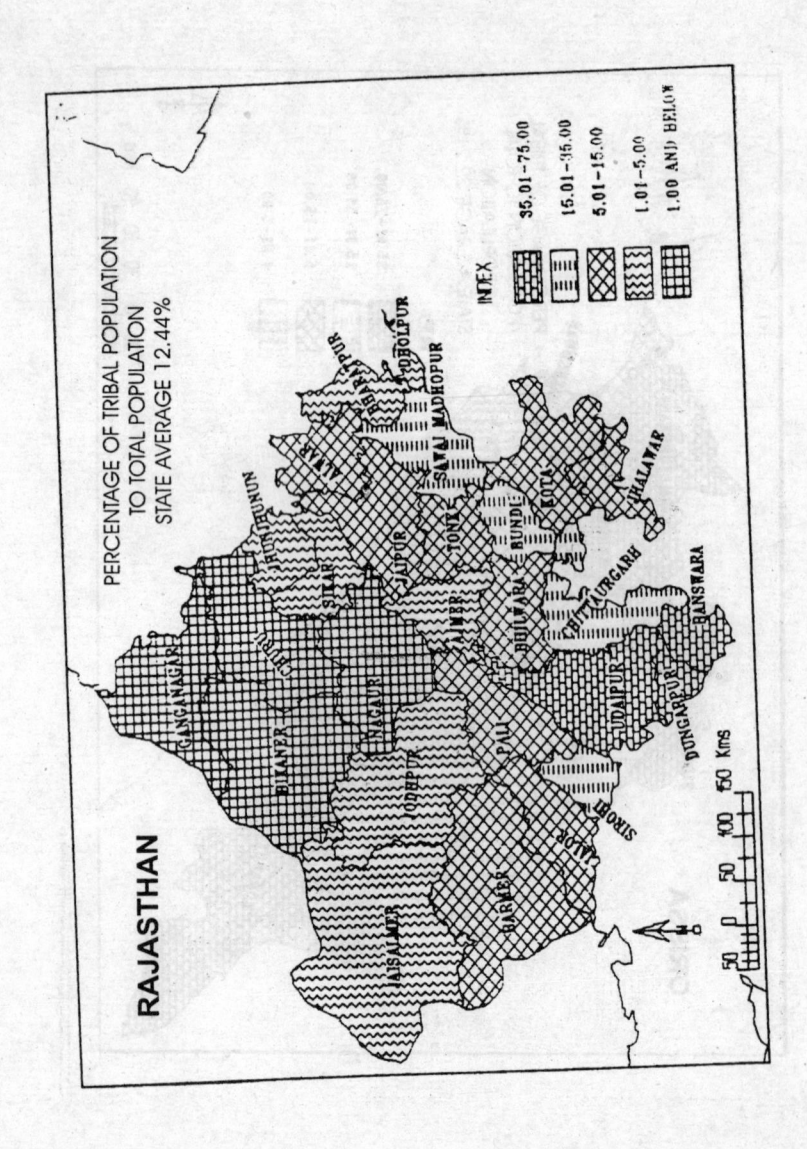

SIKKIM

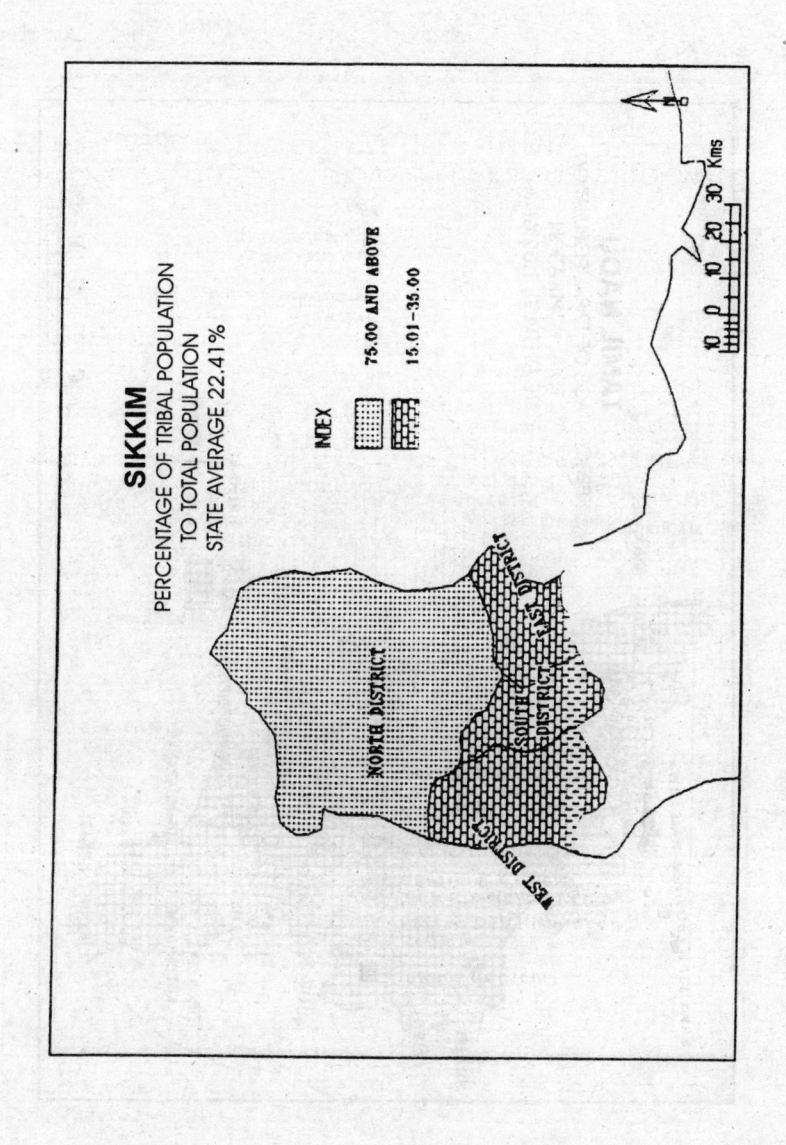

PERCENTAGE OF TRIBAL POPULATION TO TOTAL POPULATION
STATE AVERAGE 22.41%

INDEX:
- 75.00 AND ABOVE
- 15.01–35.00

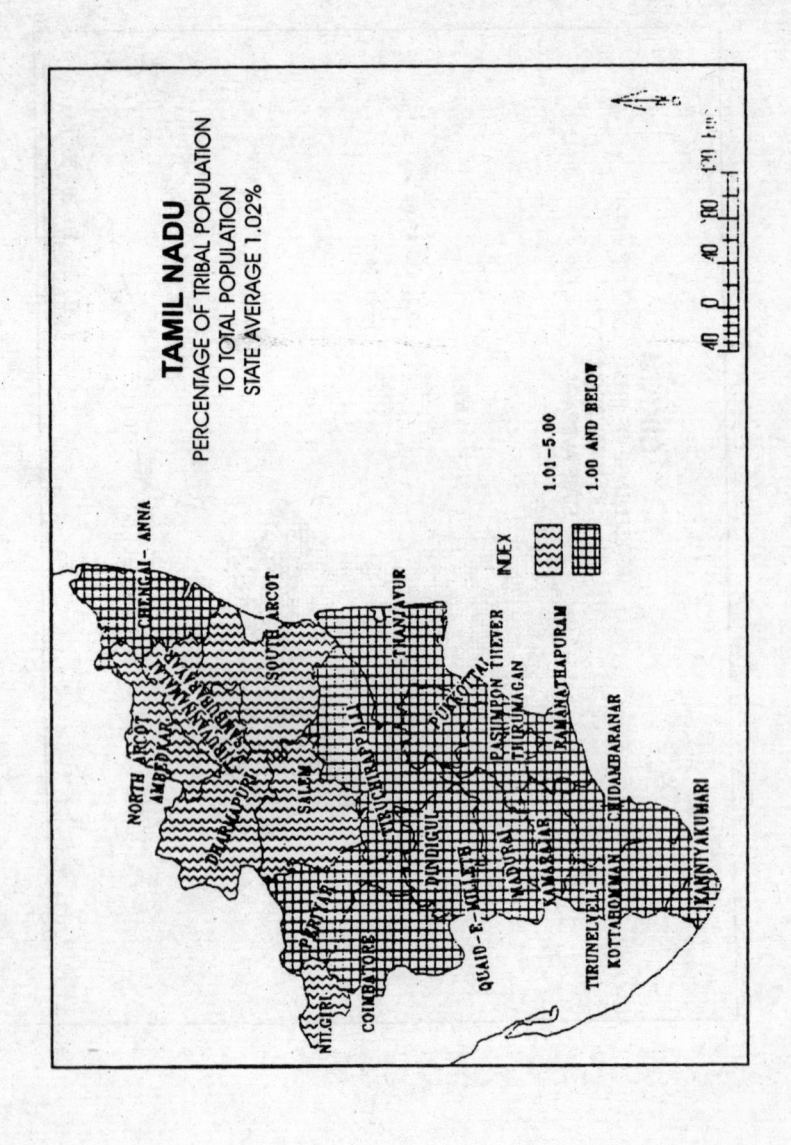

TAMIL NADU

PERCENTAGE OF TRIBAL POPULATION TO TOTAL POPULATION
STATE AVERAGE 1.02%

INDEX
- 1.01–5.00
- 1.00 AND BELOW

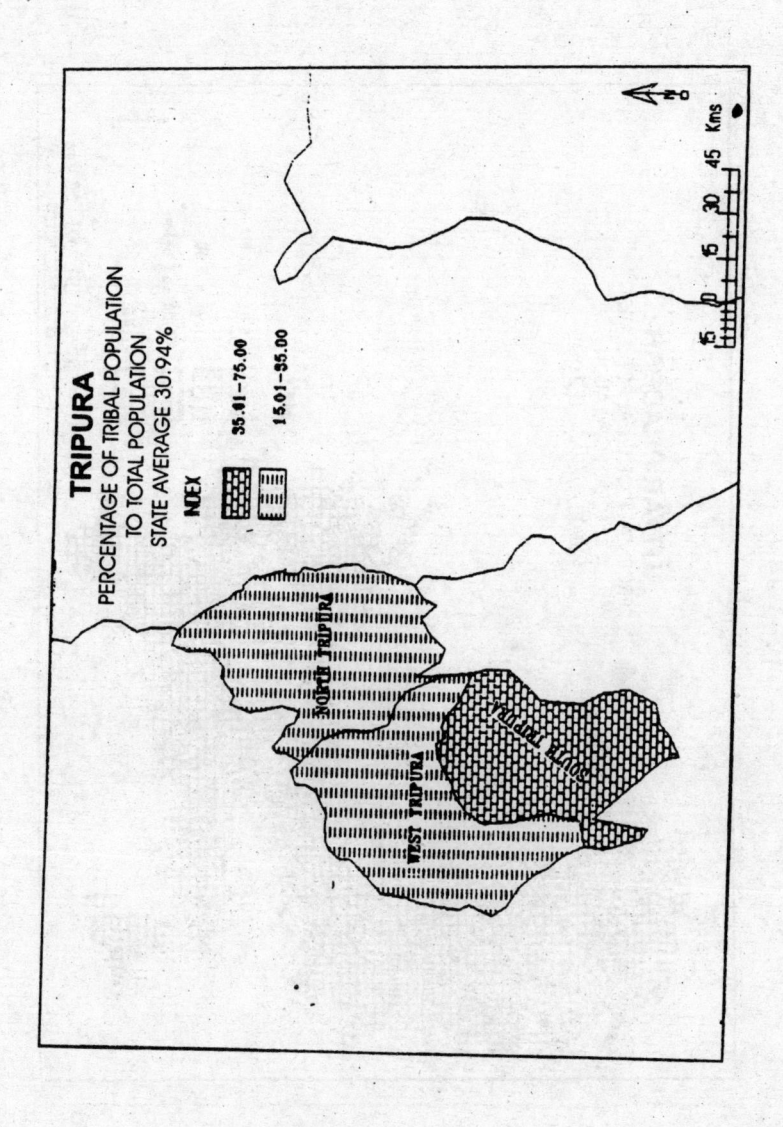

TRIPURA
PERCENTAGE OF TRIBAL POPULATION TO TOTAL POPULATION
STATE AVERAGE 30.94%

INDEX
- 35.01–75.00
- 15.01–35.00

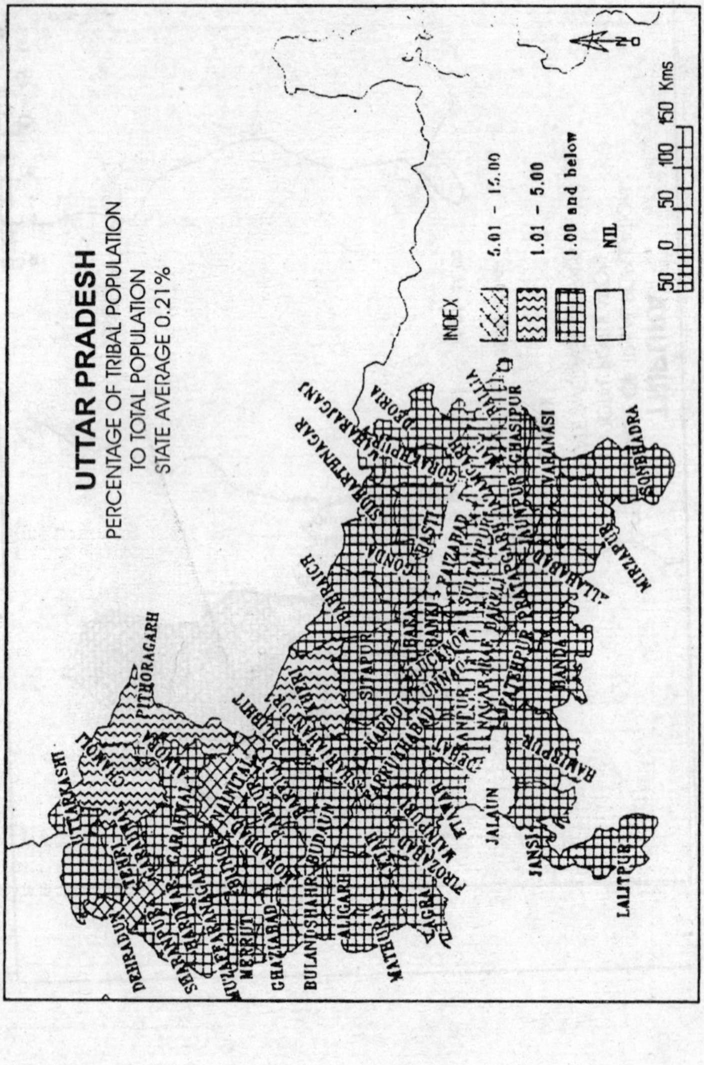
UTTAR PRADESH
PERCENTAGE OF TRIBAL POPULATION
TO TOTAL POPULATION
STATE AVERAGE 0.21%
INDEX
5.01 - 15.00
1.01 - 5.00
1.00 and below
NIL
50 0 50 100 150 Kms
N
UTTARKASHI
PITHORAGARH
DEHRADUN
ALMORA
NAINITAL
PILIBHIT
MEERUT
GHAZIABAD
BULANDSHAHR
ALIGARH
MATHURA
AGRA
BUDAUN
SITAPUR
HARDOI
LUCKNOW
FAIZABAD
GONDA
BASTI
BAHRAICH
SIDHARTHNAGAR
MAHARAJGANJ
DEORIA
GORAKHPUR
GHAZIPUR
VARANASI
JAUNPUR
ALLAHABAD
MIRZAPUR
SONBHADRA
BANDA
HAMIRPUR
JALAUN
JANSI
LALITPUR
FIROZABAD
MAINPURI
ETAWAH

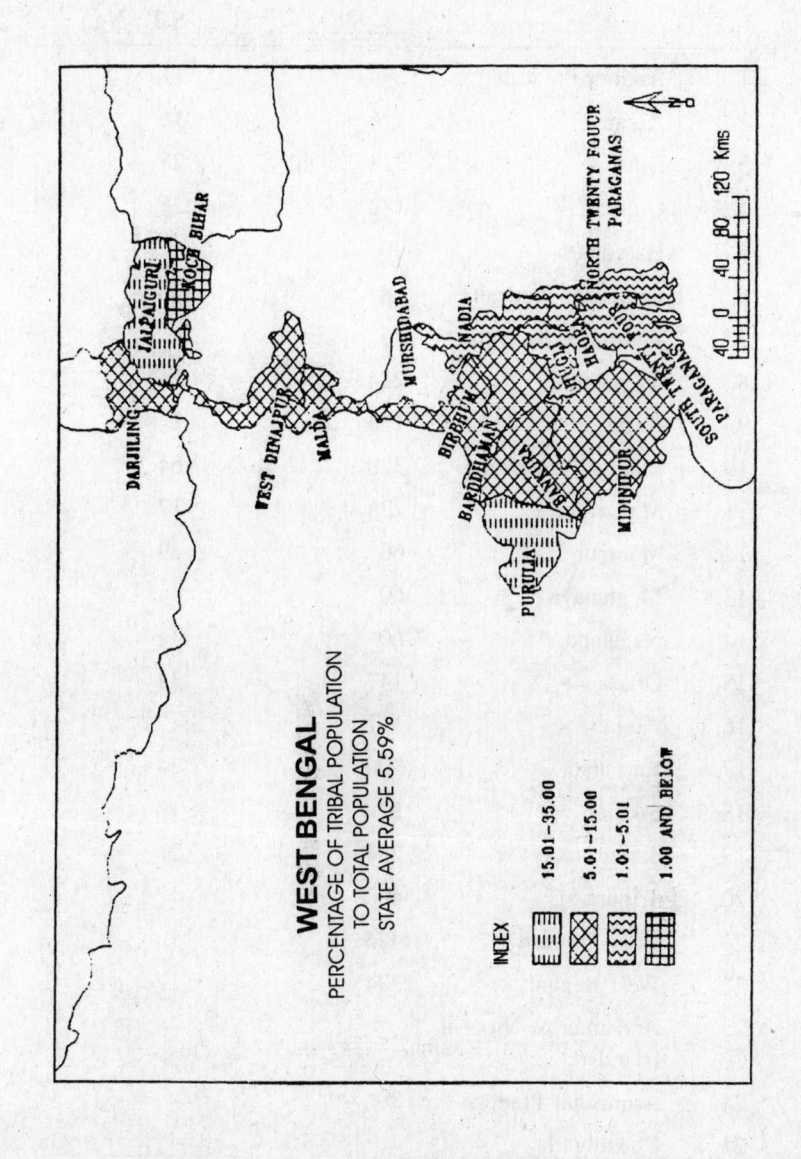

Prologue

WEST BENGAL
PERCENTAGE OF TRIBAL POPULATION
TO TOTAL POPULATION
STATE AVERAGE 5.59%

INDEX
- 15.01–35.00
- 5.01–15.00
- 1.01–5.01
- 1.00 AND BELOW

Appendix - 1
State-wise Reservation in Legislative Assemblies

S. No.	Name/ State/ Union territory	Total Seats (No.)	Seats Reserved for S.T. (No.)
1.	Andhra Pradesh	294	11
2.	Assam	126	16
3.	Bihar	324	28
4.	Gujarat	182	25
5.	Haryana	90	-
6.	Himachal Pradesh	68	3
7.	Jammu & Kashmir	76	-
8.	Karnataka	224	2
9.	Kerla	140	2
10.	Madhya Pradesh	320	64
11.	Maharashtra	228	17
12.	Manipur	60	19
13.	Meghalaya	60	-
14.	Nagaland	60	-
15.	Orissa	147	34
16.	Punjab	117	-
17.	Rajasthan	200	24
18.	Sikkim	32	12
19.	Tamil Nadu	234	2
20.	Tripura	60	17
21.	Uttar Pradesh	425	1
22.	West Bengal	294	17
23.	Andaman & Nicobar Islands	-	-
24.	Arunachal Pradesh	30	-
25.	Chandigarh	-	-

S. No.	Name/ State/ Union territory	Total Seats (No.)	Seats Reserved for S.T. (No.)
26.	Dadra & Nagar Haveli	-	-
27.	Delhi	56	-
28.	Goa, Daman & Diu	30	-
29.	Lakshadweep	-	-
30.	Misoram	30	-
31.	Pondichery	30	-
	Total	3,997	294

Appendix-2

The Second Schedule

Chapter I

In the Constitution (Scheduled Tribes) Order, 1950-

(a) for paragraph 3, substitute-

"3 Any refernce in this order to a State or to a district or other territorial division thereof shall be constructed as a refernce to the State, district or other territorial division as constituted on the 1st day of May, 1976"

(b) for the Schedule, substitute-

THE SCHEDULE

Andhra Pradesh

1. Andh
2. Bagata
3. Bhil
4. Chenchu, Chenchwar
5. Gadabas
6. Gond, Naikpod, Rajgond
7. Goudu (in the Agency tracts)
8. Hill Reddis
9. Jatapus
10. Kammara
11. Kattunayakan
12. Kolam, Mannervareu
13. Konda Dhors
14. Konda Kapus
15. Kondareddis

Prologue 69

16.	Kondhs, Kodi, Kodhu, Desaya Kondhs, Dongria Kondhs,,Kultiya Kondhs, Tikiria Kondhs, Yenity Kondhs
17.	Kotia, Bentho, Oriya, Bartika, Dhulia, Dulia, Holva, Paiko, Putiya, Sanrona, Sidhopaiko
18.	Koya, Goud, Rajah, Rasha Koya, Lingadhari Koya (ordinary) , kottu koya, Bhine koya, Raj koya
19.	Kulia
20.	Malis (excluding Adilabad,Hyderabad, Karimnagar, Khammam, Mahbubnagar, Medak, Nalgonda, Nizamabad and Warangal districts)
21.	Manna Dhora
22.	Mukha Dhora, Nooka Dhora
23.	Nayaks (in the Agency tracts)
24.	Pardhan
25.	Porja, Parangiperja
26.	Reddi Dhoras
27.	Rona, Rena
28.	Savaras, Kapu Savaras, Maliya Savaras, Khutto Savaras
29.	Sugalis, Lambadis
30.	Thoti (in Adilabad, Hyderabad, Karimnagar, Mahbubnagar, Medak, Nalgonda, Nizamabad and Warangal districts)
31.	Valmiki (in the Agency tracts)
32.	Yenadis
33.	Yerukulas

Assam

1. In the autonomous districts -

1.	Chakma
2.	Dimasa, Kachari

3.	Garo
4.	Hajong
5.	Hmar
6.	Khasi, Jaintia, Synteng, Pnar, War, Bhjoi, Lyngngam
7.	Any Kuki Tribes, including-
i).	Biate, Biete
ii).	Changsan
iii).	Chongloi
iv).	Doungel
v).	Gamlhou
vi).	Gangte
vii).	Guite
viii).	Hanneng
ix).	Haokip, Haupit
x)	Haolai
xi).	Hengna
xii).	Hongsungn
xiii).	Hrangkhwal
xiv).	Jongbe
xv).	Khawchung
xvi).	Khawathlang, Khothalong
xvii).	Khelma
xviii).	Kholhou
xix).	Kipgen
xx).	Kuki
xxi).	Lengthang
xxii).	Lhangum
xxiii).	Lhoujem

Prologue 71

xxiv).	Lhouvun
xxv).	Lupheng
xxvi).	Mangjel
xxvii).	Misao
xxviii).	Riang
xxix).	Sairhem
xxx).	Selnam
xxxi).	Singson
xxxii).	Sitlhou
xxxiii).	Sukte
xxxiv).	Thado
xxxv).	Thangngeu
xxxvi).	Uibuch
xxxvii).	Vaiphei
8.	Lakher
9.	Man (Tai speaking)
10.	Any Mizo (Lushai) tribes
11.	Mikir
12.	Any Naga tribes
13.	Pawi
14.	Syntheng

II. In the state of Assam exluding the autonomous districts-

1.	Barmans in Cachar
2.	Boro, Borokachari
3.	Deori
4.	Hojai
5.	Kachari, Sonwal
6.	Lalung

7. Mech
8. Miri
9. Rabha

Bihar

1. Asur
2. Baiga
3. Banjara
4. Bathudi
5. Bedia
6. Bhumij (in North Chotanagpur and South Chotanagpur divisions and Santal Parganas districts)
7. Binjhia
8. Birhor
9. Birjia
10. Chero
11. Chik Baraik
12. Gond
13. Gorait
14. Ho
15. Karmali
16. Kharia
17. Kharwar
18. Khond
19. Kisan
20. Kora
21. Korwa
22. Lohara, Lohra
23. Mahli

Prologue 73

24. Mal Paharia
25. Munda
26. Oraon
27. Parhaiya
28. Santal
29. Sauria Paharia
30. Savar

Gujarat

1. Barda
2. Bavacha, Bamcha
3. Bharwad (in the Nesses of the forests of Alech, Barda and Gir)
4. Bhil, Bhil Garasia, Dholi Bhil, Dungri Bhil, Dungri Garasia, Mewasi Bhil, Rawal Bhil, Tadvi Bhil, Bhagalia, Bhilala, Pawra, Vasava, Vasave
5. Charan (in the Nesses of the forests of Alech, Barda and Gir)
6. Chaudhri (in Surat and Valsad districts)
7. Chodhara
8. Dhanka, Tadvi, Tetaria, Valvi
9. Dhodia
10. Dubla, Talavia, Halpati
11. Gamit, Gamta, Gavit, Mavchi, Padvi
12. Gond, Rajgond
13. Kathodi, Katkari, Dhor Kathodi, Dhor Katkari, Son Kathodi, Son Kathari
14. Kokna, Kokni, Kukna
15. Koli (in Kutch district)
16. Koli Dhor, Tokre Koli, Kolcha, Kolgha

17. Kunbi (in the Dangs district)
18. Naikda, Nayaka, Cholivala Nayaka, Kapadia Nayaka, Mota Nayaka, Nana Nayaka
19. Padhar
20. Paradhi (in Kutch district)
21. Pardhi, Advichincher, Phanse Pardhi (excluding Amereli, Bhavnagar, Jamnagar, Junagadh, Kutch, Rajkot and Surendranagar districts)
22. Patelia
23. Pomla
24. Rabari (in the Nesses of the forests of Alech, Barada and Gir)
25. Rathawa
26. Siddi (in Amreli, Bhavnagar, Jamnagar, Junagadh, Rajkot and Surendranagar districts)
27. Vaghri (in Kutch district)
28. Varli
29. Vitola, Kotwalia, Barodia

Himachal Pradesh

1. Bhot, Bodh
2. Gaddi [excluding the territories secified in sub-section (1) of section 5 of the Punjab Reorganisation Act, 1966 (31 of 1966) other than the Lahaul and Spiti district)
3. Gujjar [exluding the territories specified in sub-section (1) of sectin 5 of the Punjab Reorganisation Act, 1966(3 of 1966)
4. Jad, Lamba, Khampa,, 1,221
5. Kanmaura, Kinnara
6. Lahaula
7. Pangwala

Prologue

8. Swangla

Karnataka

1. Adiyan
2. Barda
3. Bavacha, Bamcha
4. Bhil, Bhil Garasia, Dholi Bhil, Dungri Bhil, Dungri Garasia, Mewasi Bhil, Rawal Bhil, Tadvi Bhil, Bhagalia, Bhilala, Pawra, Vasva, Vasave
5. Chenchu, Chenchwar
6. Chodhara
7. Dubla, Talavia, Halpati
8. Gmit, Gamta, Gavit, Mavchi, Padvi, Valvi
9. Gond, Naikpond, Rajgond
10. Gowdalu
11. Hakkipikki
12. Hassalaru
13. Irular
14. Iruliga
15. Jenu Kuruba
16. Kadu Kuruba
17. Kammara (in South Kanara district and Kollegal taluk of Mysore district)
18. Kaniya, Kanyan (in Kollegal taluk of Mysore district)
19. Kathodi, Katkari, Dhor Kathodi, Dhor Kathari, Son Kathodi, Son Kathari
20. Kattunayakan
21. Kokna, Kokni, Kukna
22. Koli Dhor, Tokre Koli, Kolcha, Kolgha
23. Konda Kapus

24. Koraga
25. Kota
26. Koya, Bhine Koya, Rajkoya
27. Kudiya, Melakudiya
28. Kuruba (in Coorg district)
29. Kurumans
30. Maha Malasar
31. Malaikudi
32. Malasar
33. Malayekandi
34. Maleru
35. Maratha (in Coorg district)
36. Marati (in South Kanara district)
37. Meda
38. Naikda, Nayaka, Cholivala Nayaka, Kapadia Nayaka, Mota Nayaka, Nana Nayaka
39. Palliyan
40. Paniyan
41. Pardhi, Advichincher, Phanse Pandhi
42. Patelia
43. Rathawa
44. Sholaga
45. Soligaru
46. Toda
47. Varlil
48. Vitolia, Kotwalia, Baroda
49. Yerava

Kerala

1. Adiyan
2: Arandan
3. Eravallan
4. Hill PUlaya
5. Irular, Irulan
6. Kadar
7. Kammara [in the areas comprising the Malabar district as specified by sub-section (2) of section 5 of the States Reorganisation Act,1956(370 of 1956)
8. Kanikaran, Kanikkar
9. Kattunayakan
10. Kochu Velan
11. Konda Kapus
12. Kondareddis
13. Koraga
14. Kota
15. Kudiya, Melakudi
16. Kurichchan
17. Kurumbas
19. Maha Malasar
20. Malai Arayan
21. Malai Pandaram
22. Malai Vedan
23. Malakkuravan
24. Malasar
25. Malayan [excluding the areas comprising the Malabar district as specified by sub-section (2) or section 5 of the States Reorganisation Act,1956(370 of1956)

26. Malayarayar
27. Mannan
28.. Marati (in Hosdrug and Kasaragod taluks of Cannanore district)
29. Muthuvan, Mudugar, Muduvan
30. Palleyan
31. Palnyan
32. Palliyar
33. Paniyan
34. Ulladan
35. Uraly

Madhya Pradesh

1. Agariya
2. Andh
3. Baiga
4. Bhaina
5. Bharia Bhumia, Bhuinhar Bhumia, Bhumiya, Bharia, Paliha, Pando
6. Bhattra
7. Bhil, Bhilala, Barela, Patelia
8. Bhil Mina
9. Bhunjia
10. Biar, Biyar
11. Binjhwar
12. Birhul, Birhor
13. Damor, Damaria
14. Dhanwar
15. Gadaba, Gadba

16. Gond; Arakh, Arrakh, Agaria, Asur, Badi Maria, Bada Maria, Bhatola, Bhimma, Bhuta, Koilabhuta, Koliabhuti, Bhar, Bisonhorn Marin, Chota Maria, Dandami Maria, Dhuru, Dhurwa, Dhoba, Dhulia, Dorla, Gaiki, Gatta, Gatti, Gaita, Gond Gowari, Hill Maria, Kandra, Kalanga, Khatola, Koitar, Koya, Khirwar, Khirwara, Kucha Maria, Kuchaki Maria, Madia, Maria, Mana, Man-newar, Moghya, Mogia, Monghya, Mudia, Muria, Nagarchi, Nagwanshi, Ojha, Raj, Sonjbari Jhareka, Thatia, Thotya, Wade Maria, Vade Maria, Daro

17. Halba, Halbi
18. Kamar
19. Karku
20. Kawar, Kanwar, Kaur, Cherwa, Rathia, Tanwar, Chattri
21. Keer (in Bhopal, Raisen and Sehore districts)
22. Khairwar, Kondar
23. Kharia
24. Kondh, Khond, Kandh
25. Kol
26. Kolam
27. Korku, Bopchi, Mouasi, Nihal, Nahul, Bondhi, Bondeya
28. Korwa, Kodaku
29. Majhi
30. Majhwar
31. Mawasi
32. Mina (in Sironj sub-division of Vidisha district)
33. Munda
34. Nagesia, Nagasia
35. Oraori, Dhanka, Dhangad
36. Panika (in Chhatarpur, Datia, Panna, Rewa, Satna, Shahdol, Sidhi and Tikamgarh districts).

37. Pao
38. Pardhan, Pathari ,Saroti
39. Pardhi (in Bhopal,Raisen and Sehore districts).
40. Pardhi, Bahelia, Bahellia, Chita Pardhi, Langoli Pardhi, Phanse Pardhi, Shikari, Takankar, Takia [in (1) Bastar, Chhindwara, Mandla, Raigarh, Seoni and Surguja districts, (2) Baihar tahsil of Balaghal district (3) Betul and Bhainsdehi tahsils of Betul district, (4) Bilaspur and Katghora tahsils of Bilaspur district, (5) Durg and Balod tahsils of Durg district, (6) Chowki, Manpur and Mohala Revenue Inspectors' Circles of Rajnandgaon district, (7) Murwara, Patan and Sihora tahsils of Jabalpur district, (8) Hoshangabad and Sohagpur tahsils of Hoshangabad district and Narsimhapur district, (9) Harsud tahsil of Khandwa district, (10) Bindra-Nawagarh, Dhamtari and Mahasamund tahsils of Raipur district]
41. Parja
42. Sahariya, Saharia, Seharia, Sehria, Sosia, Sor
43. Saonta, Saunta
44. Saur
45. Sawar, Sawara
46. Sonr

Maharashtra

1. Andh
2. Baiga
3. Barda
4. Bavacha, Bamcha
5. Bhaina
6. Bharia Bhumia, Bhuinhar Bhumia, Pando
7. Bhattra

Prologue 81

8. Bhil, Bhil Garasia, Dholi Bhil, Dungri Bhil, Dungri Garasia, Mewasi Bhil, Rawal Bhil, Tadvi Bhil, Bhagalia, Bhilala, Pawra, Vasava, Vasave
9. Bhunjia
10. Binjhwar
11. Birhul, Birhor
12. Chodhara (excluding Akola, Amravati, Bhandara, Buldana, Chandrapur, Nagpur, Wardha, Yavatmal, Aurangabad, Bhir, Nanded, Osmanabad and Parbhani districts)
13. Dhanka, Tadvi, Tetaria, Valvi
14. Dhanwar
15. Dhodia
16. Dubla, Talvaia, Halpati
17. Gamit, Gamta Gavit, Mavchi, Padvi
18. Gond ,Rajgond, Arakh, Arrakh, Agaria, Asur, Badi Maria, Bada Maria, Bhatola, Bhimma, Bhuta, Koilabhuta, Koilabhuti, Bhar, Bisonhorn Maria, Chota Maria, Dandami Maria, Dhuru, Dhurwa, Dhoba, Dhulia, Dorla, Gaiki, Gatta, hill Maria, Kadra, Kalanga, Khatola, Koitar, Kaya, Khirwar, Khirwara, Kucha Maria, Kuchaki Maria, Madia, Maria, Mana, Mannewar, Modghya, Mogia, Monghya, Mudia, Muria, Nagarchi, Naikpod, Nagwanshi, Ojha, Raj, Sonjhari, Jhareka, Thatia, Thotya, Wade Maria, Vade Maria
19. Halba, Halbi
20. Kamar
21. Kathodi, Katkari, Dhor Kathodi, Dhor Katkari, Son Kathodi, Son Katkari
22. Kawar, Kanwar, Kaur, Cherwa, Rathia, Tanwar, Chattri
23. Khairwar
23. Kharia
25. Kokna,Kokni, Kukna

26.	Kol
27.	Kolam, Mannervarlu
28.	Koli, Dhor, Tokre Koli, Kolcha, Kolgha
29.	Koli Mahadev, Dongar Koli
30.	Koli Malhar
31.	Kondh, Khond, Kandh
32.	Korku, Bopchi, Mouasi, Nihal, Nahal, Bondhi, Bondeya,
33.	Koya, Bhine Koyha, Rajkoya
34.	Nagesia, Nagasia
35.	Naikda, Nayaka, Cholivala Nayaka, Kapadia Nayaka, Mota Nayaka, Nana Nayaka
36.	Oraon, Dhangad
37.	Pardhan, Pathari, Saroti
38.	Pardhi, Advichincher, Phans Pardhi, Phanse Pardhi, Langoli Pardhi, Bahelia, Bahellia, Chita Pardhi, Shikari, Takankar, Takia
39.	Parja
40.	Patelia
41.	Pomla
42.	Rathawa
43.	Sawar, Sawara
44.	Thakur, Thakar, Ka Thakur, Ka Thakar, Ma Thakar, Ma Thakur
45.	Thoti (in Aurangabad, Bhir, Nanded, Osmanabad and Parbhani districts and Rajura tahsil of Chandrapur district)
46.	Varli
47.	Vitolia, Kotwalia, Baroda

Manipur

1. Aimol
2. Anal
3. Angami
4. Chiru
5. Chothe
6. Gangte
7. Hmar
8. Kabui
9. Kacha Naga
10. Koirao
11. Koireng
12. Kom
13. Lamgang
14. Mao
15. Maram
16. Maring
17. Any Mizo (Lushai) tribes
18. Monsang
19. Moyon
20. Paite
21. Purum
22. Ralte
23. Sema
24. Simte
25. Sahte
26. Tangkhul
27. Thadou

28. Vaiphui
29. Zou

Maghalaya

1. Boro Kacharis
2. Chakma
3. Dimasa, Kachari
4. Garo
5. Hajong
6. Hmar
7. Khasi, Jaintia, Synteng, Pnar, War, Bhoi, Lyngngam
8. Koch
8. Any Kuki Tribes including:
i) Biate, Biete
ii) Changsan
iii) . Chongloi
iv) . Doungel
v) . Gamalhou
vi) . Gangte
vii) . Guite
viii) . Hanneng
ix) . Haokip, Haupit
x). Haolai
xi). Hengna
xii). Hongsungh
xiii) . Hrangkhwal, Rangkhol
xiv) . Jongbe
xv) . Khawchung

xvi). Khawathlang, Khothalong
xvii). Khelma
xviii). Kholhou
xix). Kipgen
xx). Kuki
xxi). Lengthang
xxii). Lhangum
xxiii). Lhoujem
xxiv). Lhouvun
xxv). Lupheng
xxvi). Mangjel
xxvii). Misao
xxviii). Riang
xxix). Sairhem
xxx). Selnam
xxxi). Singson
xxxii). Sitlhou
xxxiii). Sukte
xxxiv). Thado
xxxv). Thangngen
xxxvi). Uibuh
xxxvii). Vaiphei
10. Lakher
11. Man (Tai speaking)
12. Any Mizo (Lushai) tribes
13. Mikir
14. Any Naga tribes
15. Pawi

16. Raba, Rava
17. Synteng

Orissa

1. Bagata
2. Baiga
3. Banjara, Banjari
4. Bathudi, 147,969
5. Bhottada, Dhotada
6. Bhuiya, Bhuyan
7. Bhumia
8. Bhumij
9. Bhunjia
10. Binjhal
11. Binjhia, Binjhoa
12. Birhor
13. Bondo Poraja
14. Chenchu
15. Dal
16. Desua Bhumij
17. Dharua
18. Didayi
19. Gadaba
20. Gandia
21. Ghara
22. Gond, Gondo
23. Ho
24. Holva

25. Jatapu
26. Juang
27. Kandha Gauda
28. Kawar
29. Kharia, Kharian
30. Kharwar
31. Khond, Kond, Kandha, Nanguli Kandha, Sitha Kandha
32. Kisan
33. Kol
34. Kolah Loharas, Kol Loharas
35. Kolha
36. Koli, Malhar
37. Kondadora
38. Kora
39. Korua
40. Kotia
41. Koya
42. Kulis
43. Lodha
44. Madia
45. Mahali
46. Mankidi
47. Mankirdia
48. Matya
49. Mirdhas
50. Munda, Munda Lohara, Munda Mahalis
51. Mundari
52. Omanatya

53. Oraon
54. Parenga
55. Paroja
56. Pentia
57. Rajuar
58. Santal
59. Saora, Savar, Saura, Sahara
60. Shabar, Lodha
61. Sounti
62. Tharua

Rajasthan

1. Bhil, Bhil Garasia, Dholi Bhil, Dungri Bhil, Dungri, Garasia, Mewasi Bhil, Rawal Bhil, Tadvi Bhil, Bhagalia, Bhilala, Pawra, Vasava, Vasave
2. Bhil Mina
3. Damor
4. Dhanka, Tadvi, Tetaria, Valvi
5. Garasia (excluding Rajput Garasia)
6. Kathodi, Katkari, Dhor Khathodi, Dhor Katkari, Son Kathodi, Son Kathari
7. Kokna, Kokni, Kukna
8. Koli Dhor, Tokre Koli, Kocha, Kolgha
9. Mina
10. Naikda, Nayaka, Cholivala Nayaka, Kapadia Nayaka, Mota Nayaka, Nana Nayaka
11. Petelia
12. Seharia, Sehria, Sahariya

Tamil Nadu

1. Adiyan
2. Aranadan
3. Eravallan
4. Irular
5. Kadar
6. Kammara(exclding Kanya-kumari district and Shenkottah taluka of Tirunelveli district)
7. Kanikaran, Karanikkar (in Kanyakumari district and Shenkottah taluka of Tirunelveli district)
8. Kaniyan, Kanyan
9. Kattunayakan
10. Kochu Velan
11. Konda Kapus
12. Kondareddis
13. Koraga
14. Kota (excluding Kanyakumari district and Shenkottah taluk of Tiruneveli district)
15. Kudiya, Melakudi
16. Kurichchan
17. Kurumbas (in the Nilgiris district)
18. Kurumans
19. Maha Malasar
20. Malai Aryan
21. Malai Pandaram
22. Malai Vedan
23. Malakkuravan
24. Malasar

25. Malayali (in Dharmapuri, North Arcot, Pudukottai, Salem, South Arcot and Tiruchirapalli districts)
26. Malayekandi
27. Mannan
28. Mudugar, Muduvan
29. Muthuvan
30. Palleyan
31. Palliyan
32. Palliyar
33. Paniyan
34. Sholaga
35. Toda (excluding Kanyakumari district and Shenkottah taluk of Tirunelveli district)
36. Uraly

Tripura

1. Bhil
2. Bhutia
3. Chaimal
4. Chakma
5. Garoo
6. Halam
7. Jamatia
8. Khasia
9. Kuki, Including the following sub-tribes:-
i). Balte
ii). Belalhut
iii). Chhalya
iv). Fun

Prologue

v). Hajango
vi). Jangtei
vii). Khareng
viii). Khephong
ix). Kuntei
x). Laifang
xi). Lentei
xii). Mizel
xiii). Namte
xiv). Paitu, paite
xv). Rangchan
xvi). Rangkhole
xvii). Thangluya
10. Lepcha
11. Lushai
12. Mag
13. Munda, Kaur
14. Noatia
15. Orang
16. Riang
17. Santhal
18. Tripura, Tripuri, Tippera
19. Uchai

West Bengal

1. Asur
2. Baiga
3. Bedia, Bediya

4. Bhumij
5. Bhutia, Sherpa, Toto, Dukpa, Kagatay, Tibetan, Yolmo
6. Birhor
7. Birjia
8. Chakma
9. Chero
10. Chik Baraik
11. Garo
12. Gond
13. Gorait
14. Hajang
15. Ho
16. Karmali
17. Kharwar
18. Khond
19. Kisan
20. Kora
21. Korwa
22. Lepcha
23. Lodha, Kheria, Kharia
24. Lohara, Lohra
25. Magh
26. Mahali
27. Mahli
28. Mal Pahariya
29. Mech
30. Mru
31. Munda

32. Nagesia
33. Oraon
34. Parhaiya
35. Rabha
36. Santal
37. Sauria Paharia
38. Savar.

Chapter II

In the Constitution (Andaman and Nicobar Islands) Scheduled Tribes Order, 1959-)

(a) in paragraph 2, for the words " resident in the localities specifid in relation to them in that Schedule", the words "resident in that Union territory" shall be substituted;

(b) for the Schedule, substitute-

The Schedule

1. Andamanese, Chariar, Chari, Kora, Tabo, Bo, Yare, Kede, Bea, Balawa, Bojigyab, Juwai, Kol
2. Jarawas
3. Nicobarese
4. Onges
5. Sentinelese
6. Shom Pens.

❏ ❏ ❏

Appendix -3
The Constitution (scheduled Tribes) Order (Amanedment) Act, 1987

An act to provide for the inclusion of certain tribes in the list of Scheduled Tribes specified in relation to the Stte of Meghalaya.

Be it enacted by parliament in the Thirty-eighth Year of the Republic of India as follows:

Short title and commencement.

1(1) This Act may be called the Constitutin (Scheduled Tribes) Order Amendment Act, 1987.

(2) It shall be deemed to have come into force on the 19th day of September, 1987.

Amendment of the Scheduled Tribes Order, 1950.

2. In the Schedule to the Constitution (Scheduled Tribes) order, 1950 (hereinafter referred to as the principal Order) in "PART XI-Meghalaya" After item 14, the following items shall be inserted, namely

"15 Boro Kacharis

16. Koch

17. Raba, Rava"

Repeal and saving

5 of 1987

3(1) The Constitution (Scheduled Tribes) Order (Amendement) Ordinance, 1987, is hereby repealed.

(2) Notwithstanding such repal, anything done or any actin taken under the principal order, as amended by the said Ordinance, shall be deemed to have been done or taken under the principal Order, as amended by this Act.

Source-order No.43 of 1987 dt. 9th December, 1987.

Appendix - 4
The Constitution (Scheduled Tribes) Order (Amendment) Act, 1991

An Act to provide for the inclusion of certain tribes in the list of Scheduled Tribes specified in relation to the state of Jammu and Kashmir

Be it enacte by Parliament in the Forty-second year of the Republic of India as follows:

Short title and commencement. 1(1) This Act may be called the Constitution(Scheduled tribes) Order(Amendment) Act, 1991. (2) The provisions of clause(b) of section2 and section 3 shall come into force at once, and the remaining provisions of this Act shall be deemed to have come into force on the 19th day of April, 1991.

Amendment of the constitution (Jammu and Kashmir) Scheduled Tribes Order, 1989.

2. In the Schedule to the Cosntitution (Jammu and Kashmir) Scheduled Tribes Order, 1989 (hereinafter referred to as the Jammu and Kashmir Order) -

(a) after item 8, the following items shall be added, namely "9. Gujjar" 10. Bakarwal";

(b) after item 10 as so added, the following items shall be added, namely: "11. Gaddi" "12. Sippi"

Repeal and saving in relation to amendement to constitution order 32-Ord. 3 of 1991.

3. The Constitution (Scheduled Tribes) Order (Amendement) Ordinance, 1991, in so far as it relates to the amendments to the Constitution (Scheduled Tribes) Order, 1950, except as respects things done or omitted to be done before the commencement of the provisions of this section, is hereby repealed.

Repeal and saving in relation to amendment to constitution order 42-Ord. 3 of 1991.

4(1) The Constitution (Scheduled Tribes) Orders (Amendment) Ordance, 1991, in so far as it relates to the amendment to the Jammu and Kashmir Order, is hereby repealed.

(2) otwithstanding such repeal, anything done or any action taken under the Jammu and Kashmir Order, as amended by the said Ordinance, shall be deemed to have been done or taken under the Jammu and Kashmir Order, as amended by this Act.

Source : Order No. 36 of 1991 dt. 20th August, 1991.

Appendix-5
The Constitution (Scheduled Tribes) Order (Second Amendment) Act, 1991

An Act to provide for the inclusion of certain tribes in the list of Scheduled Tribes specified in rlatin to the State of Karnataka.

Be it enacted by Parliament in the Forty-second year of the Republic of India as follows:

Short Title and Commencement.

1(1) This Act may be called the Constitution (Scheduled Tribes) Order (Second Amendment) Act, 1991

(2) It shall be deemed to have come into force on the 19th day of April, 1991

Amendment of the Constitution (Scheduled Tribes) Order, 1950.

2. In the Schedule to the Constitution (Scheduled Tribes) Order, 1950 in "PART VI- Karnataka", in item 38, the following shall be inserted at the end, namely.

"Naik, Nayak, Beda, Bedar and Valmiki"

Repeal and Saving- Ord. 7 of 1991.

3(1) The Constitutin (Scheduled Tribes) Order (Second Amendment) Ordinance, 1991, is hereby repealed.

(2) Notwithstanding such repeal, anything done or any action taken under the Cosntitution(Scheduled Tribes) Order, 1950, as amended by the said Ordiance, shall be deemed to have been done or taken under the said Order as amended by this Act.

Source : Order No. 39 of 1991 dated 17th September, 1991

Appendix - 6
The Constitution (Nagaland) Scheduled Tribes Order, 1970.

The Constitution (Nagaland) Scheduled Tribes order specified in relation to the State of Nagaland. The following tribes have been included.

(1) Garo

(2) Kachari

(3) Kuki

(4) Mikir

(5) Naga

Source : Order No-88 of 1970.

Appendix - 7
The Constitution (Sikkim) Scheduled Tribe Order, 1978

The constitution (Sikkim) Scheduled Tribes Order specified in relation to the state of Sikkim. The following tribes have been included.

(1) Bhutia (including Chembipa, Doptapa, Dukpa, Kagatey, Sherpa, Tibetan, Tromopa, Yolmo)

(2) Lepcha

Source : Order of 1978.

Appendix - 8
The constition (Uttar Pradesh) Scheduled Tribes Order, 1967

The constitution (Uttar Pradesh) Scheduled Tribes order specified in relation to the state of Uttar Pradesh. The following tribes have been included.

(1) Bhotia

(2) Buksa

(3) Jaunsari

(4) Raji

(5) Tharu

Source : Order No. 78 of 1967

Appendix-9

SHEDULED TRIBES OF INDIA

The list of scheduled tribes of India according to Amendment Order No. 108 of 18th Sept. 1976 with 1981. Tribe-wise cecnsus (population)-

Andhra Pradesh

		Tribal Population (1981 Census)
1.	Andh	5,944
2.	Bagata	87,994
3.	Bhil	259
4.	Chenchu, Chenchwar	28,434
5.	Gadabas	27,632
6.	Gond, Naikpod, Rajgond	169,477
7.	Goudu (in the Agency tracts)	8,692
8.	Hill Reddis	398
9.	Jatapus	86,506
10.	Kammara	36,548
11.	Kattunayakan	399
12.	Kolam, Mannervareu	21,842
13.	Konda Dhors	139,238
14.	Konda Kapus	28,003
15.	Kondareddis	54,685
16.	Kondhs, Kodi, Kodhu, Desaya Kondhs, Dongria Kondhs,,Kultiya Kondhs, Tikiria Kondhs, Yenity Kondhs	39,408
17.	Kotia, Bentho, Oriya, Bartika, Dhulia, Dulia, Holva, Paiko, Putiya, Sanrona, Sidhopaiko	31,466

18.	Koya, Goud, Rajah, Rasha Koya, Lingadhari Koya (ordinary), kottu koya, Bhine koya, Raj koya	359,799
19.	Kulia	413
20.	Malis (excluding Adilabad, Hyderabad, Karimnagar, Khammam, Mahbubnagar, Medak, Nalgonda, Nizamabad and Warangal districts)	2,467
21.	Manna Dhora	18,964
22.	Mukha Dhora, Nooka Dhora	17,456
23.	Nayaks (in the Agency tracts)	6,532
24.	Pardhan	16,023
25.	Porja, Parangiperja	16,479
26.	Reddi Dhoras	5,281
27.	Rona, Rena	232
28.	Savaras, Kapu Savaras, Maliya Savaras, Khutto Savaras	82,101
29.	Sugalis, Lambadis	1,158,342
30.	Thoti (in Adilabad, Hyderabad, Karimnagar, Mahbubnagar, Medak, Nalgonda, Nizamabad and Warangal districts)	1,416
31.	Valmiki (in the Agency tracts)	42,944
32.	Yenadis	320,444
33.	Yerukulas	300,557

Arunachal Pradesh (1971 census)

1. In the autonomous districts -

1.	Chakma	396
2.	Dimasa, Kachari	39,342
3.	Garo	9,139
4.	Hajong	386
5.	Hmar	5,380
6.	Khasi, Jaintia, Synteng, Pnar, War, Bhjoi, Lyngngam	6,487
7.	Any Kuki Tribes, including-	13,524
i).	Biate, Biete	
ii).	Changsan	
iii).	Chongloi	
iv).	Doungel	
v).	Gamlhou	
vi).	Gangte	
vii).	Guite	
viii).	Hanneng	
ix).	Haokip, Haupit	
x)	Haolai	
xi).	Hengna	
xii).	Hongsungn	
xiii).	Hrangkhwal	
xiv).	Jongbe	
xv).	Khawchung	

xvi).	Khawathlang, Khothalong	
xvii).	Khelma	
xviii).	Kholhou	
xix).	Kipgen	
xx).	Kuki	
xxi).	Lengthang	
xxii).	Lhangum	
xxiii).	Lhoujem	
xxiv).	Lhouvun	
xxv).	Lupheng	
xxvi).	Mangjel	
xxvii).	Misao	
xxviii).	Riang	
xxix).	Sairhem	
xxx).	Selnam	
xxxi).	Singson	
xxxii).	Sitlhou	
xxxiii).	Sukte	
xxxiv).	Thado	
xxxv).	Thangngeu	
xxxvi).	Uibuch	
xxxvii).	Vaiphei	
8.	Lakher	1
9.	Man (Tai speaking)	964
10.	Any Mizo (Lushai) tribes	711

11.	Mikir	177,194
12.	Any Naga tribes	8,481
13.	Pawi	6
14.	Syntheng	611

II. In the state of Assam exluding the autonomous districts-

1.	Barmans in Cachar	13,210
2.	Boro, Borokachari	610,459
3.	Deori	23,080
4.	Hojai	2,298
5.	Kachari, Sonwal	198,619
6.	Lalung	95,609
7.	Mech	2,570
8.	Miri	259,551
9.	Rabha	138,630

Bihar

1.	Asur	7,783
2.	Baiga	3,551
3.	Banjara	411
4.	Bathudi	1,595
5.	Bedia	60,446
6.	Bhumij (in North Chotanagpur and South Chotanagpur divisions and Santal Parganas districts)	136,109
7.	Binjhia	10,009
8.	Birhor	4,377

9.	Birjia	4,057
10.	Chero	52,210
11.	Chik Baraik	40,339
12.	Gond	96,574
13.	Gorait	5,206
14.	Ho	536,523
15.	Karmali	38,651
16.	Kharia	141,771
17.	Kharwar	222,758
18.	Khond	1,264
19.	Kisan	23,420
20.	Kora	33,952
21.	Korwa	21,940
22.	Lohara, Lohra	
23.	Mahli	91,868
24.	Mal Paharia	79,322
25.	Munda	845,887
26.	Oraon	1,048,066
27.	Parhaiya	24,012
28.	Santal	2,060,730
29.	Sauria Paharia	39,269
30.	Savar	3,014

Goa

1.	Dhodia	63
2.	Dhubla, Helpati, Talvia	169
3.	Naikda, Nayaka	399

| 4. | Siddi | 42 |
| 5. | Varli | 2 |

Gujarat

1.	Barda	757
2.	Bavacha, Bamcha	3,714
3.	Bharwad (in the Nesses of the forests of Alech, Barda and Gir)	519
4.	Bhil, Bhil Garasia, Dholi Bhil, Dungri Bhil, Dungri Garasia, Mewasi Bhil, Rawal Bhil, Tadvi Bhil, Bhagalia, Bhilala, Pawra, Vasava, Vasave	2,030,438
5.	Charan (in the Nesses of the forests of Alech, Barda and Gir)	1,426
6.	Chaudhri (in Surat and Valsad districts)	219,897
7.	Chodhara	5,464
8.	Dhanka, Tadvi, Tetaria, Valvi	185,091
9.	Dhodia	449,130
10.	Dubla, Talavia, Halpati	469,855
11.	Gamit, Gamta, Gavit, Mavchi, Padvi	250,550
12.	Gond, Rajgond	1,056
13.	Kathodi, Katkari, Dhor Kathodi, Dhor Katkari, Son Kathodi, Son Kathari	2,546
14.	Kokna, Kokni, Kukna	203,511
15.	Koli (in Kutch district)	47,876
16.	Koli Dhor, Tokre Koli, Kolcha, Kolgha	62,232
17.	Kunbi (in the Dangs district)	35,214

Prologue

18.	Naikda, Nayaka, Cholivala Nayaka, Kapadia Nayaka, Mota Nayaka, Nana Nayaka	280,230
19.	Padhar	10,587
20.	Paradhi (in Kutch district)	4,416
21.	Pardhi, Advichincher, Phanse Pardhi (excluding Amereli, Bhavnagar, Jamnagar, Junagadh, Kutch, Rajkot and Surendranagar districts)	814
22.	Patelia	70,230
23.	Pomla	793
24.	Rabari (in the Nesses of the forests of Alech, Barada and Gir)	5,047
25.	Rathawa	308,640
26.	Siddi (in Amreli, Bhavnagar, Jamnagar, Junagadh, Rajkot and Surendranagar districts)	5,429
27.	Vaghri (in Kutch district)	7,806
28.	Varli	152,983
29.	Vitola, Kotwalia, Barodia	17,759

Himachal Pradesh

1.	Bhot, Bodh	22,635
2.	Gaddi [excluding the territories secified in sub-section (1) of section 5 of the Punjab Reorganisation Act, 1966 (31 of 1966) other than the Lahaul and Spiti district)	76,860
3.	Gujjar [exluding the territories specified in sub-section (1) of sectin 5 of the Punjab Reorganisation Act, 1966(3 of 1966)	28,121

4.	Jad, Lamba, Khampa,, 1,221	
5.	Kanmaura, Kinnara	47,913
6.	Lahaula	1,874
7.	Pangwala	11,202
8.	Swangla	7,162

Karnataka

1.	Adiyan	368
2.	Barda	727
3.	Bavacha, Bamcha	79
4.	Bhil, Bhil Garasia, Dholi Bhil, Dungri Bhil, Dungri Garasia, Mewasi Bhil, Rawal Bhil, Tadvi Bhil, Bhagalia, Bhilala, Pawra, Vasva, Vasave	1,867
5.	Chenchu, Chenchwar	276
6.	Chodhara	141
7.	Dubla, Talavia, Halpati	2
8.	Gmit, Gamta, Gavit, Mavchi, Padvi, Valvi	34
9.	Gond, Naikpond, Rajgond	60,730
10.	Gowdalu	6,223
11.	Hakkipikki	3,382
12.	Hassalaru	10,660
13.	Irular	313
14.	Iruliga	5,534
15.	Jenu Ķuruba	34,747
16.	Kadu Kuruba	209,677

17.	Kammara (in South Kanara district and Kollegal taluk of Mysore district)	844
18.	Kaniya, Kanyan (in Kollegal taluk of Mysore district)	528
19.	Kathodi, Katkari, Dhor Kathodi, Dhor Kathari, Son Kathodi, Son Kathari	942
20.	Kattunayakan	107
21.	Kokna, Kokni, Kukna	38
22.	Koli Dhor, Tokre Koli, Kolcha, Kolgha	39,135
23.	Konda Kapus	98
24.	Koraga	15,146
25.	Kota	75
26.	Koya, Bhine Koya, Rajkoya	27,807
27.	Kudiya, Melakudiya	1,773
28.	Kuruba (in Coorg district)	4,595
29.	Kurumans	131
30.	Maha Malasar	14
31.	Malaikudi	6,967
32.	Malasar	62
33.	Malayekandi	129
34.	Maleru	966
35.	Maratha (in Coorg district)	1,844
36.	Marati (in South Kanara district)	65,822
37.	Meda	18,684

38.	Naikda, Nayaka, Cholivala Nayaka, Kapadia Nayaka, Mota Nayaka, Nana Nayaka	1,260,158
39.	Palliyan	738
40.	Paniyan	482
41.	Pardhi, Advichincher, Phanse Pandhi	2,424
42.	Patelia	52
43.	Rathawa	10
44.	Sholaga	1,942
45.	Soligaru	16,390
46.	Toda	131
47.	Varlil	7
48.	Vitolia, Kotwalia, Baroda	13
49.	Yerava	19,241

Kerala

1.	Adiyan	8,152
2.	Arandan	95
3.	Eravallan	2,071
4.	Hill PUlaya	3,091
5.	Irular, Irulan	18,697
6.	Kadar	1,503
7.	Kammara [in the areas comprising the Malabar district as specified by sub-section (2) of section 5 of the States Reorganisation Act, 1956 (370 of 1956)	12,725
8.	Kanikaran, Kanikkar	8,803

9.	Kattunayakan	10
10.	Kochu Velan	11
11.	Konda Kapus	1,064
12.	Kondareddis	1,098
13.	Koraga	41
14.	Kota	603
15.	Kudiya, Melakudi	22,215
16.	Kurichchan	20,744
17.	Kurumbas	1,283
19.	Maha Malasar	9
20.	Malai Arayan	24,499
21.	Malai Pandaram	2,121
22.	Malai Vedan	2,435
23.	Malakkuravan	260
24.	Malasar	967
25.	Malayan [excluding the areas comprising the Malabar district as specified by sub-section (2) or section 5 of the States Reorganisation Act, 1956 (370 of 1956)	2,394
26.	Malayarayar	2,747
27.	Mannan	5,812
28..	Marati (in Hosdrug and Kasaragod taluks of Cannanore district)	22,196
29.	Muthuvan, Mudugar, Muduvan	11,213
30.	Palleyan	30
31.	Palnyan	793
32.	Palliyar	425

33.	Paniyan	56,952
34.	Ulladan	12,687
35.	Uraly	9,032

Madhya Pradesh

1.	Agariya	55,757
2.	Andh	153
3.	Baiga	248,949
4.	Bhaina	39,136
5.	Bharia Bhumia, Bhuinhar Bhumia, Bhumiya, Bharia, Paliha, Pando	195,490
6.	Bhattra	117,297
7.	Bhil, Bhilala, Barela, Patelia	2,500,530
8.	Bhil Mina	5,358
9.	Bhunjia	9,524
10.	Biar, Biyar	7,374
11.	Binjhwar	92,076
12.	Birhul, Birhor	561
13.	Damor, Damaria	1,112
14.	Dhanwar	34,386
15.	Gadaba, Gadba	3,254

16.	Gond; Arakh, Arrakh, Agaria, Asur, Badi Maria, Bada Maria, Bhatola, Bhimma, Bhuta, Koilabhuta, Koliabhuti, Bhar, Bisonhorn Marin, Chota Maria, Dandami Maria, Dhuru, Dhurwa, Dhoba, Dhulia, Dorla, Gaiki, Gatta, Gatti, Gaita, Gond Gowari, Hill Maria, Kandra, Kalanga, Khatola, Koitar, Koya, Khirwar, Khirwara, Kucha Maria, Kuchaki Maria, Madia, Maria, Mana, Man-newar, Moghya, Mogia, Monghya, Mudia, Muria, Nagarchi, Nagwanshi, Ojha, Raj, Sonjbari Jhareka, Thatia, Thotya, Wade Maria, Vade Maria, Daro	5,349,883
17.	Halba, Halbi	236,375
18.	Kamar	236,375
19.	Karku	17,517
20.	Kawar, Kanwar, Kaur, Cherwa, Rathia, Tanwar, Chattri	469
21.	Keer (in Bhopal, Raisen and Sehore districts)	562,200
22.	Khairwar, Kondar	9,894
23.	Kharia	14,374
24.	Kondh, Khond, Kandh	6,892
25.	Kol	1,670
26.	Kolam	123,811
27.	Korku, Bopchi, Mouasi, Nihal, Nahul, Bondhi, Bondeya	304
28.	Korwa, Kodaku	66,781
29.	Majhi	11,079
30.	Majhwar	6,509
31.	Mawasi	11,021

32.	Mina (in Sironj sub-division of Vidisha district)	383
33.	Munda	1,579
34.	Nagesia, Nagasia	14,471
35.	Oraori, Dhanka, Dhangad	88,819
36.	Panika (in Chhatarpur, Datia, Panna, Rewa, Satna, Shahdol, Sidhi and Tikamgarh districts).	52,979
37.	Pao	7,223
38.	Pardhan, Pathari, Saroti	18,234
39.	Pardhi (in Bhopal, Raisen and Sehore districts).	1,831
40.	Pardhi, Bahelia, Bahellia, Chita Pardhi, Langoli Pardhi, Phanse Pardhi, Shikari, Takankar, Takia [in (1) Bastar, Chhindwara, Mandla, Raigarh, Seoni and Surguja districts, (2) Baihar tahsil of Balaghal district (3) Betul and Bhainsdehi tahsils of Betul district, (4) Bilaspur and Katghora tahsils of Bilaspur district, (5) Durg and Balod tahsils of Durg district, (6) Chowki, Manpur and Mohala Revenue Inspectors' Circles of Rajnandgaon district, (7) Murwara, Patan and Sihora tahsils of Jabalpur district, (8) Hoshangabad and Sohagpur tahsils of Hoshangabad district and Narsimhapur district, (9) Harsud tahsil of Khandwa district, (10) Bindra-Nawagarh, Dhamtari and Mahasamund tahsils of Raipur district]	8,006
41.	Parja	1,408
42.	Sahariya, Saharia, Seharia, Sehria, Sosia, Sor	261,821
43.	Saonta, Saunta	3,174
44.	Saur	68,034

Maharashtra

45.	Sawar, Sawara	63,773
46.	Sonr	48,662
1.	Andh	231,871
2.	Baiga	546
3.	Barda	10,292
4.	Bavacha, Bamcha	336
5.	Bhaina	1,293
6.	Bharia Bhumia, Bhuinhar Bhumia, Pando	1,022
7.	Bhattra	124
8.	Bhil, Bhil Garasia, Dholi Bhil, Dungri Bhil, Dungri Garasia, Mewasi Bhil, Rawal Bhil, Tadvi Bhil, Bhagalia, Bhilala, Pawra, Vasava, Vasave	993,074
9.	Bhunjia	1,940
10.	Binjhwar	6,216
11.	Birhul, Birhor	212
12.	Chodhara (excluding Akola, Amravati, Bhandara, Buldana, Chandrapur, Nagpur, Wardha, Yavatmal, Aurangabad, Bhir, Nanded, Osmanabad and Parbhani districts)	179
13.	Dhanka, Tadvi, Tetaria, Valvi	55,881
14.	Dhanwar	69,809
15.	Dhodia	10,980
16.	Dubla, Talvaia, Halpati	16,019
17.	Gamit, Gamta Gavit, Mavchi, Padvi	

18.	Gond ,Rajgond, Arakh, Arrakh, Agaria, Asur, Badi Maria, Bada Maria, Bhatola, Bhimma, Bhuta, Koilabhuta, Koilabhuti, Bhar, Bisonhorn Maria, Chota Maria, Dandami Maria, Dhuru, Dhurwa, Dhoba, Dhulia, Dorla, Gaiki, Gatta, hill Maria, Kadra, Kalanga, Khatola, Koitar, Kaya, Khirwar, Khirwara, Kucha Maria, Kuchaki Maria, Madia, Maria, Mana, Mannewar, Modghya, Mogia, Monghya, Mudia, Muria, Nagarchi, Naikpod, Nagwanshi, Ojha, Raj, Sonjhari, Jhareka, Thatia, Thotya, Wade Maria, Vade Maria	1,162,735
19.	Halba, Halbi	242,819
20.	Kamar	242,819
21.	Kathodi, Katkari, Dhor Kathodi, Dhor Katkari, Son Kathodi, Son Katkari	174,602
22.	Kawar, Kanwar, Kaur, Cherwa, Rathia, Tanwar, Chattri	20,321
23.	Khairwar	2,345
23.	Kharia	11,412
25.	Kokna,Kokni, Kukna	352,932
26.	Kol	4,187
27.	Kolam, Mannervarlu	118,073
28.	Koli,Dhor, Tokre Koli, Kolcha, Kolgha	77,435
29.	Koli Mahadev, Dongar Koli	787,448
30.	Koli Malhar	177,368
31.	Kondh, Khond, Kandh	406
32.	Korku, Bopchi, Mouasi, Nihal, Nahal, Bondhi, Bondeya,	115,973
33.	Koya, Bhine Koyha, Rajkoya	447

34.	Nagesia, Nagasia	124
35.	Naikda, Nayaka, Cholivala Nayaka, Kapadia Nayaka, Mota Nayaka, Nana Nayaka	35,053
36.	Oraon, Dhangad	70,983
37.	Pardhan, Pathari, Saroti	98,685
38.	Pardhi, Advichincher, Phans Pardhi, Phanse Pardhi, Langoli Pardhi, Bahelia, Bahellia, Chita Pardhi, Shikari, Takankar, Takia	95,115
39.	Parja	806
40.	Patelia	1,045
41.	Pomla	219
42.	Rathawa	1,009
43.	Sawar, Sawara	301
44.	Thakur, Thakar, Ka Thakur, Ka Thakar, Ma Thakur, Ma Thakur	323,191
45.	Thoti(in Aurangabad, Bhir, Nanded, Osmanabad and Parbhani districts and Rajura tahsil of Chandrapur district)	209
46.	Varli	361,273
47.	Vitolia, Kotwalia, Baroda	1,013

Manipur

1.	Aimol	1,882
2.	Anal	9,349
3.	Angami	566
4.	Chiru	3,744
5.	Chothe	1,687

6.	Gangte	7,891
7.	Hmar	29,216
8.	Kabui	26,006
9.	Kacha Naga	12,754
10.	Koirao	919
11.	Koireng	948
12.	Kom	9,830
13.	Lamgang	3,452
14.	Mao	50,715
15.	Maram	6,544
16.	Maring	11,910
17.	Any Mizo (Lushai) tribes	6,544
18.	Monsang	11,910
19.	Moyon	6,544
20.	Paite	11,910
21.	Purum	6,126
22.	Ralte	1,139
23.	Sema	1,642
24.	Simte	5,034
25.	Sahte	282
26.	Tangkhul	79,029
27.	Thadou	56,457
28.	Vaiphui	15,463
29.	Zou	12,576

Maghalaya

1.	Boro Kacharis	N.A.
2.	Chakma	103
3.	Dimasa, Kachari	1,349
4.	Garo	405,449
5.	Hajong	24,331
6.	Hmar	611
7.	Khasi, Jaintia, Synteng, Pnar, War, Bhoi, Lyngngam	628,104
8.	Koch	N.A.
8.	Any Kuki Tribes including:	2,917
i)	Biate, Biete	
ii)	Changsan	
iii) .	Chongloi	
iv) .	Doungel	
v) .	Gamalhou	
vi) .	Gangte	
vii) .	Guite	
viii) .	Hanneng	
ix) .	Haokip, Haupit	
x).	Haolai	
xi).	Hengna	
xii).	Hongsungh	
xiii) .	Hrangkhwal, Rangkhol	
xiv) .	Jongbe	
xv) .	Khawchung	

xvi).	Khawathlang, Khothalong	
xvii).	Khelma	
xviii).	Kholhou	
xix).	Kipgen	
xx).	Kuki	
xxi).	Lengthang	
xxii).	Lhangum	
xxiii).	Lhoujem	
xxiv).	Lhouvun	
xxv).	Lupheng	
xxvi).	Mangjel	
xxvii).	Misao	
xxviii).	Riang	
xxix).	Sairhem	
xxx).	Selnam	
xxxi).	Singson	
xxxii).	Sitlhou	
xxxiii).	Sukte	
xxxiv).	Thado	
xxxv).	Thangngen	
xxxvi).	Uibuh	
xxxvii).	Vaiphei	
10.	Lakher	41
11.	Man (Tai speaking)	666
12.	Any Mizo (Lushai) tribes	3,291
13.	Mikir	8,129

14.	Any Naga tribes	846
15.	Pawi	37
16.	Raba, Rava	N.A.
17.	Synteng	24

Mizoram

1.	Chakma	39,905
2.	Dimasa (Kachari)	22
3.	Garo	34
4.	Hajong	85
5.	Hmar	8,645
6.	Khasi and Jaintia (Including Khasi synteng or phar, war, Bhoti or Lyngnam)	314
7.	Any Kuki Tribes, including:	20,785

   (i) Biate, Biete

   (ii) Changsan

   (iii) Chongloi

   (iv) Doungel

   (v) Gamalhou

   (vi) Gangta

   (vii) Guite

   (viii) Hanneng

   (ix) Haokip, Haupit

   (x) Haolai

   (xi) Hengna

   (xii) Hongsungh

(xiii) Hrangkhwal, Rangkhol
(xiv) Jangbe
(xv) Khawechung
(xvi) Khawathlang, Khothalong
(xvii) Kheema
(xviii) Kholhou
(xix) Kipgen
(xx) Kuki
(xxi) Lengthang
(xxii) Langum
(xxiii) Lhoujem
(xxiv) Lhouvun
(xxv) Lupheng
(xxvi) Mangjel
(xxvii) Misao
(xxix) Sairhem
(xxx) Selnam
(xxxi) Singson
(xxxii) Sitlhou
(xxxiii) Sukte
(xxxiv) Thudo
(xxxv) Thangngeu
(xxxvi) Vibuh
(xxxvii) Viphei

8.	Lakhar	16,704
9.	Man (Tai speaking)	2

Prologue

10.	Any Mizo (Lushai) Tribes	351,341
11.	Mikir	1
12.	Any Naga Tribes	23
13.	Pawi	22,997
14.	Synteng	5

Nagaland

1.	Garo	1,472
2.	Kachari	7,212
3.	Kuki	9,839
4.	Mikir	440
5.	Naga Tribes (Any)	630,973

Orissa

1.	Bagata	2,615
2.	Baiga	188
3.	Banjara, Banjari	10,925
4.	Bathudi,	147,969
5.	Bhottada, Dhotada	247,710
6.	Bhuiya, Bhuyan	207,793
7.	Bhumia	75,221
8.	Bhumij	157,614
9.	Bhunjia	9,077
10.	Binjhal	98,631
11.	Binjhia, Binjhoa	8,002
12.	Birhor	142
13.	Bondo Poraja	5,895

14.	Chenchu	44
15.	Dal	18,163
16.	Desua Bhumij	1,183
17.	Dharua	8,612
18.	Didayi	1,978
19.	Gadaba	56,911
20.	Gandia	2,263
21.	Ghara	617
22.	Gond, Gondo	602,749
23.	Ho	44,496
24.	Holva	8,883
25.	Jatapu	18,457
26.	Juang	30,876
27.	Kandha Gauda	15,189
28.	Kawar	8,549
29.	Kharia, Kharian	144,178
30.	Kharwar	1,429
31.	Khond, Kond, Kandha, Nanguli Kandha, Sitha Kandha	
32.	Kisan	227,992
33.	Kol	4,234
34.	Kolah Loharas, Kol Loharas	18,730
35.	Kolha	315,355
36.	Koli, Malhar	4,710
37.	Kondadora	17,442
38.	Kora	5,822

39.	Korua	986
40.	Kotia	19,136
41.	Koya	87,261
42.	Kulis	1,498
43.	Lodha	5,100
44.	Madia	1,066
45.	Mahali	11,767
46.	Mankidi	205
47.	Mankirdia	1,005
48.	Matya	12,122
49.	Mirdhas	28,177
50.	Munda, Munda Lohara, Munda Mahalis	338,936
51.	Mundari	24,667
52.	Omanatya	19,465
53.	Oraon	215,336
54.	Parenga	9,623
55.	Paroja	267,185
56.	Pentia	7,908
57.	Rajuar	2,314
58.	Santal	2,314
59.	Saora, Savar, Saura, Sahara	370,060
60.	Shabar, Lodha	529,209
61.	Sounti	67,872
62.	Tharua	1,034

Rajasthan

1.	Bhil, Bhil Garasia, Dholi Bhil, Dungri Bhil, Dungri, Garasia, Mewasi Bhil, Rawal Bhil, Tadvi Bhil, Bhagalia, Bhilala, Pawra, Vasava, Vasave	1,840,966
2.	Bhil Mina	27,137
3.	Damor	31,377
4.	Dhanka, Tadvi, Tetaria, Valvi	14,111
5.	Garasia (excluding Rajput Garasia)	118,757
6.	Kathodi, Katkari, Dhor Khathodi, Dhor Katkari, Son Kathodi, Son Kathari	2,553
7.	Kokna, Kokni, Kukna	2,553
8.	Koli Dhor, Tokre Koli, Kocha, Kolgha	2,081
9.	Mina	2,086,692
10.	Naikda, Nayaka, Cholivala Nayaka, Kapadia Nayaka, Mota Nayaka, Nana Nayaka	9,174
11.	Petelia	1,703
12.	Seharia, Sehria, Sahariya	40,945

Sikkim

1.	Bhutia (including Chumbipa, Dopthapa, Dukpa, Kagatey, Sherpa, Tibetan, Tormopa, Yolmo)	48,664
2.	Lecha	24,952

Tamil Nadu

1.	Adiyan	913
2.	Aranadan	141
3.	Eravallan	1,109

Prologue

4.	Irular	105,757
5.	Kadar	762
6.	Kammara(exclding Kanya-kumari district and Shenkottah taluka of Tirunelveli district)	524
7.	Kanikaran, Karanikkar (in Kanyakumari district and Shenkottah taluka of Tirunelveli district)	3,698
8.	Kaniyan, Kanyan	1,038
9.	Kattunayakan	26,383
10.	Kochu Velan	43
11.	Konda Kapus	1,624
12.	Kondareddis	31,525
13.	Koraga	421
14.	Kota (excluding Kanyakumari district and Shenkottah taluk of Tiruneveli district)	604
15.	Kudiya, Melakudi	91
16.	Kurichchan	7,160
17.	Kurumbas (in the Nilgiris district)	4,354
18.	Kurumans	14,932
19.	Maha Malasar	239
20.	Malai Aryan	470
21.	Malai Pandaram	1,026
22.	Malai Vedan	7,098
23.	Malakkuravan	7,079
24.	Malasar	4,162
25.	Malayali (in Dharmapuri, North Arcot, Pudukottai, Salem, South Arcot and Tiruchirapalli districts)	209,039

26.	Malayekandi	70
27.	Mannan	40
28.	Mudugar, Muduvan	696
29.	Muthuvan	310
30.	Palleyan	19
31.	Palliyan	1,818
32.	Palliyar	1,615
33.	Paniyan	6,393
34.	Sholaga	4,827
35.	Toda (excluding Kanyakumari district and Shenkottah taluk of Tirunelveli district)	875
36.	Uraly	9,225

Tripura

1.	Bhil	838
2.	Bhutia	22
3.	Chaimal	18
4.	Chakma	34,797
5.	Garoo	7,298
6.	Halam	28,970
7.	Jamatia	44,501
8.	Khasia	457
9.	Kuki, Including the following sub-tribes:-	5,502
i).	Balte	
ii).	Belalhut	
iii).	Chhalya	
iv).	Fun	
v).	Hajango	

- vi). Jangtei
- vii). Khareng
- viii). Khephong
- ix). Kuntei
- x). Laifang
- xi). Lentei
- xii). Mizel
- xiii). Namte
- xiv). Paitu, paite
- xv). Rangchan
- xvi). Rangkhole
- xvii). Thangluya

10.	Lepcha	106
11.	Lushai	3,734
12.	Mag	18,230
13.	Munda, Kaur	7,993
14.	Noatia	7,182
15.	Orang	5,217
16.	Riang	83,999
17.	Santhal	2,726
18.	Tripura, Tripuri, Tippera	330,872
19.	Uchai	1,306

Uttar Pradesh

1.	Bhota	32,311
2.	Baksa	31,807
3.	Jaunsari	68,348
4.	Raji	1,087
5.	Tharu	95,542

West Bengal

1.	Asur	4,286
2.	Baiga	1,606
3.	Bedia, Bediya	29,396
4.	Bhumij	233,906
5.	Bhutia, Sherpa, Toto, Dukpa, Kagatay, Tibetan, Yolmo	40,192
6.	Birhor	658
7.	Birjia	913
8.	Chakma	141
9.	Chero	1,648
10.	Chik Baraik	3,248
11.	Garo	3,206
12.	Gond	4,923
13.	Gorait	2,191
14.	Hajang	1,035
15.	Ho	3,202
16.	Karmali	1,418
17.	Kharwar	11,726
18.	Khond	639
19.	Kisan	5,370
20.	Kora	96,835
21.	Korwa	2,493
22.	Lepcha	23,409
23.	Lodha, Kheria, Kharia	53,718
24.	Lohara, Lohra	23,799
25.	Magh	1,020
26.	Mahali	50,288

Prologue 131

27.	Mahli	10,827
28.	Mal Pahariya	17,020
29.	Mech	26,959
30.	Mru	1,231
31.	Munda	230,016
32.	Nagesia	7,745
33.	Oraon	437,574
34.	Parhaiya	3,745
35.	Rabha	11,256
36.	Santal	1,666,610
37.	Sauria Paharia	4,283
38.	Savar.	37,247

Andman and Nikobar Islands

1.	Andamanese, Chariar, Chari, Kora, Tabbo, Bo, yere, Kede, Bea, Balawa, Bojigiyab, Juwai, Kol	42
2.	Jarawas	31
3.	Nicobarese	21,956
4.	Onges	97
5.	Sentinelese	N.A.
6.	Shom Pens	223

Dadara and Nagar Haveli

1.	Dhodia	13,796
2.	Publa (including Halpati)	1,872
3.	Kathodi	74
4.	Kokna	13,770
5.	Koli Dhor (Including Kolgha)	692

| 6. | Naikda or Nayaka | 67 |
| 7. | Varli | 51,337 |

Daman and Diu

1.	Dhodia	1,424
2.	Dubla (Synoynym: Halpati, Talvia)	7,435
3.	Naika (Synonym: Nayaka)	236
4.	Siddi	96
5.	Varli	798

Lakshadweep

| 1. | Inhabitants of the Laccadive, Minicoy and Amindivi Islands who, and both of whose parents, were born in those islands | 37,027 |

❑❑❑

Appendix - 10

Scheduled Tribes, with 50,000 plus population arranged in descending order of their population, 1981

Rank	Name of Schedule Tribes	State	Population	Percent of total ST population of the state
1	2	3	4	5
1.	Gond, Arakh	Madhya Pradesh	5,349,883	44.63
2.	Bhil, Bhilalal, Barela, Patelia	Madhya Pradesh	2,500,530	20.86
3.	Mina	Rajasthan	2,086,692	049.88
4.	Santhal	Bihar	2,060,730	35.46
5.	Bhil, Bhil Garasia, Gujarat		2,030,438	41.88
6.	Bhil, Bhil Garasia	Rajasthan	1,840,966	44.01
7.	Santhal	West Bengal	1,666,610	54.28
8.	Naikda, Nayaka	Karnataka	1,260,158	69.04
9.	Gond Rajgond	Maharashtra	1,162,735	20.14
10.	Sugalis, Lambadis	Andhra Pradesh	1,158,342	36.47
11.	Oraon	Bihar	1,048,066	18.04
12.	Bhil, Bhil Garasia	Maharashtra	993.074	17.20
13.	Khond, Kandha, Naguli Kandha, Sitha Kandha	Orissa	989.342	16.73
14.	Munda	Bihar	845,887	14.56
15.	Koli Mahadev, Dongar Koli	Maharashtra	787,448	13.64

1	2	3	4	5
16.	Naga tribes (Any)	Nagaland	630,973	96.94
17.	Khasi, Jaintia, Synteng, Pnar, War, Bhoi, Lyngngam	Meghalays	628,104	58.36
18.	Gond, Gonda	Orissa	602,749	10.19
19.	Kawar, Kanwar, Kaur, Cherwa, Rathia, Tanwar, Chattri	Madhya Pradesh	562,200	4.69
20.	Ho	Bihar	536,523	9.23
21.	Santhal	Orissa	530,776	8.97

Appendix - 11
Ranking of States and Union Territories by size of Scheduled Tribes Population (1991 Census)

S. No.	States/UT according to size of Schedule Tribe Population	Total ST. Population
1	2	3
1.	Madhya Pradesh	15,399,034
2.	Maharashtra	7,318,281
3.	Orissa	7,032,214
4.	Bihar	6,616,914
5.	Gujrat	6,161,775
6.	Rajasthan	5,474,881
7.	Andhra Pradesh	4,199,481
8.	West Bengal	3,808,760
9.	Assam	2,874,441
10.	Karnataka	1,915,927
11.	Meghalaya	1,517,927
12.	Nagaland	1,060,822
13.	Tripura	855,345
14.	Mizoram	653,565
15.	Manipur	632,173
16.	Tamilnadu	574,194
17.	Arunachal Pradesh	550,351
18.	Kerala	320,967
19.	Uttar Pradesh	287,901
20.	Himachal Pradesh	218,349
21.	Sikkim	90,901

1	2	3
22.	Goa	376
	Union Territories	
1.	Dadra And Nagar Haveli	109,380
2.	Lakshadweep	48,163
3.	Andaman and Nicobar Island	26,770
4.	Daman and Diu	11,724

Appendix - 12
Ranking of States/Union Territories by Scheduled Tribes Concentration

Rank in 1991	State	Percentage of Schedule Tribe Population to State Population 1991
1	2	3
1.	Mizoram	94.75
2.	Nagaland	87.70
3.	Meghalaya	85.53
4.	Arunachal Pradesh	63.66
5.	Manipur	34.41
6.	Tripura	30.95
7.	Madhya Pradesh	23.27
8.	Sikkim	22.36
9.	Orissa	22.21
10.	Gujarat	14.29
11.	Assam	12.82
12.	Rajasthan	12.44
13.	Maharashtra	9.27
14.	Bihar	7.66
15.	Andhra Pradesh	6.31
16.	West Bengal	5.59
17.	Karnataka	4.26
18.	Himachal Pradesh	4.22
19.	Kerala	1.10
20	Tamil Nadu	1.03
21.	Uttar Pradesh	0.21
22.	Goa	0.03

1	2	3
	Union Territories	
1.	Lakshadweep	93.15
2.	Dadra and Nagar Havali	78.99
3.	Andaman and Nicobar Islands	9.54
4.	Daman and Diu	11.54

Appendix - 13
List of Approved Primitive Tribal Groups

S. No.	State		Tribe
1.	Andhra Pradesh	1.	Bodo Gadaba
		2.	Bondo Poroja
		3.	Chenchu
		4.	Dongaria Khond
		5.	Gutob Gadaba
		6.	Khond Poroja
		7.	Kolam
		8.	Konda Reddy
		9.	Konda Savaras
		10.	Kutia Khonda
		11.	Parengi Paroja
		12.	Thoti
2.	Bihar	13.	Asurs
		14.	Birhor
		15.	Birjia
		16.	Hill Kharia
		17.	Korwas
		18.	Malpapaharias
		19.	Pahariyas
		20.	Sauria Paharia
		21.	Savar
3.	Gujarat	22.	Kathodi
		23.	Kotwalia
		24.	Padhar
		25.	Siddi
		26.	Kolgha
4.	Karnataka	27.	Jenu Kuruba
		28.	Koraga
		29.	Cholanaikayam (A section of Kattunaickans)
		30.	Kadar

S. No.	State		Tribe
		31.	Kattunayakan
		32.	Kurumbas
		33.	Koraga
5.	Madhaya Pradesh	34.	Abujh Marias
		35.	Baigas
		36.	Bharias
		37.	Hill Korbas
		38.	Kamars
		39.	Sahariyas
		40.	Birhor
6.	Maharashtra	41.	Katkaria (Kathodia)
		42.	Kolam
		43.	Maria Gond
7.	Manipur	44.	Marram Nagas
8.	Orissa	45.	Birhor
		46.	Bondo
		47.	Diyayi
		48.	Dongria-Khond
		49.	Juangs
		50.	Kharias
		51.	Kutia Khond
		52.	Lanjia Souras
		53.	Lodhas
		54.	Mankidias
		55.	Paudi Bhuyans
		56.	Soura
9.	Rajasthan	57.	Sahariyas
10.	Tamilnadu	58.	Kattu Naickans
		59.	Kotas
		60.	Kurumbas
		61.	Irulas
		62.	Paniyans
		63.	Todas

S. No.	State		Tribe
11.	Tripura	64.	Reangs
12.	Uttar Pradesh	65.	Bukas
		66.	Rajis
13.	West Bengal	67.	Birhor
		68.	Lodhas
		69.	Totos
14.	Andaman and Nicobar Islands	70.	Great Andamanese
		71.	Jarawas
		72.	Onges
		73.	Sentenelese
		74.	Shompens

Appendix - 14
Literacy Rate Among Generals During 1961, 1971 and 1981 Census

Sl.No.	Name of States/UTs	General			
		1961	1971	1981	1991***
1	2	3	4	5	6
	ALL INDIA	24.00	29.45	36.23	52.21
1.	Andhra Pradesh	21.19	24.59	29.94	44.09
2.	Arunachal Pradesh	-	11.29	20.79	41.59
3.	Assam	26.99	28.72	-	52.89
4.	Bihar	18.40	19.94	26.20	38.48
5.	Goa	-	-	-	75.51
6.	Gujarat	30.45	35.79	43.70	61.29
7.	Haryana	-	26.89	36.14	55.85
8.	Himachal Pradesh	21.26	31.96	42.48	63.86
9.	Jammu and kashmir	11.00	18.58	26.67	-
10.	Karnataka	25.50	31.52	38.46	56.04
11.	Kerala	46.85	60.42	70.42	89.81
12.	Madhya Pradesh	17.23	22.14	27.87	44.20
13.	Maharashtra	29.82	39.18	47.16	64.87
14.	Manipur	30.42	32.91	41.35	59.89
15.	Meghalaya	-	29.49	34.06	49.10
16.	Mizoram (included in Assam)	-	-	59.88	82.87
17.	Nagaland	17.91	27.40	42.57	61.65
18.	Orissa	21.66	26.18	34.23	49.09
19.	Punjab	-	33.67	40.86	58.51
20.	Rajasthan	15.21	19.07	24.38	38.58

1	2	3	4	5	6
21.	Sikkim	-	17.74	34.05	56.94
22.	Tamilnadu	33.41	39.46	46.76	62.66
23.	Tripura	20.24	30.98	42.12	60.44
24.	Uttar Pradesh	17.60	21.70	27.16	41.60
25.	West Bengal	29.28	33.20	40.94	57.70
	Union Territories				
1.	A and N Island	33.63	43.59	51.65	73.02
2.	Dadra & Nagar Haveli	9.48	14.97	26.67	40.71
3.	Chandigarh	-	61.56	64.30	77.81
4.	Delhi	52.70	56.61	61.54	75.29
5.	Lakshadweep	23.27	43.66	55.07	81.78
6.	Pondicherry	37.40	46.02	58.85	74.74
7.	Daman and Diu	30.80	70.75	56.66	71.20

*** Excluding population of age group (0-6).

APPENDIX - 15
State-wise distribution of tribals in India
(According to 1981 census)

S. No.	State/ Union Territories	1981 census					% of S.T. Population to total population
		Population	Scheduled Tribes population			
			Male	Female	Persons	
1	2	3	4	5	6	7
	India	665,287,849	26,038,535	25,590,103	51,628,638	7.76
1.	Andhra Pradesh	53,549,673	1,618,689	1,557,312	3,176,001	5.93
2.	Arunachal Pradesh	631,839	220,046	221,121	441,167	69.82
3.	Assam	Census was not conducted				
4.	Bihar	69,914,734	2,915,492	2,895,375	5,810,867	8.31
5.	Goa	Upto 1981 the state was with Daman and Div				
6.	Gujarat	34,085,799	2,453,566	2,395,020	4,848,585	14.22

1	2	3	4	5	6	7
7.	Haryana	12,922,618	-	-	-	-
8.	Himachal Pradesh	4,280,818	99,727	97,536	197,263	4.61
9.	Jammu & Kashmir	5,987,389	-	-	-	-
10.	Karnataka	37,135,714	926,235	895,968	1,825,203	4.91
11.	Kerala	25,453,680	131,243	130,232	261,475	1.03
12.	Madhya Pradesh	52,178,844	6,003,304	5,983,727	11,987,031	22.97
13.	Maharastra	62,784,171	2,923,955	2,848,083	5,772,038	9.19
14.	Manipur	1,420,953	196,455	191,522	387,977	27.30
15.	Meghalaya	1,335,819	537,635	538,710	1,076,345	80.58
16.	Mizoram	493,757	231,261	230,646	461,907	93.55
17.	Nagaland	774,930	332,943	317,942	650,885	83.99
18.	Orissa	26,370,271	2,939,863	2,975,204	5,915,067	22.43
19.	Punjab	16,788,985	-	-	-	-
20.	Rajasthan	34,261,862	2,150,767	2,032,357	4,183,124	12.21

	1	2	3	4	5	6	7
21.	Sikkim	316,385	38,211	35,412	73,623	23.27
22.	Tamil Nadu	48,408,077	264,288	255,938	520,226	1.07
23.	Tripura	2,053,058	297,612	286,308	583,920	28.44
24.	Uttar Pradesh	110,862,013	121,506	111,199	232,705	00.21
25.	West Bengal	154,580,647	1,559,288	1,511,368	3,070,672	5.63

Union - Territories

1.	Andaman & Nicobar Island	188,741	11,586	10,775	22,361	11.85
2.	Chandigarh	4,516,105	-	-	-	-
3.	Dadar and Nagar Haveli	103,676	40,486	41,228	81,714	78.82
4.	Goa, Daman and Diu	1,086,730	5,512	5,209	10,711	0.99
5.	Delhi	6,220,406				
6.	Lakshadweep	40,249	18,865	18,895	37,760	93.8
7	Pondichery	604,471	-	-	-	-

State-wise distribution of tribals in India
(According to 1991 census)

Sr. No.	State/Union Territories	1991 census					% of ST Population to total population
		Population	Scheduled Tribes population				
			Male	Female	Persons		
1	2	8	9	10	11		12
	India	846,302,688	34,363,271	33,315,109	67,758,380		8.08
1.	Andhra Pradesh	66,508,008	2,142,817	2,056,664	4,199,481		6.31
2.	Arunachal Pradesh	864,558	275,397	274,954	550,351		63.66
3.	Assam		1,461,560	1,412,881	2,874,441		12.82
4.	Bihar	86,374,465	3,357,563	3,259,351	6,616,914		7.66
5.	Goa		199	177	376		0.03
6.	Gujarat	41,309,582	3,131,947	3,029,828	6,161,775		14.92
7.	Haryana	16,463,648	-	-	-		-
8.	Himachal Pradesh	5,170,877	1,102,40	108,109	218,349		4.22
9.	Jammu & Kashmir	7,718,700	Census not held				
10.	Karnataka	44,977,201	976,744	938,947	1,915,691		4.26

1	2	8	9	10	11	12
11.	Kerala	29,098,518	160,812	160,155	320,961	1.10
12.	Madhya Pradesh	66,181,170	7,758,174	7,640,860	15,399,034	23.27
13.	Maharastra	78,937,187	3,71,7783	3,600,498	7,318,281	9.27
14.	Manipur	1,837,149	322,720	309,453	632,173	34.41
15.	Meghalaya	1,774,778	760,234	757,693	1,517,927	85.53
16.	Mizoram	689,756	329,817	323,746	653,565	23.15
17.	Nagaland	1,209,546	545,156	515,666	1,060,822	87.70
18.	Orissa	31,659,736	3,512,891	3,519,323	7,032,214	22.21
19.	Punjab	20,281,969	-	-	-	-
20.	Rajasthan	44,005,990	2,837,014	2,637,867	5,474,881	12.44
21.	Sikkim	406,457	47,504	43,397	90,901	22.36
22.	Tamil Nadu	55,858,946	293,012	281,182	574,194	1.03
23.	Tripura	2,757,205	434,225	419,120	853,345	30.95
24.	Uttar Pradesh	139,112,287	150,420	137,481	287,901	0.21
25.	West Bengal	68,077,965	1,938,955	1,869,805	3,808,760	5.59

Union - Territories

S. No.	State/Union Territories	1991 census				
		Population	Scheduled Tribes population			% of ST Population to total population
			Male	Female	Persons	
1.	Andaman & Nicobar Island	280,661	13,750	13,020	26,770	9.54
2.	Chandigardh	642,015	-	-	-	-
3.	Dadar And Nagar Haveli	138,477	54,102	55,278	109,380	78.99
4.	Daman And Diu	1,271,394*	6,073	5,651	11,724	11.54
5.	Delhi	9,420,644	-	-	-	-
6.	Lakshadweep	51,707	24,160	24,003	48,163	11.54
7.	Pondichery	807,785	-	-	-	-

* Including Goa

Source:

1. Census of India 1981, Series-1, Part-II-B(iii). Primary Census Abstract (Scheduled Tribes), pp. XIX-XXI and 4-15.
2. Census of India 1981, Series - 1, Part-II-B(i), Primary census Abstract (General Population Tables), pp. XXX-XXXIII and 4-23.
3. Census of India, 1991, Series-1, Paper-1 of 1993, Union Primary Census Abstract for S.C. and S.T., pp.11, 44-67.
4. Census of India 1991, Series - 1, paper-1 of 1992, Vol-II, pp15-19.
5. Mehta, Prakash Chandra : Bharat -Ke-Adivasi, Shiva Publishers Distributors, Udaipur, 1993.

Appendix - 16
Ranking of States and union Territories by size of Scheduled Tribes Population (1991 Census)

S.No.	State / Union Territory	Total S.T. Population
1.	Madhya Pradesh	15,399,034
2.	Maharastra	7,318,281
3.	Orissa	7,032,214
4.	Bihar	6,616,914
5.	Gujarat	6,161,775
6.	Rajasthan	5,474,881
7.	Andhra Pradesh	4,199,481
8.	West Bengal	3,808,760
9.	Assam	2,874,441
10.	Karnataka	1,915,927
11.	Meghalaya	1,517,927
12.	Nagaland	1,060,822
13.	Tripura	855,345
14.	Mizoram	653,565
15.	Manipur	632,173
16.	Tamil Nadu	574,194
17.	Arunachal Pradesh	550,351
18.	Kerala	320,967
19.	Uttar Pradesh	287,901
20.	Himachal Pradesh	218,349
21.	Sikkim	90,901
22.	Goa	376
Union Territories		
1.	Dadra and Nagar Haveli	109,380
2.	Lakshadweep	48,163
3.	Andaman & Nicobar Island	26,770
4.	Daman & Diu	11,724

Source : Census of India 1991, Series-1, Paper-1 of 1993, Union Primary Census Abstract for S.C. & S.T.

Appendix - 17
Ranking of States and Union Territories by Scheduled Tribes Concentration (1991 Census)

Rank	State / Union Territory	Percentage of S.T. Population to total state Population 1991.
1.	Mizoram	94.75
2.	Nagaland	87.70
3.	Meghalaya	85.53
4.	Arunachal Pradesh	63.66
5.	Manipur	34.41
6.	Tripura	30.95
7.	Madhya Pradesh	23.27
8.	Sikkim	22.36
9.	Orissa	22.21
10.	Gujarat	14.29
11.	Assam	12.82
12.	Rajasthan	12.44
13.	Maharastra	9.27
14.	Bihar	7.66
15.	Andhra Pradesh	6.31
16.	West Bengal	5.59
17.	Karnataka	4.26
18.	Himachal Pradesh	4.22
19.	Kerala	1.10
20.	Tamil Nadu	1.03
21.	Uttar Pradesh	0.21
22.	Goa	0.03
Union Territories		
1.	Lakshadweep	93.15
2.	Dadra and Nagar haveli	78.99
3.	Andaman & Nicobar Island	9.54
4.	Daman & Diu	11.54

Source : Census of India 1991, Series-1, Paper-1 of 1993, Union Primary Census Abstract for S.C. & S.T.

Appendix - 18
Percentage of Main Workers in Primary, Secondary and Tertiary Sectors among Total population and Scheduled Tribe population (1991 Census)

S. No.	State / union Territory	Percentage of Workers					
		Primary		Secondary		Teritary	
		Total Population	S.T. Population	Total Population	S.T. population	Total Population	S.T. population
1	2	3	4	5	6	7	8
	INDIA*	67.53	90.03	11.97	3.85	20.50	6.12
	STATES						
1.	Andhra pradesh	71.25	90.40	10.48	4.79	18.27	4.81
2.	Arunachal Pradesh	67.44	87.16	8.66	2.98	23.90	9.86
3.	Assam	73.99	89.38	5.56	1.68	20.90	8.54
4.	Bihar	82.36	90.47	4.64	3.29	13.00	6.24
5.	Goa	32.29	21.98	21.98	37.59	45.73	40.43
6.	Gujarat	59.76	86.63	17.86	6.56	22.38	6.81
7.	Haryana	58.84	-	13.18	-	27.98	-
8.	Himachal Pradesh	69.28	79.22	9.99	6.46	20.73	14.32

1	2	3	4	5	6	7	8
9.	Karnatka	67.37	85.29	13.17	6.44	19.46	8.27
10.	Kerala	48.02	87.93	18.17	3.91	33.81	8.16
11.	Madhya Pradesh	77.54	94.36	8.37	2.35	14.09	3.29
12.	Maharastra	61.51	87.47	15.80	5.40	22.69	7.13
13.	Manipur	70.00	86.94	9.66	1.77	20.34	11.29
14.	Meghalaya	74.81	82.15	3.73	2.48	21.46	15.37
15.	Mizoram	65.99	71.13	5.07	3.44	28.94	25.43
16.	Nagaland	75.26	83.20	3.48	2.17	21.26	14.63
17.	Orissa	75.83	91.48	7.51	3.83	16.66	4.69
18.	Punjab	56.08	-	14.84	-	29.08	-
19.	Rajasthan	71.63	92.39	9.87	2.53	18.50	5.08
20.	Sikkim	68.40	70.60	11.12	8.42	20.48	20.98
21.	Tamil Nadu	61.81	87.10	16.18	4.96	22.01	7.94
22.	Tripura	64.08	89.28	6.41	1.29	29.51	9.43
23.	Uttar Pradesh	73.01	84.36	9.98	6.41	18.01	9.23
24.	West Bengal	56.46	90.85	17.82	4.80	25.69	4.35

	Union Territories	3	4	5	6	7	8
1	2	3	4	5	6	7	8
1.	Andaman & Nikobar Islands	34.50	21.07	25.14	58.43	40.36	20.50
2.	Chandigarh	4.46	-	27.82	-	67.72	-
3.	Dadra & Nagar Haveli	71.81	85.88	16.13	7.75	12.06	6.37
4.	Daman & Diu	37.32	46.16	25.40	31.01	37.28	22.83
5.	Delhi	2.85	-	32.43	-	64.72	-
6.	Lakshadweep	25.02	29.30	25.27	24.26	49.71	46.44
7.	Pondicherry	39.24	-	19.99	-	40.77	-

* Excludes figures of Jammu & Kasmir where 1991 Census was not taken.

Sources : *Census of India 1991, Series - 1 of 1993, Union Primary Census Abstract for S.C. & S.T.*

Appendix - 19
Literacy Rate Among Scheduled Tribes During 1961, 1971 and 1981 Census

Sl.No.	Name of States/UTs	Scheduled Tribes			
		1961	1971	1981	1991***
1	2	7	8	9	10
	INDIA	**18.53**	**11.30**	**16.35**	**29.60**
1.	Andhra Pradesh	4.41	5.34	7.82	17.16
2.	Arunachal Pradesh	-	5.20	14.04	24.45
3.	Assam	23.58	26.03	-	49.16
4.	Bihar	9.16	11.64	16.99	26.78
5.	Goa	-	-	-	42.91
6.	Gujarat	11.69	14.12	21.14	36.45
7.	Haryana	-	-	-	-
8.	Himachal Pradesh	-	15.89	25.93	47.09
9.	Jammu and kashmir	-	-	-	-
10.	Karnataka	8.15	14.85	20.14	36.01
11.	Kerala	17.26	25.72	31.79	57.22
12.	Madhya Pradesh	5.10	7.62	10.68	21.54
13.	Maharashtra	7.21	11.74	22.29	36.79
14.	Manipur	27.25	28.71	39.74	53.63
15.	Meghalaya	-	26.45	31.55	46.71
16.	Mizoram (included in Assam)	-	-	59.63	82.71
17.	Nagaland	17.91	27.40	42.57	61.65
18.	Orissa	7.36	9.46	13.96	22.31
19.	Punjab	16.46	-	-	-
1	2	7	8	9	10
20.	Rajasthan	3.97	6.47	10.27	19.44

21.	Sikkim	-	-	33.13	59.01
22.	Tamilnadu	5.91	9.02	20.46	27.89
23.	Tripura	10.01	15.03	23.07	40.37
24.	Uttar Pradesh	-	14.59	20.45	35.70
25.	West Bengal	6.55	8.92	13.21	35.70

Union Territories

1.	A and N Island	11.10	17.85	31.11	56.62
2.	Dadra-Nagar Haveli	4.40	8.90	16.86	28.21
3.	Chandigarh	-	-	-	-
4.	Delhi	-	-	-	-
5.	Lakshadweep	22.27	41.37	53.13	80.58
6.	Pondicherry	-	-	-	-
7.	Daman and Diu	-	12.73	36.48	52.91

*** Excluding population of age group (0-6).

Appendix - 20
State-wise Distribution of Tribals in India

S. No.	State/ Union Territories	Total population	1981 Census S.T. Population Male	Famale	Persons	Total Population	1991 census S.T. Population Rural	Urban	Persons
1	2	3	4	5	6	7	8	9	10
	India	665,287,849	26,038,535	25.590.103	51,628,638	846,302,688	62,751,026	5,007,354	67,758,380
1.	Andhra Pradesh	53,549,673	1,618,689	1,557,31	3,176,001	66,508,008	3,880,254	319,227	4,199,481
2.	Bihar	69,914,734	2,915,492	2,895,375	5,810,867	86,374,465	6,153,659	463,255	6,166,914
3.	Gujarat	34,085,799	2,453,566	2,395,020	4,848,586	41,309,582	5,663,178	498,597	6,161,775
4.	Haryana	12,922,618	—	—	—	16,463,648	—	—	—
5.	Himachal Pradesh	4,280,818	99,727	97,536	197,263	5,170,877	212,940	5,409	218,349
6.	Jammu & Kashmir	5,987,389	—	—	—	7,718,700	—	—	—
7.	Karnataka	37,135,714	926,235	895,968	1,825,203	44,977,201	1,629,496	286,195	1,915,691
8.	Kerala	25,453,680	131,243	130,232	261,475	29,098,518	309,764	11,203	320,967

1	2	3	4	5	6	7	8	9	10
9.	Madhya Pradesh	52,178,844	6,003,304	5,983,727	11,987,031	66,181,170	14,652,730	746,304	15,399,034
10.	Maharashtra	62,784,171	2,923,955	2,848,083	5,772,038	78,937,187	6,405,814	912,467	7,318,281
11.	Manipur	1,420,953	196,455	191,522	387,977	1,837,149	578,930	53,243	632,173
12.	Meghalaya	1,35,819	537,635	538,710	1,076,345	1,774,778	1,312,093	205,834	1,517,927
13.	Nagaland	774,930	332,943	317,942	650,885	1,209,546	933,145	127,677	1,060,822
14.	Orissa	6,370,271	2,939,863	2,975,204	5,915,067	31,659,736	6,670,506	361,708	7,033,214
15.	Rajasthan	34,261,862	2,150,767	2,032,357	4,183,124	44,005,990	5,220,549	254,332	5,474,881
16.	Sikkim	316,385	38,211	35,412	73,623	406,457	83,486	7,415	90,901
17.	Tamil Nadu	48,408,077	264,288	255,938	520,226	55,858,946	505,208	68,986	574,194
18.	Tripura	2,053,058	297,612	286,308	583,920	2,757,205	839,264	14,081	853,345
19.	Utter Pradesh	110,862,013	121,506	111,999	232,705	139,112,287	271,028	16,873	287,901
20.	Punjab	16,788,985	—	—	—	20,281,969	—	—	—
21.	W. Bengal	154,584,647	1,559,288	1,511,368	3,070,672	68,077,965	3,612,448	196,312	3,808,767
22.	Assam		Census not taken place			22,414,322	2,777,308	97,133	2,874,441

	Union Territories								
1.	Andman & Nicobar Islands	188,741	11,586	10,775	22,361	280,661	26,268	502	26,770
2.	Arunachal Pradesh	631,839	220,046	221,121	441,167	864,558	518,222	32,129	550,351
3.	Dadra and Nagar Haveli	103,676	40,486	41,228	81,714	138,477	105,864	3,516	109,380
4.	Chandigarh	451,610	—	—	—	642,015	—	—	—
5.	Goa, Daman, and Diu	1,086,730	5,512	5,209	10,711	1,271,379	9,281	2,819	12,100
6.	Delhi	6,220,406	—	—	—	9,420,644	—	—	—
7.	Lakshdweep	40,249	18,865	18,985	37,760	51,707	21,478	26,685	48,163
8.	Mizoram	493,757	231,261	230,646	461,907	689,756	358,113	295,452	653,565
9.	Pondichery	604,471	—	—	—	807,785	—	—	—

Source
1. Census of India 1981, Series-1, Part -II-B(iii) Primary census abstract (Scheduled Tribes), pp XIX-XXI and 4-15
2. Census of India 1981, Series-1, Part -II-B(i) Primary census abstract (General Population), pp XXX-XXXIII and 4-23.
3. Census of India 1991, Series-1, paper 1992 of 1992 Vol. II, p-19, Final population tables.

Appendix - 21
Tribal Commissions and Committees on Tribal Development

S. No.	Name of the Committee	Chairman	Setup by	Constituted on	Report submitted
1	2	3	4	5	6
	In fulfilment of Constitutioal requirements				
1.	Backward classes commission	Kaka Kalelkar	President of India	29.1.1953	30.3.1955
2.	Scheduled Areas and Scheduled Tribes Commission	U.N. Dhebar	Do	28.4.1960	October
3.	Backward Classes Commission	B.P. Mandal	Do	1.1.1979	December,1980
4.	Commissioner f or Scheduled Castes and Scheduled Tribes		Do	1950	Annually
	Constituted by the Parliament				
5.	Parliamentary Committee on* the Welfare of Scheduled Castes and Scheduled Tribes	Member of Parliament (Shri K. Pradhani) in 1991-92)	Parliament	18.12.196	Till the end of 1991-92 reports on variaous subjects submitted.
6.	Joint Committee on the Scheduled Castes and Scheduled Tribes Order (Amendment) Bill 1967.	A.K. Chanda	Do	26.3.1968	15.11. 1969

1	2			6
Related to tribal development				
7. Advisory Committee on the Revision of the Lists of Scheduled Castes and Scheduled Tribes	B.N. Lokur	Deptt. of Social Security	1.6.1965	27.7.1965
8. Committee on special Multi purpose Tribal Blocks	Verrier Elwin	Ministry of Home Affairs	1.5.1959	30.3.1960
9. Special Working Group on Co-operatin for Backward Classes	M.P. Bhargava	Do		Sept., 1962
10. Committee on Tribal Economy in Forest Areas	Hari Singh	Deptt. of Social Security	7.5.1965	March, 1967
11. Study Group on Tribal Labour	L.P. Vidyarthi	Ministry of Labour and Employment	24.12.1966	28.8.1969
12. Working Group on Administrative Arrangement and Personnel Policies in Tribal Areas	Maheshwar Prasad	Ministry of Home Affairs	17.10.1978	28.8.1979

1	2	3	4	5	6
13.	Working Group on Monitoring and Evaluation of Tribal Development and Development of Backward Classes	Dr. Bhupinder Singh	Ministry of Home Affairs	July,1978	July, 1979
14.	The commission for Scheduled Castes and Scheduled Tribes	*	Do	21.7.1978	Annually
15.	Committee on Forests and Tribals in India	B.K. Roy Burman	Do.	9.4.1980	6.9.1982
16.	Study Team on Working of the Co-operative Organisations	K.S. Bawa	Ministry of Agriculture	3.12.1971	24.9.1973
17.	Study Group on Relief of Indebtedness Land Alienation and Restoration in Tribal Development Agency Area	P.S. Appu	Ministry of Agriculture	Dec., 1971	October, 1972
18.	Committee on Orientation of Forest Education in India	K.M. Tiwari	Ministry of Home Affairs	5.12.1982	December, 1983.
19.	Committee on Forestry Programmes for Alleviation of Poverty	C.L. Bhatia	Do	12.3.1982	October

1	2	3	4	5	6
20.	Large sized Multi-purpose Societies (LAMPS) - Cadre Management	B. Bandopadyaya	Do	30.10.1980	September,1984.

Related to Planning and Development

1	2	3	4	5	6
21.	Study Team on Social Welae and Welfare of Backward Classes	Renuka Ray	Committee on Plan Projects	5.1.1958	9.7.1959
22.	Study group on the Welfare of the Weaker Sectins of the village community	J.P. Narayan	Ministry of C.D. and Co-operation	8.12.1960	12.10.1961
23.	Study group on tribal Development Programme	P.Shilu AO	Planning Commission	26.10.1966	19.9.1969
24.	Task Force on Development of Tribal Areas	L.P.Vidyarthi	Planning Commission	5.4.1972	-
25.	Working Group on Tribal Development during Medium Term Plan	D.L. Mandal	Ministry of Home Affairs	3.2.1978, July	July,1978

1	2	3	4	5	6
26.	Natinal Committee on Development of Backward Areas	B. Sivaraman	Planning Commission	30.11.1978	June, 1978 (The committe submitted a separate report on Development of Tribal Areas)
27.	High Power Panel on Minorities Scheduled Castes and Scheduled Tribes	Dr. Gopal Singh	Ministry of Home Affairs	May, 1980	1983
28.	Working Group on Tribal Development during Sixth Plan	B.G. Deshmukh	Planning Commission	8.7.1980, 1980	1983
29.	Working Group on Tribal Development during Senth Plan S.	Narayanaswamy	Do	4.10.1983	December, 1984
30.	Working Group on Development and Welfare of Scheduled Tribes during Eighth Five Year Plan	S.S. Verma	Do	2.9.1988	November, 1989

* The Commitee consists of 30 members; 20 from Lok Sabha and 19 from Rajya Sabha. The tenure is for one year. This is now a standing Committee of Parliament.

+ The Special Offices (Commissioner for Scheduled casts and Scheduled tribes) appointed by the President under Article 338 of the Constitution has been submitting annual reports since 1950.

ADIYAN

Dr. Bindu Ramchandran

The Adiyan are notified as a scheduled tribe inhabiting the Manantavady Taluk and adjoining areas of Wayanad district in Kerala. They were subjected to worst from of bonded labour till 1976. The landlords addressed the tied labourers as 'kundalpanikkar' and the payment was known as *'kundalpanam'*. Bonded labour was referred to as *'kundalpani'* or *'ballipani'*. *'Bally'* was the wage received in kind often as paddy and *'kundal'* was the annual reward given to the labourers by their landlords. In addition to the normal wage the labourers were also allowed to harvest a small patch of land by themselves for their own use. They were a landless agricultural labourer community devoid of any other skill for their subsistence. Their culture and economy were languished by the traits of bonded labour system.

Luiz (1962) has observed that their name has originated from an old rule that they should maintain a distance of *'ar'* (six), *'adi'* (feet) to avoid pollution. The very name Adiyar connotes their subservient position as tied labourers. They were also known as *'ravular'* which means the descendants or *'ramaswami'*. Local communities address them as *'adiyar'*. Adiya language has close affinity to Kannada belonging to the Dravidian family of languages. Now most of them are bilingual. They can also speak Malayalam and use the malayalam script.

The traditional manner of recruiting the tribals as bonded labourer was by advancing loans at the *Valliyoor Kavu Bhagavathi* temple (situated in the Manantavady taluk of Wayanad) in the last week of March. The system was that a tribal pledged not only himself but the members of his family as well against loan and until the debt was discharged all of them were bound to work for the creditor for which they got only daily meals and a pittance in kind (Mathur, 1997-98).

ORIGIN

There are many myths and legends about the origin of Adiyan. According to one, "they are the descendants of a *Sivadwaja Brahmin* who ventured on a *prothiloma* union (violating) the rule of hypergammy) with a pure non-Brahmin girl". Another legend is that they are the progeny of a Brahmin who lost his status by eating rice offered to Siva and there by committed an *'anacharam'* (violation of a restricted custom). They also claim that at one time they were *pujaris* (priest in the *Bhadrakali* temple). It is perhaps true that they came to kerala with the Chettis and Brahmins of Mysore and continued to be their agricultural serfs (Luiz, 1962: 27-28).

SOCIAL DIVISION

Family among the Adiyan is matrilineal in descent and matrilocal in residence. Nuclear family is the basic social and economic unit. Husband is the head of the family and division of labour in a family is based according to age and sex.

The society of adiyan is endogammous and divided into clans and phrateries. In their vernacular these matrilineal clans are known as *'Mant'* and phrateries as *'Chemmem'*. Each Mant and Chemmem are associated with a place name or the direction one points. Each Chemmem is exogammous in nature.

The three Mant (clan) are (a) Thirunelli mant, (b) Badak mant, and (c) Pothur mant. Among the three mant, Thirunelli mant is having higher social status. There are nineteen Chemmems is thirunelli mant with its own gods and goddesses. Badak mant have six Chemmems and Pothur mant have four Chemmems respectively. The chemmems of thirunelli mant are kottla, cheruvali, ulankuttu, muthukuttu, kuppala, kalankot, muthira, momatta, idamalai, madacheri, kachala, kadamala, naalapadi, maragavu, saitya, thirumunda, karai and kallumalai.

Chemmems of Badak mant constitute *bayanattila, kunduru, puthuru, poothadi, anjila* and *panalila*. Where as Pothur mant consisted of four Chemmems i.e. aevila, vellachal, onpathukudi and pavadalam.

The members of a Chemmem are considered as borthers and sisters and no marriage is allowed i.e. Chemmems are strictly exogammous. Among the thirty one Chemmem, some are treated as siblings and marriage is prohibited between them.

Siblings Chemmem which do not intermarry are as follows-

Kottala	....	Cheruvali
Ulankuttu	....	Muthukuttu
Kallala	....	Kalakotte
Muthira	....	Momattae

Idamalai	....	Madacheri
Kachala	....	Kadamalai
Nalappadi	....	Maragavu
Saintya	....	Thirumunda
Karae	....	Kallumali
Puthuru	....	Poothadi
Anjila	....	Panalila
Aevila	....	Vellachal
Onpathukudi	....	Pavadalam

SOCIAL RITUALS

The Adiyan have a cephalous political structure in which *'naattumoopan'* (chief) is the supreme authority. In the former days, they worked under a non-tribal land lord, called *'jammi'*. Under a land lord there will be atleast fifteen houses in a hamlet, From Adiyan the jammi selects a person who has the ability to control others. Others accept him as their leader and they are obliged to obey his orders. The landlord gives him a ring called *'vala'* (bangle) as the symbol of power. After getting approval from the landlord, others call him as *'moopan'* or *'nattumoopan'*.

The traditional political organisation of adiyan constitute social functionaries and religious functionaries. Social functionaries includes naattumoopan, kunnumoopan (chief of the hamlet), and chemmakkaran (chief of the clan). Religious functionaries includes *'kanaladi'*, *'karimi'* and the *'thammadikkaran'*. A group of adiya hamlet in a specified territory constitute a *'naadu'* headed by a *naattumoopan*, who invariably belongs to the mant which has high social status among the three. The territory of a *nattumoopan* is demarcated between hills and rivers. In wayanad there are three *nattumoopan* for adiyan vannathithodu (2) between vellalodi and chembanakki, and (3) between anamala and bavali.

Naattumoopan functions as judge, mediator and also officiate as priest in religious rituals and ceremonies. He has the supreme authority over the people of the hamlet. The position of the *nattumoopan* can be hereditary or non-hereditary. In hereditary cases it is either from father to son and then from elder brother to younger brother.

There will be *kunnumoopan* or *kuntumoopan* under each *naattumoopan* for managing the affairs of the 'kuntu' (hamlet). He is responsible for taking decisions during exigencies. If he fails to find a solution then only that matter is referred to the council of *naattumoopan*. The position of *kunnumoopan* in also not hereditary. A man efficient in the affairs of the society will emerge as and then *naattumoopan* approves it.

Decisions of disputes and other problems are taken by *'chemmakkaran'* and he is an important person as far as members of each Chemmem is concerned. Adiya descent is reckoned through matriliny and the position of *chemmakkaran* devolves from the person to his sister's children.

Naattumoopan is assisted in rituals and ceremonies by two religious functionaries called *kanaladi* and *karimi*. Kanaladi is also known as *cheriyamoopan*. The position of kanaladi is hereditary/non-hereditary from father to son or from elder brother to younger brothers. The assistance of officiating burial rites and related duties are limited to karimi. They belong to a particular clan and the members of kachala, idamala, naalappadi, can only become *karimi*. They act as messengers to inform the news of death in a hamlet. In addition to the above mentioned socioreligious functionaries a religious leader called *'thammadikkaran'* can also seen in their society.

The adiyan who are interested to study the *sastra* are brought in a particular section called *'kanaladi'*. Like any other member *naattumoopan* does not enjoy any extra economic benefit being the leader of the community. The fine imposed and other gifts received by him are shared with all other assistants equally. He has to work for his livelihood.

Among the Adiyan fine is always given in the from of *'thappubala'* (brass bangle) and the amount is measured in terms of the number of *'bala'*. One bala is equivalent to fifty paise. If a person is unable to pay fine at the meeting, then the clan leader pays it or the *naatumoopan* takes the responsibility of paying it.

LIFE CYCLE

Marriage

In the dialect of adiyan marriage is referred to as *'kanyala'*. Attainment of puberty is considered as the age for marriage. Pre-puberty marriages at the age of twelve known as *'thalikettukanyala'* were practiced earlier.

The usual form of marriage among the adiyar is described as one of service. As a preliminary step of fixation, boy's father, elder sister's husband and mother's brother visit the girl's hamlet, If they agreed to proceed that proposal, then the boy and some of his close relatives visit to the girl's house. The boy must carry articles such as paddy, chilly, salt, betel leaves, onion and firewood. It is a kind of payment known as *'kolubally'* (kolu means firewood and bally means paddy).

After reaching the girl's house the boy presents the *kolubally* to the girl's mother and he distributes betel leaves to the invitees. He brings a *'thali'* (sacred thread) with coins (below ten in number) to tie around the girl's neck. Thali is handed over to the girl's father and he asks one of the women to tie it. Generally thali is tied by the boy's sister. It is customary to bring/ *'mookubettu'* (nosestud), *kathala* (earstud), *'kadagam'* (bangle) and new dress to the bride. The thali is not destroyed or removed till puberty ceremony. After *'thalikettu'* (tying of thali) a feast is given to the invitees. Then the boy's party returns to their native hamlet.

Once this thali ceremony is performed, the boy has to observe certain rules and regulations. He must go to the house of the girl's once in a week usually on sundays with *'kolobally'* when he reaches the girl's house, her parents entertain him and give him an axe to collect firewood from the nearby forest. If the bundle is also small the girl's relatives tease him.

The boy stays there and he is given *'nookan'* (rice-with curry). It is served by the girl's mother. This custom continues till marriage. He visit all sundays with *kolubally* and returns on monday. Even though he stays there every week he avoids physical contact with his would be bride or wife. Marriage is conducted only after the attainment of puberty. *Kolubally* cannot beequated with brideprice. In many cases even after the payment of *kolubally* many girls refuse to marry the betrothed boy and ran away with another one.

Before marriage the consent of the *chemmekkaran* and *naattumoopan* is indispensable. Naattumoopan collects brass bangles from both the parties. It is known as *'bethanum'* Unless this is paid, naatumoopan willnot give his consent for the marriage. The number of bangles depend on the quality of disputes. It is considered as a customary payment to *nattumoopan* and to his assistants for settling the disputes at the time of marriage. He may sometimes impose *'thappu'* (fine) on both the parties depending upon committed by then and they are freed from such offence through *'thappedukkal'* (imposition of fine). Fine paid by the groom goes to the girl's Chemmem and the fine paid by the bride goes to the groom's Chemmem.

Marriage ceremony always begins at night. It is concluded at the house of the *Chemmakkaran*. It is his responsibility to conduct the function in his *Chemmem*. When the bride leaves the home for marriage, elders bless her by sprinkling rice in her head. This is known as *'ariyidal'*. The groom's party carries a *'thudi'* (a kind of musical instrument) and *'Cheeni'* (a musical instrument) along with them. As this beating progresses, one of them starts performing a dance called *'paygavanattam'*. The dancer is called *'paygavan'*. He has a different dress. A red mundu with a belt is tied over the mundu. Besides this dance they sing many songs narrating the myth of their ancestors. After reaching the bride's residence, the bridegroom distributes betal leaves and *arecanut* to all the invitees. *Naattumoopan* and his assistants sacrifice a fowl and roast it. This is to avoid all problems at the time of marriage.

After taking bath, bride and groom are covered in a canopy of white dress on both sides of their way and walk over another white cloth spread on their way. This is known as *'paavadapudikkal'*. After that they are seated in the *'pandal'* (temporary shed). Then the *Chemmakkaran* of the groom calls the groom's sister for tying *'thali'* (sacred thread). After thali tying ceremony *naattumooppan* breaks a coconut and dips a betel leaf in the coconut water and sprinkles it on the bride and groom. After marriage a feast is given to all the invitees. Serving is carried out by males only.

When they reach the groom's residence, The party is received by the groom's relatives. A ceremonial bath is given there also. It is believed that only after this bath she is admitted in their *Chemmem*. On the second day of marriage, the couple enter a separate room with some of the old women of the house. The women advised than about the future life. This is known as *'buddiparayal'*.

Adiyans are monogamous by custom. One is permitted to have a second wife only after divorce. If one husband marries another married woman, it is considered as a fault and he will have to pay fine. Fine is paid in the form of brass bangles which is around sixteen in number.

When the groom is unable to pay *kolubally*, he serves for the parents of the bride. The service is rendered till marriage is conducted. Elopement is an approved form of marriage among adiyan. If the eloped couple are previously married, it is the duty of the *'karimi'* and *nattumoopan* to protect them upto a function called *'kunnukayattal'* (taking the new couple to the hamlet). It is a function for giving social recognition. One who breaks the rule for exogammy will have to give thirty brass bangles as fine. They are excommunication if they are not willing to give this fine.

Birth Ceremony

Like other ceremonies, the birth ceremony is not at all important among Adiyan. There is no difference in the ceremonies for male and female child. When a woman gets labour pain she is confined to a room and seek the help of *'bethikarathi'* (midwife) who helps the mother in child birth. The midwife cuts the umbiac cord with a knife. The knife is not washed for five days. The newly delivered woman is considered to be polluted for five days. No one enters that room and no male members have their food from that house for five days.

On the fifth day, the *'bethikarathi'* cleans the house with cowdung, washes all the clothes and mats used by the mother and the child in river water, take her bath and returns. Then she breaks a coconut in the name of god and distributes the pieces to all children and present there. This is the only religious ceremony performed in order to remove the pollution associated with child birth. The *'bethikarathi'* is given betel leaves, are canuts lime, paddy, salt, oil, chilli, coconuts, soap and rupees forty by the mother-in-law on the fifth day.

On the fifth day *bethikarathi* ties a black string around the waist, on the ankle and on the arm of the child. In olden days they used to feed the newly born child at home. It is the child's father who keeps the child on his lap and feeds him first followed by others. During this ceremony the child is named.

There are no special ceremonies connected with the first hair cutting and ear boring. Either the father or mother cuts the hair of the child after one year. It there is any vow it is done in the temple.

Death Rituals

A death in a settlement is first informed to the *kuntumoopan* and to the *naattumoopan*. Naattumoopan arrange two *karimis* (assistants) to two directions for informing the relatives of the dead. A wooden stick called *'kuntham vadi* is also carried by the *karimi*. Kins are not allowed to touch the dead body. That right is bestowed to *karimis* of idamalai Chemmem. After the crops is given bath, *Naattumoopan* sent two *karimis* to collect bamboo stretcher called '*padi*' to take the corpse to the burial ground. Then *Naattumoopan* asks for '*thappubalai*' (brass bangles given as fine). Three '*thappubalai*' are given in the name of three '*mant*', eight are given tot he father's relatives of the deceased, and six are given to the *Chemmakkaran* of the deceased. These *thappubalai* are collected by *Naattumoopan*.

The corpse is given bath in hot water in a sitting posture facing east. Turmeric paste and oil are applied on the body. After bath, if the diseased is a female, the corpse is covered by black sari, and if the deceased is a male his face is shaved and applied sandal paste. The corpse is then taken to the courtyard and laid down keeping head towards south. Rice, coins, six *thappubalai* and a bell metal lamp are kept close to the head. The body is covered with white cloth. *Naattumoopan* and *kanaladi* start reciting mantras. The *karimi* then lay the corpse on '*padi*' made for the purpose and '*thappubalai*' are tied on the four corners of the stretcher. Then '*kuntumoopan*' throw few coins upwards. This is repeated by *Chemmakkaran* of the deceased, brothers and father of the deceased, if alive and lastly *Naatumoopan*. the ownership right of these coins goes to *karimis*.

Then the four *karimis* takes four sides of the reed stretcher containing corpse and it is taken to graveyard. They dig a is lowered in to the grave and pushed into the cellar. Before covering the grave, a *thappubalai* is placed under the head of the corpse. A soil heap of six inch thickness is prepared on the grave and thorns are kept over it. This thickness is prepared on the grave and thorns are kept over it. This is in order to keep the dead man's soul confined to the grave as the soul is believed to be trying to return with the living ones.

Karimi stands on the head portion of the grave and then he sprinkle water which was kept in a piece of reed with grass on the body of *Kuntumoopan, Chemmakkaran*, and close relatives starts observing death pollution. The duration of pollution and the subsequent observances varies in accordance with financial status of the family.

The *Karimis* exchange knife and axe by standing two opposite sides of the grave. The relatives take bath after the burial and everybody return to the dead person's house and *Naatumoopan* and others settles the payments towards the burial. Twenty seven *thappubalai* are given for preparing '*padi*', ten for digging grave, one for bringing sandal paste smeared over the forehead and eight for other related rites. *Nattumoopan* asked *Kuntumoopan* to fix a date for the observance of pula within three days and the assembled persons disperse.

FAIRS AND FESTIVALS

Adiyar usually celebrate Hindu festivals and celebrations like Onam, Vishu and Karkidakam- 14 in addition to their own festivals. *Naaduneekkal*, thera/vellat ..... etc are the important festivals of their own. *Naaduneekkal* is considered to be one their important festival. They do it in order to avoid *'kulirupani'* (smallpox) which they believe is caused by the wrath of *'maariyamma'* (a female goddess). It is celebrated before 30th *'edavam'* (May - June).

There/vellat is usually celebrated after harvest. *Chemmakkaran* presides over the function which lasts for two days. People give rice, banana, coconut, and cash to the *Chemmakkaran*. Now a days they also celebrate the important social celebrations of the neighbouring Hindus.

❑ ❑ ❑

REFERENCES

Bindu, B. (1998): Socio-economic change among three wayanad tribes. A study of Adiyan, Kattunaicken Mullukurumba in eco-cultural context. (Un published Ph.D thesis)

Luiz, A.A.D. (1962): Tribes of Kerala. Bharathiya adimjati sevak sang, New Delhi.

Mathur, P.R.G. (1971): Tribal situation in Kerala. Kerala Historical society, Trivandrum.

Singh, K.S. : The Scheduled Tribes. Oxford University Press, Oxford.

Photo of Adiyan

AGARIA

Dr. Prakash Chandra Mehta

The Agaria are a small ethnic group of Madhya Pradesh with a population of 55,884 in 1981. They are chiefly concentrated in the Sarguja. Shahdol, Sidhi, Bilaspur, Mandla, Raigarh and Rajnandgaon district of Madhya Pradesh. An offshoot of the Gond tribe. The Agarias have adopted the profession of iron smelting.

The Agarias have mainly two endogamous sub tribes viz *Patharia* and *Khuntia*. The Patharia place a stone (Pathor) on the mouth of the bellows to fix them in the ground for smelting, while the Khuntias use a peg of Khunti. Other smaller sub division are Kalha Agaria, Asur Agaria and Mahali Agaria.

The Agarias are divided into a number of 'Gots' (clan). The 'Gots' are exogamous groups which are generally totemistic, named after plants, animals, birds, insects, etc. Member of same clan are known as 'Gotiar'. The clan is a very important functional sub-structure for them.

In this tribal group few taboos separate relatives from each other. A women should avoid all the real or classificatory elder brothers or her husband. The relatives coming in this category do not talk to each other directly and the women in expected to observe *purdah* before them.

Life Cycle

Pregnant women continue to work as usual till an advanced stage of pregnancy in Agarias. When a women becomes pregnant for the first time her mother goes to her taking a new cloth and some luxurious food, which it is supposed to strengthen the child and mother. Delivery generally takes place at home. At the time of delivery some elderly and experienced women of the tribe are called to assist. After delivery the *Nerua* (umbilical cord) is cut with sickle and it is burried in a pit at home. After delivery medicinal *Kada* (decoction), is made from barks of *Mahua, Jamun*, roots of *Tendu*, popod, palm, atigan leaves and raw sugar. This kada is given as food for five days. On third day rice and *tuver dal* given to the mother. They celebrate *Chhathi* on 6$_{th}$ day and *Barhi* on 12th day. In this ceremony the nursing women and child take bath and wear new clothes and worship family goddess. After that she can starts their routine domestic work.

Marriage

The most popular form of marriage in known as *Bihav* which is formally arranged by the parents of the bride and the bride groom and it is celebrated with all the prescribed rites and ceremonies. The marrital age in this tribal group is 17-18 years for boys and 16-17 years girls. Betrothal is known as *Phaldan*, in this ceremony the boy's father along with some elderly relatives come to the girls house. They carry with them new *sari*, coconut, *gud,* money, bidi, etc. The first day of marriage in known as *Madawa* and *Magarmati*, second day as *tel* and third day *barat*. On third day the *barat* procession persons go to the bride's house with the bridegroom where the marriage is performed. The couple and *barat* returns to bride groom's home after marriage.

Gauna ceremony may be held after one month to three years of marriage. Other ways for acquiring a mate are known as *Paitoo, Odheria* and *Guravant*. Remarriage for widow and divorce is permitted.

Death

When a person dies, the news is conveyed to the near relatives through somebody. The dead body is laid on a bier and covered with a piece of new cloth. All the male members go in procession to the cremation ground. Then the pyre is lit by the eldest son or nearest relatives. On the third day, they go to collect ashes and bones which are carried to the *Ganga* or the *Narmada* or any near by river. The relatives shave hair, moustache and beard and take bath and perform some religious rites. On 13th day they arrange a death feast, but those who can not afford can arrange it after 4 to 12 month. Children and those who die of small pox or pregnancy period are buried.

Occupations

The Agaria traditional and main occupation is iron smelting. They also make a few agricultural implements. In this tribal group some families collect forest produce and are engaged in cultivation also.

Now a days Agaria are members of three panchayat viz, 1. Caste panchayat, 2. Village council, and 3. Modern gram panchayat. In the traditional caste panchayat only Agaria are members. The head of this panchayat known as *Gauntia* and other are *panch*. The function of this panchayat is to try cases of breach of social code and organise festivals.

Religion

The religion of the Agaria is animistic in character. Their gods and goddesses are *Budha deo, Dulhadeo, Loha sur, Shitalamata, Kankali mata,* etc. They also worship sun, moon, river, tree, hills and animals. Every year on *Dashahra* festival they offer a black hen to *Lohasur* and every three year a black goat. Their main festivals are *Hareli, Dashahara, Diwali, Holi, Nayakhani, Pitar pola,* etc. They believe in magic and witch craft. The magician among the tribe is knows as *Bhumaka*. The *Bhumaka* stand between mankind and all malignant forces.

Agaria's folk dance are of several kinds. They are *Karma*, in Karma pooja, *Pandaki* in Diwali, *Bihavanch* in marriage. *Rahas* in holi, etc. Their folk songs are Karmageet, *Suageet, Vivah geet,* fag and fog dance. They also have a love song known as *Dadaria,* in this song young girls put some question and young boy gives some answer in song. Agarias popular musical instruments are *Kingari, Dhol, Timaki, Mohari, Thali* and other local musical instruments.

❑ ❑ ❑

AKA

Dr. Prakash Chandra Mehta

The Aka tribe is mainly concentrated in the Kameng district of Arunachal Pradesh. The area inhabited by the Akas lies to the east of the Sherdukpens as far as Khari-Dikarar river. It is bounded on the west by the land of the Sherdukpens, on the east by the Bargnis, on the north by the Mijis and the south lies the Darrong district of Assam. The Aka land is hilly country interested by a number of streams like the Bichom. Tengapani and the Kheyang being the notable. During rainy season the Akas put temporary suspension bridges for crossing these rivers. Their village are located both in the valley as well as on hill tops.

In their own dialect the Akas call themselves Hrusso. The term Aka is derived from the Assamese word Anka literally meaning painted. They are so termed because of their custom of smearing their face with a mixture of the resin obtained from the Pinus excelsus and charcoal. The Akas speak their own dialect belonging to the Tibeto-Burman group. According to 1981 census, the population of the Aka Nagas was enumerated as 2,947.

Religion

The Aka religion is shamamistic animism, Due to proximity to Buddhist neighours, they were influenced to an appreciable extent by Buddhism. Some of their villages have chortens and prayer flags too. But still they cannot be identified with the Buddhists since Buddhism has not made any lasting impact on them. Recently they are showing inclination toward the Vaisnavism of Srimat Sankardeva cult of Assam. The Aka priest as they call him as *Shaman* is important in every social event. A *shaman* is distinguished from the others by the fact that he wears a yak's tail on his back and his pill box hat is covered with tiger or leopard skin. Any young person having supernatural power can become a *Shaman*. The *Shaman* is not hereditary. According to the Akas *Bhusluao* is the supreme creator who is creator of all living being. After creating all human beings he taught people the different mode of life then social customs and traditions including dances and sent them to different places. In addition to the supreme creator, they have a number of spirits both benevolent and malevolent whom they worship for happiness.

Occupation

The main occupation of the Aka is Jhuming of the slash and burn cultivation. The principal crops they produce from their jhum field are rice, mustard, chilli, sweet potatoes, millet, *urad*, Indian corn, etc. Other subsidiary means of economy depends on collection of forest produce, fishing and hunting, while handicraft and weaving considered as one of the essential work intermingled with their culture. They possess considerable proficiency in the art basketry in which particularly the menfolks engage during their leisure hours. They make baskets of different shapes and sizes with bamboo. There are different names for these baskets used for different purposes. Wood carving is almost absent among the Akas, but they love to make designs and single stylized drawing on wooden frames combs and tobacco pipes.

Dwellings

The Aka houses are well made structure of wood and bamboo standing generally about 1.8 meters to 2 meters off the ground on stout wooden and bamboo piles. The space between the floor and the ground serves as an enclosure of shed for domestic animal such as pig and goats. The walls and flooring in the houses of poorer persons are made of split bamboo, while wealthy persons use of rough planks for the walls and flooring of their houses. All houses are roofed with thatch. A house is divided into three of four rooms with a *verendah* at either end. The occupants of a house usually are three or four connected families, each family living in a separate room. Wherever families of two bothers live together they occupy two sides of the main living apartment called *Uluri* without any partition. Each family however has its own hearth. The small compartment opening to the Veranda in front is at all times reserved for guests and is known as *Ihumona*. The houses of a Aka village are usually, scattered.

Rituals

In any society it is song must and dance that reflects depth of philosophical thinking the culture and creativity. This is very much applicable for the Aka society also. The musical instruments, played generally be men in accompaniment of the dances, and songs are the drums, a stringed instrument and cymbals. The Akas have no organized dance party, but everyone of either sex is a dancer. The small boys and girls observe the dance movement of their elders and gradually learn these by imitations. There is no age at which an individual begins or ceases to take part in dances, but generally the young men and women are the dancers. The dancers get no remuneration. They young men and women may dance separately or in a group. There are several types of Aka dance but only the principal dances are discussed here. The most important Aka dance is *Niuksidou* Dance. This dance is not associated with any festival, but is associated with the death ceremony and with the marriage ceremony. The dance is performed when bridegrooms party arrive at brides villages in order to entertain them. This entertainment continues till the party leaves with the bride. The Akas believe that when a person dies the soul of the decased tries to return to its previous home. The some of a deceased man may return within ten nights and that of a deceawed women within eight nights. The soul, if it succeeds to return, is believed to cause harm to the other inmates of the house. So the villagers, generally youths, assemble in the bereaved house after desk, and keep vigil throughout the night. This they do for eight and ten nights for the death of a woman and man respectively and during this period they sing and dance inside the bereaved household. The singing and dances have two purposes. It caves them from getting fatigues on such long vigil. The sound created by the singing and dancing in groups and the assemblage of so many persons in the house are believed to frighten away the soil of the deceased. Only difference in the dance on the above two occasions being the wordings of the song while the movements usually remain the same. The boys during the dance wear a long white garment which hangs from the shoulder to the knees and over it a black coat. They put a bamboo ring cap. The girls wear a purple coloured coat over a long white gown and they deck themselves with a protrusions of silver ornaments and bead necklaces around their necks, big silver car bulbs and a silver filler as well as coloured waist bands. Thus attired, the boys and girls stand in separate rows. One or more from the boys group come forward to give group. Thus this rotation of dances by boys and girls continues to the accompaniment of the playing of drums, cymbals and stringed instrument. *Dogohdou* dance is associated with head hunting and hunting of animals.

□ □ □

REFERENCES

Elwin. vermier, (1969) : The Nagas in the Nineteenth Century. Oxford University press. Bombay.

Ramunny. M., (1988) : The World of Nagas, No-them Book Center. New Delhi.

Sen. Spira, (1987) : Tribes of Nagaland. Mittal Publications. Delhi.

BHILS - I

Mrs. Sonu Mehta

In the tribal heritage of India, the Bhils have an special identity and substantial contribution. They constitute about 1 crore population which is about 15 per cent of the total tribal population of India. Bhils stands third in population after Santhals and Gonds. The concentration of Bhils in the country can be observed in four states viz. Rajasthan, Gujarat, Maharastra and Madhya Pradesh, while they can also be seen in the sountern and eastern part of the country i.e. Andhra Pradesh, Karnataka and Tripura. Hence the Bhils are met with in a long irregularly shaped triangle of country in North-Western India. The base of the area is in Khandesh (Maharastra), some 90 miles from Bombay and its narrow apex reaches up along the bridge of the Aravali Hills in Udaipur. Throughout this territory, which is over 400 miles from north to south, the Bhils show considerable local variations in customs, traits along with language also. There are at one extreme, the Bhilalas of Khandesh, who claim relationship with the Rajputs and the near naked aboriginal "black Bhils" of Jhabua at the other end. There local differences have been fostered by the lack of communication.

Bhil is a major tribal group of central India. The concentration states are Gujarat, Rajasthan, Maharashtra and Madhya Pradesh. In Rajasthan Bhils can be seen throughtout the state, Groups but their concentration is in southern part of the state viz. Banswara, Dungarpur and Udaipur Districts having more than 50 per cent of the Bhils.

In Gujarat state the Bhils can be seen in Surat, Dang, Bhuruch, Vadodra, Panchmahal, Mehasana, Ahmedabad, Kheda, Banaskantha, Sabarkantha and Kuch District, while about 75% Bhils are residing in Bhuruch, Vadodara, Sabarkantha and Panchmahal District.

The Bhils concentrated district of Maharashtra are Dhule, Nasik, Jalgaon, Ahmednagar and Aurangabad where more than 50 per cent Bhils can be seen.

Similarly Madhya Pradesh is the home of tribals. In this state Bhils stands second after Gonds. The Bhils concentration area of the state are Dhar, Jhabua, Khargon and Ratlam District. They constitute the western tribal region of Madhya Pradesh. In those area more than 50 per cent Bhils are residing. The population of Bhil includes sub-tribal groups of Bhil, Bhilala, Barela and Patelia. While in Rajasthan, Gujarat and Maharashtra population of Bhil includes the sub-groups viz. Bhil, Bhil-Garasia, Dholi Bhil, Dungri Bhil, Dungri Grarsia, Mewasi Bhil, Rawal Bhil, Tadvi Bhil, Bhagalia, Bhilala, Pawra, Vasava and Vasave.

Demography

According to the census, 1931 return there were 363,124 Bhils in Central India, out of these 144,836 returned (written) themselves as Hindus and the remaining 218,288 retained their allegiance to their tribal religion. The true strength of the Central India Bhils has hitherto not been estimated. Certain tribes allied to the Bhils were paraded under different labels in the caste table as separate castes or tribes. The strength of Bhils group of tribes is considerable. If we amalgamate, as we should, the figures for a number of the allied tribes. The details are given below:

S. No.	BHIL Groups	HINDU			TRIBAL		
		Persons	Male	Female	Persons	Male	Female
1	Bhil	144,836	73,939	70,897	218,288	109,666	108,622
2	Bhilala	187,145	94,926	92,219	6,630	3,363	3,267
3	Barela	38,517	19,647	18,870	108	59	49
4	Mankar	20,430	10,058	10,372	49	26	23
5	Nihal	11,529	5,766	5,763	702	350	352
6	Patlia	8,268	4,280	3,988	11,140	5,812	5,328
7	Rathia	37,260	19,028	18,232	-	-	-

The tribal population constitute only 3.6 per cent, while the Bhils constitute one-tenth of the total population of the Central India.

According to census of 1971, the total number of Bhils residing in the country inculding sub-groups was 5,172,129, while in 1981 the census figure rose upto 7,367,972. Hence during the decade 1971-81 an increase of 2,195,843 Bhils have been observed. The increase in Bhil population was 29.80 per cent which is much more higher than the national average growth of 2.5 per cent per year, but this is just equal to the growth rate of the other tribal groups. Similar trend have been observed during the decade 1981-91. Now the Bhil population has grown about one crore i.e about 15 per cent tribals belong to Bhil or its subgroups.

The above table shows that the highest number of Bhils are residing in the Madhya Pradesh in other words we can say that Madhya Pradesh is home land of Bhils. Second credit goes to Gujarat and third to Rajasthan, while forth position goes to Maharashtra. Hence from the above table it can be said that Central India is the "Home Land" of the Bhils.

The special feature is that the Bhils have their concentration with adjoining boundaries of the said states i.e they reside on the adjoining boundaries of Rajasthan, Gujarat, Madhya Pradesh and Maharashtra. Hence about 98 per cent Bhils are residing in the Central part of the country. In other words it can be said that 'Bhils' are the tribals of Central India. Very few can be seen in Andhra Pradesh, Karnataka and Tripura also.

State-wise Bhil Population according to 1981 census have been discussed below :

S. No	State	Population	Percentage to Total Bhil Population
	India	7,367,972	100.00
1	Andhra Pradesh	259	0.0035 (Neg.)
2	Madhya Pradesh	2,500,530	33.94
3	Gujarat	2,030,438	27.56
4	Rajasthan	1,840,966	24.98
5	Maharshtra	993,074	13.48
6	Karnataka	1,867	0.035 (Neg)
7	Tripura	838	0.01

Gujarat

Gujarat is also Bhils dominated area and out of its 17 district, 11 districts have Bhils i.e. in Gujarat Bhils can be seen throughout the state, but whatever may be. According to 1961 census, the district-wise Bhil population is discussed below in the table.

S. No.	District	Population Rural	Population Urban	Person
	Gujarat	1,085,682	38,600	1,124,282
1.	Surat	95,091	683	95,774
2.	Dang	23,701	-	23,701
3.	Bhuruch	267,555	14,869	282,424
4.	Vadodara	113,890	4,946	118,836
5.	Panchmahal	398,117	4,875	402,992
6.	Mehasana	672	2,887	3,559
7.	Ahmedabad	3,199	5,390	8,589
8.	Kheda	9,610	2,574	12,184
9.	Banaskantha	50,633	1,737	52,370
10.	Sabarkantha	122,683	379	123,062
11.	Kutch	531	260	791

The table shows that Panchmahal, Bhuruch, Banaskantha, Sabarkantha and Vadodara having high concentration of Bhils. This trend have been observed during the census of 1971,1981 and 1991 also

Rajasthan

The Bhils stands second largest tribal group in the state constituting about 40 per cent of the total tribal population and comes after Mina tribe. Though they can be seen throughout the state, but their concentration is in the southern part of the state i.e. Udaipur, Banswara and Dungarpur where more than 50 per cent Bhils are residing. This area also have been included in the Tribal Sub Plan Area (TSP)of the state for special Development of the tribal groups.

The principally state Mewar can be said as 'home land' of Bhils in the state.

The Bhil population according to the census conducted in Samvat 1974, Kavirai Shymala Das has quoted in his book "Vir Vinod" the details are-

Bhils - I

S. No	Area	Population
	Mewar	134,429
1	Udaipur	2,883
2.	Girwa	12,393
3.	Magra, Sarada	24,332
4.	Salumber	8,253
5.	Kanor	4,166
6.	Bansi	4,204
7.	Jhadol	6,381
8.	Dharayawad	23,815
9.	Kherwara, Bhomat	34,169
10.	Kotra, Bhomat	13,833

From the above table it can be said that princially times this part has concentration of Bhils. This trend continues till date.

At the time to 1961 census the Bhil population was 906,705, while after two decades it goes upto 1,840,966 which is just double. It shows a heavy increase in the Bhil population which is much more high than the national growth rate. This appendix also reveals that Bhils can be seen throughout the state whatever the number may be. The Bhil concertation area in the state are Banswara, Dungarpura and Udaipur Distric of the Southern Rajasthan. The similar trend have been observed during the census 1991.

Change is a natural age old pheomenon. After existance of human being on the earth series of changes have been observed by the Anthropolists, Sociologist and other scientists. They recorded them time-to-time. Such historical changes can be seen in past history of human development. The factors responsible for a series of change may be a number and different from each other. Hence change is not a rendom phenomenon. But it takes a lot of time. The effect of few changes can been seem immediately, while the effect of few can take a long duration.

The change is culture, traditions, traits and habits take very long time or duration for a change. In other words we can say that social change take long duration and their effect can be observed.

By nature some groups can adopt new devices in early age and they developed their skill in short time. This can be seen in Hindus and other upper caste of the society in camparison to the tribal groups. The late development or change is responsible due to their isolation, because a person feels fear when he sees some thing new or abnorm. Hence the tribals are living since long in solution they have a fear to adopt new devices which may harmful for them. By rapid education and means of communication, the contact to isolated groups make easily.

Hence by the effect of changing devices Bhils could not be saved, they have also join steadly the main stream of national life. Now we can see the effect of changing face in the Bhil soicety easily.

Inhabitation

The Bhils today observe the age old settlement pattent of scattered inhabition. In this pattern each house is away from other house. In thses houses filed are surrounded by their hutments. The scattered pattern of settling having a special feature of vigilance i.e. on the crops as well as animals. Bhils always like to settle outside the village or far away form the village, they do not like to live within the vilalge. This type of age old concept is also prevailing in the recent years also and can be seen throughout the Bhil region today. On the other hand such a pattern of scattered living is highly disadvantageous for comminity development needs. For the community development need they have force to go nearby village which may be far away or near to their settlings.

The age old **Pal** settelements also exists. **Pal** is a endogamous. Isolation is the cahraterstic mark of the borader stratification pattern among the Bhils. Generally **Pals** having 10-15 familes among the exceptional cases, it may be upto 100 families.

Today the Bhils also living in the plain. The plain area Bhils are better-off in comparison to **Pal** or remote Bhils. The Bhils of western Rajasthan lives in plain area having a better economic condition in comparison to Southern Rajasthan Bhils. The Bhils of western Rajasthan having economic land holdings and a different type of housing pattern as compared to scattered habition Bhils of Souhtern Rajasthan. Similar situation can also be seen in Nothern Gujarat and Southern Gujarat Bhils along with Maharasthara. Now a days the educated Bhils like to reside in a collective village or near settlings so they can get essential community services provided by govt. at par.

The Bhils prefer nuclear family, so they live in a single hut, which serves as a multipurpose room for them. Their hut is also having a varanda and a courtyarel or fancing by plants. In the fancing, they tie their livestock like Bullock, Cow, Goat and others. After marriage of their son, they construct another hut for this new couple. Such sort of fregmentation of familily carriesout till the marriage of last or youngest son.

The Bhils usually construct their houses by earthen material which is easily available at local site without any cost i.e. they use such material which they can get free. Generally they thath roofs of huts with bamboos and calverts (**Kelu**). Hence their house may be constructed without any cost i.e. free. In the huts they do not get any sort of ventilation. Only a single door is sufficient for their hut. In front of hut, they construct a varanda with the same material i.e. mud and stone serves as a guest room. Such sort of housing pattern can be seen througout the Bhil region. Now a days well to do Bhils also construct **pucca** houses in the plain area. The **pucca** houses can be seen in the plain area of Gujarat and Maharasthara state, while in Rajasthan and Madhay Pradesh such type of houses can be seen in very few cases, due to the extreme poverty of Bhils.

In the urban areas, the Bhils reside in a mixed locality. Hence the urban areas Bhils behave i.e.reside like the upper caste Hindus and avail all facilites like them.

The Bhils of **Pals** or scattered inhabition fulfill their essential needs inculding food, fuel and shelter are largely metout from the produce within the locality. They produce grain which is sufficient for their livelihood except hard times. In case of surplus produce, they exchange it from their essential house hold needs.The Bhils of such type of habition metout their other requirements from the nearby village. Hnece the Bhils generally fulfill their requirements from the nearby village, while the Bhils of urban area fulfill their are requirements from the local market. Hence the Bhils of all regions fulfill their requirements on a routine age old patten.

The Bhils of **Pal** or scattered inahabitation generally use the community facility, nearby village like school, health centre, etc.

Village Panchayat

The tribal groups having a strong social organisation known as **Jati Panchayat**. The similar organisation pattern has been followed througout the Bhil region of the country. They obey the decisions of their **Panchayat**. The **Panchayat** generally give economic punishment i.e. impose fines and in some case they may be physically punished or both the punishment also. Hence in the Bhil society the **Panchayat** organisation have extreme interference in their routine life. They go for their any sort of greviences in their local **Panchyat**. The head of **Panchayat** named as 'Gameti' or 'Patel' or 'Mukhi' according to the regional pattern. The post of 'Patel' or 'Gameti' is ancestral. After the death of Patel or Gameti, his son will be the next Patel.

In the Bhil Panchyat the local disputes are generally solved in their panchayat viz marriage, land and other sort of criminal disputes. In the marriage disputes regarding bride price known as 'dapa' is generally setteled in their village Panchayat in other words the dispute of 'dapa' is generally solved by the mediators like Patel and other resourceful persons of the **pal** or village. They have too much fath in their Panchayat. In some cases it was observed that they have punished by the law of court, but after completing the punishment of the court they obey the punishment of their Panchayat also.

Now a days in the educated Bhils, the effect of their panchayat is reducing day by day. They belive in the court of law and do not bother their social organisation i.e. panchayat. This practice can be generally seen in the nearby urban inhabitations or in urban area Bhils througout the Bhil region.

After the amendment in the Panchyati Raj Act through 73rd and 74th amendment, the village panchayat have more powerful by this. The effect of Bhil panchyat also reduces, but the participation of Bhil women also involved which was not previously seen in anywhere of the Bhil region.

Family

The Bhils like nuclear family in which husband, wife and their unmarried childern live together. They do not prefer joint family as can be seen in Hindus. When a grown-up son marries, he separate from his parents and estableshes new family. For establishing the new couple, the father of boy construct another hut for him and give a part of a land for his survial by this way fragementation carried out till all his sons married. Hence the separation is complete in this respect that the son and the father do not work on the common farm, but a separate piece of land is allotted to the son for his maintenance. The head of family is father or the eldest male member of the family in the absence of father.

In Bhil family, the paraents generally live together with their youngest son. This sort of family system can be seen througout the Bhil region. This age old family system is still contunued or observed in the cahnging face. This sort of family concept can be seen now a days in the Hindus. Hence the Bhils feel that this short family system is more convenient in comparison to join family. In Bhils family no disputes can be seen generally if disputes arises in the family will be between the husband and wife. By this way the Bhil women enjoys more freedom in his family as compared to Hindus.

In Bhil family the relationship is as usualy can be seen in other societies or groups like Hindus. They called them according to the realtionship and prevalent names in the region.

The Bhil prefer monogamy, but polygamy can be seen in many families. Polygamy practies can be seen in rich Bhils, becuse the marriage criteria is bride price (**dapa**) which a rich Bhil can efford. Hnece polygamy practice in the Bhil society is restricted by the bride price, becuased due to economic constraints they do not able to pay a huge amount for a women. The prefer polygamy, because they get more free workers. This situation can be seen throught the Bhil region. No change have observed on this practice.

Clan

Every society having clans. Hindus also observe a number of clans. Similarly the tribal groups also observe clan system in the groups and sub-group. Clan system is very important in setting the marriage relations. The clan system plays an important role in the **Pal** and **villages** i.e. in a pal or village persons reside in them belongs to single clan or two three clans. Hnece the Bhil society observe clan system very seriously. The clan system among the Bhils can be seen througout the Bhil region weather it may, reside in Rajasthan or in the remote of Maharastahra.

Bhils are organised into a number of patrilineal exogamous groups or clan locally known as **atak** that rests on the "fiction of common descent from a founding ancestor who lived so far the distant past as to be mythological".

Each clan is distinctively named and cansists of the totality to related individuals from the same ancestors. Each clan has its own terms. The totem may be plant, bird or animal. All clan members invoke their respective totemic gods and goddeses locally known as **Devata**. During their hard times and difficulties or on the ocassion, they perform ceremony. They also observe the ranking of clan i.e. lower and upper groups in the society, they do observe marrital relations with lower groups i.e. clans

The prevalent **clans** in the Bhil region are detailed below.

Angari, Amrat, Ahari, Uthed, Udavat, Katara, Kapaya, Kaluva, Kalasua, Kasauta, Kuriya, Koted, Khakhad, Kharadi, Gamar, Gameti, Gogara, Goda, Gorma, Gugra, Chadana, Chavana, Charpota, Joshiyala, Dana, Dabi, Damar, Damor, Dindor, Dungri, Dodiyat, Tanwar, Tabayar, Tawad, Tejot, Nanoma, Dama, Dayama, Parmar, Pandor, Pandot, Pargi, Bhagora, Rathore, Rangot, Miyada, Manat, Relawat, Rot, Varada, Solanki, Makwana, Hirata, Hirot, Bhuriya, etc. Hence the Bhils are divided in a number of clans. Bhils observe may clans as resemble to Rajputs, becuause they believe that their ancestor were Rajputs of the said clan groups.

Sharat Chandra Rai in his book given refernce of prevalent totems observed in the area of Jaisamand Bhils. Komari explained 43 clans which observe their totems, 17 trees and plants, 17 animals and 7 other items prevalent in the Bhils of Jhabua, Madhay Pradesh. Some of the prevalent totems among the Bhils are :

Clan	Totem
Harayat	Kalika Mata
Dhari	Bhulya
Katara	Malo
Kharadi	Ambav
Damar, Bhagora, vodavat	Kanyalo
Dama, Nanama, Hela	Thur
Tejot, Parmar	Peepal Hen
Goda Damor	Vajed

Hence the number of clains are day-by-day increasing and througout the Bhil region they observe it strictly.

Language

language is a special feature of a creature, by which they can express their thoughts, talks and communicate their views. It is not necessary that every language may have special script or codes of representation. It is only a medium to communicate their view by orally or in written form. Language do not represent the origin of any caste, person or a group, but it represents only the area specification in which a person or groups belongs, in other words language represents the regional identity of a person or a group or sub-group. Keeping in view this identity Bhils have their own langugage but this language have not any special form of code (**Lipi** i.e. script) representation. This can be written in **Devangari Lipi**.

In the view of Stephen Funch " that the tribal groups of Western. Centre India belongs to the Indo-uropean speaking part of the Indian population". There is evidence to suggest as Coppers and Jug-blunt that Bhils have their own language which was not of the Indo-Aryan family.

hence in the view of experts Bhils have their own language they named it **Bhili** or **Bhilodi**. This language is spoken througout the Bhil area but the pronunciation differnt from region-to-region. This language is spoken in adjoining Bhil areas of Gujarat, Madhya Pradesh and Maharastra states.

Accroding to George A., Grearsion" the area of Bhil language is a triangle inculdes the top or Aravil ranges and base inculdes the southern part of Khandes Districts".

Historically first of all Father S.S Thompson has used this language and published the Bhils grammer in 1895. On the basis of Bhil language, Thomson has classified that Bhil belonging to the Kolarian tribes. He further analysie that several of the words used by the Bhils are simply corrupt forms of Gujarati words. According to Thompson's analysis of Bhili language 80 per cent of the words derived from Sanskrit, 10 per cent from Arabian and Parsian and rest 6 per cent having uncertain origin. The Thompson distionary having a collection of 2,956 words, out of them 2,483 of Sanskrit, 295 of Arabian and Parsian and about 178 words of disputed origin. Griorson made similar observation. He also emphasized the Gujarati basis of all Bhili dialects. Similarly Sh.P.G Shah has also supported the view and according to him" Bhili is similar to modern Gujarati and it in origin and use it shows Aryai". In support of Bhili two concepts are there (1) Bhili is corrupt (vibhasha) from Rajasthani and Bhili is corrupt (vibhasa) of Gujarati and greater effect of Gujarati. Hence it can be said that Bhili dialect or language is infeunced by the neighbouring languages viz. Marathi, Malvi, Vagri, and Mewari, because most of the Bhilis of these area use the language which non-tribal families /person speak, so their language have greater effect of this language also. Sniti Kumar Chatarjee has also supported the views of Thomson according to him "Bhili" is a mixed format of Rajasthani and Gujarati". Sh. Naratom Swami and Sh. Mathura Prasad Agarwal both have considered Bhili as a principal dialect of 7 Rajasthani dilects. They have also included 4 sub-dialects of Bhili viz. Garasia, Bhilodi, Bhili and vagdi. Hence Bhili language having a vaste scope and having 28 sub-groups, each group having regional identity and speciality.

Dr. Nami Chand Jain has also prepared a Bhili-Hindi Dictionary, in this he has inculded 4,500 words of this language.

According to George A. Griorson the Bhili speaking persons were 2,689,109 out of them 163,872 used pure Bhili (**Parinisth Bhili**) and rest 1,526,872 speaks sub-Bhili diclects (**Knisth Bhili**).

The Details of Bhili speaking persons from 1891 to 1951 are detailed below:

Year	Persons
1891	3,942,175
1901	1,198,843
1921	1,855,617
1931	2,000,000
1941	2,330,270
1951	2,233,000

According to 1961 the Bhili speaking persons in the state of Rajasthan, Gujarat, Madhya Pradesh and Maharashtra are detailed below:

Rajasthan	385,412
Gujarat	41,030
Madhya Pradesh	650,629
Maharasthara	212,766

In Rajasthan, the **Vagri** speaking persons have been inculded, because **Vagri** is also dialect of Bhili.

Hence Bhili a perfect single language with simple literature, but it has no specific **Lipi**. Bhili is written in Devnagri **Lipi** (script).

Hence the Bhils of India having a specific language,but local and Hindi language effect can be seen throught the Bhili region. The educated and youngest among the Bhils now a days like to speak Hindi and other regional languages also, becuase they are getting their education in the medium of Hindi or in other regional languages like

Gujarati and Marathi. In Madhya Pradesh Bhil also speaks **'Nimadi'** which is also a dialect of Bhili.

Food Habits

In the ancient time Bhils were fully dependent on forests. They use forest produce as their food along with the animals of the forests, which they can kill easily, they eat them, after passing a long time and their attention towards agriculture, they have adopted a change in their food habits.

The Bhils of rural area generally use staple food i.e. maize, jowar and other small millets which they prefer to eat. But by the introduction of fair price shops (control commodities scheme), they have adopted to eat wheat in their regular diet. Due to strict control over forest policy they do not get forest produce easily and in ample, so they have forced to reduce their dependancy on forest produce and change their eating behaviour.

Now a days Bhils have fully adopted the changing behaviour and made a drastic change in their eating habits. They take wheat, Maize or Jowar and rise as a cereal in their regular diet. Bhil use a least amount of fats like oil. Generally they do not use **Ghee** i.e. butter fat. They use a minimum quantity of oil in their daily use. Similarly they do not use spices, on the name of spices they only use salt and chillies. They also use Garlic and onion in their regular food. Bhils do not use sugar, they use it casually. They use **Gaggery** (**Gur**) powder in their daily life. Bhils are also found of tea. They use **Gur** on the place of sugar in the tea. Bhils prefer **Rabdi** which is common preparation made by boiling flour in butter milk (**chhach**). Pulses of **gram** and **urd** (Black gram) and green vegetables are taken if available easily. By custom and tradition they are non-vegetarian. They eat flesh of hare, mutton, dear and other animals and birds such as partridge, sand-grouse, etc. They also use fish.

Bhils genearlly take meals twice a day. In genral Bhils do not use fruits, but plums and mangoes are seasonal fruits are taken in plenty, the forest fruits are common items of use. They do not habitual to buy fruits from the market, because they are not in a position to efford it.

The '**Bhagats**' among the Bhilis are strictly vegetarian even they do not use liquor.

Bhils are very much fond of liquor. In Bhil society all members of the family use the liquor in plenty, becuase they extract it their own level.

Generally they use **Mahua** fruits for the extrection of liquor which is readily available to them without any cost. They also use tobacco, bidi and opimum and like the other intoxicants.

Bhils prepare special diets on the festivals and other important occasion, but the items are limited. But now a days the well do Bhils celebrate the occasion very cheerefully and preapare a number of dishes. This sort of changing eating habit pattern can be seen throughout the Bhil region of the country. They are developing their habits similar to Hindus.

Life Cycle

Generally Bhil couple like the child. Every couple wishes that they must have a child whether it may be male of female i.e. boy or girl. In Bhil society no difference have been observed in male and female child both of them given equal importance. During pregnancy of women, Bhils do not observe any ceremony. After the delievery they celebrate it. Usually on the birth of son they beat metal plate (**Thali**) and on the birth of girl they beat winniong fan (**sup**). They observe purification ceremony after the birht of 5 to 7 days. On this day the mother and child took bath and **Suraj Punjan** ceremony is observed for the welfare of child and mother. On this day a feast is also organised and songs also sung by ladies. The nearer relatives gives presents to the mother and child. During the delivery period they try to fed the mother in well and give her nourishing diet whatever they can efford.

The Bhils also observe naming and **mundan** cermonies. Hence we can esily see the effect of Hindu culture on the Bhils, Now a days Bhils are comming nearer to the Hindu culture and they observe most of the rituals followed by Hindus.

Marriage

Marriage among the Bhils is not a sacrament. Like the Hindu marriage it is not indissoluble. In Bhil society child marriage is not prevelent. For a Bhil, both male and female marriage is a mark of adulthood and maturity.

In Bhil society different forms of marriages are prevalent among them. They prefer marriage by elopment and traditional marriage which is performed by full rituals by the parents of girl and boy. The prevailing marriages are:

(1)   Marriage by traditional (**Morbandiya Vivah**)
(2)   Marriage by elopment

(3) Marriage by trial (**Perviksha Vivha**)
(4) Marriage by purchase
(5) Marriage by service (**seva vivah**)
(6) Marriage by exchange
(7) Marraige by concent
(8) Marraige by Rigidness (**Huth vivah**)
(9) **Nata** Marrige

The most prevalent marriages in the Bhil society are traditional and elopement. In traditional marriage all the ceremaories are performed right from **sagai** to **vidai** in the houses of boy and girl. But the criteria for this marraige is bride price locally known as **dapa**. Before **sagai**, birde price is settled between the girl and boys father, if any dispute arises the matter has to be decided by the patel of both sides. In this sort of marriage all rituals are performed according to Hindu marriage.

In elopment, the boy and girl run away from their house and marry, but he marriage is recognised by the society after payment of bride price i.e. **dapa** to the boys father and payment of panelty imposed on them to their panchyat, if any dispute arises is to be solved by the **Patels** of both the villages.

Marriage by exchange means ones sister marriage to each other. The poor Bhils perform such type of marriage. In this bride price is not paid from both sides.

Widow marriage is also prevalent among the Bhils. It is performed in simple manner.

Nata marriage is prevalent among the Bhil society. In this case a married Bhil women can marry with any other person whom she likes, but the criteria for this is bride price. The women can only marry after bride price is paid to his previous husband. This amount is known as **Jagdha** and the women is known as **Jadha-ki-Aurat.** Such type of marriage is known as **Nata.** In exception **Nata** can be seen in unmarried girls also.

Hence among the Bhils women have freedom to marring with any person which she likes, but payment of bride price is necessary. By this way there is check of their marriage by the society. This pracatice can be seen throught the Bhil region.

In conclusion it can be said that Bhils are observing age old marriage traditions throught the Bhil region right from Rajasthan to Maharashtra and Madhya Pradesh. The local traditions may be differ according their culture and rituals.

Status of Women

In Bhil society women enjoys more freedom than the Hindu society. The Bhils like the female child from the very begining, becuase female chile right from the early chilhood helps the family in their domsetic work. During the teen age they go for work out- side the home and also helps their parents on the economic front i.e. they works on the filed as well as go on the labour work. Hence by this way the female helps their parents from the early age.

In the Bhil society bride price (**Dapa**) is also prevalent. So far the marriage purpose of women i.e. girl is a asset for their parents. They demand 'Bride Price' what ever the desire. Generally bride price (**dapa**) becomes a hurdle in their marriage, this dispute is generally solved by the **Patels** or **Gameties** of the socitey. Hence for the marriage of a girl they get a handsome amount. In case of **Nata** they also get **dapa**. Hence in the Bhil society **dapa** is main creiteria for the marraige. Hence **dapa** provides the Bhil girl as a shield or protection in their in-laws house.

In Bhils society the newly married girl enjoys full freedom. In Bhil society after the marriage of the boy, the father construct a hut for their son and give him a piece of land for his survival. So the bride enjoys full freedom in their husbands house. In Bhil society no-disputes between the mother in-law and daughter in-law has been observed. Both of them enjoys full freedom and liberty.

In Bhil society the women have to work very hard. She have to work from early morning to late night. Right from cooking, fuel collection, water collection, field work or labour work along with the child rearing and family management. Hnece we can say that women status is better in comparison to upper caste Hindu societies and they prevail freedom more then other caste women, but they have do drudgery right from the early age.

The Bhil girl have full freedom to choose their life partner, but the bride price is also a restriction for them. Now a days the educated parents do not like to take bride price, but they have imposed a lot of restrictions on their female child.

Hence the similar position of the Bhil women can be seen throughout the Bhil region. In the changing economic pattern they are also facing a number of restrictions impsoed by their parents and their society.

In Bhil society the women can re-marriage or divorce. Widow marrige is also permissible by the society. But for that bride price is also a hurdle form them, in remote areas the Bhils today take bride price accroding to their desire.

In Bhils society the females have no property right. The position of the women confirms to the form of marriage. In a polygamous family, the position and status of a wife are accorded in realtion to the degree of preferences she gets from his husband. However if she is the senior most, then she enjoys higher status in the family relating to social matters and rites. The relation ship between co-wivas is often strained. No family ritual can be performed in her absence.

The widow's position hardly arises in the Bhil society. She can takes remarriage **Natra** after expiry period of mourning. Only old women who do not want to remarry, remain widows. The widow has been given full respect in the family. The traditional Hindu attitude towards widow is absent among the Bhils, she is free to participate in any social function. So in Bhil society widow's can also enjoys full freedom, while in the Hindu societies their are a number of restrictions imposed on them.

Overall we can say that in Bhil society the status of women is better in comparison to other societies.

Education

Education makes a person polite and well behaved, but the Bhils have deprived from very begining by this facility due to their isolation and non-contact to upper castes. The rulers never payed any attention towards their education.

In the begining of this century, the position of Bhil was very worst. Regarding this feature Eraskaine expeained the 1901 census situation. In the Mewar Residency. He has written "Education is paratically non-exixtent but there are few schools in Udaipur and Dungarpur at which Bhil childern attained the school. The latest cencus report does not give the number of literate Bhils., but tells that only 340 Animists (307 males and 32 females) were able to read and write. It may be said that in 1901 among the Bhils sixteen in every 10,000 of the males and two in every 10,000 of the females were literate,

The literacy percentage of Bhils of Rajasthan during last three decades have been given below. This represents an increasing trend in all the decades.

S. No.	Year	Bhil Population	Literate	Percentage of Bhil literacy to Total Bhils	State Percentage of literacy (General)
1	1961	906,705	24,225	2.67	15.21
2	1971	1,437,937	67,320	4.68	19.07
3	1981	1,840,966	121,430	6.60	24.38

Source - *Census of India 1961,1971 amd 1981 Social and Cultural Tables.*

According to 1981 census out of 6.60 per cent literarcy, only 5.81 males were literate, while only 0.41 per cent female were literate. The ecucation status of Bhils of Rajasthan is detailes in the Appendix-I

Hence the overall review of the situation, the educational status of Bhils is a question of review. The female literarcy is less than one per cent. The similar situation can be seen throught the Bhil region. So the Bhils are deprived by the reservation policy of the Government. They do not pay more attention towards their education, because they need labour force for their work. Now a days many voluntany agencies and Govt. is making efforts to educate/literate them, but the effect seems very low in the Bhil area.

Religion

Most of the Bhil worship Hindu dieties along with their own local dieties. They workship Shiva, Ganesh, Human, Durga, etc. The temple of Bhils known as '**Devra**'. Bhils do not workship regularly, but they workship in hard times. They are supertious and believe in them blindly. They have very much faith in their local priest known as '**Bhopa**' In hard times or in any problem they consult him and obey his advice. They also believe in '**Bhopas**' treatment. This situation can be seen throught the Bhil region. Some Bhils observe Sikh, Jain, Buddh, Christian and Muslim sects also. The details of Bhils according religion at the time of 1981 census in Rajasthan is given in Appendix - II

From appendix -II is can be said that most of the Bhils (99.2%) of Rajasthan observe Hindu religion. Alongwith Hindu religion they believe in Animism.

Economy

The Bhils in the past as a whole have been law-less and independent earing their livelihood from forest and forest produce. If they did not get enough to eke out a living through forest, then they adopt theft and burglery as a profession. At a later stage i.e. about a century before they adopted agriculture as occupation. Initally they do shifting cultivation and adopted this practice for a long time.

Due to strict forest policy of the govt. they have settled at one place and leave the practice of shifting cultivation and started the settled farm practice. For their settlement govt. played a very important role and allotted land to the Bhils. But the misery is that they are not perfect in cultivation i.e. in agriculture, low tertility of land or hilly or barran land, poor irrigation facilities or lack of irrigation facilities, small holdings and economic constraints behind them for low production. So they do not get surplus marketable produce. Hence the economic condition of Bhils is very miserable and they face extreme proverty, in few cases the Bhils of plain area have economically better than hilly area Bhils.

In hard times i.e. in famine time there condition goes very critical and they are hand to mouth in these days.

Even all family member do hard work on their fields and larbour front, but they get only for the survival not any sort of surplus amount. Hence throughout the life they face economic constraints and deprived by the essential needs.

This situation can be seen throughout the Bhil area. The position of Nothern part of Bhils of Gujarat is better in comparison to Bhils of Southern Gujarat. The position of Madhya Pradesh and Maharashtra is similar with Rajasthan.

The change in occupation on this tribal group have been due to urbanization and industralization. Due to this effect the Bhils of adjoining area migrated to the urban area or industrial area where they get job. They have setteled in the big cities or in the nearby area and come to their native place once or twice in a year. Hence few of the Bhils have changed their occuption, but they are facing other sort of problems.

The occuptional pattern of Bhils in Rajasthan according to 1981 census have been detailed in Appendix - III. This appendix reveals that 87 per cent Bhils are engaged in agriculture and allied agriculture occuptions, while only 13 per cent have adopted other occupations. The appendix-III reveals that among the Bhils only 45.73 per cent are working, while 54.27 per cent are dependent. But in fact that working population in this society is more in comparison to other groups.

Hence a changing pattern have been observed during this centuary, but their economic situation goes worst. The govt. of India and state govts. have launched a number of schemes / programmes for their economic upliftment and included Bhil area in Tribal Sub-Plan Area or in other special schemes, but the desired results are still awaited.

Social Change

The Bhils have adopted the Hindu culture in other words they are coming nearer to Hindus. A time will come when they merge their culture in Hindu culture and lose their speical identity. This a question of their cultural survival. There culture must be preserved.

Now a days the remote Bhils are observing their age old cultural traits, but on them Hindu effect can be seen easily. They perform their marriages according to Hindu rituals and observe all rituals similar to Hindus right from **sagai** to **vidai** of bride.

The Bhil male and female both like to wear ornments. Male use ornaments in ears and hands. They use rings in ears known as **long, Murki** and **kada** in Wrist or in leg. They wear chain or some **Tabiz** in their neck also. They like to wear rings in their fingures. Ladies in Bhil society are very much fond of ornaments. The wear a variety of ornaments from head to toe viz **Bor** on head **Rakdhi, long** in nose, **Toti** / rings in ears, In neck chain and **Hansli** in wrist bangles, etc. Usually their ornaments are made of cheap meterial like silver, brass, ranga and fancy items. The women are very fond of decoration. Generally they wear cheap and decorative ornaments. In Bhil society the male and female both like tottoting. This a cheapest mode of decoration.

The young Bhils are using the latest design ornaments.

Their dressing patterns are also changing. The old and remote Bhils use their traditional dresses, while the young Bhils use the modern colthes.

The Bhils participate in the fairs very actively. They fully enjoy the fairs wheather it may be local or regional. From the fair they buy the goods/ articales of their daily use and meetout their essential needs from these fairs. In fairs some of young boys and girls may choose their life partners also. Hence throughout the Bhil region Bhils actively participate in the fairs.

Similarly Bhils also enjoys the local festivals. They celebrate the functions with full of joy and cheerfully. They generally perfom the activities like Hindus. The Bhils of urban area also celebrate the festivals as other caste persons. The mode of celebration can not be differentiate. Hence regarding the celebration of fairs and festivals they have adopted the changing pattern.

The Bhil are very much fond of arms, usually the remote Bhils like the age old arms like **lathi**, bow, axe, etc. The well to do Bhils like guns also. But they do not know about their restrication of licence etc. So generally every family keeps the essential age old traditional equipments in their house for safety purpose. Axe is a multi purpose arm, it can be used as safety measure, while on other hand it can be used as a tool for cutting wood.

The Bhils very much like dances and songs. In this society male and female both join dances together. Their dances are pecular and full of joy. They generally perform traditional dances. Bhils of Rajasthan play **Ger, Gavari,** etc They use to go for folk dances, On the occasion of **holi** they enjoy for a month with dances and use plenty of liquor. During the dance they use their traditional musical equipments like **Dhol, Kundi, Thali** (metal plate), etc. The dance and musical instruments changes according to local needs in other words the dances of Maharashtra are different than Rajasthan and Madhya Pradesh. Hence regarding cultural traits their is separate identity which represents their local and regional idendity. In few cases a change have been observed i.e. they also sing flimi songs and inculded some latest trend in their dances. They celebrate may functions with songs and dances specially marriage ceremonices.

Hence the social life is changing through the passing of times Urbanisation, education, industralization and means of communications are the major factors behind it. Perhaps a bit change in the living pattern can be seen, but the change is slow and in process. This change can be seen thorought the Bhil Area.

Hence Bhils are effected by the modern devices and are coming nearer to the national main stream. The misery with them is their poor or lack of knoweldge, criticil econimic condition and illetracy deprived them from the rapid change. One another factor which is hurdle in their rapid development is their age old concepts and views.

❑❑❑

APPENDIX - I
Tribe-wise population of Rajasthan

S. No.	Tribe	1961	1971	1981 Male	1981 Female	1981 Person	Percentage of total S.T. Population
	Rajasthan	2,351,470	3,125,506	2,150,767	2,032,357	4,183,124	100
1.	Bhil, Bhil Garasia, Dhoil, Bhil, Dungari Garasia, Mewasi Bhil, Rawal Bhil, Tadvi Bhil, Bhagalia, Bhilala, Pawra, Vasava, Vasave	906,705	1,437,937	929,087	911,879	1,840,966	44.01
2.	Bhil-Mina	2,063	17,076	13,766	13,371	27,137	0.65
3.	Damor, Damaria	14,534	14,795	15,937	15,440	31,377	0.75
4.	Dhanka, Tadvi, Tetaria, Valvi	-	157	7,378	6,733	14,111	0.34
5.	Garasia (Excluding Rajput Garasia)	62,509	52,268	60,225	58,332	118,757	2.84
6.	Kathodi, Katkari, Dhor Kathodi, Dhor Katkri, Son Kathodi, Son Katkari	-	1	1,236	1,137	2,553	0.06

Bhils - I

S. No.	Tribe	1961	1971	1981 Male	1981 Female	1981 Person	Percentage of total S.T. Population
7.	Kokna, Kokni, Kukna	-	2	91	74	165	0.004 Negligible
8.	Koli Dhor, Tokre Koli, Kolcha, Kolgha	-	166	1,075	1,006	2,081	0.059
9.	Mina	1,155,620	1,532,331	1,091,451	995,241	2,086,692	49.88
10.	Naikda, Nayaka, Cholivala Nayaka, Kapadia Nayaka, Mota Nayaka, Nana Nayaka	-	32	4,800	4,374	9,174	0.22
11.	Patelia	-	1	931	772	1,703	0.04
12.	Seharia, Sehria, Sahariya	23,299	26,939	20,821	20,124	40,945	0.98
13.	Unspecified	186,740	43,801	3,969	3,494	7,463	0.18

Source:-
1. Census of India 1961 Vol.-I part V-A (ii) Special Tables for Scheduled Tribes pp. 40-97 & 186.
2. Census of India, 1971 Social and Cultural Tables (Table VII & VIII) Part II-C (i), Series -18, Rajasthan,pp.604-693.
3. Census of India,1981, Series -18, Part -IX Special Tables for S.T.pp 8-15.
4. Mehta, Prakash Chandra : Bharat -Ke-Adivasi, Shiva Publishers Distributors, Udaipur, 1993.

APPENDIX-II
Categories-wise and district-wise distribution of scheduled tribes of Rajasthan
(According to 1981 census)

S. No.	State/District	All Scheduled Tribes	Bhil	Bhil-Mina	Damor, Damaria	Dhanka, Tadvi	Garasia	Kathodi, Katkari
1	2	3	4	5	6	7	8	9
	Rajasthan	4,183,124	1,840,966	27,137	31,377	14,111	118,757	2553
1.	Gangangar	5,095	525	45	6	898	74	23
2.	Bikaner	1,496	423	-	-	2	23	-
3.	Churu	5,619	82	5	-	285	5	8
4.	Jhunjhunu	23,077	94	27	-	440	-	3
5.	Alwar	143,858	369	1	-	1,267	2	2
6.	Bharatpur	56,716	514	1	-	-	-	-
7.	Sawai Madhopur	348,130	1,132	76	28	52	22	4
8.	Jaipur	380,199	1,668	40	22	7,593	22	7
9.	Sikar	36,552	11	-	-	708	14	-
10.	Ajmer	23,183	17,608	15	1	2,159	8	12
11.	Tonk	92,477	7,612	2	5	3	1	2

Bhils - I

1	2	3	4	5	6	7	8	9
12.	Jaisalmer	10,680	10,532	48	3	-	8	-
13.	Jodhpur	28,288	37,559	179	2	74	34	5
14.	Nagaur	2,984	221	-	-	43	1	-
15.	Pali	69,694	15,069	66	2	10	20,223	1
16.	Barmer	57,038	56,344	19	1	-	1	-
17.	Jalor	72,361	57,111	14	1	-	70	-
18.	Sirohi	125,245	51,420	16	4	41	58,484	1
19.	Bhilwara	121,664	69,113	12	5	25	103	5
20.	Udaipur	809,156	392,709	2,147	1,153	18	38,325	1,919
21.	Chittourgarh	223,864	80,687	191	530	185	277	10
22.	Dungarpur	440,026	131,871	3,305	22,240	4	192	9
23.	Banswara	643,866	582,723	20,875	7316	51	838	-
24.	Bundi	118,030	23,760	5	2	-	-	-
25.	Kota	231,316	49,950	36	55	247	30	379
26.	Jhalawar	91,601	51,863	7	1	4	-	162

Categories-wise and district-wise distribution of scheduled tribes of Rajasthan
(According to 1981 census)

S. No	State/District	Kokna	Koli Dhor	Mina	Naika, Nayaka	Patelia	Seharia, Sehria, Sahariya	Percentage of S.T. to total population
1	2	10	11	12	13	14	15	16
	Rajasthan	165	2,081	2,086,692	9,174	1,703	40,945	12.21
1.	Gangangar	18	1	2,950	406	3	20	0.25
2.	Bikaner	-	-	456	556	-	-	0.18
3.	Churu	1	-	4,960	200	-	4	0.48
4.	Jhunjhunu	1	-	22,265	213	-	-	1.90
5.	Alwar	4	159	141,939	100	-	-	8.12
6.	Bharatpur	4	128	55,819	13	-	168	3.01
7.	Sawai Madhopur	7	505	346,097	64	-	12	22.67
8.	Jaipur	12	233	368,025	2,283	1	7	11.12
9.	Sikar	9	1	35,560	263	-	-	2.65
10.	Ajmer	11	-	11,860	433	35	-	2.23
11.	Tonk	-	1	84,702	64	-	-	11.80

Bhils - I

1	2	10	11	12	13	14	15	16
12.	Jaisalmer	1	-	36	31	-	-	4.39
13.	Jodhpur	4	31	672	1,338	-	-	2.40
14.	Nagaur	2	-	2,341	324	-	-	0.18
15.	Pali	6	57	33,865	197	8	-	5.47
16.	Barmer	2	-	451	17	3	-	5.10
17.	Jalor	12	231	14,834	1	21	11	8.01
18.	Sirohi	1	439	14,550	21	102	1	23.11
19.	Bhilwara	15	21	51,837	441	26	10	9.28
20.	Udaipur	12	-	370,519	177	31	178	34.33
21.	Chittourgarh	12	55	140,578	496	137	474	18.16
22.	Dungarpur	7	5	81,971	29	9	-	64.44
23.	Banswara	8	-	29,544	46	348	5	72.63
24.	Bundi	2	31	93,826	265	114	1	20.11
25.	Kota	6	168	138,687	1,026	497	39,808	14.83
26.	Jhalawar	7	13	38,297	178	367	247	11.67

Source:- 1. Census of India,1981, Series -18, Part-IX, Special Tables for S.T. pp 8-195.
2. Mehta, Prakash Chandra : Bharat-ke-Adivasi, Shiva Publishers Distributirs, Udiapur,1993.

BHILS - II

Dr. D.B. Mandal

India is a land of 635 tribal communities inhabiting at diferent eco-cultural set-up. In tribal India the Bhils occupy an important psoition. Numerically they hold third position among the tribal population in India, numbering around 7,367,973 (1981 census). The Bhils are inahbited over large teritory of Western part of India and mostly they are concentrated in Western Madhya Pradesh, Eastern Gujarat, Southern Rajasthan and Northen Maharastra. A small number of Bhils are also scattered over the states of Tripura, Andhra Pradesh and Karnataka.

The largest concentration of Bhils in Madhya Pradesh was 2,500,530 (1981 census) and about 95% of Bhils were found in the districts of Jhabua and Dhar, of which a segment of Bhils population have already been migrated towards forest and fallow land areas in other districts prior to sixty in search of cultivable land for livelihood. Bhil population of Mahdya Pradesh includes other endogamous sub-groups known as Barela, Patelia, Bhilal, etc.

In this paper an attempt has been made to depict the life and culture of Bhils of Malwa region especially those who had migrated recently to Guna and Shivapuri districts from the native place of Jhabua and changes observed among them.

The Bhils as one of the largest native scheduled tribes in India are widely distributed over a vast area of Aravali ranges of hills and also scattered in plain forest area of adjacent districts. The state boundaries pose no bar to dispersed Bhil settlements. Large number of Bhils have settled recently in the Sahariya dominated area of Guna and Shivapuri districts of Mahdya Pradesh. They have spread over the central uplands area of Madhya Pradesh since long and bulk of them inhabiting in the region covered by forest clad and hilly terrain of the Vindhyas, Satpura even in Chambal plateau.

History

Accroding to Erthoven, the original home land of the Bhils were the hilly country between Abu and Asirgarh, from where they migrated towards Southern, Northern and Eastern plains on account of famine. In the opinion of Sir Jhon Malcolm Marshal the north-west region of Malwa was the original homeland of the Bhils from where they were pushed towards the hilly tracts by the invaders of that days. According to Tod (1881), the Bhils were the ancient inhabitants of Aravalli where they are largely distributed even today.

The original inhabitant of Mewar were the Bhils prior to the conquest by the Rajputs and the Bhils had kingdom at Southern provinces of Rajasthan. Many of the princely states such as Dungarpur, Banswara, Deolia are named after the Bhils Chieftains who had control over the regime of these areas.T.B Naik said that the Bhils were the oldest inhabitants of Mewar. The Rajputs had better connection with Bhil's chieftains than with other Hindu communities. Incidence of admixture between two groups and many Rajputs married with the Bhil women found all over Bhil land. Bhilala is a highest status group among the Bhils rose as a results of marriages between the Bhils and the Rajputs. There were both commensal and connubial realtions between them. Tod writes that the Rajputs would still take food and water from the Ujala Bhils.

The Malwa Land

Malwa is a distinct landscape located in north-western part of Madhya Pradesh having its historic, political and cultural identity since long. Geo-physiographic features and climatic scenario add uniqueness of this region. The ethnic groups living in this area shared the peculiar socio-cultural tradition and moving up at different stages of livelihood.

According to Singh(1971) Malwa region forms a distinct physio-historio-cultural entity lying almost in the heart of India and landmass with a population of 12 million inculding huge tribal and non-tribal pouplation. Malwa region covers 18 districts of Madhya Pradesh adjacent to some areas of Rajasthan and Maharshtra. Bulk of Bhils are inhabiting in the western part of Malwa region. The term 'Malwa' has been derived from the word 'Malva' originated from the Sanskrit word 'Ma' for the goddess Lakshmi and 'Lav' for 'part' which means fertile land of Malwa. Mathur (1964) said that the name Malwa was derived probably from 'Malvas' a tribe who formerly lived in South Punjab and Rajasthan states. The Important tribals and its sub-groups in Malwa region are Bhil, Barela, Sahariya, Karku, Mina,

Bhilala, Patelia, etc.

Demography

The Bhil is one of the most important indigeneous and mumerically dominant tribe who live in varied eco-cultural region. At present day, the term Bhil is used in derogatory sense. Untill last half of this centuary, these people were known as Bhil, but since then some segments of Bhil have refused to be addressed by that name.The Bhils who have been living in the plains and have been acculturated to a great extent and here established close contact with the wider society have opposed the term Bhil as a whole.They splitted into different sub-groups and are now called by different names, according to their life style. According to Wilson the term 'Bhil' is derived from the Dravidian ward 'Billee' means a 'bow' which is the characteristic weapon of this tribe. The Bhils of Madhya Pradesh themselves as 'Palvi' perhaps due to their clsoe association with forest and were lived in leaf-clad. Bhils of Rajasthan generally address themselves 'Gameti'. They speak in Bhili language, which belongs to the Indo-Arya family of languages. However they also speak in Hindi and Malwai with others.

Bhils are divided into different endogamous sub-group such as Bhilala, Dhali, Bhil, Dungars Bhil, Ujala, Langatiya, Mankar, Garasia, Bhil-Mina, Mewasi Bhil, Tadvi, Rawal, Bhogolia, Pawara, Barela, Dhankar, Patelia, etc. Bhils sub-gropus are known by different names at different places becuses of their habit, dress and ornaments as well as on account of cultural assimilation. Acculturated Bhils do not have commensal and connubial relation with the Bhils of Jungle area. The Bhils of present day may be classified as cultivating Bhil living in plains, admixture of cultivating Bhil living in plains and the wild Bhil, who still live in forest and hilly area and maintaining traditional way of life.

Dwelling

In general the Bhils live in a separate hamlet in the multi-enthnic villages or live isolately away form the other communities, preferably closer to the forest. They live scatterly in group of a few huts. Huts are having one room with a small courtyards made up of some walls and stone palte (**Patti**) on thatched roof. Bhils differ considerably from the caste Hindus, but their manners and way of life closely resemble to those of Sahariya tribe of this region. They maintian a distance from the neighbouring communities and talk less with other groups. Language barrier keep themselves aloof from others . Their poor- economic condition compelled them to migrate from the native place. As the Bhils are reorganised a good farmers, they migrated towards follow-land. For cultivation the immegrants Bhils cleared large forest belt between Biswanwara and Bamari of Guna district. Slowly large number of Bhils, both affinals and consoguineal relatives settled for cultivation. These people have established good contact with the service castes like potters, balcksmith, **Bania**, etc. A staple food of the Bhil is **Roti** (bread) of maize, jowar or wheat. They take pulses, vegitable, curry, fish, meat, egg, etc. Occasionally they take rice. Variation of food pattern of these people have been observed according to seasonal crops. Millet is mainly consumed in the winter. **Puri** and **Khir** (sweet) is usually perpared in the ceremonial occasions and festivals. **Gruel** of maize flour is also consumed during busy season of cultivations. **Dal-Bati** is another popular delicious food of the Bhil, preapred casually out of wheat flour. Besides, they consume edible roots, tubers, fruits and leaves which they collect from the forest. Liquor especially prepared from the mahuwa plays an important role in Bhil life. In connection with festivals and socio-religious ceremonies they consume huge liquor irrespective of sex and age. Both men and women also smoke **Bidi** and chew tabocco.

Dress

Men generally werar short dhoto, shirt, kurta or vest bands and turnbon, **Pathat** and women wear shirt, gahaghra, bodice, kachli, and **Lugral** (stole) through out season. The Bhil dress pattern is considerably varied from the local people. The male usually wear loin clothes at home and at agricultural operations. But during festive ocassion they must wear white turbon and shoe. The Bhils of different groups use traditional colour and style of turbon which make their affinity and identity. **Ghaghra** and **Kachli** of red colour are the common dress of rural Bhil women. Married women use **Lugra** to cover their face and head before the aged persons. The bride wears deep red **Ghaghra**, yellow **Lugra** and blouse and bridgeroom wears yellow **Dhoti**, short, red turbon and shoe. Bhil women are fond of ornaments and is a mark of wealth. They wear huge ornaments of silver and allay metals at their neck, ear, arm, wrist, fingers, waist, ankle, toes, forehead and nose. Men wear ear rings only. **Bor** is a cocoon like typical ornaments of Bhil women which is worn at their hair partening after marriage. Besides glass and toe bangles are used by the married women. Tattooing with traditional designs are still common among the original Bhils and get tattoo by the Muslim women on their arms, legs, chest and forehead. The size of tattooing is becoming shorten. The Bhil women are tatooed on their body as a part of adornment as well as folk beliefs.

Social Organisation

The social organisation of the Bhil is characterised by the presence of diverse social groups recognised on the basis of kinship, territory, culture-contact, etc. Family is the smallest social and economic unit of the Bhil. Their descent system is patrilineal and residence is partrilocal i.e. after marriage a woman moves to her husband's house. Succession of authoruity is always patripotestal. Neolocal kind of residence is common among the Bhil, in which the newly married couple live in independant hut in close proximity to the natal place of the boy. Nuclear type of family is predominant. Though families of extended nature are present, but rare in ocurance. The headman of a village and well to do Bhils are ivariably found to have more than one wife. "**Kutum**" is the consenguineal group consists of a few families closely related through kinship and come farward to rendering mutual help and co-operation during rites of passages. The principal is that to exchange reciprocal help under kinship obligation. Divorce is common among the Bhil and men are not afraid to pay the Jhagda (compensation). Childern are the liablility of the biological father. Step childern do not get any share of property.

Bhil tribe of Madhya Pradesh is divided into a number of endagamous sub-groups. Each endagamous group is again divided into number of tolemistic clans, Clans like Mogar, Ahir, Gangada, Pipalse, Shinde, Sonami, Wagh, Bijar, Solanki, Chowhen are among the Bhils. Some of these clans like, ahir, solanki, mali, barda, mori, shinde, etc. have been borrowed from non-tribal groups. Many Rajput had married Bhil women in the past and stayed with the people. Some clans like ghunia more, magar are derived from the animals and brids. likewise a few clan names are associcated with trees and plants. Another set of clans have originated from the native settlement which bears the name of the ancestor's. Inter-marriage within the clan is stricitly prohibited. Clan exogamy is the rule. The memebrs belonging to a clan showed their respect and reverace towards the symbol of clan and devako by not killing on eating the animals. Some of the Bhil clans like **Mode** is again sub-divided into sub-clans as **Dharya** (sward), **Kalami** (Kalam tree), **Kekdyas** (crab), **Soglaya** (sagan tree), etc. Likewise Pamar clan is also divided into pipariya, dharya, Khaliya, sotariya, gahariya and so on. These mother clans are probably represented the territorial association and might have originated from one village. Many of the Bhils clan are similar among the Patelia, Mina and Sahariy's. Most of thses clans are respected and worshipped by its members on the occasion of life cycle rituals. Clan though named after the animate and inanimate objects mostrly associated with female deities like **Kalaimata, Sheetalamata, Chamundi devi, Khama mata,** etc. Marriage is not allowed within one's clan, mother's clan and mother's clan. So a Bhil has to avoid at least three clans for selection of a mate. Usually they has to avoid 4-6 generation gap to acquire mate from maternal side. These clan constraints are followed in case of **Natra** (remarriage) marriage. Solidarity and co-operation of family as well as lineage members is maintained through the worships of clan deities,. The Bhils are aboriginal people, their strong belief towards clan can not be violated as breach of taboo might invite harm to those people by the supernatural power.

Pal is a territorial grouping consisting of multi clan habitation. The Bhil can opt for both village (**Pal**) endogamy and exogamy. Bhils of a **Pal** maintain solodariy and intergration through receprocal help and observing traditional rites and rituals. Among the Bhil a **Pal** member has his own identity in respect of association with a habitat. The dwellers of a Bhil **Pal** is called as **Palia Bhils**, where as **Khabi Bhils** are refer to who live out side the **Pal**. The **Kalia Bhils** are treated as impure and are traditionally place lower than **Palia** or **Ujala** Bhil. Both groups prefer to marry within their own groups. Another group of Bhil who embracced the **Bhagat faith** are known as **Bhagat Bhil.** They are vegetarian and do not take liqour. They curtailed both commensal and connubial relation with other groups of Bhil. In the changing situation the Bhil of Madhya Pradesh still remain out side the caste system.

Life Cycle

Birth

Bhil observe number of rituals in connection with life cycle. After the child birth pollution period is observed for five days. They celbrate **Dora** and **Jalwai** rites together on 5th day. Both mother and child are bathed and dressed with new clothes. In the evening two earthen pots with a coconut is worshipped by the house owner at courtyard. At the time of male child **Thali** (matalic plate) is beaten loudly and a **Supra**, winnowing fan, is beaten is case of female child. Pregnant women observe certain restrictions, as she is not allowed cremation ground as well as go outside during eclipse. Purificatory rite i.e. **Jatjowarna** is held on '12th day when mother goes to well with a new earthern pot with some **Jowar** seeds inside the pitcher. **Chokhe** (rice feeding) and **Mundan** (head saving) rites are simple and observed at the age of six months or later. An old experience woman of the same tribe or from other community serve as **Dhai** (midwife) during delivery.

Marriage

Marriage is a socially approved rite of a man and woman for sexual gratification as well as social ritual and economic co-operation.**Dej-San** (bride price) of Rs.500/- is paid to the father of the bride. Among the Bhil bride price is fixed before the marriage and setteld in the presence of **Panch**. Both the parents of boy and girl along with village headman consume liqour in connection with **Sagai** rite. Marriage rites such as **Sagai, Fera, Tel, Mondap, Logan**, etc. are performed by the Bhils. The marraige are usually held in summer season. The boy's father takes initiative in search of bride.

The marital alliances are generally arranged by the parents throught matchmaker (**Bhanjaro**). Maongamous type of marriages are common. Though ploygamy is rare, but socially allowd. They paractise part puberty marriage through negotiation, mutal consent or by elopment. Marriage symbol of the Bhil woman is Kandora (waist belt) or **Bore** (ornament of fore head), lac and glass bangles. Marrirage is performed at bride house .Cross -cousin marriage is prevalent only among the tadvi Bhil. Sarorate is allowed. The female is not permitted to marry a man belonging to the caste/tribe whom they consider as inferior.

Widow remarriage is known as **Natra**. Both widower, divorcee or umarried man can marry a widow and vice-versa. No formal rites are performed. Only a set of dress, ornaments and glass bangles with a token bride price is given to the girl. **Ladi** a simplest form of marriage without formal ceremonies is mostly practiced by the poor Bhil. No feast is given to the villagers. **Bhagadi** is the marriage by where the bride run away with her paramour in the forest. This type of marriage is adopted by those Bhils who can afford much expenditure. The couple has to pay a fine of Rs.

500/- and more to the council for readmission in the village (**Pal**).

Divorce is permitted among the Bhil society through the tribal council. The incidence of divorce is frequent among the traditional Bhils. If the husband divorces, the wife he tears off the end of his turban and give it to her. If the wife deserts the husband she tears off the end of her **Sari**. A divorce woman may marry again or allow to live with another man as wife. She is called a **Ghar-ghesi**. The man who lives with her has to pay all marriage expenses of the first husband along with a fine to the council for community feast. The nature and amount of fine called **Jhagda** are decided by the council members. In case of extra marital sex realtionship an amount is charged as fine from the accused. Among the Bhils pre-marital sex-relation is intolerable to some extent.

Death

Generally the Bhil used to bury the corpse, but creamte in case of unnatural death such as small pox, cholera, leprasy at time of delivery, etc. After death the body is brought out side the house and kept in a sitting posture and cover with a new white cloth. The head covered with a red turbon. The eldest son is the chief mourner who throws a handfull of earth on the carpse and cover the grave with soil. From 3rd day of death women of the mourn's house will wail at morning for 5 days. Purificatory rite **Kharache** is observed an 11th day, the cheif mourner shave his head and beard and take bath in the river. On 12th day Nukta (Parsadi) i.e. community feast is given to the villagers. In case of child death a small dinner is given to relatives on 7th day.

Economy

In the Sahariya's dominated area of North Madhya Pradesh, the Bhils are known as hard workers and good farmers. Cultivation is their primary occupation. Besides cultuivation most of them depend on subsidiary sources of subsistance such as labourer, cattle rearing and grazing, preapring charcol, etc. According to 1981 census, 71% of Bhils were cultivators, 25% labourers and remaining 4% were engaged in other occupation in Madhya Pradesh. Most of the Bhil families possess a patch of land of cultivation in the forest clad and produce single crop only on account of scarcity of water.

The economy of the Bhil was different in the early stage than it appears today. The Bhils were a tribe of food-gathers and hunters in the post. Later they cultivated millets on hills slopes by slash and burn method. Untill 1950 they were engaged in shifting cultivatin and only a section of Bhils owned land and used ploughs for cultivation. The intoduction of settled cultivation brought significant change in their economic as well as social development. Bhils are now no more nomadic in nature. Most of them posses cultivable land either as owners or teanants and are leading settled life. During the slack season, they irrespective of sex are engaged as labourers in the construction works in roads and building in forest and agricultural fields. Besides, they are also engaged in the collection of forest produce like fire wood, honey, mohuwa, flower, gum, tubers, roots wild fruits, leaves, grass, etc.They consume the edible forest produce as food and use the same for domestic purpose. Extra porduce is sold off to the traders and in return get cash or food materials in exchange for the same. Bhils in forest areas are also engaged in non-agricultural pursuits like preparation of charcol, wood cutting, etc.

From cultivation, they produce insufficient grains in the unfertile land which last ofr a few months in a year. Under draught conditions they completely depend on labour. Their economics conditions is miserable because, most of them have small pieces of land. Secondly, many of them have either mortagaged or sold off their land to the other in lieu of cash money. Besides indebtedness and drinking habits force them to remain in exterme hardship.

The landless Bhils are mostly engaged as share cropper. First the owner of the land get two third of the yield, while the owner provides all the implements, seeds as well as bullock except the labour. The labourer gets only one third of the yield (**Tecsribatai**). In case of **Batai** system, the yield is divided into equal shares and land owner gets half of the produce. In winter they produce crops like gram, linseed, weat, pea, dhania, onion, etc. and grains like maize, jowar, urad, tuwar, millet like Kulthi, etc. are produced as kharif crops. Agricultural innovation and new jobs opportunities have brought some changes in the socio-economic status of the Bhils.

Changes

In the present s~enario, the Bhil has imbided by the number of traits of the local Hindu society through cultural contact, which not only influnced them to borrow some elements of culture, but also changed their pattern of life as per reference groups of the area. The nature of habitation of the Bhil was different in the past in comparison to present day's settlment. In the past, they used to live in a small hut isolately in the forest and hill slopes and secured their food through collection and gathering as well as also paractising hunting with bow and arrow. Previously they used to live scatterly and a few huts wre erected on their farm land. They were semi-nomadic in anature and practising shifting cultivation for livelhood. In course of time some have migrated to plains and used to live in cluster of huts (**Pal**) for settled cultivation. Plough cultuvation has brought a signigficant change in more stable economics pursuits. By and large the Bhils have changed their life sytle through cultural contact and modernisation. Formation of **Pal** (hamlet) with the families of uni-clan people his declined and multi-clan or castes people are now living along with Bhils. Besides agriculture, they are also engaged in subsidiary occupations like labourer, fishing domestication of animals, trade and collection of forest produce, etc. They conjunct the traditional economy with the market economy. A few educated Bhils are also engaged in service. The system of **Hali** (Serfs) is now being abolished. Moreover,economically they are being self-dependent and avoid to go to the **Sahukar** (money lender) for debt. In the past many of them either sold or mortagaged theri land and ornaments in lieu of money or food grains.

The important rreason of change in Bhil life is attributed to their contact with the non-tribals. Affluent sections of Bhils have established commensal relationship with the non-tribals, who are considered hierarchically equal or higher than the Bhils. Many castes Hindus and trading communities had arrived in the Bhil areas long ago and interpersonal realtionship have developed in various aspects of life. Traditionaly the Bhil had no notion of untouchability, but due to assimilasion with caste Hindus, they have looked down upon the untouchable castes like Namar, Dhankar, Jatana, Kanjar, etc. So called advance Bhils have left some off the customary paractices like folk dances, drama and songs whcih were not merely the sources of entertainment of the Bhil life but also connected with the customary rites asociated with birth, marriage and other rituals. Instead of traditional dresses and ornaments they adorn themselves according to local fashion and dresses. In marriage they perfer marriage by negotiation than marriage by elopment. Besides the traditional priest, they are also inviting the **Brahman** priest for **Satyanarayan puja** and marriage ceremonies. With the introduction of Panchyat Raj, the traditional tribal council and leadership pattern become weaker and shaky in the post independence period. Though the Bhils profess animism, but many of them worship the

Gods and Goddess of Hindu pantheon. **Hanuman** and **Mahadeo** are two supremen deities worshipped by them. They observe almost all the local Hindu festivals and participate in the festivals like Holi, Diwali, etc. It has been observed from our study that the migrant Bhils have acculturated themselves faster in comparison to native Bhils. Becuase the former had to establish necessary contact and realtionship with the neighbouring people for their safty and settlement in the strange situation. They struggled hard for livelihood in the new environment and economical pursuits.

❏ ❏ ❏

Appendix
Distrubution of Bhil Population in India and States

	Population (census 1981)	Percentage
India	7,367,972	100.0
Madhya Pradesh	2,500,530	33.93
Gujarat	2,030,438	27.55
Rajasthan	1,840,966	24.98
Maharastra	993,074	13.47
In other states (Karnatak, Tripura and Andhra pradesh)	2,964	0.07

BIRHOR - I

Dr. Pratibha Kumari

Birhor, a primitive tribe of Chhotanagpur plateau of South Bihar belong to "*Forest - hunting*" type (Vidyarthi 1968, 76-78) from the point of view of ecology and level of Socio-economic integration. On the organisational level two classes of the Birhor have been indentified: migratory and settled. The former is known as '*Uthlu*' and the later is called '*Janghi*' Birhor. The name '*Birhor*' is derived from the words '*Bir*' meaning jungle and '*Hor*' meaning man, thus the words mean the people of jungle equivalent to the Bushman. The most important characteristic features of the hunter gatherer society is that they live in '*Bands*' (or Tanda as Birhors call it) used here to designate the unit. A band or Tand includes number of households or individuals having nuclear families belonging to same or different clans.

Ethnically they belong to Proto - Australoid group and linguistically to Austo Asiatic mundari group. They also speak *Sadari* and *Hindi*. *Sadari* is a linguafranca of chhotanagpur.

The earliest definite reference to this people an be found in colonel Daltons "Notes of a Tour in the Tributory for the year 1864.

Forbes (1872) also gave clean cut account of this people as an aboriginal tribe of this plateau living on the tops and spurs on maonkeys, birds, jungle roots and herbs. Bradley Birth (1903) and Risley (1905) also gave some account of Birhor life. During the period of 1910-1920, S.C. Roy, the celebrated Indian anthropologist did some field work among the Birhor of Ranchi district and wrote a monograph depicting the life and culture of nomadic Birhor.

In South Bihar are mainly distributed in the Ranchi, Gumla, Hazaribagh and Giridih districts. They are also distributed in West Bengal, Madhya Pradesh and Orissa, According to 1981 Census Birhor population was 4,377. In 1991 contimated population of Birhor was 4,984 in Bihar. In West Bengal they number 658 persons (1981 Census). In Madhya Pradesh they are distributed mostly in Raigarh district and their population is 561 (1981 Census) and they speak Chhathisgarhi language. In Orissa, the Birhor are concentrated in the districts of Sundergarh, Kalahandi, Keonjhar, Mayurbhanj and Sambalpur and their population was number 142 according to 1981 census.

Literacy rate among Birhor is 5.76 per-cent (8.65% male and 2.68% female) respectively.

OCCUPATION

Birhor were totally dependent on forests for their livelihood, when they were nomads. But after their settlement in different colonies at the fringe of forests and due to the implementation of different forest policies, they are no more nomads and living a sedentary life, but they have continued their foraging and trapping habit, besides the manual labour work on wages. They still fabricate rope from chop (*Bauhinia scandens*) fibres collected from the forests. These days they are preparing rope and its articles with hemp fibres and plastic twins taken out of used grains bags or sacs. Both gender make ropes and rope articles used for agriculture and cosmetic purposes. Usually women collect forest produces e.g. edible roots, lettuces, flowers, fruits, medicinal plants, but the collection of honey, chop bark and trapping of small games like hare, patridges, wild cocks are done solely by the menfolk. Hunting and trapping is a taboo for the women. Rope and rope articles are generally bartered with grains or paddy from their peasant neighbours. Birhor ladies hawk these articles from village-to-village, when the menfolk for labour work or in the forest for getting small games. The games are sold in village hat or to the truck drivers. For the economic reason Birhor rarely consume the trapped game as it fetch good cash. So they prefer vegetarianism except on some festivals when the sacrifice of fowl is done and meat is consumed by the family.

There has been induced change in their economic life after their settlement in colonies made by the Government which resulted in their involvement in wage labour work. They have to face the financial uncertainties as they do not get the wage labour work regularly and it causes a type of bewilderness. It is still the forest which provide them food, when there is no grains at home. But with the thinning of forests and industrialization heir collection and hunting work have been effected. Many times they return with empty hands. Chop have been effected. Many times they return with empty hands. Chop fibres are not available these days as much as it happened to be in earlier days. Besides, consumption of *Mahua* (*Bassia latifolia*) as liquor has become a regular feature of Birhors, which is sold by their village neighbours belonging to different castes. A good sum of their hard earned money is spent on the liquor.

Few old Birhors of both gender of the colonies have taken up begging as one of their mode of livelihood. They can be seen begging at village market, in villages and at town markets of the district. It was never being observed when they were nomads and forest dwellers. Their existence is from hand to mouth every members of the family whether old or young contribute his or her labour for the sake of economic gain except the children below six or seven years. Children above 6-7 years accompany their mother in collection work. Boys of 10-14 years go in forests along with their father or tanda men for trapping the game. They also rear cattle on share basis. The cattle are given by their neighbours who are cultivators for the rearing purpose. A type of symbiotic relationship is maintained between the Bithors and their neighbours belonging to nearby villages who are mainly cultivators.

A number of schemes like goatary, trench digging, basketary, house construction, deep boring, land levelling, etc. were being implemented by the State Government Welfare Department, to improve the economic condition of the Birhor, but they did not bring expected, result.

SOCIAL DIVISION

The Birhors are patrilineal people. A Birhor word for lineage is *Khut*. For the Birhor a linegage is addressed after the name of the head of the living agnates. The patrilineal descent group includes families which most often are co-resident in a band. S.C. Roy has mentioned 37 symbolic clans of Birhor. There is hardly any social integration between the different clans forming the tribe. Even the different families of the same clan living at a distance from one another don't recognize the idea of collective responsibility. It is to be noted that the Birhor terms *khunt*, *'Killi'*. or *'Paris'* are of Munda origin. The names of the Birhor killi or paris are in some cases identical to the Munda and Santhal tribes of South Bihar. Some prevalent clan names are *Saoria, Hembrom, Murmu, Mahali, Hansda Bhuinya, Soren, Magahiya, Tanti, Kisku, Todu, Beherwar, Banadwa, Golowas Matkorwa, Raosa*, etc. The Birhors of Hazaribagh and Giridih district have twenty types of clans. Clan exogamy is strictly maintained. It is worth to note however that all totem taboos have to be strictly observed only by married men, for it is not until he is married that a Birhor is considered to become a full member of his clan. A woman must not however kill the totem animal or destroy the totem plant of her husband clan.

Birhor family is of nuclear type. Daughters are not entitled to share the fathers property with their brothers. In the absence of a son or son-in-law the daughter is entitled to the fathers property, provided she bears the funeral expenses. In the absence of children or a son-in-law the nearest agnates of the deccased enherit the property, failing a near agnate, men of same clan living in the '*tanda*' will take the property.

LIFE CYCLE

The life cycle from conception to death among the Birhor is quite interesting because it contains a certain important features which distinguishes them from other tribal group.

The normal attitude of Birhor towards pregnancy is that of rejoicing. Certain herbs are used both for fertility and antifertility purposes. The elderly Birhor men and women have good knowledge of herbal folk medicines which include both roots, slens, leaves, tendril, seeds of certain plants as well as organ of birds and animals collected from the forest.

There are a number of taboos which a pregnant woman must maintain, e.g., must not be present at a burial place nor even touch a dead body, must not go near rivers of streams where spirits of women who died during pregnancy or in child birth are supposed to dwell, must be inside the house when lighting flashes are been or a thunder is heard, must not cross a river, must not lie down in the courtyard or open space lest spirits may not harm her life etc. During wife's pregnancy her husband too must abstain from eating the head of any animal of fowl sacrificed to any spirit or the head of any animal or fowl obtained by hunting. The practice of *couvade* is unknown among Birhor.

BIRTH RITUALS

One end of the hut is partitioned off to serve as the lying in room and where the delivery takes place. Soon after the birth a new door is open on the wall for the use of parturient woman for some period i.e. for a week or few weeks varying among different clans. If the placenta is delayed in coming out the type of grass locally known as '*Satti Patti*' is tied around the ankles to facilitate delivery. Root of certain plants are suspended from the women's neck on a string. Naval string is cut by an arrow kead.

These days razor is also used. Naval chord is buried just out side the threshold of the hut keeping it in a leaf cup.

Mahua liquor (*Bassia latifolia*), Kurthipulse (*Dolichos biflorus*) are given to new mother to drink on the first day of delivery. Kurthi Pulse is consumed as it is supposed to hasten the flow of milk at her breasts.

On the seventh day from the date of birth, *chhathi* ceremony is performed is meant for the final purification of the other members of the *tanda* and the prelioninary purification of the new born child and its mother and the family members. Until then there will be no *Puja* on the *Chhathi*, day the members of the *tanda* of the child clan have their *nails* pared and their beard and edges of the hair round the head shaved. The women of the clan also have been nails pared. *Nails* of the mother and baby are being pared first of all. Finally the baby will have its head shaved. Then the men first, after them women folk also go for the purification bath. The assembled guests are then treated *to rice or Mahua beer.* Before they begin drinking the eldest member of the clan takes up in his hands a leaf cup filled with rice beer.

Generally on the twenty first day after birth, but in some clan later, the final purification ceremony is performed e.g. *Tanti, Mahali, Hansda, Magahia.* The baby's head is shaved and mat used by baby and its mother is cast aside. The new door of the lying in room is then closed up. Whole house is cleaned and all family members take a ceremonial bath. the chief of the family sacrifices a red fowl and a libation of rice beer to the spirits of his ancestors and prays for the health and longevity of the baby. The mother with the baby in her arms goes to the *Thaans* or spirits seats of her husbands's family and then to '*Thaans*' of the other families of the *tanda* and bows down to all the ghosts of the '*thaans*'.

Naming Ceremony

Name of the child is selected on the '*Chhathi*' day in the following manner. A bowl of water is placed in the open space in front of the hut. A handful of rice and a blade of tender grass (Dub) are placed on the ground as witness of the ceremony. A grain of Til (*Sesamum*) seed to represent the baby is first dropped into the water of the bowl and then a grain of unhusked rice representing the paternal grand father of the baby is similarly dropped into the same bowl. If the grains sesamum and paddy float on till they meet, the baby is named after his paternal grand father. If they sink out without meeting the process is repeated, the name of the relatives in whose name the grain meet is selected for the child. Name is also derived from the day of the week on which the child was born.

Among Birhor there was system of separate of dormitory both of for young girls and boys. These days this institution is not maintained. There is no special puberty rite among Birhor, but there are certain taboos in menstrual condition of a female, she must not sit on the same mat with other persons, must not walk across a hunting net. During this period there will be no sacrifice or *puja* offered to the spirits house.

Marriage Rituals

Among Birhors marriages are performed in the months of *Paus* and *Magh* (January-February). Marriage age of girls 16 to 19 and that to boy is eighteen to twenty. For negotiation purpose, male members of the family or *'tanda'* go to the girls *tanda*. They have good and bad omens for which they strictly follow. If they happen to be dead body, dead mat, they are taken as good omens, but if a branch of tree breaks, while on the way or if they meet jackal, snake,cat on the way these are considered as bad omens. In such situation they come back to their home and after drinking water they again start for girl's village.

Both boy and girl sees each other. After taking their consent, marriage is fixed and bride price is given which is known as "*Dali taka*". Bride price includes Rs. 5/ - to Rs. 10/ - alongwith new cloths for girl's rice. After giving bride price, a bangle or an ordinary metalled ring is given to the girl. After this ritual of betrothal ceremony, same is repeated for the bridegroom. The relatives of the girl's are offered rice beer of *Mahua* liquor. After this ceremony date of marriage is fixed.

'Mandap' made of *sal (Sherea robusta)* wood is erected at the home of bride and bridegroom both is the morning of marriage day. Mandap or shade is erected under the guidance of *'Pahan'* the priest of the community. Grains of rice are thrown in all direction to avert the difficulties. Two unmarried girls digout some clay and it is front of the door. The groom is bathed by his brother-in-law and the groom puts on new cloths. Then *'Barat'* or grooms party starts for the brides *tanda*. At the time of *'Barat'* or grooms party starts for the bride's *tanda*. At the time of 'Barat' departure a number of *'puja'* is performed by the *pahan*. New cloths are given to the bride by her in Laws. Girl stands up in the basket in the 'Mandap' and covers her face. Boy removes the cloths from her face and puts on vermillion and the girl also applies vermillion on the right feet of the boy. After the end of this ritual marriage feast is offered which consists of rice, pork and rice beer of *mahua* liquor.

After the return of the *Barat* party at the grooms *Tanda* new couple are offered rice cooked with jaggery. After getting some gifts or money from her in laws bride eats the rice. It is the most common custom of marriage among the Birhor. This type of marriage is known as *Sadar Bapla* in the Birhor language. Marriage feast is also given by the grooms family after the marriage at the grooms *Tanda*.

Other forms of marriage prevalent among Birhors are *Nam, Napan Bapla, Udra Udri Bapla, Bolo Bapla* or marriage by intrusion, *Golat* or marriage by exchange. Levirate and sorrorate form of marriages are also in practice among the Birhor. In the *Nam*, '*Napan Bapla*' type of marriage, when the girl and the boy develop close relationship, the girl is permitted to live with her lover at his home. When the girl's father get the bride price, then the community men assemble and marriage takes place by applying vermillion to the girl with the boy. In "*Udra-Udri Bapla*" both the boy and girl stealthily flee away form the village. After sometimes, if they are found out, they are tied in marital bond after giving bride price, Feast is also arranged by the couples family. Cases of desertion of wife are found among Birhor divorce and remarriage is approved by their society.

Death Rituals

Among the Birhor dead body is buried usually. Sometimes it is burnt in the few Birhor *tandas*. They believe in natural death as well as the wrath of evil spirit causing death. A person breathing hid last is laid on new cot or on old mat. Family members including wife or sister pourdrops of water in the mouth of the dying person. When the person breathed his last, every one goes out of that room so that soul must be freed as they think. All ornaments of the deceased are taken out. The corpse is taken to the burial ground or '*Sasan*' on a ladder like structure made up of '*Sal*' Wood. The female members of the family accompany the man carrying the corpse upto some distance, then they come back to their *tanda*. At the burial ground the eldest members of the family put the soil on the corpse fust of all. The headman of the tandalers few enchantations and put thorny bushes and stones on the burial day. The widower shaves his head and beard. The persons who visited the burial ground annoint paste of turmeric and mustered oil on their body after their return from burial ground. It is considered that it purifies their body, Death pollution is observed for eleven days. If economical condition permits, feast is offered to the *tanda* families with on the twelveth day or after a year of the death.

Political organization

Traditional headman of Birhor *tanda* is known as "*Naya*" or "*Pahan*" who look after religious and political issues. The post of "*Naya*" is not strictly inheritable, but a Naya's son can become the naya after the death or retirement (due to old age) of his father. From early childhood '*Naya*' is not strictly inheritable, but a Naya's son can become the Naya after the death or retirement (due to old age) of his father. From early childhood '*Naya*' beguns to giving instruction to his son with all the rituals and observances of the band or tanda. Usually the head of living male agnates of a lineage is the *Naya*. But it may not be the case of all lineages of all bands or tandas. To assist the *Naya*' there is another man though not related to the same lineage. He is known as *Kotwar*. In case social offenses such adultery, theft, etc. Meeting is called by the '*Naya*' which includes, '*Kotwar*' and four five elderly persons of the tandas. Woman is permitted to participate in the meeting directly, but her version is accepted. Practically Birhor woman have no role in the Political Council of the tanda like other tribal woman. A fine of some money is charged on the offender as penalty. Sometimes the offender and his family is forced to leave the tanda in case of serious offenses like violation of taboos maintained by entire tanda families or involvement is sexual liasons. The Birhor rarely takes helps of village panchayat for their *tanda* problems. They solve their problems within their *tanda* with the help of '*Naya*' and other elderly persons.

Birhors of few tandas of Bishanpur block of Gumla district have accepted christianity and they help of the local church authorities to solve their problems. Their socio-politic and religious organization is controlled by christian missionaries of Block which include. Persons of other tribes like Oraon, Munda, etc.

Religious Life

Unlike the agricultural tribes of chhotanagpur, Birhor don't have a clear conception of hierarchy of pantheon. They don't have sacred groves. They are the animist and see gods in nature. They worship nature in all here forms. Inspite of constant and continuous efforts of the christian missionaries they have not converted to christianity except very few member about fifty to sixty. They always resisted conversion and christian mission. The Birhor pantheon aries from one band to the next and is quite extensive in each band. The pantheon of gods can be divided into three groups. They always resisted conversion and christian mission. The Birhor pantheon aries from one band to the next and is quite extensive in each band. The pantheon of gods can be divided into three groups. They are (i) The *ora bonga* or house god, (ii) *The Hapram* (ancestors), and (iii) *The Tanda bonga* (gods of clearing). In addition there is *Condu Bonga* and some spirits associated with individuals which are considered malevolent. In every Birhor colony four or five small huts are seen having mould of clay. These are the shrines of ancestral spirits. Here ancestral spirits are worshipped and sacrifices are made by the head of the household female of the family is not permitted to worship at the shrine. Ancestral worship is performed elaborately on last night of *phalgun* month on Holi festival, Every propitiation ceremony of involved as sarifice. This may be a simple dropping of a bit of food (rice grains) or drink (rice beer) in the name of the God or it may be the sacrifice of *chicken* or even pig or *goat*. Only clan member can take the offering of rice beer and cocked sacrificial fowl. Their sacred centries known as '*marai*' where sacrifices and offering are made. In the place '*marai*' where sacrifices and offerings are made. In the place 'marai' all deities of baongas are symbolized with earthen mounds (pendas).

Birhor claim that they observe festivals like *Sarhul, Dushera, Jitia, Karma, Holi, Noakhani* (Newgrain festival) and *Chulhauti Puja* (hearth worship).

Noakhani festival and Hearth worship

It is observed in the month of October when New grain crop up in the fields on that day women worship hearth as it is considered a sacred place and the abode of deities by the grace of when the hearth may continue to cook food. Head of the family offers cooked food to the ancestors and fowl is sacrificed. Bitten rice *(Chura)* of new paddy is also offered alongwith rice beer. Noakhani festival is observed only by those Birhor who cultivate millets and cereals, very few Birhors are cultivators. They first offer new grain to their ancestral spirits and then the grain millets are consumed by the family. On the *Jitia* festival no hunting is done by the men folk of the *tanda*. Ladies keep fast. No sacrifice of fowler pig is done. Only vegetarian food is cooked. The festival comes on any day of *Bhadra* (September) month. After the propitiation of ancestors all family members take food. *Sahul* and *Karma* festivals are also celebrated by Birhor like other tribes e.g. Munda, Oraon, Santhal, etc.

On Sarhul festival, they propitiate all the deities of their pantheon. Fowls are sacrificed by the '*Naya*' or '*Pahan*' of the *tanda*. After worship every family of he tanda takes (Prasad) of rice beer and sacrificed fowl. Men and women sing and dance. In *'Karma'* festival *'Pahan'* places the three branches of *'Karam'* tree *(Adina cordifolia)* on the earth. Young girls and boys come there to worship the *'Karam twig'* in the evening and perform some rituals under the guidance of *'Naya'*. At night drinking of rice beer and dancing and singing are carried out by the tanda families.

In all the religious performance women are not allowed to participate directly. They only assist the men. The religious life of Birhor is primarily a household affair. More sacrifice are carried out by the household head or the adult head of a household under the direction of *Naya*.

Birhor are facing many problems. Their problems and socio-economic life are much different from the rest of the tribal communities in the region. Many Governmental schemes either failed or proved beneficial upto very little extent for the socio-economic developed of this tribes. Very careful planning as well as careful implementation are needed for getting fruitful results.

❏ ❏ ❏

REFERENCES

Badle Birth, F.B. (1969): Chotanagpur; A little Known province of Empire, London: Meth Elder and Co.

Census of India. (1981): Apical Tables for Scheduled Tribes, Series-4 Bihar, Part IX(III).

Dalton, E.T. (1872): Descriptive Ethnology of Bengal, Calcutta, Government Printing Press.

Forbes, L.R. (1872): Report on the Roy atwaran Settlement of the Government Farms in Palamau, Calcutta, Government Press.

Prasad, N. (1961): Land and people of Bihar, Ranchi. Bihar Tribal Welfare Research Institute.

Risley, H.H. (1991): Tribes and Casts of Bengal, Vol II, Calcutta.

Roy, S.C. (1925): The Birhor: A little Known Jungle Tribe of Chhotanagpur; Man in India Ranchi.

Singh, K. S. (1994): "Birhor" in the *Scheduled Tribes; People of India, National Series* Vol. III, Oxford University press.

Sinha, D.P. (1958): "Cultural Ecology of the Birhor. A Methodological Illustration". In *Journal of Social Research Vol - 1 Ranchi.*

Vidyarthi, L.P. (1960): "The Birhor: A Study in Ecology a and wandering" in W.F.C. Wallace (Ed). *Selected papers of the Anthropological and Ethnological Sciences);* Philadeephea.

William, B.J. (1967): "Birhor or Hazaribagh" in *Contribution to Anthropology and Band Societies No.* 228, National Museum of Canada.

Birhor - I

Photo Birhor

BIRHOR - II

A.K. Sinha
and
B.G. Banerjee

Since the Fifth Five-Year Plan, The Central Government had felt the need the development of the tribals. Hence, the Integrated Tribal Development Programme was initiated. Inspite of this there are some tribal groups whose population is very less and lead an extremely poverty-ridden level of living. These people, living on hard labour and marked by pre-agricultural economy, are better known as primitive tribes.

Madhya Pradesh is the largest state of India (443,443 sq km). The census figure of 1991 places the total population of Madhya Pradesh at 66,181,170. Percentage of tribal population in the state is 23.27, while the national proportion constitutes 8.08 per cent. Here the total number of scheduled tribes is 46, with a total population of 15,399 lakhs.

During the fifth Five-Year Plan, in Madhya Pradesh five backward tribes (*Abujhmaria, Baiga, Saharia, Bharia, Pahari Korwa*) were identified as primitive tribes. Subsequently, the *Kamar* and the *Birhor* were included in the same list during the sixth and seventh plan respectively. Presently the population of Birhors living in Madhya Pradesh is 1,021. They are also found in many other states of India with varied population - size for example in Bihar (4,377), Orissa (142), West Bengal (658) and Maharashtra (212).

The Origin

There is one folktale about the origin of the Birhor. It goes like this : A lady, named *Koltin,* were two sisters.The Birhors are the descendants of the elder sister, while the younger sister gave birth to another community called the *Mahakul.* It is said that Koltin had illicit sexual relations and as a result became pregnant. She gave birth to a male child. Her parents came to know about her illicit relationship and one day when she was sleeping with her baby in the hut, her parents burnt the hut with a motive to kill them (mother and the child). Next day, in the morning, the villagers rescued the mother and the child from the *debris.* The boy was brought up in the village but without any process of socialization (i.e. initiation and birth purification ceremony). The child gradually grew up in cultural isolation and the villagers looked down upon him and prevented him from participating in sacred/religious ceremonies of the community. The villagers did not even hesitate to abuse him by saying "*Majha Majha Ati Hai Sala Manjhai*" (why does he come again and again). From these reproachful terms the child came to be known as *Majhi*. He then started dwelling in the *Biru hills* and thus the term Birhor was coined. The descendants from him are known at present as *Birhor - Majhi*.

Initially the Birhor tribe had no permanent place of dwelling and led a nomadic or semi-nomadic life. In the year 1990, the Government of India decided to rehabilitated them into a settled life and hence they were provided with permanent settlement areas and houses. Five acres of land for agricultural purpose, under the *Indira Awas Yojna*, was distributed to each Birhor family.

Demography

The distribution of this tribe in madhya Pradesh has been shown in Appendix-1. It reveals that the number of females is more than that of the males and 71.53 per cent of their total population inhabit in the district of Raigarh. The number of Birhors in the districts of Mandla and Surguja, which is 35 and 27 respectively, stand second and third in position. In other areas, their population is extremely low.

The Birhor tribe is found in 31 villages (24 villages under Dharamajayagarh project and 7 villages under Jashpurnagar project). According to the socio-economic survey conducted in the year 1993, by office of the Dy. Commissioner, Jashpur Development Authority, the total population of the Birhor tribe was 1,021 (details of which are presented in Appendix-2).

Race and Language

Anthropologists have racially classified this tribe under the Proto-Australoid group. Linguists consider their language to be one of the *Austro-Asiatic* (Mundari) group. It is noteworthy that, while communicating with other tribes and caste group they fluently speak *Chhatisgarhi* dialect which is almost the *lingua france* of Eastern Madhya Pradesh. Thus the Birhors are bilingual. The native connotation of the Birhor dialect is *Birhori*.

Life Cycle

In a Birhor household all the members usually get up early in the morning and after completion daily chores, consume *Basi* (stale food) and commence their day with ropemaking except adult males who indulge in ploughing, sowing, winnowing and harvesting of crops during the agricultural period. The females mainly engage themselves in ropemaking. During the agricultural period, females also work in ploughing, sowing, etc.

The male members leave for the agricultural field after having taken their midday meal. After 2-3 hours of work, they make themselves little free for rest and there after set out for the jungle to collect firewood. The children simply roam about here and there and the youth go to study at the Adult Education Centres. The females indulge in cooking and the elderly people gossip and exchange jokes with one another by assembling at a definite spot.

Birth Rituals

Life is recognized and perceived not by birth but by pregnancy. Besides, to understand the social life of any community, rituals and customs should also be included in the study of life-cycle which runs through pregnancy and end up at the cremation ground.

Among the Birhors, there is a belief that if a woman stops menstruating the month after she indulges in sexual intercourse she is normally presumed to have conceived. Pregnant women have to follow certain taboos:

- She is not supposed to step out of her house during lightening.
- Abstaining from collecting leaves of a tree.
- Abstaining from entering the *Sarana* (sacred place).
- Abstaining from treading places, declared as spiritual by *Baigas* or the spots of spirit-dwelling.
- Crossing of river is also not permitted.
- Change of place is restricted.

In scientific parlance all these taboos appear to be quite rational. Normally, a pregnant woman is not offered any special diet due to the fact that their economic condition is very low in absolute sense. During this period a woman continues to work like any other Birhor woman. But in the ninth month of pregnancy she keeps herself away from heay tasks, like fetching water from the well, picking up of heavy load, etc. She is supposed to consume only fresh food during the ninth month of her pregnancy.

Child delivery takes place in a traditional manner in a completely natural habitat i.e. the child is born under a tree in the jungle. Child birth inside a house is tabooed because the child may become victim of malevolent spirits. If, accidently, any pregnant woman gives birth to her child under a roof, she is considered unholy. In this case a *Baiga* (a religious specialist) is summoned to purify the house. The *Baiga* attempts to remove the *ill - effects* of the house by taking a round of the woman and also the house with turmeric powder, accompanied by breaking open a coconut. The relatives and the other members of same community are offered the *Bakra Bhat* (mutton - rice) as penalty feast and apology.

When a pregnant woman feels the labour pain, she informs her-husband or any other elderly people in the house. A midwife is called by her husband. After the delivery the midwife cuts the umbilical cord with the help of a bamboo strip. After this the mother and the new-born baby are brought to the newly built *Jhala* (hut) in the courtyard. After 6-7 hours of child birth, the woman is offered *Kaansa* (nutritious drink). 1-2 hours later she is fed with the usual meal.

As the name suggests the *chhatti* rites are celebrated on the sixth day of childbirth. On this occasion of *chhatti*, both the mother and child are given a bath. Previous to this day they are not given a bath. The baby and the mother are kept under the supervision of the midwife. The christening of the child is performed on the day of *chhatti* for which there is no special paraphernalia. The elderly people do the needful. Usually christening is done according to a suitable data and festival. The midwife is offered rice, pulses and *saree*. On the day of *chhatti,* the mother and child are brought to the *parchhi*, a thatch made over mud-walls by the side of the house, where they live for three months. Unless and until the period of *chhatti* is over the woman may be confined and restricted from doing normal household activities. The woman does not touch the household utensils and it is for the other members of the family to assume the responsibility of cooking day males. Till the period of *chhatti* and christening is over, the woman is considered defiled and ritually impure.

As the child attains five months of age, in the case of males, and four months, in the case of a female, all the relatives are invited to a feast. The child is given a bath and adorned with a new cloth. The mother takes the child in her *lap* and goes to the place of worship where the *Baiga* propitiates the deity with the offering of a fowl. Thereafter, the child is fed with rice, followed by a feast to the relatives.

A child largely depends upon the breast milk of the mother for 2-3 years. in case another child is born, breast feeding is stopped after six months. Birhor children hardly wear any cloth. During the first year of a child's life he/she is made to walk the help of the parents. He/she is adorned with dress only when the child grows up. A child normally lives in the family as a result of which he/she acts in the same manner as his/her parents do. When a female child attains the age of 9-10 years, her parents get her *tattooed*. Tattooing is done on both the arms, back and chest (below the neck).

Dress and ornaments

The Birhors wear simple clothes. The working dress of male member consists of a *kopni* or loin cloth (a narrow cotton strip of cloth passed between the legs and tied with the waist belts), a portion being hung in front. The usual dress comprises of a short, coarse piece of unsewn cloth (dhoti) and short kurta (sewn sleeveless shirt). When at home they generally do not put on any cloth on the upper part of the body. They do not use shoes or any footwear. The females use a type of coarse saree without any under garments. This cloth covers both the upper and lower part of the body. Modern shirts and trousers are becoming popular among the male labourers. The Birhor females prefer *tattooing*. Glass bangles, ear-rings, finger rings as ornaments are in common use among the Birhor females.

Literacy

The percentage of literacy of the Birhor tribe was 1.60 per cent according to the 1981 census. The level of literacy for males 3.30 per cent whereas among the females none was found to be a literate.

Marriage Rituals

The Birhor children attain adolescence while living in a environment free from the binding of elders. An adolescent boy is easily distinguished from and adolescent female. Just after the attainment of adolescence the girls are trained in household chores and domestic duties. On the other hand, an adolescent boy begins to take interest in socio-economic activities and forest, following the other members of the house; the growing boy gradually becomes habituated to the consumption of *tobacco, guraku* (tabacco mixed with molasses used in smoking) and use of *biris* (crude from of a cigarette) at a tender age.

In this way, the child gradually goes beyond the period of adolescence and enters into the age of youth. With the onset of menstrual cycle the age of marriage of a girl is determined. The menstruation is feferred to as *Mundi Mijna* in native term. During menstruation, the girl has to observe certain taboos, she does not cook food for seven days, she does not enter the place where paddy is stored and her clothes have to be kept on ground itself. She is not supposed to hang them, and she is also not supposed to go to the *Sarana (Devesthal)*. Boys and girls are free to meet each other during the period of adolescence and no restrictions are imposed on them.

Among the Birhors, boys and girls are considered to have attained the age of marriage when they are 17-18 and 12-14 years respectively. A Birhor boy is accepted as a full-fledged members of the same clan are considered to be brothers. Among the Birhors, three types of marriages are accepted i.e. *Biha, Udariya* and *Churiahi*.

Biha

Biha is the most prevalent form of marriage among the Birhors. *Biha* is a form of marriage by negotiation. After the selection of a girl is made by the parents, the boy is sent to take the final decision. When both the parties agree, then the groom's family proceeds towards the finalization of the negotiation i.e. the *Phaldan* ceremony with 50 kg. of rice, a sack full of *Tai Murra*, 2 bottles of country liquor and clothes for the bride and her mother. Also the date of marriage is finalized on this day. The marriage takes place in the month of *Magh* (February-March) and *Phalgun* (March-April) since the standing crops are ready for harvest by this time which ensures subsistence and financial resources for the marriage ceremony.

The marital customs and marriage rituals among the Birhors continue for either three, five or seven days. The seven-day long rituals are performed by those families who are economically well off. In case the ritual continues for a week, the *barat* (marriage party) leaves on the sixth day and in case of five-day long celebration, the *barat* leaves on the fourth day. Economically poor families usually perform a three-day long celebration, the *barat* leaves on the second day.

The *Marwa* (marriage spot) is constructed at both the bride's and groom's place. It is made by *Sarai* wood (*willow*), outside the house. Mango leaves are fastened with the *marwa*. On the first day of marriage celebration, the *Baiga* places mango leaves, a lamp, a coconut, turmeric and incense sticks there and performs the *puja*, while chanting hymns. Thereafter, he digs out some clay from the ground and offers five handful of clay to the mother of the groom / bride. Offering of clay to the mother of the groom/bride indicates the onset of the marriage rituals. The *Baiga* worships in order to ward off evil spirits and other undesired phenomena. All the relatives are invited to the marriage.

Next day, a mixture of some oil and turmeric powder is smeared on the bodies of the bride and groom. This is repeated again on the bride's body on the 'main' days (marriage day), the groom is given a bath and made to wear new clothes. Thereafter the *barat along* with the relatives proceed. They carry with them some necessary items like *flour, jaggery, coconuts* and clothes for the bride and her mother. On reaching the village the barat is greeted by the bride's family and after that the custom of *samdhi bhent* (exchange of gifts by the male parents-in-law) is solemnized. The *panigrahan* (marriage ceremony) among the Birhors takes place either in the morning or in the evening. An oil lamp is lit and the bride and groom take seven rounds of the lamp. After the feast at night the people accompanying the baral disperse for their respective places, the groom's family returns home with the bride and the bride lives with her parents-in-law for five days. Thereafter, the newly-weds again go back to the bride's place to stay for five days there. During this period of stay at the bride's place the *pila dhuluana* ritual is performed. The newly married couple return to their home after the stipulated days and the bride starts living with the family of parents-in-law as permanent member.

Udariya

According to the custom, if a young man falls in love with a girl and if their parents do not permit them to marry, then they decide to elope at an unknown place and live as husband and wife. When they are spotted by members of the tribe, the couple is accorded social recognition as a married couple only after the *Bakra Bhat* (grand feast).

Churiyahi

When a Birhor woman becomes a widow, then her brother-in-law or any other male member of the village offers a *churi* (bracelet) to her and keeps her as his wife. This form of marriage is similar to that of the *churiyahi* marriage prevalent in Chhatisgarh. The consent of the widow and other related matters are decided mutually in presence of the *panch* (village council).

After marriage the son with his wife shifts to a new residence. The aged parents continue to earn their livelihood from cultivation and rope-marking till they are physically capable enough to do so. When they find themselves physically incapable of working, they go to their son and daughter-in-law and start living with them. Normally the Birhors consider themselves infirm and disabled due to old age after attaining the age of 50-55 years. They may suffer from various diseases also. Their ability to work ceases.

Death Rituals

In the event of death of any member of their community the Birhors believe that is was due to an evil affect which had befallen on them. This warrants them to change their dwelling. Due to this reason, it is difficult to compel Birhors to lead a settled life. After a prolonged and concerted efforts of the State government nowadays they have started leading a settled life and do not prefer to shift to a new place in the event of death of any member of their community. They practice ancestor worship with the sacrifice of a *hen and liquor.* The Birhors believe that if they do not do so, the soul of the deceased ancestor may cause harm to them.

When a person dies, a bamboo structure in the form of a stretcher is prepared on which the dead body is placed. Four persons carry it to the burial ground. A trench of about five feet long and three feet deep is dug out and the dead body laid down in the grave with its head facing towards the north and feet towards the south. The son of the deceased person initiates by pouring five handful of clay in the grave. Thereafter other persons join in filling up the grave. His clothes and other possessions are kept at the place of *burial.* After the *burial,* they throw cereals like, *Kodo, Kutki* (small grains eaten by poor people), paddy, maize, bajra, etc.) over the graveyard. In the event of death of a child, he/she is buried under a *mahua tree (Bassia latifolia),* bearing sweet smelling flowers which are used in the preparation of an alcoholic liquor) in the jungle. Behind this there is a strong belief that the bark of *mahua* secretes milk, and hence the child shall be able to drink milk from the *mahua tree.* After the burial the mourners take a bath and return home. After three days of death, all the relatives of the deceased are invited and *Dashgatra* rites are performed. On the eleventh day the members of the village and the relatives are given a feast by the family of the deceased person.

SOCIAL ORGANISATION

The Birhors are an endogamous tribe. They are divided into

various patrilineal exogamous clans. These clans are totemic in nature. Totemic objects as indicated below may be a tree, a bird, or an animal.

Clan and Totem

Clan	Totem	Clan	Totem
Badi	Banyan tree	Kosandi	Kosa (Tasar) tree
Baghel	Tiger	Sonwani	Swan
Bandi	Bam fish		

The members of different clans enjoy equal social status. A woman after her marriage is a member of the clan of her husband and gets back to her father's clan whenever she becomes a widow or is divorced.

Family, among the Birhor consists of husband, wife and their unmarried children. So nuclear family is the only type in a Birhor community. A father is the head of the family. He is the most important member and is also responsible for procuring the sources of subsistence for the entire family. A mother looks after her children and is in charge of domestic duties. Adult sons assist their father. Usually after one year of his marriage the son builds a new hut and establishes - a new and separate household.

The Birhors maintain denotative type of kinship system for reckoning their relatives. They have separate terms of address. All the members of a family and the members of the same clan are called *Kutumb*, whereas the members of other clans are known as *Saga*. Here is a list of terms of reference:

Kinship

Kinship term	English equivalent	Kinship term	English equivalent
Aaja	FF	Aaji	FM
Bau/siani	W	Beti	Z
Chacha	FB	Chacha	FBW
Dada	B	Dai	M
Dau	F	Fufa	FSh
Fufi	FS	Gearjian	DH
Lihikin	ZW	Mama	MB
Mami	MBW	Mausi	MS
Sari	WS	Sara	WB

(F=Father, M=Mother, B=Brother, S=Sister, Z=Son, D=Daughter, H=Husband W=Wife)

Different kinds of relationship that are found within kin-members have been classified under the following three categories.

(a) Joking relationship

This brings two kinsmen quite close to each other. They have the right to joke and tease each other. The Birhors maintain this relationship between the ego and alter as under:

(i) A man with his wife's younger sister
(ii) A woman her husband's younger brother
(iii) Between the parents-in-law
(iv) Grand-parent with grand-children (irrespective of generation different and sex).

Avoidance

It has been found that avoidance of one kind or another is observed between daughter-in-law and parents-in-law; between a woman and her husband's elder brother. This relationship prevents the above stated kins from becoming too close and familiar.

The Birhor generally do not share jokes with their parents. They do not utter slang or abusive words in the presence of their parents.

Sahiyan Patana or Gaighati

To develop the traditional bond of friendship *Sahiyan patana* is arranged. It occurs between persons of two different clans or two communities. They claim it is due to love and affection towards an unknown person. After making this type of ceremonial relationship, both the families maintain a congenial tie and try to oblige each other in customary exchange of gifts and services. One may enter into this kind of ritual kinship on a specific festive occasion especially during *nawateohar* and marriage ceremony.

POLITICAL LIFE

The Birhors have their own traditional *Panchayat*. The *mukhia* is the head of the community *panchayat*. A decision is usually taken by the consensus of opinion of all adult male members present there. Next to the *Mukhia* (the-man), the *baiga* (religious priest), the *pujari* (*Baiga's* assistant), the *guniya* (sorcerer and the *jhankar* (village messenger) play important role in the *panchayat*. Any dispute in the village is settled by the *panchayat*. In case they fail to arrive at a decision, the case is referred to the statutory *panchayat*. When the statutory *panchayat* also fails, then only the matter is reported to the police. A Birhor handcuffed by the police is expelled from the community and allowed re-entry only when the members are appeased by throwing a feast arranged by the expelled person. Some offences and punishment prevalent in Birhor society are given below:

S.No.	Offence	Type of Punishment
1.	Tribe exogamy	Expulsion from the tribe and acceptance of marriage after offering a feast of mutton and rice.
2.	Clan endogamy and prohibited sexual intercourse	Excommunication but after giving a feast and fine ranging from Rs. 500/ to Rs. 1,000/- they are readmitted into the community.
3.	Illegitimate relation	A feast of goat meat and rice and a fine of Rs. 1,500/- to Rs. 2,000/- as per the seriousness of the offence.
4.	Rape case	The two persons are persuaded to get married, if the man refuses he is penalised by fine of Rs. 500/- to Rs.1,000/- as per the severity of the case.
5.	Handcuff	Expulsion from the community and re-entry is permitted on offering a feast.
6.	Delivery inside the house	Feast of goat meat, rice and *handia* (locally made beer)

RELIGION

The religion of the Birhor may be seen through their series of worships and ceremonies of numerous gods, deities and spirits. They believe in supernatural powers and worship them for their well being. They also worship their ancestors and various objects of nature. They do so with the belief that these forces would protect them form any unforeseen danger. The main deities, gods and goddesses they worship are: *Thakur Deo, Mahadeo, Sarpen deo, Dhartimatia, Diharin.* Besides these they also worship the evil spirits to ward off their evil effects. Baiga is the religious head who performs worship on different occasions. The ingredients in the worship are *coconuts, chandan* (sandal wood), incense sticks, flowers, etc. Animal or bird sacrifice is an essential part of their worship. They generally offer hens for this, but the colour of the hens varies with the deities. Some of those are as:

Diharin Devta - Black hen
Thakur Deo - White hen
Sarpen Deo - Red hen

According to 1981 census 84.67 per cent of Birhor were Hindus, 13.55 per cent were Christians and rest 1.60 per cent were followers of 'other religion'.

The Birhors now live in mud houses and not in *jhopri* (hovel) which was made of branches of trees designed in triangular shape. The main entrance was without any door. Changes have also place in the manner of constructing their houses. They build their houses with a mud wall and tiled *khapra* (baked tiles) roof instead of *Khadar* and *chhind* shrub. They now use wood for making windows and doors. One interesting thing that can be easily visualized here is that though the houses are provided with windows, the Birhors always keep them closed. They stress that these are too ventilated for them and make them more chilly, especially in the winter season. Instead their traditional leafy huts were warm and cosy. Besides these news have created some fresh demands on their poor economy. Purchase of warm clothes etc. to cope up with the changed circumstance is an additional burden on them from their own resources.

Besides their traditional dress, *shirts* and *blouses, petticoat* are slowly becoming popular. Though they are using modern pullovers, *sarees,* etc. yet these are not permitted to wear on *religious* and sacred occasions. Besides tattooing their interest is increasing towards glass bangles, anklet, earrings, lace for hair, etc.

They have taken fancy to vessels and other utensils of brass and aluminum for their household. They use modern match boxes at present along with their traditional *thondi* and *chakmaki pathar* (flint stone) for fire making. They now own transistor-sets, searchlight, bicycles, etc.

At present they not only consume rice, various roots and forest products but have also taken to potato, tomato, brinjal and other vegetables. These crops are produced by them through plough cultivation in their own fields.

Rope-making in also widely practiced by the Birhors. Along with it, they are gradually being introduced to a settled life and plough cultivation. A few families have started grocery shops as business. It is seen that a few are also interested in getting Government jobs in military or army services.

□ □ □

Appendix - 1
Distribution on Birhor in Madhya Pradesh

S. No.	Name of the District / Tehsil	Rural area Male	Rural area Female	Urban area Male	Urban area Female	Total
1	2	3	4	5	6	7
1	Bastar	10	8	-	-	18
2	Betul	-	1	-	-	1
3	Bilaspur	8	11	-	-	19
4	Durg	-	1	-	-	1
5	Indore	-	-	2	2	4
6	Jabalpur	1	1	3	1	6
7	Mandla	11	24	-	-	35
8	Mandsaur	2	1	-	-	3
9	Morena	1	-	-	-	1
10	Narsinghpur	1	-	-	-	1
11	Raigarh	197	205	-	-	402
12	Raipur	6	11	-	-	17
13	Raisen	-	2	-	-	2
14	Rewa	1	-	-	-	1
15	Sagar	1	-	-	-	1
16	Satna	1	-	-	-	1
17	Sehore	4	3	-	-	7
18	Shahdol	1	1	-	-	2
19	Sidhi	1	1	-	-	2
20	Surguja	9	16	1	1	27
21	Tikamgarh	6	5	-	-	11
22	West Nimar	-	1	-	-	1
	Total	261	291	6	4	562

Sources: Census of India, 1981, Series - 11 Madhya Pradesh, Part IX (4)

Appendix - 2
Distribution of the Birhor in Raigarh District

Project	Block	Village	Family	Person
Dharam-jaygarh	Dharam-jaygarh	Bandhanpur	1	1
		Dhodgaon (Bassantpur)	7	25
		Dumarpara (Nekana)	2	12
		Jamarga	7	24
		Jamargi	5	6
		Jamargidih	3	18
		Khamhar	5	14
		Kumhichua	26	80
		Majhidera (kida)	24	85
		Ongana (khalbora)	24	79
		Ruwaphool	13	29
		Sakarlia	4	11
		Siwar	6	25
		Tejpur (Kekranara)	2	6
	Gharghora	Bichhinara (Indira nagar)	1	3
		Kaya	1	9
		Kotrisal	3	14
		Raikera (Baigapara)	3	13
	Lailunga	Jhagarpur	12	47
		Kurra	8	25
		Buldega (Darripari)	15	53

Birhor - II

Project	Block	Village	Family	Person
	Pathalgaon	Kokiyakhar (Kukurbhuka, Sawatoli)	5	18
	Tamnar	Kachakowa (Sitapara)	15	45
		Korakel (Bankheta)	16	50
	Total	24	208	692
Jashpurnagar	Bagicha	Bhitghara (Siurinarayan)	13	47
		Ghoghar (Dhengurjor, Janakpur)	31	110
		Peta (Khosardand)	8	19
	Duldula	Jhargaon	8	41
	Kansabel	Baiga Amba (Pogad)	9	34
		Bataikela (Dabnipani)	5	21
	Kunkun	Behrakhar (shankernagar)	20	57
	Total	7	94	329
	Grand total	31	302	1,021

Sources: Dy. Commissioner, Jashpur Sarvattomukhi Development Authority, Jashpurnagar, Letter No./42/Yojna Birhor/96 dated 22.94.96.

❑ ❑ ❑

BHOTIA

Dr. Alok Chantia

Those tribe groups who are engaged in trading, the Bhotias are a restless people who are almost semi-nomadic due to their trading way. They are spread over in eight districts (Chamoli, Tehri, Uttar Kashi, Dehradun, Pauri, Almora, Nainital and Pithaura garh) These districts cover 5,000 miles and it lies in the N.E. of the Division between latitude 28° 59' and 30°49' north and longitude 79°2' and 81°31' East. It is bounded on the North by Nainital on the south and by Garhwal and Nepal on the west and east respectively.

The origin of Bhotia tribe is based on the word "Bhotia" which is used for all six nomadic trading group. Bhotia word is originated by "Bhot" word which is similar to a tibetan word "Bod", So the exact origin of Bhotia tribe is still in confusion.

The Bhotia are sturdy people having marked mongoloid traits. They are of medium stature the mean being 160.18 Cm and are mesocephalic (51.0%) to brachy cephalic index being 79.89 their nose varies from leptorrhine (56.0%) to mesorrhine (41.0%). The mean nasal index being 70.20. They possess Hypsicephal (96.6%) and acrocephal (70.0%) types of head associated with mesoprosopic (37%) to mesane (59%) type of face. Their complexion is medium yellow brown with ruddy cheeks and dark brown eyes. They have black in colour.

Cymotrichous hair with scanty beards and moustaches while their eye slits are oblique and an epicanthic fold is commonly observed among them. The blood group analysis of the Bhotia shows a high frequency of group B(50.69%). They also exhibit trends in the finger and palmer prints which are characteristic of the yellow brown stock.

Linguistically they belong to the *Tibeto-Burman* family and five dialects are spoken them. Rankas or shokiya khun: Bayansi in bayans valley: Chaudansi in *Chaudans*; Darmi in *Darma* valley and Bhotia or *Hunia* spoken by scattered groups of Bhotias, *Hunias* and *Khampas*. The Bhotias can be classified in-to the following subdivisions: Jethoreas who speak the *Ranka dialect* and live in *Johar* and *Malla Danpur*. Among them are vary few traders, their occupation being mostly agriculture, The marchas the tolchas and the Rawats are found in Johar and have forgotten their own language are found in *Johar* and have forgotten their own language and use the *kumaoni language*. The other sub divisions are the *Darmi, Chaudansi* and *Byansi* Bhotias who inhabit the areas of *Darma, Chaudans, Byans* respectively and speak their own dilects known by their place names, but according to shering (1906) Bhotias are classified in six following subgroup *shoka,* (Pithoragarh), *Dharmi* (Dharchula), *johari* (Munsayari) *Tolcha, Marcha* and *Jad* (Chomli & Uttarkashi district).

After the Indo-China war (1962) their occupation have been changed. Now they are in Govt. Service, but mainly are in agriculture. They produce-Wheat, Barley, Tumeric, Ginger Uaa & fafra (like wheat) potatoes, Groundnut, etc.

The family is organised on a patriarchal basis and is governed by the types of marriage contracted both monogamy and polygyny are present among Bhotia and the composition of the family changes accordingly.

A peculiar position pertains regarding the habitations of the Bhotias conditioned as they are by the dual forces of climate and occupation as they have to shift their abodes in relation to the weather and their trading habits and their villages, called *kheras* are therefore temporarily occupied for short periods of time.

MARRIAGE RITUALS

Among the Bhotias, different types of marriage are practiced, but the arranged marriage is very frequent and this marriage is known as *"consent marriage"*. This type of marriage is completed in different steps. First step is *"CHAMAI KHARMO"*. In this process the consent of girl for marriage is taken. The meaning of *chamai kharmo* is" to cheat a girl at mental level for her consent about marriage". This process is done by a relative woman of girl and this woman is known as *"TARAM"*. After the consent of the girl a traditional wine *"CHYACTI"* is given by groom side to the bride side under the process of *"VINTI"* Both side worship their local God & Goddess with *chyacti* and then they take it as prasad. This whole process is known as *sagai (THOMI).* At the time of thomi, marriage data is fixed and this fixed data is known *"DHAMI SYASYA"*).

On the marriage day the functional role of *"TISYA"* (Real or cousin sisters of groom) is very important. They go in *Barat* with their traditional dresses and abucket on their back. In this bucket they keep *Chyacti, Dhalam* (Cake) and other material which is must for marriage.

Barat is received by the every village man of the bride side in the village.

At the bride's home "Shaknu" ritual is performed in this ritual God & Goddess is worshipped by *Chyacti* and *Dhalam* (cake). Then both these things are distributed between the both side as *prasad*.

Laye (Goad Bharai): This ritual is performed by the groom's side at the time of marriage and some amount is given to the bride's mother.

Khato

It is another ritual at the time of marriage in which groom's side gives a white cloth (1.5 mater long) to the every relatives of bride this white cloth is known as *KHATO*. They keep khato on their heads and worship the God for the welfare of new couple. Then marriage is completed and they start "*RANG BANG*" for two or three nights at the bride's home.

After the completion of *Rang Bang* bride comes on groom's home with her friends (*SYASYA*) and then again all old men worship the *Dhalam* and groom's mother gives a piece of *Dhalam* and cup of *chyacti* in which she dips a coin. This ritual is similar to the *saptpadi* of Hindus. They queer characteristic of Bhotia's marriage is the absence of *Brahmin* or *Purohit*. Elopement and kidnapping marriage is also practiced.

Birth Rituals

Among Bhotia tribe the birth ritual is celebrated in following manner:

At the time of birth, "*Chyacti* and *Dhalam*" is given to God & Goddess and every relative takes it as *prasad* then a Dinner (Bhoj) is organised.

Chhushimo

It is a ritual which is celebrated on eleventh day of the child's birth, on that day mother and child takes sacred bath for their normal life and on the same day Naming ceremony of child is performed. In the local language it is known as *CHHUSHIMO*.

Muliyakormo

It is performed on the twenty second day of child's birth. On that day mother - child again take sacred bath and worship the God. From this day mother can do domestic work and behaves like a holy woman.

Bhumo
This ritual is concerned with child's movement on the ground and it is celebrated after the completion of the third month of the Child's birth.

Pushyavomo
Mundan is known as *pushyavomo* which is celebrated at the 3rd or 5th or 7th year of the age of the child.

Death Rituals (Gavan)
They practice same death ritual as Hindu does but their ritual's name are different. The span of *Gavan* ritual is three days. The first day only cremation is done.

Chesa
It is the name of *Shamshan* (cemetry)

Amlugra
It is a woolen cloth in which dead body is wrapped.

Chao
It is an important ritual which is performed on the second day of cremation. The bones of the dead person is collected from the *chesa* and it is kept inside the ground of the village with a hanging pitcher of water and flour and *Ghee*. This work is done by any experienced old man *(ARMICHA)*. In the same day a dinner is given in the night to those persons who were present in the cremation.

GHARCHYOMA (CURTAIN) CEREMONY
It is the final and third day ritual of *Gavan Sanskar*. In this ceremony every village man is participated except the family members of the dead man. On the third day or at the *Gharchyoma* ceremony they gather in an open place and form two groups for dancing. Both groups are separated by - litting the fire. This fire is considered as a curtain between the two groups. This ceremony shows that dead soul (First Group) and life (Second group) is not connected to each other in the world. Both are different matter. Here fire is the symbol of world *(curtain)* which separates the dead soul and life. So this ceremony is performed for creating a difference between *dead soul and life*

Yak has an important role in *Gavan Sanskar*. It is used for the *vedai of soul*. The *Chao* is kept on its back and it is left in the Jungle. When it comes back again in the village. village men think soul of dead man in now free from the world.

At the time of *Gavan Sanskar* women donot use the *ornaments and bangles in right hand* and men donot use any sacred work.

CULTURAL TRAITS

Among the Bhotias the important village Gods worshiped are *GOBALA, CHIPULA* and *HARDEOL* who are specially worhsipped thrice a year in the month of *Kartik Bhadon* and *Jeth* respectively. Goats are sacrificed to these Gods and liquor is placed at the shrine and much dancing and singing goes on. The bhotias of *Chaudans* and *Byan* erect shrines called "*SAITHAN*" for their Gods, consisting of a stone kept at the base of a tree trunk with red and white strips of cloth tied to the branches. The God *Gabila* is worshipped by all though various villages have various God.

The Kutiyals worship a god called "*GULACH*". The Gorbials protitiate "*Kungr*" the God of rain. The God Chan is worshipped for protection against diseases whereas in Darma a deity which is both male and female called "*KIBANG RANCHIM*" is worshipped when his flocks fall sick the Bhotia worships Gods "*Sidhuwa*" and Bidhuwa" and for lost sheep the God" *Runiya* is importuned.

They celebrate many festival. It is in two part. In the first they celebrate religious festival- Eisth *Devta pujan, Atma pujan, Gabala pujan, Chanta Karna pujan*, etc. In the second part, agricultural festival is celebrated. *Mati puja, Navu sano, Nu, Dhalam* etc. They also celebrate *Lohusar day* (15 february) - a tibetan new year day.

POLITICAL ORGANISATION

They have a panchyat with 5 to 7 members. Trade disputes and other controversial matters are amicably settled by an ingenious custom called "*ANTARA BAIRNA*". A goat is sacrificed and the meat is cooked, while intestines are cleaned. The two disputants are asked to stand together and the intestine is wrapped round them. This signifies fact that they were born from the same womb and should consider themselves brother and cease to quarrel. Thereafter friendly relations are established and much feasting and merriment takes place.

Now acculturation is making rapid head way among the Bhotias and breakingup their peculiar brand of culture.

❏ ❏ ❏

REFERENCES

Bisht, B.S. : Bhotia tribe of Uttarakhand, 1992, Vivek Prakashan. Delhi
Vanya, Jati : Bhotia tribe of Almora district, Journal from Delhi. 1955
Hasan, Amir : A bunch of wild flowers.

BOKAR

Dr. Prakash Chandra Mehta

A member of the Adi group of tribes, they are found in West Siang district of Arunachal Pradesh. It is believed that they first lived in place called *Pui* adjacent to Tadadego. As per folk story prevalent among them they believe that they had been pushed south by Tibetans. In course of their migration southwards they settled on both sides of *Tungu La Pass* in *Yumi* and *Nayu valleys*. Gesing is the largest of the Bokar village. For full account of their social and cultural life is similar to Adi's.

❏ ❏ ❏

BOMDO

Dr. Prakash Chandra Mehta

Bomdo are a small subgroup of the Adi tribe of Arunachal Pradesh. They are found in East Siang district. According 1981 Census their population was only two persons. Interestingly the tribe is shown to have a population of 294 persons in 1971, persons returned mostly from East Siang district. Therefore, it is likely that most of them have returned themselves as Adi in 1981 Census. They have adopted Adi's culture.

❑❑❑

BORI

Dr. Prakash Chandra Mehta

Bori is an important constituent of the Adi tribe of Arunachal Pradesh. Their population as per 1981 Census was 1,885 persons. They are found on both banks of the Siyom and Sike rivers in West Siang district of Arunachal Pradesh. They have also adopted similar rituals to Adi's.

❏ ❏ ❏

BONDA

Ramesh Prasad Mohanty

The Bonda Highlanders are the most primitive and aggressive tribal people of Orissa as well as in the eastern India. Among the plains people, they are popularly known as *Bonda-paraga*. But they call themselves as *'Remo'*, meaning 'human'. They speak a very difficult Auto asiatic language which is indigenous. Hence, it is not ordinarily understood by the plains people. They call their language as *'Redo-sam'*. By this word, they mean 'human-language'.

The whole Upper Bonda people are confined to only 32 villages located at a height of about 3,000-4,000 feet above the sea level in the remote and high elevated alluring hill ranges of Eastern - Ghats falling under the Khairput block of the district of Malkangiri of Orissa. All these 32 villages are spread out sporadically in approximately 135 sq. kms. and are collectively known as Bonda-hills or *Bonda-Ghati* which has a characteristic and distinction of its own as a sensation is felt of being very high up amidst the clouds, out of the way, above the world while walking inside the hills.

According to 1981 census, the Bonda people constitute a total number of 5,895 population, but a survey made by the Bonda Development Agency (BDA) in 1996, shows that the upper Bonda constitute only 5,313 population.

Elwin writes that "their country is the wild and mountainous region north west of the *Machkund* river, and they have preserved themselves comparatively unaffected by the march of civilization. In fact by the plains men and the officials, the Bondas are regarded as entirely savage, almost as the classic savage type: the strange dress and appearance of their women, their violent homicidal ways, their unfamiliar tongue ..., the inaccessibility of their abode, separate them from the rest of Orissa" (1950:1). Thus, they can be termed as the people of the "*Stone Age Insitu*" , whose culture persists in its purest form; however, with very minimal level of change due to their inaccessive habitat. They feel themselves as if the first human beings of the earth and the whole human civilization originated from themselves and from their homeland also. So, they do not care the people other than themselves and even do not hesitate to be aggressively oriented leading to homicidal offenses towards others who intrude into their country or villages and impinge on their rights, self respect or stresspass on their properties or interfere in personal matters. (cf. Mahapatra, 1992:1)

Some of the most important characteristic features of these people are (i) Rude and ruthless manner of expression (ii) Spirit of independence and sence of freedom. (iii) Aggressive and violent propensities leading to homicidal offenses (iv) Unconventional dress pattern (v) Excessive consumption of *sago-palm* juice and other country liquor irrespective of age and sex (vi) Dormitory life (vii) Declining growth rate (viii) Pre-agricultural level of technology combined with extremely low level of literacy. (ix) Consumption of stale carcasses, cow dung-beetle, date-palm grubs, silk worm, etc. (x) Marrying of elder girls to very younger boys maintaining an age gap of about thirteen years, and (xi) Unhygienic health condition, they do not take bath for months and even years together, they do not even clean themselves with water after defecation.

One of the most important eye catching characteristic features which immediately separate them from the rest of the world at the fist sight of an outsider is the strange and unique dress pattern of their female population who are almost more than half clad-they wear a self made skirt, called *Nodi*. This piece of cloth hardly reaches their thighs and is even not to sufficient length to go round the waist or to cover up the genital. They keep themselves bald and use some colourful necklaces of beads to cover up the upper part of their body. But it is not because of their poor economic condition, rather it is their tradition, the way of life.

The Hill-Bondas are divided into two exogamous sections such as (a) the *Barajangar* group, and (b) the *Gadaba* group. The *Barajangar* group or the country of twelve confederacy constitutes 12 villages which are situated at the hilltops within the hill ranges and are thought to be the original bonda villages from which the rest villages, being branded as *Gadaba* group have emerged out of population explosion. These daughter villages are not necessarily situated on the hilltops. Of all these villages, *Mudulipada* is considered as the central and the capital of the whole Bonda country where their chief deity *Patkhanda-Mahaprabhu* is propitiated in a great *banyan tree* and the chief (*Naik*) of the Bonda country occupies his throne. However, the people of *Gadaba* tribe, another primitive community justaposed with the Bondas, do not acknowledge the authority of the *Naik of Mudulipada;* they have no interest in the cult of *Patkhanda Mohaprabhu*; and they may even keep their festivals in different dates and even perform in a different way of varying degrees of cultural values also.

The entire upper Bonda tribe is divided into two exogamous moities or Baish namely *cobra* (Ontal) and *tiger* (Killo/Druka) of which the people of *cobra group* are most numerous and both these moities share common exogamous clans (*Mada*) named after village functionaries, like, *Muduli, Kirsani, Badnaik, Dhangada-Majhi, Chalan, Dora, Sisa* etc.

The entire upper Bonda tribe is divided into two exogamous moities or Baish namely *Cobra*) (Ontal) and *tiger* (Killo/Druka) of which the people of *cobra group* are most numerous and both these moities share common exogamous clans (*Mada*) named after village functionaries, like, *Muduli, Kirsani, Badnaik, Dhangada-Majhi, Chalan, Dora, Sisa,* etc.

The Bonda people are basically individualistic in nature. And they prefer to establish separate households soon after their marriage. So, their family forms are primarily nuclear (68.9%) in nature. These households are followed by single-member (13.5%) and sub-nuclear households (10.6%). Supplemented nuclear, polygynous nuclear and lineal joint families are also found, but their percentage is found to be very low.

Patrilineality, patriarchy and patrilocality are the rules of descent, authority and residence, but the female voice is highly respected by the male members due to their high economic importance in the society. Seniority in age of the wife is also an important factor for this.

Marriage Rituals

There are separate youth dormitories for both the boys and girls, known as, *Ingersing* and *Selaniding* respectively. While selecting life partners, the boys of one village go to the *Selaniding* of other villages as village exogamy is strictly observed and though, the real aim of Bonda dormitory is marriage, they are free to have sexual experience; however, not of intercourse, which the boys call "*Breast Play*" This comes to them naturally as the younger boys or husbands do not get pleasure with their old wives and the girls marry in a late age to very young boys who are not physically matured.

The Bondas mainly practice two types of marriage (*Dosing*), namely, arranged marriage (*Salak-Boyi-Dosing*) and capture marriage

(*Wai-Boyi-Dosing*). Payment of birds price (*Ginning*) is prevalent in both the cases, but while a cow, a bullock and about 20-30 kgs. of cereals are the prescribed amount of bride price in case of an arranged marriage, it goes upto 3-15 or even more number of cattle and cereal weighing about a quintal or so in case of a capture marriage. However, *the amount depends upon the nature and severity of the capture made by the groom's party.*

One of the most important features of Bonda marriage, as mentioned earlier, is that an elderly woman aging about 20-25 years-old marries a boy of about only 7-10 years-old thereby maintaining an age gap of approximately 13-15 years and takes the responsibility to make her child husband young out of her own effort in economic pursuits. And in turn, the boy welcomes the responsibility of looking after his wife when she become old welcomes the responsibility much earlier than himself due to maintenance of long age gap between them. This is why such a long age gap is maintained between them. This is why such a long age gap is maintained between the spouses for becoming economically helpful to each other during their deserted period, i.e, old - age of the wife and childhood of the husband. But unfortunately, *in many cases, the old wives cannot avail the support of their husbands during their old-age* as the men hardly survive after their late forties due to high frequencies of homicidal offenses among themselves. However, *the wife acts as the guardian of her husband, especially when her husband is a child.* The child-husband feels to be a subordinate to her wife at the initial stage because of his ignorance on life. They start *conjugal* life only when the *child-husband becomes physically mature or suitable to have sex.* Thus, it can be concluded that at the initial years of marriage, a Bonda husband treats his wife as a motherly person and fears her as a guardian and then accepts her as his wife only when he become physically mature and understands his role as a husband.

Birth Ritual

Couvade is not practiced, but the husband observes certain restrictions regarding his food taboos and his movement outside the village during the pregnancy of his wife. As bareness is not tolerated either by the wife or the husband, a child irrespective of sex is highly intended, but the birth of a female child is more joyful. Because, culturally *she bears high economic importance over a boy child.* Hair cutting ceremony is observed when the child attains 3 years of age, but ear lobing, which is a must, is held during infancy. The name giving ceremony is not strictly observed and the names given to the children are based on the days in which they are born. So, names of either sexes are confined to only seven possibilities and thus, identical names are very common with a number of members of a family. For example if a male baby takes birth on *Somabara* or Monday his name bacomes *Soma* which turns to be *Somabari* for a girl child. Like-wise, the names become *Mangala* and *Munguli* for a boy and a girl respectively if they are born on *Mangalbara* or Tuesday. Similarly, the names for a boy and a girl would be *Buda* and *Budi*, *Guru* or *Gurubari* or *Laxmi*, *Sukra* and *Sukri*, *Sania* and *Sanaki*, *Adior Hadi* and *Adibari*, if they taken birth on *Budhabara* or wednesday, *Gurubara* or Thursday, *Sukrabara* or Friday, *Sanibara* or saturday, and *Rabibara* or Sunday, respectively.

Death Rituals

Cropses are *cremated* and the ritual impurity continues for *ten days*. On the second day of the death, the wife of the deceased person goes to the cremation ground to ascertain whether the death is natural or due to some other reason like, *sorcery*. She ascertains the possibilities by hammering a piece of bone from the pyre with a pebble. If the bone brittles, the death is considered normal, if not, due to *sorcery* and when it is concluded that the death is due to *sorcery*, the cuplrit is tried to be found out through *magico-shamanistic* ways and is made punished either through severe revengious *black magical* and *sorceric ways* of high importance of through the village council where the culprit is supposed to give penalty the village council where the culprit is supposed to give penalty - preferably cows, to the wife of the deseased.

It is a general practice among the Bonda people to sacrifice a cow (preferably an old one, which is invalid and therefore useless for agricultural purpose) on the tenth-day of death ritual of an adult member. If the dead has only one, who is supposed to observe the rite but does not won a cow or is unable to purchase the same for performing the rite, he is granted some months, upto a year or two if the kins who are related by *Soru brotherhood* (a socio-religious bond among the Bonda within or outside their own village) permit him. Within that stipulated period, the concerned person is expected to perform the ritual where in the *Soru-Brothers* are given a feast. If the person, is unable to arrange the feast within the period sanctioned by the *Soru-brothers*, he may contract a loan from any one of his community members and for this he may become a bonded labour (cf. Mohanty, 1996: 110-111).

Food

The Bondas are very fond of red ants, and even more fond of date-plam grubs. The dung beetle, silkworm and rats are also eaten with keen interest and enthusiasm. Though they do not take milk or milk products, they consume beef and even stale carcasses of a day or two and like to have semi-roasted games. Sacrifice of a cow, which is required for almost all the *ritualistic* and *shamanistic* observances, is a day-to-day activity. So, when a cow is sacrificed and as the beef cannot be consumed in a day by the family members, it is preserved just above the hearth and consumed piece by piece until it comes to an end.

Both the men and women are very fond of *sago-plam juice* (Sapung) and other country liquors (*Sagur*) which they brew out of different fruits like mango (*Uli*), jackfruit (*Unkusuin*) and banana (*Unsungdak*); berries like, amla (*Singer*), dete-plam (*Bulura*), and blackberry (*Idra*) and from flowers like, mahua (*Bawh*). They also prepare country bear (*Pendum*) from flowers like, mahua (*Bawh*). They also prepare country bear (*Pendum*) from different cereals like rice (*Kerang*), millet (*Same*), maize (*Makah*) and other locally available cereals, like, rice (*Kerang*), millet (*Same*), maize (*Makah*) and other locally available cereals like *Khankadaki, rigdar* and *widar.* It is very important to mention here that the Bonda infants are also fed with different country liquors as milk is fed among the children of the plain people and, thus, a Bonda is habituated to drinking since its childhood and even from mother's womb as consumption of liquor irrespective of sex in a important aspect in their daily food habit.

Occupation

The Bondas are unusually a self-sufficient community (Elwin: 1950:) and they never like to come down the hills to interact with the plains people, their economy is primarily of subsistence type that includes practice of crude methods of sweden cultivation, food gathering and hunting combined with paddy cultivation in few available terraces. They also rear cattle, pigs and poultry and grow fruit bearing trees, like, mango (*Uli*), jackfruit (*Unkusuin*), tamarind (*Titim*) in their village sites.

Barter system is preponderant over cash economy. Salt and dry chillies are the most important marketable items. They procure these commodities from the external markets like Khairiput, Mathili and even very distant markets namely Malkangiri, a walk of about 50 kilometers in the jungle. They get these provisions in exchange of blacksesame (*Alsi*) and some indigenous variety of cereals and pulse crops produced in their swiddens.

Agricultural and hunting implements constitute the most important and valuable household materials. Musical implements are also considered equally important and valuable items, but these are possessed by a very few households. However, bows and arrows are considered as the vary important personal assets at the individual level, for which a Bonda man may kill a person, no matter, whether he goes to jail or leaves the earth. Traditionally, whenever, he goes out of his home, he takes a bunch of arrows in his grip with the bow hanging by his shoulder and a sharp knife (*unsunk*) hanging behind his back. He turns very furious when he seen any person climbing his sago-palm tree for its juice without his knowledge. In that case, immediately, he lifts up his bow, aims and shoots down the thief. If he is counter-attacked, he shoots to kill. All the while, he makes a lot of noise and remain silent only when he takes out the encroacher's lever, which it is said that the Bonda were once eating in the remote past (ibid: 117).

Religion

The Bondas are primarily animistic. At the some time they are also Hinduistic. But they go against some of the strict norms of Hindu religion, like consumption of beef. They Bondas cannot think of their existence without this.

As mentioned earlier, the *Patkhanda Mahaprabhu*, the prime Hindu deity of the Bondas, is worshipped in a great banyan tree in the form of a sword which they call the sword of a hero of *Ramayan*. Sun and moon are worshipped with a number of *demi-gods* presiding over different streams, forests, swiddens, villages, homes, etc. who are thought to be responsible to create ups as the intermediaries between such *supernatural powers* and human beings. Furies and ghosts of the recently deads are considered as malevolent entities who are responsible for crop failures. They destruct village settlements, kill domestic animals and create diseases among the family members in order to cool down their outrage. So, the Bondas fear such ghosts and furies and do not go out of the home in night, if however, they go, they go in groups by singing songs to ward off those beings of the unseen world. The demigods who are believed to reside in jungles, strems, swiddens, etc. are worshipped in different shrines, mainly at the *Sindibor*, the meglithic stone platform of menhir like stone slabs located in each village, where the important religious rites are carried on.

The Bondas consider different malevolent deities to be the cause of different diseases and have deep faith in their indigenous practices for curing such ailments through shamanistic ways, which however, very often proves to be unsuitable. And since the Bonda are self-sufficient and allopathic in nature, they never like to come down the hills to avail the modern medical facilities even when they suffer from very serious illness or health hazards.

Political Organisation

Law and order are maintained in the society through the village functionaries. In each clan there is a head called *Munda* who is responsible to solve minor cases relating to the members of his group. However, the cases relating to homicidal offence, adultery, divorce, land, crop etc. are referred to the *Munda of Badnaik* clan who acts as secular headman of the village and enforces law and order in the society. He conducts the trials of social offence at the *Sindibor*. He is assisted by the *Kirsani Munda* and sub-assisted by the *Chalan Munda*. All these functionaries enjoy hereditary positions. But they can be removed from their chairs by consensus if found unsuitable.

For the Bonda, the problems of survival is increasing from day-to-day. heavy denudation, though, has caused these people agrarian, the yield they get from agriculture is very meager which cannot substitute the produces they were collecting from the local forests a few decades ago. This cause an alarming starvation, malnutrition, transhumance, increasing debt bondage syndrome and over consumption of country liquor that very often leads to increasing number of *homicidal offence*. However, all these problems for survival can best be solved through creation of agro forestry with usufruct right under social forest schemes, but, however, a through study of their whole social system be first studied before an action plan is prepared for them and the palm must be based on their socio-cultural values and customary norms with whom they are familiar and well acquainted, otherwise such plans may not be successful.

❑ ❑ ❑

REFERENCE

Elwin, V. (1945): "The Bonda Murderers" Man in India, vol.XXV, No1, Ranchi.

Elwin, V. (1950): Bonda Highlanders, Oxford, Oxford University press.

Hutton, J.H. (1935): "Bondo paraga". Tour Note of the Census Commissioner for India, Census of India-1931, Vol-1, India Part-III, Simla.

Hutton, J.H. (1951): Bonda Paraga", Caste in India, Bombay: Blossary.

Mahapatra, L.K. (1992): Model Feasibility Survey in Bonda Hills. Koraput District, for Extensive Terracing and Alternate land use Modules for Rehabilitation of shifting cultivators Insitu, (Project Report) Bhubaneswar: NKC Center for Development Studies.

Mahapatra, Krishna. (1977): "The Bondas Today: Introductory Ramarks" Research Proceedings vol. 5, No. 122 Delhi: Dept of Anthropology, D.U.

Mahapatra, L.K. & R.P. Mohanty (1997): Development insitu of the Hill Swiddeners: A Case Study of the Bonds in Orissa (Project Report), Bhubaneswar: NKC Center for Development Studies.

Mohanty, R.P. (1992): "Beliefs & Practices Associated with Liquor Preparation among the Bonda Highlanders" in Man & Life, vol. 18, No.1 & 2, Calcutta: ISRAA.

Mohanty, R.P. (1993): (a)"Profile of Bonded Labour system in India with special reference to an allopatric Tribal Community of Orissa, Vision, Vol. XI, No.3 & 4, Bhubaneswar, JNISES.

Mohanty, R.P. (1995): "Bonda" Encyclopedic Profile of Indian Tribes, New Delhi: Discovery.

Mohanty, R.P. (1996): Bonda Highlanders of Orissa - A Socio-Cultural Profile, Fourth World Vol-4, Bhubaneswar: NISWASS.

Mohanty, U.C. (1963): "Bonda", Adivasi, Vol. No.3, Bhubaneswar: THRTI.

Patnaik, N. (1984): Bondas and their Response to Development Bhubaneswar, THRTI.

14. Nanda, B.N., 1994 Contours of Continuity and Change - The Story of Bonda Highlanders, New Delhi: Sage.

BOT

Dr. Prakash Chandra Mehta

Bot, or as they are also commonly known, *Boto or Botpa*, are found in *Kadakh* area of Jammu and Kashmir. Located at a height of 10,000 to 12,000 feet above sea level, Ladakh is surrounded on the north by the Great Karakorram ranges and on the sough by the Great Himalayan ranges. The area actually forms an extension of the Tibetan plateau. Cut off by the two high rising mountain ranges there is absence of humid air resulting in desert like condition in the area. Hardly any greenery is visible in the vast stretches of this desert mountains, except near the river banks. Climate is extreme wintry and rainfall very scanty. Understanding the ecological setting of this isolated part of the country is vital to understanding the people who reside in Ladakh.

Introducing the identity of the people of Ladakh, Cunningham (1964, 19) observed that "Ladak is inhabited by a peculiar race of people, who call themselves *Bot-pa* (the name is spelt Bod, but pronounced Bot), who speak a peculiar language called Tibetan, and who profess the religion of Buddha, under a peculiar hierarchy of monks called *Lamas*. The name of Tibet is entirely unknown to the people as well as to the Indians, who call them *Bhotiyas* and their country Bhutan. The use of the names of *Bot* and *Bhutan* is not probably older than the tenth or twelfth century, when the Buddhists, having been expelled from India, the hill country in which they settled the Buddhists, having been expelled from India, the hill country in which they settled naturally acquired the name of Bauddhasthan or Bauddhthan, and *Bod-tan or Bot*".

In Kashmir (Gauhar and Gauhar: n.d.) they have long been known as *Bhutias* or *Botas* and their land as Botun. They belong to the same racial stock as Tibetants and closely resemble them in features. *Boti* is the name of the language and *Bot* for people (Dalton: 1978 Reprint, pp 95-100: Crooke: 1974:II:61-63).

Bot are numerically and politically the most dominant member of the ethnic groups found in Ladakh. Their total population is about 75,000 constituting about 40% of the total population of Ladakh. Due to inhospitable terrain and lack of agricultural land, the Bot villages are very sparsely distributed forming clusters wherever opportunities exist for settlement. They occupy land in Leh area by the banks of the great Indus river which flows through the valley before vanishing into Pakistan. They are also found in large numbers in *Nubra* valley, the *Zanskar* valley, and in small numbers in *Purig* and other valleys and foothils of Ladakh. They speak a dialect known as *Ladakhi*, which has been classified by Grierson as *Bhotia*.

The Bot have history of migration from Central Tibet. It is believed that they have migrated in different waves at different points of time settling in the valleys where scarce water could be located. In course of time these migrants were known and identified by the valley names. Thus *Nubrapa*, ('Pa' meaning of) refers to *Bot of Nubra* valley. Zanskarpa, Rongpa, Stodpa etc., also represent Bot residents of these areas. The Bot migrants had also spread to other areas of Ladakh, as far as *Skardu* and *Kargil*.

Bot are Mongolian by race, and like the Tibetans are Buddhist by religion. They share same cultural values as those found in Tibet and in spite of the great distance their temporal matters are still controlled by the monks of Lhasa. Their Buddhism however, rests lightly on them, as they continue to remain faihful and loyal to their early primitive religion (*bon chos*) in which the spirits (*lhas*) and serpents (*lhus*) control their day-to-day life. The form Mahayana Buddhism of Tibet as introduced by *Padma Sabhava* from India which blends both the great religion Buddhism with the everyday belief in the spirits and ghosts, remains their religion today. Governed by inhospitable terrain, harsh climate, lack of economic opportunities, the Bot is surviving by the dictates of their religion and overlordship of the monasteries (gompa).

The Bot society is divided into two different classes, the *Rigzang* or the upper class and the *mangrik*, or the common gentry. *Rigzang* comprises of the *Gyal-rig*, or the class to which the king belongs and the *zering*. or the class of noble men. Though today the concept of the King, the nobles and the gentry or the subject has lost relevance, the descendants of the *rigzang* continue to adhere to the titles to show their heritage and pristine glory. The common Bot stil offers full respect to the decedents of the king and other functionaries.

The *Mangriks* constitute the majority of the Bot society, the rigzang being only a few in number. Rigzang comprised of such functionaries as *Klon* (prime minister), *Lonpo* (ministers), *Amchi* (medicine-man), *Trakshos* (royal dancers) etc. *Mangrik*, on the other hand included the peasants and the herdsmen and constituted the economic backbone of the society. Besides there are such functionaries as *Onpo* (astrologer), host of high and low order lamas. In Ladakh, there is also a third class who provide service to the Bot society. They are known as *Mon, Garra* and *Beda*. They serve the Bots in various functions and are looked down by the former.

The Bot society is not organised on the basis of clan or any other similar structure. The primary unit of their society is the family. They have a concept of *khangchen* (or ancestral house) which owns the property and where the *chotkang* (place of worship) and the *Ihato* are situated. The head of the household, usually the eldest son resides in the *Khangchen* and is recognised by the Bot society as the head of the social kin group comprising mainly the immediate blood relatives.

Bot is very important to keep in view the ecological condition existing in the area. Due to lack of rain, and the existence of desert like condition land for cultivation is extremely scarce. Besides, the onset of early winter and its continuance for more than nine months a year, leaves very little time for agriculture. As a result agricultural land is held as extremely precious, and is not believed to be divisible. Those who have extra hands, or those who could be spared during lean agricultural period, are engaged in tending livestock and collection of freewood. These two activities are extremely important for any household, as whithout, as without the butter, milk, frozen meat, frozen curd, and fire wood it would be impossible to survive through the severe winter. Both agriculture and tending livestock or collection of firewood are, therefore, vital to a Bot.

Based on the cardinal principle of indivisibility of agricultural land Bot society has adopted a social system which seems suitable to their ecology and need for survival. In Bot society the developmental cycle of the domestic group begins with sometime it is customary for the father to move out of the *Khangchen* along with his unmarried children to a small house outside leaving the ancestral house, the properties to the eldest son, who by tradition is only allowed to inherit property. In case however, for a small family the parents may stay together. Due to suh harsh conditions, it becomes difficult for younger brothers to get married and setup their domestic group. From childhood, based on behavioural compatibility the parents motivate one of their sons to join the ranks of the lamas, first as trainees at about eight or nine year of their age, to later as full fledged lama (monk) staying in *gompa*. When the eldest son is married, one of the immediate brothers is also motivated to stay with him in an arrangement of polyandrous union. Accepting one brother as second husband by the wife on the elder brother is quite an acceptable social norm. Similarly while the eldest daughter is given away in marriage she takes along with her all the valuable jewelleries, most important being *perek*, head gear studded with precious gems, like turquoises etc., which were brought by her mother. As arranged marriage is very expensive, it becomes difficult for the younger daughters to get married is very expensive, it becomes or are married by capture. For respectable families, earlier the tradition was to send the younger daughter as *nun* (*chomo*) to the local monastery to be engaged in the service of God. There is also the system of *magpa*, wherein the husband moves to wife's family and stays there permanently. This option is resorted to by a Bot when he has no son and one or more daughters. Instead of marrying off the daughter, it is customary to bring in a husband and hand over all property to him in course of time. Younger sisters of the wife also share the husband in this system of polgynous marriage. All sisters stay together with *magpa* in their own *khangchen* as one domestic unit. In case of polyandrous marriage the eldest brother is the socially recognised father all their children.

A few members of the different *khangchnes* living in the vicinity constitute the second important social group known as *Phosphoon*. Structurally *Phosphoon* is a king of association of member with eight to ten khangchen, related or unrelated, bound together by a feeling or brotherhood emerging from their acceptance and worship of a common tutelar deity, (*or lha*). Members of *Phosphoon*, stay together through the harsh climate of Ladakh helping each other by right and tradition on all important occasions like birth, marriage and death. Every *Phosphoon* has a leader (*lardak dakpo*) who keeps the tutelar deity in his house. All members of the *Phosphoon* assemble once a month to pay respect to the *Ihato* (deity's abode) under the direction of a lama. Till recently *Phosphoon* is an exogamous unit. In interior parts of Ladakh, for instance, in *Zanskar*, it is still considered incestuous to marry within the *Phosphoon*.

Agriculture is the mainstay of Bot economy. Due to shortage of available land every Bot tries to cultivate every inch of land they have. They begin work as soon as the snow starts melting using all the manpower they have. Most of them own about 0.5 to 1 hectare of land. Some also own grazing land and fallow for growing grass. Before embarking upon important stages of agricultural operations propitiation of important deties is common, Grim, barley and wheat are the chief crops grown. The snow melted water is canalised to irrigate the field which at times is rather a difficult and arduous process. menfolk perform the arduous tasks, the women undertaking comparatively lighter work, like weeding. *Shupla* is the most important religious rite performed by Bot before harvesting. Organised at village level by Lama, the village and tutelary deities are propitiated jointly for bumper harvest. Similar propitiation is done at family level also. Both men and women jointly reap the harvest. Land in Ladakh is not very fertile. As a result the crops produced is hardly sufficient to keep body and soul together.

Bot rear a number of livestock to augment their income or for use in agricultural operations. They keep such animals as *yak, dzo* (hybrid or yak and cow or their progenies), cow, pony, horse, donkey, sheep and goat. A Bot has to be extra careful to tend these animals through the severe winter. Ponies and yak are used as pack animals to transport merchandise from one place to another using the mountainous tracks. Earlier Leh lied on the Silk Route from Srinagar to Leh. Bot would carry goods, like salt, iron, pashm, wool, spices, etc., upto the Changthang area and bringing back silk. copper and other necessary items, Bot would rarely slaughter an animal unless faced with starvation. They use wool from sheep to make garments, yak and goat hair are used to make blanket and carpet; *cow,dzo dzomo* (female dzo) as draft animals.

The Bot are Budhist by religion. They follow Lamaism or Tibetan Buddhism, a form of Mahayana Buddhism incorporating the tantrik or mysticism elements. Prior to the advent of Buddhism they had complete faith in *bon religion* of Tibet. It revolved around propitiating devil, ghosts, spirits and a host of *Ihas* and *Ihus*. Buddhism prevalent in Tibet incorporated these mystic and mythological elements into classical Buddhism and made it acceptable to the society. As a result Bot revere Lord Buddha as their supreme deity and has accepted the overlordship of monastery. In every day life, however, the *Ihas* and the *Ihis dominate their life*. The *Iha* are spirits which moves from one place to another and controls the destiny of every Bot. *Ihu*, on the other hand, are believed to be serpents who reside in earth or spring and must be propitiated. Both are considered extermely malevolent and unless appropriately propitiated bring destruction to the family. Every family has a *Iha* as it tutelary deity. The phosphoon, and the village as a whole also have separate *Ihas*.

Bot society which remained cut off from the outside world till the

Chinese aggression, is witnessing tremendous change in all fornts. Their traditional value system is giving way to the modern concepts. With the advent of foreigh tourists army, govt officials, traders and modern means of communication, Bot society is witnessing new dynamism. They have taken to fromal education, business and trade, and are in a position to travel to other parts of India when severe winter sets in. Polyandrous marriages are avoided, in the younger generation opting for monogamous marriages setting up nucelar families. With new economic opportunities becoming available a Bot has not longer to depend upon the scarce agricultural land for survival. Even the younger brothers now hope to setup their own famileis as the rigours of traditional social system do not manifest itself as rigidly as in the past.

❑ ❑ ❑

BUGUN

Dr. Prakash Chandra Mehta

Bugun, also known popularly as *Khowa*, are a small, but important tribe of West Kameng district of Arunanchal Pradesh. According to 1981 Census they had a population of 625 persons.

Regarding origin of the tribe, it is believed that they have originated from a single group called *'Achinpimbu'*, In course of time this group developed into an endogamous group. They are divided into various clans which are exogamous in nature.

Bugun or Khowa are Mongoloid by race. They are fair complexioned, well built and have short to medium height. It is customary for males to tie their in *a knot* at the top of the head.

They live in long houses which are usually 25 to 30 metre in length and only 4 to 5 metre in breadth. The house is erected on a raised bamboo platform and do not have any room or partition within the structure. The walls are made of bamboo split and the roof is covered with banana leaves.

Agricultural is the mainstay of Bugun economy. They practice shifting cultivation on the hill slopes. In this type of shifting cultivation. Known as *jhum*, the slash and burn technique is used. They cultivate in the land for three to four years. The land is then allowed to remain fallow for three to four years to regain fertility. During this time they move to another plot returning back to the original plot after three four years. This sometimes results in splitting of the original village group.

Every Bugun household keep livestock. Cow, horse, pig, goat, fowl, are the usual livestock. A few household also keep the important animal *Mithum*.

Bugun are Buddhist by religion. They have a village council to settle their family and all local disputes.

❑ ❑ ❑

DAMOR

Dr. Prakash Chandra Metha

The Damor are a small tribe. They migrated from Gujarat state and are largely located in the Simalwara Block of Dungarpur of Rajasthan adjoining Gujarat. The Damors have a population of 31.337 (1981).

The Damors of the border of Gujarat and Rajasthan in the district of Dungarpur speak Gujarati of mixed from. A majority of them speak *Vagri* which is local dialect spoken by rest of the population of Dungarpur district.

The Damor are taken to be a branch of the Bhils. The identity of Damors is largely due to habitation and forming interior villages on hills bordering Gujarat from where they migrated Damor in the state of Rajasthan have been demarcated a separate identity like Damors.

Damors also called Damarias and have no sub-groups.

Clans (Moieties)

Damors have two moieties. One upper Damor and other lower Damor. Both groups treat themselves superior but marital relations are restricted between them. Both the groups are ecogamous and have their own clans.

Most of the clans have similarity with Rajputs clans. They believe that their ancestors were Rajputs and due to some social sin, they were debared from the caste and fallen into group of tribals.

Damors prefer nuclear family in which father mother and unmarried sons and daughters live together. Generally parents prefer to live with their youngest married son. Joint family is rare. They are patrilineal and partilocal.

Birth Rituals

In the Damors first delivery generally takes place in the house of girl's parents. The succeeding deliveries take place in the house of parents or at their own house. An elderly women of the family acts as midwife. Usually the period of confinement is limited to twelve days after the delivery. On the twelfth day the mother worships the sun with her relative and neighbours known as *"Huraj Puja"*. Sister of the husband has specific role to play after the birth of the child.

Namkaran

The Damors invite Brahmin to perform the Namkaran ceremony. This ceremony is performed after the third of fourth month of the birth of the child. The role of the *Bhuva* is important in the name giving. Damor usually name the child on the basis of week days or after ancestors or totems.

Mundan

Like high caste Hindus *Mundan* ceremony is observed among the Damors. Generally the *Bhuva* accepts the hair of the new born. In this ceremony. *Bhuva*, presents cloths to the infant. Such presents are also given by relatives.

Marriage rituals

When there is no male child in the family, a husband may either be permitted to marry another women or to adopt brother's or sister's son. Sometimes son-in-laws can also be accepted as successor.

The marriage age varies between 12 to 15 years, both in case of male and female. The negative checks are clan exogamy, sapinda restriction i.e. there is no preference for cross cousin or parallel cousin marriage, they can not marry out of Damor tribe and a boy can marry a *Bhagat* or *non-Gnagat Damor* irrespective of his category of orientation. *Dapa* or bride price has to be paid for marriage.

Polygyny does not exists in this tribal group, but exceptions can be seen. Pre-marital relations are not permitted in the society. In case of deviation of this rule, the offenders have been punished. The proposal for marriage is initiated by the parents of the boys. The instances of marriage by elopement can be seen. Generally marriage is performed by a *Brahmin priest* on Hindu pattern. Usually, after marriage the spouses live in a separate house.

Widow marriage is prevalent among Damors, Generally levirate marriage is popular. If the husband younger brother refused to marry with his *Bhabhi*, then the widow can marry with other person of her choice. In widow marriage *Dapa* is also taken by bride father. The window marriage is arranged in a simple manner.

Divorce is permitted in this tribal group, Husband and wife both can seek divorce, Husband wishing to seek divorce is allowed, but bound to compensate bride price to his wife. This *Jagda* is settled by the *Panch* of *Jati Panchayat*. If the divorce is sought by wife no compensation is paid. In such a matter no *Jagda* is taken for divorce.

Death rituals

The dead body is cremated among Damors. The dead body of a child or that of a person died by smallpox is buried. thirteen days of mourning is observed. In the mourners house no food is cooked, food and drinks are supplied by near kin to the family. The first ten days after death is observed as pollution period. On the 13th day the members of the tribe assemble at the residence of deceased person and turban tieing ceremony is observed and a feast also given to guests. The eldest son of the deceased also gets turban called as *Sora-Pagdi* from the villagers, which is sign of his recognition for succession. In Damors ashes are dispersed in holy rivers or nearby ponds according to their economic status.

Occupation

The Damor economy is largely based on agricultural. Generally, they have 3 to 4 bigha of land. The quality of land is poor. In hard times they go for labour. Out of working force 95.21 per cent were engaged in agriculture and rest of population in other occupations. Lack of education and poor agricultural techniques have kept the Damor economy largely to a stage of subsistence.

Religion

With the passage of time the Damor have accepted Hindu god and goddesses. Some of their deities are of local importance. These are *Kairing Mata. Kandia Mata. Dhuli Mata* and *Kalka Mata.* The Hindu gods worshipped are *Mahadeo. Genesh, Rama Krishna, Ganga* and *Ranchodji.* They also worship *Khatri Mata* of Gujarat and sacrifice animal to her at the time of any epidemic among the cattle. This deity also assists in curing snake-bite.

In many ways Damors have been Hinduised by the impact of *Bhagat* movement on their social life. The *Bhagat* Damors do not eat any thing before bath. After bath, they offer prayers to their *Guru* and Hindu god, specially *Ram* and *Krishna.* They also observe fast on certain days. Bhagat Damors are strictly vegetarian and they do not take alcoholic drink.

Fairs and Festivals

Most of the fairs and festivals of Damors are the fairs and festivals of the High caste Hindus. The mode of celebration of festivals are similar of high caste Hindus. They do not have any special fair and festival as their own.

Social Organisation (Traditional Panchayat)

In matter like out-casting a member, dispute over an extra martial relation, question pertaining to the formulations of reformation in the tribal organisations and feasts as part of social punishment are some of the main functions of the Tribal Inter-village organisation consisting of 80 village.

The Damor traditional panchayat can be seen at the level of clan and village. As the clan level, minor disputes pertaining to marriage and bride price are brought. The head or chief of the Panchayat is known as *Mukhi* like the *Patel.* The village panchayat is usually convened to decide cases of development, land disputes, criminal cases, etc. The post of *Mukhis* is hereditary. Now the cases are lodged in the law court, hence the power of traditional panchayats are decaying and their importance is dwindling.

Bhagat movement has effected their social life. They are fully vegetarian and do not take liquor. The development programmes have effected their social life. With development programmes, their economic condition has been improved to some extent. Effect of Urbanisation can also be seen on their social life. Their socio-economic life is changing.

❏ ❏ ❏

REFERENCES

Vyas, N.N. Damors (1967) : A Border Tribe of Rajasthan. Tribe ed. Vol. IV (1). June 1967, Tribal Research Institute and Training Centre. Rajasthan. Udaipur. p. 15-16.
Mehta, Prakash Chandra (1993) : Bharat-ke-Adivasi - A Socio-economic analysis. Shiva Publishers Distributors. Udaipur.
Mann. R.S. (1966) : Some aspects of cultural life of Damors, Vanyajati, Vol. XIV (2). April 1966. p. 76.

JUANGAS - I

Ramesh Prasad Mohanty

The Juangas, one of the most primitive tribal communities of Orissa, are largely concentrated in the districts of Keonjhar and Dhenkanal constituting 97.29 per cent of their total population of 30,876 (1981). They inhabit the contiguous hill ranges of high peaks extending from west Keonjhar to Pallahara of Dhenkanal and its adjoining areas which covers in the "Central Hill-belt of India". (Mc Dougal, 1963:1).

While the district of Keonjhar is located in the northern part of the State of Orissa between 20°1' N and 22°10' N latitude and 88-11' E and 86°22' E longitude 20°29' N and 21°41' N latitude and 84°16' E and 86°20' E longitude with an area of 1,082.70 sq. kms.

The Juang people belong to the proto-Australoid racial stock and speak a South *Mundari* dialect, specific only to themselves. They call themselves as *'Juang'*, meaning, *man'* who are otherwise known as *Pattoas* by the neighboring communities, meaning the 'people of leaf dress'; the women were wearing leaf dress a few decades ago.

The Juangs are divided into two sub-tribes known as *Thaniyas* or the people of the original Juang-land, and *Bhagudias* or the excommunicated Juangs of the past who have fled away from their homeland and settled in Dhenkanal area. Thus, the Thaniyas consider themselves superior to the *Bhagudias* and their tradition persists in its purest form due to geographical isolation of their habitat from the plains. On the other hand, the *Bhagudias,* who, otherwise claim their superiority over the *Thaniyas* due to their being highly acculturated with Hindustic ideology, are not regarded much by the *Thaniyas.*

The Juang belt of *Thaniyas* is confined to Keonjhar district and is known as *Juang-pirhs* or Juang-country which is sub-divided into four sub-pirhs of exogamous territorial units, namely *Jharkhand, Satkhand, Rebena* and *Kathus.* The people of *Jharkhand-pirh* consider themselves to be the first in the ladder of social hierarchy of all the sub-pirhs due to their inaccessive settlement with very minimal level of change in their traditional cultural values.

SOCIAL DIVISION

Each sub-tribe is divided into a number of totemistic exogamous clans or Bok named after grains, trees, animals or birds and places. Mc Dougal notes 18 clans based on all these four categories, namely, *Banim, Barum, Dumuria, Dwarsunia, Gungi, Hatishilia, Kundui, Liom Nachim, Panasanasia, Rodua, Samana, Sara, Sarom, Sayn, Synytem Tangar-Paria* and *Temerem* (1963:433-444).

In Keonjhar, the villages are mostly of uniclan in nature for which marrying within the clan or village is considered as incestuous thereby indicating the practice of both clan as well as village exogamy. Thus the members of one clan or village are thought to be consanquines, who are referred to as *Kutumb* (consanquines), and they refer to th affine as *Bandhu* - only with whom spouses can be exchanged. Hence the Juangs have two type of villages namely *Kutumb* (consanquinal) village and *Bandhu* (affinal) village.

The institution of kinship in Juang society is based on descent and marriage. By descent, one person is related to all his consanguines and by marrying he is equally related to his affines. They use both classificatory and descriptive kinship are prevalent among themselves. While joking relationship exists between a man and his elder brother's wife, a man and his mother's or father's father, a man and his wife's younger sister, a woman and her brother's wife's brother and a woman and her husband's younger brother through dialogue, metaphors and allegories; avoidance is very strictly observed between a woman and her husband's elder brother, a man and his wife's elder sister which are stereotypic in nature.

Though patrilineality, patriarchy and patrilocality are the rules of descent, inheritance of property, authority and residence, female voice is not neglected due to their high economic importance. However, in religious matters the women are least associated.

The Juang family is a significant co-residential, corporate unit with economic, ritual, socio-cultural and political affairs. It is considered as a *jural unit,* i.e. considering a single legal personality which is based on large families of bonds between father and son or that between full brothers are the ideal. The average mean size of 189 households of *Gonasika* area is found to be 4.18 and the family types are mainly of four types' viz, (i) extended (ii) nuclear (iii) sub-nuclear, and (iv) broken.

Each village is characterized by the presence of youth dormitories

(Majang) located at the centre of the village, where the unmarried boys (Kangeriki) sleep after initiation and both the boys and girls learn *Changu* dance, one of the most important characteristic features of this tribe. Most often, this tribe is known after this *changu* dance.

There is a separate dormitory for girls called *Melabasa* or *Dhangidibasa*. "However, the *Dhangidibasa* is not a feminine counter-part of the *Majang* as it lacks special associations paralleling those associated with the latter" (ibid: 190).

The dancing visits relating to mate selection are only exchanged between the *Bandhu* villages as any type of sex relationship is considered as incestuous (*Begudang*) among the members of *Kutumb* villages or clan members.

Life Cycle Marriage

Mainly, there are five type of primary marriage forms prevalent among the Juangs. In order of frequencies these are: **(i) Marriage by** capture (*Digar kania*) (ii) arranged marriage (*Gotang kania*) (iii) marriage by payment (*Tonkayoti*) (iv) love marriage without elopement (*Monamani*), and (v) marriage by elopement (*Dhoripara*). The child marriage (*Wadikania*) which was practiced before a couple of decades, has lost its importance in the present days.

Though monogamy is the rule, polygyny is not absent. Both junior sorority and junior levirate are practiced.

As bareness is never tolerated either by the husband or by the wife herself, procreation of a child irrespective of sex is highly intended, but birth of a male child is more valued even though both have equal economic importance. This is because a male child is more useful in day-to-day life and also during old-age of the parents.

Birth

While a midwife (*Satruani*) assists for easy delivery, the medicine man or the shaman (*Raulia*) is consulted in difficult cases. The period of ritual impurity in child birth varies from one to six days in different villages. The mother can take her ritual bath for purification just after the day of delivery in Keonjhar district, but in Dhenkanal it is six days after which the mother becomes ritually pure.

Naming Ceremony

The name giving ceremony (*Nimicha*) is performed either on the sixth or seventh day of delivery. The name of the father's father or father's brother is preferred for a male baby, but the name of father's sister of father's mother is the ideal one for a female one. However, a number of children are found with the names of different trees, flowers, birds, beasts and the days of the week.

Mundan

Hair cutting for boys and ear and nose piercing for girls are not associated with any ritual among the Juangs of Keonjhar area, which, however, are associated with rituals in Dhenkanal area. This happens primarily because the Juangs of Dhenkanal are juxtaposed with many Hindu communities and hence, are observed to have assimilated with such communities.

Death Rituals

It is though that death occurs mainly due to evil effects of the spirits and when a death occurs, the news is immediately spread out among the consanguine and relatives through loud wailing of family members. The corpses are cremated in normal cases, but buried in suicidal, snake bite, murder and labour pain cases. The ritual pollution period continues only for 2 days in case of the Juangs of Keonjhar district, but it lasts for about 11 days for the Juangs of Dhenkanal area because of their adoption of Hindustic cultural traits.

Economy

The Juangs of Keonjhar area mostly carry on sweden cultivation and are in the pre-agricultural level of technology and those living in Dhenkanal area are agrarian in nature who have also taken to basketry as their main source of income. In Keonjhar, the crops, chiefly sesamum and mustard which are produced in swiden plots and hill slopes, have higher yield and grater market value than the paddy produced in scantily available terraces.

Only the fruit bearing trees like mango, jackfruit, tamarind, etc. are domesticated at sweden plots and around the edges of the village only when these are individually owned. Their diet is greatly supplemented by fruits, roots and tubers collected from the local forests. They depend on this source for a long period of a year subject to ritual restrictions. And large game animals are almost always hunted communally if available.

The Juangs of either sex are very much addicted to different country liquors and beer (mada) prepared out *Mahua* flower, *sago-plam, date-plam*, rice, maize, and other indigenous cereals, like, *akogang, kasola, jinjozi*, etc.

As earlier said, sesamum and mustard are the major produce with greater market value, these are primarily used for barter purpose in the markets like Janghira, Suakati, Kenjhar, Telkoi, etc for obtaining paddy, livestock, clothes, pottery, axe and arrow heads, and salt which are not abundantly available in their internal economy. Crops are also sometimes converted into cash economy required for transaction with the far away external economy.

In the north-western peripheries, the Juang-pirhs are juxtaposed with the Bhuyan-pirh, another numerically major primitive tribal group of Orissa. But since the *Bhuyans* consider the Juangs as untouchable, the interaction in almost all shears between these two groups is very minimal. *Bathudia* and *Gonds,* though are the other two adjacent communities of the Juangs, they do not interact remarkably with the Juangs. However, the milkmen (*Gauda*) who have been staying within the Juang habitat since the regime of the feudatory rulers of Keonjhargarh, are intimately associated with the Juangs in socio-economic peripheries.

The Juang is in transition. The Juangs of Dhenkanal district have left the practice of sweden cultivation under the pressure of restriction of the government rules and as earlier mentioned, they have taken to basketry and have become agrarian in nature. But the Juangs of Keonjhar belt are less affected by such rules and still subsist on sweden cultivation. However, they have become agrarian to a little extent and have taken to rearing of domestic animals under the compelling situations.

Religion

Though the Juangs trace their origin from the mythological stories of Hinduistic nature, they are primarily animistic. As they live amidst the hills and forests, their beliefs and religious practices are confined to only some benevolent natural deities namely sun god and Earth goddess in addition to a number of malevolent demigods, ghosts, and spirits dwelling on hills, forests, streams, paddy terraces, villages, etc. The ancestral spirits are thought to guide every walk of their life.

Among the benevolent deities. Sun god (*Dharam Deota*) and the Earth Goddess (*Basumata*) are the supreme deities in hierarchical order which are propitiated at the beginning of each religious rite.

The *Gramasiri* is the prime village deity who occupies its place in front of the Majang being installed in the form of some long pointed menhir like stone emblems. *Thanapati*, another village deity is of subsidiary importance who is also found in hills and jungles specified to some particular villages. *Kanchuni* and *Bhimabudma* are thought to be the deities of their traditional musical instruments namely *changu* and its other varieties, who reside in the *Majang*.

The abnormalities in the day-to-day life are normalized through shamanistic and sorcoric ways by a person called *Raulia* who is assisted by Naik, Dangua and *Adhikari*, the sub-functionaries.

Fair and Festivals

The festivals like *Pushpunei, Magha jatra, Amba nua, Manchuri, Gudabua, Kimiyang* and *Pirpuja* are the most important occasions which are observed with great enthusiasm in addition to the observance of some Hindustic festivals like *Raja Parva, Gamha Purnima* and *Gurubar Osha*, etc. However, these Hindu fair and festivals are observed among some households or Gonasika area of those who have more of less come in contact with the caste Hindu people of their locality.

Political Organisation

Law and order are maintained by secular heamen, namely *Pradhan* at the village level and Sardar at the *Pirh* level. The unsolved cases of the court of *pradhan* are referred to the court of *Sardar*, the maximal traditional judicial are referred to the court of *Sardar*, the maximal traditional judicial unit. However, the *Pradhan* is now called as member and performs a number of duties relating to modern politics in addition to his traditional assignments. *Dangua* who acts as a messenger, is an integral part of their political organisation. Though *Nagam* is a sacerdotal head, in many villages he activity takes part in political affairs, but voice is not always final.

The accused are punished and the fine includes few bottles of liquor, animals like goat or birds like fowl etc. and few measures of rice depending upon the nature and gravity of the fault.

As change is inevitable, the Juangs who were once, other-wise, described in different time phases as "people of the leaf", (Samuells, 1856 cited by Raut, 1969:1) people of the "Stone age *institute"* (Dalton, 1872, ibid: 1-2), can no more be termed as such since they have experienced tremendous change under the pressure of modernity of the outer world. However, though the Juangs of Keonjhar belt are still having many primitive characteristic features as per the present day criteria and facing an alarming threat of series diseases and have more or less stagnant growth rate, impoverished economic condition, slow growth of literacy rate etc. The Juangs of Dhenkanal belt are incomparably better off because of their unhostile habitat and the scope of mixing with the caste Hindu peoples of the locality. The development efforts which have started through micro projects during seventies, would take many more decades to bring the Juangs of Keonjhar belt into the main stream.

❏ ❏ ❏

REFERENCE

1. Bose, N.K. (1928): "Marriage and Kinship among the Juang" Man in India, Vol. III
2. Bose N.K. (1929): "Juang Association", Man in India, Vol. X.
3. Bose N.K. (1930): "Juang Ceremony", Man in India, Vol.X.
4. Dash, J. (1988): "Role of Kinship in Social Life of Juang of Keonjhar district, Orissa", Adivasi, Vol. XXVII, No.2, Bhubaneswar, THRTI.
5. Elwin, V. (1943): "An Anthology of Marriage Sermons (Juang of Pallahara)" Man in India, Vol. XXIII, No, 2.
6. Elwin, V. (1948): "Notes on Juang", Man in India, Vol XXVIII No. 1-2.
7. Mc Dougal, C. (1963): (a) "The Social Structure of Hill Juang: A Precis". Man in India, Vol. III.
8. Mc Dougal, C. (1963): (b)The Social Structure of Hill Juang (un-published Ph.D.dissertation), New Mexico, University of New Mexico.
9. Mc Dougal, C. (1964): "Juang Categories and Joking Relationship", South-Western Journal of Anthropology, Vol. XX No. 4.
10. Misra, K.C. (1982): "Some Aspects of Juang Folklore" Adivasi, Vol. XXI, No. 1-4, Bhubaneswar, THRTI.
11. Patnaik, N. (1986): "The Juangs of Orissa: Their Work and Food Intake, Demography and Fertility" Adivasi, Vol. XXI, No. 3, Bhubansewar, THRTI
12. Patnaik, N (1989): The Juang, Bhubaneswar: THRTI.
13. Rout, S.P. (1966): "Some Aspects of Juang Marriage" Adivasi, Vol. XI No. 3 Bhubaneswar: THRTI.
14. Rout, S.P. (1969): Hand Book or the Juang, Bhubaneswar: THRTI.

JUANGAS - II

D.B.Giri

The Juangas is well known in Anthropological literature. This tribe is identified as one of the primitive tribes of Orissa. The Juang tribe was studied the first time as early as in 1856 by Samuells. He gave an account of their dress pattern only distinguished the females as wearing only the long branches of leaves, covering only the lower, private parts. While the upper parts were covered only with necklace of earthen beads. Interestingly, he mentioned hunting being their chief subsistence activity.

Dalton's study in 1872 reveals more interesting facts about Juang settlement. he mentioned that the Juangs were inhabit and customs the most primitive people and considered them to be survival of the *'Stone age'*. According to him their huts were amongst the smallest that human beings ever deliberately constructed as dwellings. He also mentioned the dormitory (community hall) was much bigger in size. In Hunter's (1877), statement, the Juangs were wandering freaks and that they loved roaming around in the woods, collecting wild products which they bartered for food as well. He also discussed about the Juang leaf dress and their economy which still centered around chase.

After a brief full, the Juangs were again brought into academic focus by Bose (between 1928 and 1930) in his descriptive notes on Juang marriage, kinship organisation of some ritual aspects, were published in the journal of Man in India.

Kinship

Later, the kinship terms were analysed in detail by Dash (1988). Who opined that segregation of Juang villages into two effective exogamies groups such as *Kutumba* (agnates) and *bandhu* (affinal) villages was chiefly due to the practice of shifting cultivation which required co-operative labour. He also opined that kinship terms (classificatory and general) categorise, the kin members, pattern their inter-personal relations, and assign reciprocal rights, duties, privileges as well as obligations to them.

Macdougal (1963) has studied the social structure of the Juangs According to their relationships are defined by the criteria of locality, kinship and age of sex.

Coming back to the historical prospective, it was Elwin (1948), after Bose, who carried out extensive fieldwork among the Juang of *Kendujhar, pallahra* and *Dhenkanal*. He mentioned that the Juangs of *Kendujhar* and the adjacent of *Dhenkanal* are (bhagudias) the highlands to the plains.

Juangs and their features

Although there are as many as 55 tribal communities inhabiting the Kendujhar district, the principal one the Juangs, who is the target group of may study. The tribal population of the district is about 45%. There are 124 Juang village in the district with 4,068 families and their total population is about 19,000 (family and population statistics are latest unpublished information form ITDA Kendujhar). The density of population in the district is 161 per sq. km, while in the study area it is less than 20 per sq. km. as per my findings. Out of the total Juang population in Orissa 51% are Kendujhar, while 45% are in *Dhenkanal*. It is well known in literature and also know from among the Juang population was found have decreased in 1921, 1931, 1951 and 1971. It was more alarming in 1951 when the population was recorded to be 4,473. This has prompted the state Government to take special measures for these endangered tribals and following this concern, a micro project called Juang development Agency (JDA) was started in 1981 at Gonasika village (initially the JDA functioned from Kendujhar under the ITDA between 1974 and 1981) with the objective about economic development and raising them above the poverty line. The term Juang is explained as 'man' by the Juang themselves. The Juang are medium in stature with brachycephalic head prominent cheek bone and broad one having little depression at the root. Their hair is relatively black and coarse, while the skin colour varies between brown and dark brown. They are fairly well built show slight mental timidity. There language known as Juang, belong to the north mundary group.

Leaf Apron (Dress)

One of the striking features of the Juang is their past attire the leaf dress. historically they are known to have put on leaves to cover their lower parts. While the females wore leaves of *shorea roubusta* (Sorgi) the males wore the bark of careya *arborea (tumboi)*. It was Johnstone, the then superintendent of Kendujhar state who banned leaf dress and forced the Juangs to wear cloth. No one affect Elwin has reported about the prevalence of leaf dress. It is totally gone from the Juangpirh, but even now people remember nostalgically about their much possessed dress. Because of their typical leaf dress, the Juangs were also addressed as *patua* (wear of leaf) by their caste neighbors. The leaf-dress meant sat (truth) for the Juang (Rath and Girl, 1998).

Settlement Pattern

A Juang settlement is generally located on foot hill/hills slopes and close to stream. Previously, when the settlements were frequently shifted from place-to-place within the village boundary proximity to the swidden patch was the chief consideration. This saved time and also made watching of standing crops much easier. Now, the Juangs have stationery villages as the state government has issued them permanent pattas (legal document of land holding). However, house sites are changed in case any chronic disease afflicts the family members in a place.

The Juangs have no term for village in their language and refer it by the *Oriya*/Hindi term *gaan*. The village is regarded as the minimal territorial unit and may consist of one or more wards in a definite locality. The traditional and or old Juang settlement is a uni-clan village although at present the Juangs villages have become *Multi-clan*. As the clan is exogamous the *uni-clan* villages are naturally exogamous and labelled as *Kutumb* (agnatic) village distinguished from *bandlhu* village (relatives with potential marital alliance). These terms are again Oriya terms and hence are adopted probably from their caste Hindu neighborers.

A typical Juang village conforms to a shapeless cluster of massive type with the street not forming a integral part of the design. The dormitory is situated preferably at the middle of the village and the houses of the individual families are dispersed around it. It is the biggest house in a village. It has a *veranda* which runs round on all sides. All the wooden pillars of the mandaghar (youth dormitory) are beautifully carves, with these at the entrance being exceptionally carved with special designs. Human as well as animal figures are curved on these poles. The interior of the dormitory has a raised wooden platform at the back where communal paddy grains are stored in straw grain bins. At the middle the sacred fire is kept lit day and right throughout the year. The musical instruments (*changu*) are kept hanging from deer horns which are fixed to the walls, with simple floral paintings and geometric designs. These decorative aspects (paintings, carving etc.) are virtually absent in individual houses in front of the dormitory is specious ground of *plaza* of the size of a badminton court where the youths perform *changu dance*. By its side is the *Gramsiri* (Village duty under a flowering tree which oversees all activities.

The Juang houses are small is size varying between 15' to 8' and small as 6' by 3'. The walls are raised with wooden poles suck into the ground vertically close to each others and plastered with mud and cowdung mixed together. The roof is thatched with the wild grass of Alang (Heteropogen Contortus). Of late, roofing is being done with tiles, if one can afford it, cows and goats and also pigs which are few in number, are kept in separate sheds made of wooden plants and poles. These sheds are either adjacent to the house or one little away. Hens in some cases along with goats are kept inside the house in a corner of the sleeping space opposite to the hearth.

A juang house which is without windows is divided into three distinct parts, each portion having a name of its own; one portion is called *daala* or the store where a wooden platform is raised for keeping grains and cereals. The portion opposite to the *daala* is called *ukusung* (kitchen). In between these two is left a small portion called *kelang* where paddy is dried and husked and also serves at the sleeping place.

A settlement site is selected by divination. The religious head (Dehuni, Boita or Nagam) of the village, goes to a new patch of land, selected randomly and makes invocations to the *Dharam Deota Basuki mata* (High gods) and *Rusi Rusiani* (Superme ancestors) to tell him whether or not to build houses at the proposed new settlement. He then leaves a legs-tied chick in a hole on the new site and leaves the place to come back home. The next morning if the chick is found to be alive then the site is believed to be auspicious for their settlement.

Political Organisation

In recent times the Juang Development Agency has sponsored a village representative member is now a part of the village council. Besides, there are ward members who represent village at the Panchayat. The traditional village council among the patriarchal Juangs consists of mainly three traditional leaders *Dehuri, Padhan, Dangua*. For disputes and quarrels *Dehuri, Padhan, Dangua*. For disputes and quarrels *Dehuri, Padhan* and Member or representative of statutory *Gram Panchayat* decide disputes and quarrels in the village *Dangua* is also a part of the decision making elites.

The *Dehuri* who is also known as *Boita* or *Nagam* is the ritual head of the village. An elderly person, as he is, his chief role is to officiate in all the communal of the village and also distributes taila lands (swidden patches). In all cases among the villagers he consults other village elders and gives due consideration to their opinion.

Padhan is the second most powerful and immediate associate of the *Dehuri* in the village. His office is believed to have been created by the then Rajas of Kendujhargarh. Even after the merger of the princely state of Kendujhargarh with the state of Orissa in 1948, the Padhan's office continued. His principal duty was to collect tax from all the families of the village, to allot land to each family and to inform the important matters to the government. During *Raja's* time the *Padhan* used to be extremely powerful and responsible for reporting the village affairs to the *Rajas*. In judicial affairs he had a status of *Padhan* which is only restricted to traditional village affairs and not tax collection or any other Government related duties.

Dangua is the co-ordinator between the *villagers* and *Dehuri* and *Padhan*. He informs the villagers about the decisions taken by the *Dehuri* and *Padhan* regarding observance of various rituals and other festivals in the villages. His duties are mostly restricted to rituals. Like the *Dehuri* and *Padhan* he is also an elderly person of the village.

The member is a relatively new entry into the village political set-up. He does much of the duties earlier performed by the *Padhan*. The member is the village representative in all government affairs. He is elected by his own villagers. He reports important village matters to the government and plays a pivotal role in bringing government sponsored development programmes to the village.

The office of the traditional leaders is non-hereditary and they are selected by divine consent, that of the *gramasiri* (village deity). However, preference is given to a member of the lineage of *Dehuri* and *Padhan* to succeed them. Once selected they continue till their death, while the *Dangua* may join them at any point of time or may leave them whenever he desires. No remuneration except ritual shares is paid to these offices. The *Dehuri*, however receives a day's free agricultural labour from each household of the village, in the first year of his office.

The political system is, however, under change because of government interference. Now a dispute which is not easily settled within the village council, is refereed by the aggrieved to the police station. The younger generation is slowly becoming indifferent to the importance and significance of the village council.

Social Organisation

Family (Kutumali) is the smallest group characterised by common residence, economic co-operation and reproduction. The nuclear family comprising parents and their unmarried children is most basic and common among the Juangs although in individual cases, in case of Dasarathi Juang of Guptagana village for example, there may be one or more additional persons related as older parents of the couple living with them. The extended family type which embraces an older man, his wife or wives, his unmarried children, his married son or sons and their wives and children is a new feature noticed as in case of *Suka Juang* of Guptaganga. This element is, however rare.

The next larger social group is the lineage (*baunsa*) which comprises a number of families which are related to one another by blood and the members are able to trace their descent from a known ancestor. In fact, in earlier days when the village size was not more than 5-10 families, the Juang villages were inhabited by the household which were consanguineously related to one another. As number of household increased in a village with the passing of time, the descent could not be traced from a known ancestor, but the members nonetheless, traced their common ancestry from a fictions ancestor and all of them belonged to a *bak* (clan), which is strictly exogamous. Now no Juang village remains a lineage, but all the members belong to a *kutumb clan* (members related by blood with patrilineal descent). In a way, village exogamy is synonymous to clan exogamy. For marital convenience, therefore, the entire Juang society is bifurcated into a moiety division of two halves, a set of clans which can marry in only a set of other clans known as the bandhu clans. The clan identity of a male is made through a suffix called bak, while that of a female through dae. But since it is a patrilineal society clans are usually referred to as bak. Most of the baks are totemic, bearings names of animals such as elephant. (Hatisilabak), bear (Banaebak), rabbit (Nachingbak), dove (Baningbak), fowl (Sankoibak) etc. and plant species Slechera Oleosa (Barumbak), Diosphyros melanoxloan (Temrebak), Ficus semicordata (Samnabak), Ficus glomerata (Dumuriabak), paddy stock (leombak), etc.

Among the juangs the village as a cohesive unit is more functional than the clan. It is the ecology and productive technology which contribute to the evolution of a social system characterised by patrilocality and patrilineality and clan organisation has nothing to do with the Juang Social system. The exploitative technology as related to environment seems to play a greater role in making the social organisation what it is in this case of Juang social system.

The *ganar* (also known as gurunda) technology and swidden cultivation requiring co-operative labour probably produced *kutumb* villages of patrilineal and patrilocal lineage groups.

Economic Life

The Juangs are recognised as one of the primitive tribes of Orissa based on three criteria one of which is pre-agricultural technology-use of hand-hoe in swidden cultivation. Shifting cultivation in the life-line of the Juang economy, although other forms of subsistence activities such as collection of minor forest produce (MFP), settled agriculture and wage earning have become subsidiary sources of income. Hunting remains only in ceremonial form; on days following the occasions of *amba nua* (first mango eating ceremony) and *asadi* (first niger sowing ceremony). Besides clandestine hunting trips (against Forest Department rules) are also undertaken throughout the year. Hunting by means of traps is common.

The Juangs identify five principal types of crop-raising lands namely *ekan* (Swidden land), *bila* (wet land) *gadak* (plain unirrigated cultivable upland), *bakadi* (Manured land attached to settlement) and muji bakadi (kitchen garden). While mixed cropping is carried out in the ekan, paddy is cultivated in *bila* and *gadak* in the later quite infrequently. The *bakadi* is used for maize and mustard cultivation, while the *Muji bakadi* is meant for cultivation of leafy and other vegetables. Except ekan all other land types are individually owned. While paddy cultivation in bila may be carried on twice in a year, that is, in winter and summer sowing period only summer corp in cultivated in ekan and gadak. In *bakadi*, on individual plots maize is sown in late summer (June and harvested in late rains (September), while mustard is sown in late rains and harvested in midwinter (December).

Most of their time throughout the year is spent in swidden cultivation activities. Although, communal help is extended on remuneration, if needed, family labour is generally employed for all swidden activities. No labour is sought from out side the community, that is juangs employ Juangs only, although they may work outside their community. The labour charged per individual and per day, during the field work ranged between Rs. 7/ and Rs. 10/- within meal of rice and *curry*. Women do most of the agricultural work except ploughing and sowing. It is believed that the soil would lose fertility, if women do such works Similarly, women are forbidden to climb fruit-bearing trees. Nevertheless, women are the major work force in not only the economic life, but in social sphere as well. They, however, play an insignificant role in politics and rituals. The Juangs are very poor and almost everyone lives below the subsistence level. A major part of the agricultural produce is consumed, while crops such as maize, mustard and niger are cash crops, exchanged after harvesting and during scarcity times, for paddy or rice, in the local weekly market at *Gonasika*. Some amount of these crops are also kept for home consumption. The agricultural food lasts for about 4 months in a year. The MFPs such as mango, mahua, jack fruit and seeds and abony take care of their hunger for about 2 months, while the rest of the period in intermittently spent in hunger and earning source is found out from outside the village i.e. wage earning in public construction works.

Even with these efforts the Juangs remain indebted to the local money lenders (caste people who provide money of paddy whenever a Juang needs by taking a promise from him that the loan would be repaid in the form of the standing crops. In this way the Juang remains indebted most of the time.

In a work on *shifting cultivation* Mohanty has pointed out its uneconomic nature. Taking a case study he finds that in shifting cultivation the requirement of seed and labour per acre is much high in comparison to what is required for the same amount of land in wet cultivation. But the yield per acre in shifting cultivation is much less than that of the wet cultivation. While the investment is double in comparison to wet cultivation, the yield is half in comparison to the latter. Similar picture also emerges from present investigation. Taking 3 case studies in Guptaganga village. I have found that with variables such as land, labour and seed remaining constant, the net yield of paddy (other crops converted into paddy value) from swidden is less than half than the yield from wet agriculture.

The carrying capacity of the land under swidden cultivation is not more favourable. In a study in the *Juangpirh*, Bose has shown that the land could take care of about 35 persons, while there are actually 82 persons to feed. These indices clearly indicate the below subsistence status of Juang economy.

Juang Religion

Religious beliefs and practices for a Juang are something which a human being cannot do without. Belief in supernatural power is firmly entrenched in the Juang psyche although some erosion is marked among the younger generation. Any uncommon object in nature is a supernatural according to the Juang and he attributes the occurrences of this uncommon object as the wish of the *Dharam Deota* (Almighty, High God) and therefore to be revered. Many things are happening is the eco-system in which the Juang lives and the cause and consequences of these events are all attributed to the supernatural beings.

Belief in all ages is truth for Juang belief is lief the survival and continuance of which is dependent of on *Karma* (deed). A pious man with good *Karma* goes to the heaven after death. While and evil man would be thrown into the hell which they believe lies below the earth's surface. There are three physical spheres heaven (swarga), hell (*narka*) and the earth (*basuki*). All gods and goddesses reside in heaven, all human beings on earth, while all demons are resident of the hell. It is the belief that man is reborn according to *Karma*. We are all children of the Almighty who keeps a watchful eye on everybody. He understands all our problems and does the needful. The concept of rebirth for a Juang, according to Elwin (1948), means that one is born again in a family as his or her grand child. This motion is found to be partially correct in that coincidental death of a grand parent and birth of grand child in a family is viewed as a grand parent being reborn.

Living amidst hills and forests the Juangs believe in various deities, ghosts and spirits guiding every walk of their life. In order to get ride of the evil intervention of the spirits and ghosts and to protect themselves and their scantly earthly possessions the Juang tries to establish a friendly relation with the spirit through its propitiation by means of appropriate rites and rituals. While all Gods and Goddesses and benevolent spirits are collectively known as *Kailong*, the malevolent spirits and ghosts do not have any common name, but individual names.

The Juang pantheon includes at the top the *High Dharam Deota* and *Basukimata*, Characterised by their benevolent nature No ritual activity would commence without uttering first the names of this due who are known to the husband and wife. The *Dehuri* would start saying 'Oh. Dharam Deota above and Basukimata below'.

Nest in rank are the superme ancestors of the Juangs Rusi and Rusiani, who are believed to have taught and directed the Junags to lead a life which they have been doing through the ages. Their names find mention in most Juang myths. Many phenomena on earth are believed to be their creation. They are believed to have possessed the power of truth and have handed over the same to their children. oblation of *Mahuli* (liquor of madhuca indica) to the ancestors is a must on all ritual occasion.

Next in order are the pirh (regional) known as *Baitarani patta* followed by *Gramasiri* (village deity) Both these goddesses are powerful and protect regional and village life and property, respectively, Below them, there are local deites and benevolent spirits. They are Gangarajia/Bengarajia, *Nagasiria, Baula Patta, Rangahanta Pokhari, Dhana, Khapuri, Kandranin Mandani, Sebadak, Badham Budha, Jambala Tuli* and *Kanchuni* (gods and goddesses and Anading *Akling, Kachua, Jhinkpani* and *pitasuni* (benevolent spirits).

The malevolent spirits include *Dhania Manga, Lunga Jhuri, Daumati, Angana Thunit and Alungmuni Thunti*. These spirits reside in places such a forest water hill and ant hill. There are various ghosts as well including *Kaka Sirguni, Sirguni, Jogini, Baghiya, Thuna, Bouti, Bara Bulari, Stat Bhauni* and *Churdi*.

While Dehuri is the ritual performer for deities and benevolent spirits the malevolent spirits and ghosts are propitiated by the Raulia (the village shaman). Offering to these evil elements includes black chicks preferably, while to the deities goats, sheeps, chicks and pigs (to the ancestors only).

The important religious occasions of the Juangs include, *puspunei* (new agricultural year and new cake-eating) held in January. *Amba Nua Khia* (New mango eating) in march April. *Tertia* (First sowing of paddy) in June, *Asadi* (First niger sowing, new Kusum-fruits eating). October and Kalarab (new pulses and vegetable eating) held in October-November. Hindu rituals such as Gamha purnima have become an integral part of the itinerary of Juang ritual observances in a year. Many more Hindu religious elements (deities and occasions) are slowly entering the Juang religious system which is surely under its influence and on transition to change.

Youth Dormitory

There are two youth organisation (dormitories) in Juang society one for the unmarried boys (*Kangers*) and the other for the unmarried girls (*Selans*). The boy's dormitory is known as *Majang* or *Mandaghar*, while the girls dormitory is called *Melainjyan* which is now structurally non existent.

Life Cycle

From birth till death human beings pass through various stages which involve a number of rituals and other observances. The Juangs are a case in hand.

Birth

Birth in a Juang family is viewed in sense that bringing a bride is essentially for begetting children. Barrenness in woman is condemned and the man is permitted to remarry again as *Rangia Juang* (40) of Upara Baitarani says "he was suggested to remarry by his first wife, as she failed to deliver a child". Women bearing numerous children are esteemed by the other villagers. For economic reasons, a male child is preferred to a girl child, even though interestingly women share a greater part of the work load-both household and economic. The Juangs are aware of the fact that birth is the result of the physical union between a man and woman. They say "unless the field is ploughes and the seed how can one expect the harvest"

During pregnancy a woman should *abstain* from eating *slaughtered meat* or *offered meat*. She should not see smoke of a funeral pyre nor should she see a lightening of hear thunder. Intense labour pain is attributed to the evil-eye or ill-will of some malevolent spirits dwelling on hills, forests and streams. For this, the spirits(s) is propitiated by summoning the village *shaman (Raulia)*. After birth, the mother is advised from being exposed to rain or cold. She is also forbidden to work for first 7 days. The child is similarly not allowed to be seen by outsiders. If a male child is born, he midwife (*Sutrunihari*) is given an extra amount of one or two rupees and a brass bangle for her services.

In the name giving ceremony (nimincha) which is performed after 5/6 days of the child's birth (sometimes it takes place after 3/4 months). The child is blessed for a happy future, free of disease and other problems. In naming the child the names of the ancestors are always preferred.

The period between childhood and adolescence is the period of *socialization* for every Juang. He or she imitates the activities of the adults while playing with fellow mates.

Marriáge

Marriage an important phase in a man's life is equally interesting among the Juangs. A marriage is generally from the boy's side, if the girls parents are satisfied with the boy's competence to maintain a wife without giving her mental and physical torture, the marriage takes place. The bride is taken to the groom's village by the groom's team on a auspicious day. The couple is blessed by the grooms parents. The moment they enter the boys village. The next day, the *Dehuri*, *Padhan* and other elderly members of the village sit together and perform a ritual to propitiate the ancestors who are prayed to bless the newly married couple. After that a fun-making occasions called *'Uaa Baungan* (bathe-taking) takes place. The couple, on the next day (3rd day) are involved in a fun-making occasion called *Kadalata* in which the sisters-in-law and brothers-in-law throw mud and water at each other. This completes the marriage of the couple, who return home the bride cooks food and the couple eat together.

Arranged marriage is the most common form of marriage prevalent among the Juangs. Marriage by capture is still prevalent, although the Juang Tribal Council in its meeting at *Gonasika* on 17.2.95 had banned this form of marriage. Marriage by elopement is infrequent. Girls marry between 15 and 17 years of age, while the boys marry between 18 and 22 years of age child marriage is non-existent, while widow marriage may take place if both parties willing.

Bride price is paid by the *groom*. But now the system is slowly changing and because of outside caste contacts a couple of marriage instances such as that of Suna Juang of Jantari village, have shown that dowry is slowly entering Juang marriage system. The usual bride price includes 2 *Khandi* (40 Kg) rice and 3 *Khandi* (60 Kg) paddy, besides cloths and one rupee to the girl's parents.

Important factors which determine a marriage are (i) both the marriage mates must not belong to one bak (clan) (ii) not only clan is exogamous but each has a number of associated *Kutumb* (non-marrying) clans in which marriage is not permissible (iii) the marrying mates, if possible should stand in proper generation to each other (iv) within the own or alternate generation the factor of kinship relation should also be noticed, and (v) forescasting its future sanctity and success by reading omens.

Death

The last stage in life-death has a devil association for the Juang. It is always feared and believed to be the work of hostile a spirits black magic, witchcraft of deities. A dead man is immediately cremated in the forests near a stream adjacent to the settlement.

Returning from the funeral ground, all sprinkle little of water (kept in a broken gourd and where in a copper coin is dipped), to purity their body. The funeral feast (sudha) is held only after the concerned family can make necessary arrangements for it. It could be held on any day within 11 days of the death. The feast includes all the blood relatives (and important affinal kins, who pray for the peaceful existence of the dead's soul). The Juangs believe that the spirit of their ancestors (deceased) live inside their house under the *daala*.

Amid such a situation, the Juangs find themselves at the road cross of tradition and modernity, without being very sure about which way to go. Let what may the situation be and let what may the direction be, what the Juang ultimately wants is enough to eat and be left alone is peace.

❏ ❏ ❏

REFERENCES

1. A few facts on the Juang (leaflet), ITDA, Kandijhar, 1987
2. Bose, N.K. (1928): Marriage and kinship among the Juangs man in India. Vol. 8(4): pp. 233-242
3. Bose, N.K., (1929): Juang Association, Man in India Vol. 9 pp. 47-53
4. Bose, S. (1996): Land use survey in Juang village, Man is India 41(3) pp. 172-183
5. Bose, S. (1996): Land use survey in Juang village, Man in India 41(3) pp. 172-183
6. Dalton, E.T., (1872): Descriptive Ethnology of Bengal, Calcutta.
7. Dash, J. (1988): Role of Kinship in the social life of Juangs of Kendujhar district, Orissa, Adivasi Vol. 28(2) pp. 22-28
8. Dash, J. (1989): Juang Kinship terms: An Analysis, Adivasi. Vol. 29(3-4) pp. 29-38
9. District statistical Handbook: Kendriyhar, 1993 Govt of India, p. 8.
10. Elwin, V. (1948): Notes on the Juangs, Man in India Vol. 28(1-2) pp. 1-143.
11. Hunter, W.W. (1877) : A statistical Account of Bengal (19) London Trubner and company.
12. Macdougal, C. (1963) : The social structure of the Hill Juangs.
13. Mishra, K.C. (1982) : Aspects of Juang folkore, Adivasi: Vol. 21(1-4) pp. 11-38
14. Mohanty, B.B. (1986) : Shifting cultivation in Orissa: with a case study among the Juangs, Adivasi Vol. 26(4) pp. 17-26
15. Mohapatra P.K. (1989) : Myths of Juang- An Anthropological analysis Adivasi. Vol. 29(3-4) pp. 21-23
16. Rath, A, Giri D.B. (1998) : Traditional Juang Attire, The eastern Anthropologist. Vol. 51(1) pp. 33-40.
17. Report of sixth group monitoring meet, New Delhi: Govt of India, 1986.
18. Rout, S.P. (1969) : Hand book on the Juang Adivasi. Vol. 11 (1-2) pp. 1-97.
19. Samuells, E.A. (1856) : Notes on a forest race called puttooas or Juang. Journal of Asiatic Society of Bengal. Vol. 25 pp. 295-303.

❑ ❑ ❑

KADU KURUBA

Dr. H.M. Maralusiddaiah Patel
and
Dr. A. Chandrasekar

The Karnataka State, a region inhabited predominantly by Kannada speaking people is situated in the west central part of peninsular India. It consists of narrow elongated belt between the Arabian Sea and the Western Ghats with strikingly exquisite and enchanting coastline of about four hundred kilo-meters and the hilly tracks of Western Ghats with its magnificent ranges of scenic beauty and evergreen forests.

The state is situated between 11°31' and 18°45' north latitude and 74° 12' and 78° 40' east longitude and lies in the west central part of peninsular India. It is bounded by on the north by Maharashtra State on the north-west by Goa, on the east by Andhra Pradesh, on the south and south-east by Tamil Nadu, on the south west by Kerala and on the west by the Arabian Sea. The Western Ghats rise in a series of terraces, but the general elevation is lower as compared to the stretch in the north. This fact has strong influences on the geography of the brodering territories, in the form of the forested hill country of the Malnad. The range appears to be haphazardly placed hills. The deeply dissected edge of the ghats edge with their deep gorges, waterfalls, rivers captures and the watersheds, interlacing with denser evergreen and semi-evergreen forests, constitute the core of the Malnad. The Karnataka state is known for the rich heritage of a varied wealth of flora and fauna. Some parts of the state have a variety of rich forests as in Chikmagalur, Uttara Kannada, Shimoga and Kodagu districts.

History and origin

The population of Scheduled Tribe in Karnataka was 1,825,203. according to 1981 census Tribes in India comprise 7.76% of the total population of the country that means 51.63 million persons, according to 1981 Census, were enumerated as belonging to the communities notified as Scheduled Tribes under the provisions of the Constitution of India. During 1981 period the tribal population had grown by 25.4% compared to 25.8% growth for the population as a whole. The *Kadu Kuruba* is a Scheduled Tribe, they are mainly concentrated in the district of Mysore.

They are mainly living in the *dense forest* and their traditional occupation is collection of *forest produce* available in the forest like *honey, tree bark, tamarind, fruits soap nuts, roots, nuts* and *resin*.

Mysore district in situated in the southern part of the Deccan Peninsula and forms the southern most part of Karnataka State Physiographically, the region in which the district is situated may be classified as partly maidan and partly semi-malnad. The district, with an area of 11, 954 sq kms, lies between 11°30' and 20°50' latitude and 75°45' 77°45'. East longitude. The extreme south forms a Terrain of dense forests. The soil of the district predominantly red sand loams derived from pure sandy soil to typical black cotton soil. The taluks of *Heggagdedevana kote* and *Hunsur* are hilly terrain and contain *red shallow soil.*

The drainage is towards east and comprises mainly of the Cauvery river basin besides those of *Kabini, Lakshmanathirtha* and *Suvarnavathi* which are tributaries of *Cauvery*. The *Cauvery* which is the life blood of the district, Kabini enters the districts at its south western angle in *Heggadadevana Kota* taluk. Emerging from the dense jungles of *Kakanakote*, it flows north-east and winds its way to Sargur, from where running east wards its receives the water of Nugu and Gundal dam. It is a perennial river and a dam has been built across the river near Bidarahally in H.D. Kote taluk. The climate of the district is moderate throughout the year. The temperature during the winter (Nov-Feb) ranges from 16.1°C to 31.3°C, while that in summer ranges from 19.7°C to 35.1°C. The rainy seasons extends from May to October with a maximum annual rainfall ranging between 620 mm to 880 mm at *H.D. Kote* and *Hunsur* taluks.

The Kadu Kurubas are mainly concentrated in the *Piriyapatna, Gundaplet, Hunsur* and *H.D. Kote* taluks of Mysore districts and in Coorg district. In kannada the term "Kadu" means forest and "Kuruba' generally means *shephered*. They are living in the forest and their traditional occupation is basketry and food gathering. According to Iyer the *kurumbas* are said to be the modern representatives of the ancient *kurumbas* or *Pallavas* who once very powerful in south India. Very little trace is left of their former greatness anywhere. In the seventh century AD., the power of the *Pallava* kings was at its zenith. It gradually declined owing to the rise of the *konga chalukya* and *Bhola chiefs*. The final overthrow of the Kuruba sovereignty was effected by the *Chola* king Adoni about the seventh of eight century A.D. This led to the dispersion of the *Kurumbas* far and wide, and many fled to the hills of Malabar, the Nilgiris, Coorg, Wynad and Mysore.

Thus with the lapse of time have became wild and uncivilised, and have moved to their comparative isolation, lost their ancient culture. Both the civilized and the wild *Kurumbas* must have been identical, but the present difference is the result of geographical distribution and environment. The name *"Kurumbranad"*, a taluk of *Malabar*, still atlests their former greatness. They may be regarded as the very oldest inhabitants of the land who can contest with their Dravidian kinsman and priority of occupation of the Indian soil. The terms Kurumba and Kuruba were originally identical, though the one from is in different places employed for the other and has occasionally assumed a special local meaning (Iyer 1948: 19).

The Kadu Kurubas are lives in the interiors of forest in thatched huts (*Padi*), in settlements (*haadi*) the huts are low, with wattled walls and wild grass roofing. In each settlement, there is shrine (*ambala*) where they conduct their worship, social gatherings and sessions of the tribal council. The household goods consists of vessels made of mud and aluminium. Their mother tongue is *"Kuruba bhase"* with large admixture of *Kannada, Tamil* and *Kodava* language.

Their total population was 8,192 as per the 1971 census. As per the 1981 census their population was increased by 209, 677. The are also called as *Betta Kuruba*.

The Kadu Kurubas are short stature, head length is of medium type with narrow and low facial height with small nasal length. They are non-vegetarian with wild boar, pig and goat. Now the youngsters started smoking beedi and cigarettes.

Occupation

They are specialised in catching elephants by specific methods like *Kedda*. They are also expert in maintaining the elephants and are most preferred to serve as elephant keepers *"mahouts"* in the Department of Forest", Government of Karnataka, During the Maharaja's period once in ten year they were catching the elephants by using the specific method "*kedda*" and the same is continued by the Department of forest.They used to be shifting cultivators long back before the department of forest stopped this practice. Some of them are engaged in protecting crops near the fields. They construct the small hunts in the tree top watch the wild animals. At night, they light a fire near the field to prevent elephants and wild animals destroying the crops. They also sit on tree tops to watch and beat drums when elephants approach the fields. Their manner of driving away elephants and wild animals are usually by running towards them with blazing torches, making loud noise and beating on tins and drums.

Clan

According to Nanjundaiash (1931), there are two endogamous groups among the Kadu Kurubas (1) Betta Kuruba, and (2) Jenu Kuruba. The formers are again divided into three groups (i) Ane (ii) Bevina, and (iii) Kolli. The Kadu Kurubas are divided into two sections, the *Munpadi* and *Yalpadi*. The *Munpudi* means families belonging to *three Hamlets*. The *Yalpadi* means families belonging to *seven Hamlets*. Members of the same sections, do not inter-mary (Iyar: 1948), Now these groups are not found among the Kadu Kuruba.

Marriage Rituals

When a girl attains puberty, she is to live in segregated hut near the hut for seven days. Daily she has to take bath and she is fed with good food and fruits. On the eights day after giving a ceremonial bathe she returns to her native hut and she can attains, her usual duties. The temporary segregated hut would be burnt down after the pollution period, (within 7 days). Marriage among the Kadu Kuruba is very simple. There are tow types of acquiring mates (1) negotiation, and (2) elopement. Marriage by negotiations is the predominant type of marriage among these types. In this type of marriage the boys parents find out the brids and keep the proposal in front of "Yajaman". In the *'chavadi'* (villagers meeting place). *Yajamans* asks girls parents opinion and after marriage date will be fixed. On the marriage day, all the relatives and friends gather at *chavadi*. Boy's parents has to give one *saree, on white cloth*, betel leaves (5 *kavalige* = 100 leaves), *betel nuts and beads necklace*. The *Yajaman* brings her to *Chavadi*. Bride and Groom distribute the *betel nut* and *betel leaves* to *Yajamans* and to all the gatherers. A feast is given to all.

Marriage by elopement takes place when a boy and a girl fall in love when they decided to lead a married life, they run away to some other place and come back after a few weeks. Then the *Yajaman* and parents accepts their marriage, then the parents of both have to give a feast to the villagers in the presence of the couple and *Yajamans*. The cross cousins and uncle-niece marriage are prevalent and are settled by negotiation. They are monogamous. The residence after marriage is partilocal, divorcees, widows and widowers are allow to remarry. Most of the families tend to be nuclear. The rule of inheritance is male equigenture, but the eldest son succeeds to the status of the deceased father.

Birthrituals

Among the Kadu Kurubas the newly born child and mother are kept in *separate seclusion shed* for seven days. On the fifth day she is given a *ceremonial bath* and she is allowed to enter in the house. On that day. The parents give a feast to their own people. The baby is taken to the ambala, where a string of heads or string is tied round the child neck and the name is pronounced by the father. They keep the grand parents name only. Male children are named *Mada, Choma,. Mara, Manja, Hanuma* and female children, *Madi, Manji, Mari* and Hanumi. The Post natal restriction continue for three to five months. The babies are tonsured after the eleventh month.

Death Rituals

The dead are buried in a lying posture head facing west. If adults would be cremated. The pollution period lasts for ten days on the eleventh day, the perform *thithi*. The worship the dead and put the food items in the name of the dead on that day.

The Kadu Kuruba's are pure animists, believing in ghosts and spirits. They follow Hinduism. They worship deities like *Mugappaji, Bommannadevaru Madappa* and village deities like *Mariyamma* and *Kaliyamma*. They are started celebrate *Ugadi*. Deepavali and Gowri festivals.Still in some villages "Medicinal man" are giving treatment for some diseases and their oral traditions is rich. They are considered to be good sorcerers in there area.

Their traditional occupation is basket making collection of forest produce and shifting cultivation. They used to do *Kumri* of shifting cultivation in the forest and growing coarse grains, minor and millets. Now-a-days due to the restriction from the department of forest, they stopped Kumri cultivation. They still cultivate small kitchen gardens. According to 1961 census their total literacy was 7.51 per cent. They have greatly benefited by the Hill Area Development Programme, IRDP and other Govt. Sponsored programmes.

❑ ❑ ❑

REFERENCES

Iyer. L.A.K., (1929): The Kadu Kurubas, Man in India, 9(4), PP 223-229.

Iyer L.A.K. (1948): the Betta kuruba, the Coorgs Tribes and Castes. Madras Govt Press. PP 19-22.

Misra, P.K., (1983): Tribal Mobilisation in Tribal Movements in India, Vol.2 ed: K.S. Singh, New Delhi, Manohar Publication. PP 325-337.

Nanjundiah H.V. and Iyer LAK (1931): Kadu Kuruba. Mysore Tribes and Castes, Vol. IV Mysore, PP 68-73.

Maralusiddaiah H.M. et al., (1996): The Kadu Kuruba. The Encyclopedic Profile of Indian Tribes. Ed: Sachidananda et.al Discovery Publication House, New Delhi.

Maralusiddaiah H.M. (1996): The Kadu Kuruba. The Encyclopaedia of Dravidain tribes, ISDL Thiruvananthapuram.

Maralusiddaiah H.M. (1996): The Profile: The Kadu Kuruba. The Social Welfare, Vol.45 No-8.

Singh K.S. (1994): The Kadu Kuruba, the People of India. Vol. IV Scheduled Tribe. Oxford University Press. New Delhi.

Photo of Kadu Kuruba

KOYA

Dr. A.K. Kapoor
Rajesh Khanna
Pramod Mishra and
P.K. Patra

The tribe that has been dealt here is known as 'Koyas' of Malkangiri Sub-Division, Koraput District (Orissa). They pronounce themselves as 'Koyae' but earlier Rev. John Cain (1876) had mentioned as *'Koie'*.

Glassford's report and Colonel Haigh's report to Jagdalpur furnishes a good record of the Koya Tribes. Census report of 1871 of the Madras presidency has also dealt with Koyas. Report of Rev. J. Cain (1876 and 1879) furnishes a interesting work regarding the Koya tribals.

Cain (1876) has shown the Koie contrary to be extending from the banks of the Indravati, Bastar, down to the neighbor-hood of Kammam, etc. He has reported that the Koies, whose population is about 100,000 persons, are widely distributed in *Hyderabad Bastar*, the *East Godavari* District and *Rampa Agency* of Madras, and the *Malkangiri* Taluk of Koraput, District, is what according to the new nomenclature.

Cain (1976) has mentioned in his language the distribution of Koies as "All these in the plain have tradition that about 200 years ago they were driven down from the plateau in the Bastar Country by famine and disputes, and this relationship is also acknowledged by the *Qutta Kois* i.e. *Hill Kois*, who live in the high lands of Bastar". Grigson considered that the Malkagiri Koyas were actually *Bisonhorn Marias*. Inter-marriages still takes place. He wrote, "between the *Marias* of Sukna and the *Koyas* of Malkangiri, and the Sukna Class intermarry with the class of Dantevada and jadelpur plateau. In 1941 there were nearly 28,000 of these *Malkangiri Koyas*, and this affinity to Marias is obvious".

Grigson (1908) named the Jagdalpur Plateau Koie (Bastar Plateau) first in him memorable book. "The *Muria* Gonds of Bastar". Elwin (1950) has wrote, "At the 1941 census thousands of *Maria* returned themselves as *Muria*, because they thought it sounds more respectable. many others in the south have for time past taken the title of *Dorla*. Others again are known as *Koya*, and a few call themselves as *Gond*". The famous *Bisonhorn* marriage dance, the class nomenclature and customs clearly justifies that Koyas and *Bisonhor maria* are all the same and belongs to one tribe. It has been cited in the book "Jaypore in Vizagapatnam" that Koyas are immigrants from Godavari which is located extreme south to *Malkangiri,* was in Vizagapatnam district in Madras presidency.

The work of Elwin (1950) gives a descriptive report or the *Marias* of Bastar. It can be seen that the traditions, customs and appearance of *Koyas* and *Marias* are all the same with slight improved modifications in the later. At present the *Koyas* of *Malkangiri* sub-division can be divided in two different forms, if carefully observed. They can be classified as Malkangiri Eastern Koyas and Western Koyas of Motu villages. The Western Koyas have come in contact with business people from *Bhadrachalam* and *Quanta* areas, so they have tinge of modern civilization and Telegue influence. The whole tract has one custom, one language and one tradition, but with tittle variation in the ritual procedures.

Geographical Situation

The Koyas are distributed widely in about 4,747.9 Sq. kms. in the Malkangiri, *Motu,* Venkettapallam Police Station areas of Malkangiri subdivision excepting the Mathli Police Station, where they are very negligible in member. It is one of the hottest area of the Koraput district. It has been observed that soils are suitable for paddy (Orization), Maize (G. Maize), Jawar (Sorghum Vulgare), *Ragi* (Eluensine corcase), *Mestha* (Hibiscus eazalinus) and *Hibiscus subdarffa, Til* (Seasaumum oriental) under dry farming. legume like *Biri* (Phesolous mungo), *Moong* (Phetolous aureous) are also grown. The growth of forest is very fast due to its heavy rainfall and suitable soil.

Koya Village

A Koya Village is generally attractive and charming surrounded by large lofty *Mohwa* trees in the life of Koyas. There is no proper road to enter into the village. A zigzag narrow wailing path leads to the villages. It runs all through raised large bands of the paddy fields. The houses in the Koya villages are not regularly arranged, but are always irregular and isolated. This gives an impression of the temperament and independent nature of the tribe. It is to be noted here that Koyas in the valley have the same language, if minutely observed (anthropological perspective) they differ in dress and some other activity, thus the authors have described in two different names as *East* and *West Koyas* where needed. The village around *Malkangiri*, *Padmagiri* and *Balimella* road upto *MV-64* come under *East Koyas* and thereafter *Kalimella, Motu, Padia* group of villages may be classified as *West Koyas*.

The primary difference between the Eastern Koyas with Western Koyas is that the latter has very large house, isolated and may be in paddy fields too. The houses are surrounded by fencing. The general site of houses is the same as Eastern Koyas. The house is always surrounded with a family vegetable garden.

Koyas have the clans ro '*Kuda*' or *Banso*' e.g. *Madkami, Padiami, Madhi, Sodi, Koashi, Dulhar, Kunjami* and *Wanjami*. They claim that the don't have intermarriages in the 'Kuda'. There is no difference between the Eastern and Western Koyas as regards the Kuda. The most reasonable feature in Koyas family is equal distribution of food.

Social Functions and Ceremonies

The Koya society follows strictly the ceremonies of life and society. The form may very from one place to other but aim is one. The procedure followed in the ceremonies are not at all the same from village to villages e.g. the marriage functions. There have been different procedure adopted to make it a social. It all ends probably when husband and wife spend a night in a house. The mode of ceremonies are aiming at co-operational sublimity and love of the pair in the path of life and fertility.

Birth and Name Giving Ceremony

When the sings of delivery approaches, the women is housed in a separate room with shade and pressure of men is forbidden; with the relaxation to wadded. The Weddes does all the necessary rituals to save the child and the mother from the evil spirits. Two or more ladies are accompanied by a old lady is the team of nurses present during delivery. The old lady cuts the umbilicus of the new born with the help of narrow head and piece of earthen pot. Mother and child are given bath with water and Tumeric.

The day when the child has to be named, all the village ladies take their bath and assemble in the house along with the old lady. The lady who has cut the umbilicus holds the child and starts singing a song to which other ladies recite. She starts with the name of dead forefather and says, we dont's know in which you bless him etc. Then she keeps some rice over a bread and breaks into two. If it ends with equal division then the child will be named after him; if it doesnt's she throws the rice and starts again singing with another name.

In another places it may differ. Two *'Phiel Jhadu'* sticks and two *Mouwa* leaves are tied with Tumeric socked threads. The leaves are then plucked with two cooked rice, the name of the person by which the child to be named is cited. If the child holds the stick over the shoulders, then he is named after him.

In another place, a femoral long bone of a poultry is given to the child and is holded by the hand. The name is cited, if the child cries with the bone touching ear and mouth, then the name is given.

After the name is given is sacrificed and feast is organized and is attended by the village ladies. No male has any share. The name giving ceremony starts when the child starts crying.

The Maturity Ceremony

The maturity of a girl is known as *"Erata'*. When a girl matures, some relations got a nearby forest away from routine way and make as small hut like over a tree, without the knowledge and look of the villagers the girl is taken to that tree. With the girl an old lady accompanies and she also stays in another tree just near by. Then the villagers are informed that the girl is staying in such forest thus for 7 days no male goes to that area. The old lady cooks for the girl. Both of them sleep in different places during the night. First day the girl eats with one finger, second day by two fingers, third day with three finger, fourth day with four and on fifth day by five fingers. Last day she is given bath with Tumeric. The utensils and the hut over the tree used by girl are burnt except the water pot which is broken near a road cross. Within these 7 days no *Puja* or festivals are allowed in the village. Sowing or even harvesting is stopped.

The Koyas think that the matured within 7 days if walks over the earth it will not give any fruit even she touches any plant no fruit will come out.

The Establishment of Love in Koyas

Koyas marry not because they are related, but because they love each other. The marriage ceremony is equally adopted as other tribes with dances, drinks and feasts so as to keep the tie a permanent marital relationship with romance and happy life.

The domestic life is guarded and fenced with festivals, rituals and religious ceremonies which aims at binding the partners in their adventure of fertility and love. These sanctions are in rich way reinforced by the opinion of the society that expensive charges one's mind, and dreads the possible supernatural disasters that follows adultracy of divorce.

The marriages are known as "*Pendule*' and expensive rich marriages which run for several days are known as "*Saukari Gate Pendule*" to the Koyas.

The 'Pendules' may be classified as:
1. Pendule (The regular wedding).
2. Lagitata (Marriage by Capture).

The marriage ceremony possibly aims at union of boy and girl, there is no fixed ritual excepting equal distribution of expenses to both parties in terms of drinks and food accompanied by dances.

Pendule (The Traditional)

The traditional marriage between boy and girl of well to-do families where every thing is regular and socially approved, where the choices has been made by the children with the subsequent consent of the parent is an elaborate affair. There is a complicated ritual procedure which follows with several visits of *Kutumb* (family relatives), house of bride and bridegroom with exchange of goat, poultry, bullocks, pendum, rice, *gruel* and *Kal*. It is not clear actually at what point the marriage ends.

Cain (1876) has reported regarding the marriage ceremony of Koyas. He said, 'the Kois generally marry when of fair age, but in fact marriages are not known. If they be bridegroom is comparatively wealthy he can easily secure a bride by a peaceable arrangement with his parents and friends, and having fixed upon a suitable young, girl, he sends his father and friends to consult with the head-man of the village where his future partner resides. A judicious and liberal bestowal of a few rupees and *arak* obtain the consent of the guardian of the village to the proposed marriage. This done, the party watch for a favorable opportunity to carry off the bride, which is sure to occur when she comes outside her village to fetch water or wood, or it may be when her parents and friends are away and she is left along in her house. (the head-man is generally consulted, but no always, as only a few weeks ago a wealthy widow was forcibly carried off from the house of Chief Koie of a village near Dummagudem, and when the master of the house opposed the proceedings he was knocked down by the invading party). The bridegroom generally anxiously awaits the return home of his friends with their captive, and the ceremony is proceeded with that evening, due notice having been sent to the braved parents. Some of the Kois are polygamists, and if not infrequently happens that a window is chosen and carried off, it may be a day or two after the death of her loss. The bride and bridegroom are not always married in the same way. The more simple ceremony is that of causing the women to bend her head, down and then having made the man lean over her, the friends pour water on his head, and when the water has run off his head to that of the women they are regarded as man and wife. The water is generally poured out of a bottle-gourd. But generally on this important occasion the two are brought together, and having promised to be faithful to each other, drink some milk. Some rice is placed before them, and having again reserved their promises, they eat the rice. They then go outside the house, and marach round a low heap of earth which has been thrown up under a small pendal erected for the occasion, singing a simple song as they proceed. Afterwards they pay their respects to the elders present, and beg for their blessings, which is generally bestowed in the form of 'May you' be happy! May you not fight and quarrel task of devouring the quantity of provision provided for the occasion, and having well caution and drunk, the ceremony is concluded. If the occasion, and having well caution and drunk, the ceremony is concluded. If the happy couple and their relatives are comparatively wealthy, the festivals last several days.

Some don't object to be seen away with wife of another man, and in former years a husband has been known to have been murdered for the sake of his wife. Even at-present more disputes time the government Officials have not been able to stop this practice".

99 year after the observation recorded by Cain, the present authors find the key marriage ceremony is the same in the Koya society, but these days there have been different ways of marriage in the tract. It differs from area to area and family to family.

These days the bridegrooms are 14 to 16 years old age on an average and the girls are 18 to 21 years. Girls are always more aged than the boys. This may be due to the fact the girls are attractive with full physiological development of the body.

The Koyas are polygamists as said by Cain (loc. cit). Every Koya wants to marry two or more wives. The widows are allowed to marry, the first professing goes to brother-in-law, if no she can he married to any one. In general at the age of 21 to 26 the Koya young men wants to have second wife. If the question asked why he needs a second wife'. He replies that the first wife is busy with children and household-job; thus he needs a servant so why not a second wife. Our personal quarries with young Koya friends that they are much attracted with the firm, round and large breasted girls and they need them as their wives.

Before getting a second wife generally the husband asked jokingly how she would like if he gets another wife to help her. She replies, if you can manage both us and feed us, you can have'. But still they quarrel. It so happens that after getting second wife she may desert within few weeks. The relation of daughter-in-law and mother-in-law does command the action to some extent. The marriages amongst Koyas are generally cross-cousin.

In some places the marriage ceremony takes place at the "brides house" and in some places "bridegroom's house"

Budra Madkami of Tamasa Village is the son of Village *Peda. Budra* when grew up his parent decided for his marriage. Thus the father went to his brother-in-law's home near by village called chetaguda and asked, there is one flower blooming in your garden; can we have the pre village to pick it up and keep on our head! The parent of the girl replied, 'if it is so why you have come bare handed? Have you got anything with you for us to eat? Then gave rice, pendum, one goat to the brides father's Kutumb.

In another occasion at *Singarjakuntta* Village which witnessed a similar marriage engagement ceremony. The *Kuda* was greeted. They were given a mate to sit just on the yard of the house. They were given a mate to sit just on the yard of the house. At about 11.00 A.M. they were all called to take meal with their *Kutumb*. The *'Kutumb'* only consists of males. That went and stood in a line before the house very humbly and respectfully. The old lady of the house accompanied by other ladies came out with water pots and gave bath to every member one after the other. The water was poured by the ladies and rubbed the body gently and helped all in the bathing. Then they all were given new clothes to change the loin clothes. Then again they stood in a line, the ladies washed the hands and face of the guests. With quite discipline one after the other all entered the *Verandah* of the house and sat on one mate on line, at the same time cooked rice was served to them with *Pendum* and mutton. After the lunch there was Exchange of words and the marriage was settled. It was a cross-cousin marriage settlement.

The marriage takes place from the February last week to April. The Koyas Calendar is governed by his hard working period of rainy season; November December harvesting period, January month go on preparation of rice, house constructions and in the February they remain busy in the collection of *Mahua* flower for food and wine (Pendum) for the marriage.

The variations in the regular pendule has been listed as following:

Pendule Type - I

Before one day of the marriage schedule day the *Kutumb* people and friends of the bridegroom village go to get the bride. They are accompanied by young girls, young boys and some elderly people of the bridegroom Kutumb and village. They carry pig, rice and pendum, First the bridegroom party give feast to the bride village people with rice and Pendum, Generally on the river side of water place the feast is carried on. In the evening the bride party give a dinner to the bridegroom party.

Before leaving the parent's house the girls is given a bath with Tumeric and new clothes are given. The girls goes to each house of the village accompanied by friends and asks for blessings, the girl naturally weeps and the ladies too; but consulate her with blessings and give some money in her and with individual capability. The friends sing songs with sorrow; speaking her child days, her departure, her activities wish them to fetch water, long and dance, etc., They feel sorry that next year, in the Mahuwa flower collect on they will be very much grieved in her absence. The girl replies all that with her tears only - with no language. The friends then drink pendulum and sing the songs of marriages.

In the evening the bridegroom party with bride and her party towards their village. The friends of the girls are also accompanied with them. The girls make lot of fun of fun all the way. They walk very slowly and sit down for hours together in the way with pretendence and again start singing songs. They say 'out girls quite innocent who doesn't known even to eat, we don't know how much troubles you will give her', the boys then reply'. In our house the rice is plenty We have door to our house, we have birds, pigs and Cattle, you will the bride the boys run and stand before and request them to walk. When a river falls before, the girls refuse to cross it, and ask the bride not to walk; thus the boys carry, her.

Before the entrance of the village a small hut is always prepared where the bridge stays with her friends before the marriage.

The women folk of the bridegroom village work and cook, but the bride women folk don't work and only sing songs and drink Pendum frequently, Before the feast the boy and the girl are made to sit at one place and are offered rice and vegetable separately after half eaten, the plate (leaf plate) are exchanged. After the bridegroom and bride has taken food others start eating. After the feast is over all of the them enter to village of bridegroom.

Reaching the village the bridegroom side party girls and boys dance in two parties with boys. Here they are typically dressed with *Bison* homes and with drums, etc. which is the real '*Koya snake Dance*' and is the mark of unity of Koya civilization.

The two village girl complete in songs, they criticize the bride and bridegroom and praise the deeds.

The day of marriage to declare as men and wife depends on waddace; he declares looking at the star position. Before the union he worships rice, Tumeric, oil, etc. The ladies keep water in 9 new pots. The bride and groom stand on a *Nolkgall*. They pour water on each other. The bridegroom drags bride into the house. He is obstructed by the Sister-in-law and has to satisfy with pendum and gets the way with a laugh and smile.

The girl's friends leave the village with sorrowful songs with deep sense and ask her to be happy and live well.

Pendule Type II

Around Bbubanpalli village, the marriage, ceremony is slightly different. The girl comes to the house of would be husband with his family members and *Kutumbs*. First day the girls dance and invite the boys to dance. After the dance they are offered rice, pendum etc. Second day, the bridegroom is asked to sit on a *Yolgall*, then both of them are moved around an earthen pot 3 times, then they are given a bath. Now clothes are given to change, and are asked to sit on a mate. The girl is given a "*Kulla*' and boy a '*musula*' to make rice out of paddy. The Waddace enchants some verses and declares them as wife and husband, it ends with feasts and dances.

Pendum Type III

The Koyas of *Poteru* a slightly different marriage system. The bridegroom leans over the bride and water is poured on the bridegroom, when water flows over the bride, the marriage is declared. After seeing the bride from the house of the bridegroom she is allowed to run away, and the bridegroom has to run after her and carry her back to his house.

Pendule IV

The bride and bridegroom sit with the both hands folded over reach, water is poured over it, and the wadace declares marriage after puja.

The Waddace does Puja to satisfy the evils like *sani* and the *Rabu* over the girl and brings peace and fortune to the new married couples.

Pendule Where Boy Goes to the Bride for Marriage

In those places where the boy goes to the village of girl, returns with his *Kutumb* after the marriage ceremony along with the girl. The party generally halts at one stream, or river where water can be available. Food is prepared, Pendum is supplied, and also seen when the husband or wife refuges to take the kind of food supplied where the *Kutumb* of the Opponent advocate and council, but still quarrel which are unavoidable.

Just at the time of sun-set the brie and bridegroom enter the village and then they are brought near their door where the bride is given bath, after that the husband pulls the wife to his house. At times it so happens that the *Kutumb* of the girl pull the roof of the house and go away; in such way quarrel to come to end. But in some places no quarrel is witnessed, everything goes peacefully and happily. After that the dance continues whole night in the village.

Lagitata (Marriage By Capture)

There are also very simplified marriage procedures; Koya youths are very independent in selecting out their life partner and also careful. If a boy likes a particular girl and due to circumstances, financial difficulties or harvest failure is not able to set a marriage or also the parents are against the marriage, he arranges half a dozen of his friends and kidnaps the girl from *bazzar* dance woods or from some ceremony and them binds himself to the so called marriage. The dramatic, turbulent, exciting marriage by capture as suggested may be the typical Koya method of uniting a man and women.

When this happens the girl, of-course, is expected to make a great deal of fus, she weeps, screams, but some how or other she usually fails to make a very effective resistance and its taken directly to the would be husband's house. It has seen when a youth is asked", do you like to get your lever with Lagitata" he smiles and then laughs and takes great pleasure in it. Some of the youth described that some girl bite during kidnapping and even kick at them. *Budra* informed that it is very escape. The procedure is really very interesting to see. All of a sudden a group of youth jump on one girl, two of them (one would be husband) and another friend drag the girl catching her arms and all other women prevent near by and sought for help and run away and inform the parents of the girl where about the youth if they know. Sometimes quite resistance may also come if the girl in question is in live with another youth or wife of another one.

Next day the bride's mother and father come to the home of bridegroom with wine to see the girl and naturally a quarrel starts later subsides with a feast and offest of food, etc.

❏ ❏ ❏

REFERENCES

Cainm, John Rev. (1876) : The Bhadachallam Taluka, Godavari, District, South India. The Indian Antiquary supplement, pp. 301-303; 357-59.

Cain, John Rev. (1879) : The Bhadachallam and Robapalli Talukas. The Kois. The Indian Antiguary, pp; 33-66.

Verrier, Elwin, (1950) : Maria Murder & Sucide 2nd Edition Oxford University Press.

Grigson, M.V. (1908) : The Maria Gonds of Bastar - Oxford University Press.

Photo Koya Tribe

KAMARS

Dr. Nilanjan Khatua

The Kamar is a dominant scheduled tribe of Raipur district in Madhya Pradesh During the sixth five year plan, Kamar was identified and included in the list of "Primitive" groups of M.P. The Kamars inhabit in the hill district of Vilaspur, Durg, Surguja and Raipur of Madhya Pradesh. However, they are mainly concentrated in *Gariaband* and *Dhamtari* tahsil of Raipur District. According to 1991 survey by Kamar tribal development agency, Gariaband they constituted 13,110 person in Raipur. According to the census 1981, has total population of Kamar is 17, 517 in madhya Pradesh and 5,939 in Maharashtra.

Origin

The Kamar narrated the following myth of their origin: In the beginning God created a man and women, in whom two children of opposite sex, were born in their old age. Mahadeo However, created a massive deluge over the earth in order to destroy a jackal who had offended Him. One day the old man went for a hunting. While shooting an arrow to a deer, it said, dear hunter it will rain for seven days and there will be great flood. It was a great surprise for him to hear this from a talking dear. So the old man returned to his house and told it to his wife. They put up their children in a *Jhapi-box* made up of bamboo providing with food for twelve years. When the deluge struck every thing went down the water excepting the bamboo box. A generation passed. Mahadeo wanted to create man on the earth. So he made a bird out of the dirt of his body and sent the bird in search of a man int he deluge. The bird discovered the bamboo box (Jhapi) and brought them to Mahadeo. Mahadeo asked them, "who are you"? "the boy and the girl said "We are a pair of brother and sister. So Mahadeo separated them for twelve more years and disfigured their faces with pox marks. Now they could not recognise each other and married. The Kamars are the children of this couple.

History

Russel and Hiralal (1916) have pointed out, "In Bengal and Chotanagpur the term kamar is merely occupational, implying a worker in iron, and similarly kammala in the Telegu country is a designation given to the fire artisan castes". Christoph conferrer Haimendorf has pointed out the existence of a few families of Kamar, aboriginal blacksmiths in the country of the hill Reddis. About them he says, "There can to my mind be no doubt that they are a purely aboriginal population" Dubey* 1951) has mentioned the traditional occupations of the Kamar, according to one of their legend, are all connected with the axe, bow and arrows i.e. *dahi* and *beora* cultivation, collection of forest produce and hunting".

M.A. Sheering (1879) depicts a picture, about the Kamar in this way "The Kamar are found in the remote jungles of Raipur, where they lead a wild life, subsisting on game and on the product of forest. They have a great aversion to agriculture".

Social Division

Russel and Hiralal (1916) mentioned that there are two subdivisions of Kamar tribe like the *Bundhrajiya* and *Mkadia*. The latter are so called because they eat monkeys. Whereas in the monograph of the Kamars. Dube (1951) it is stated that two arbitrary division, the Paharpatiya i.e. the dwellers of the hills and the *Bundhrajiya* i.e. the dwellers of the plains. Recent study (1997) reveals that the Kamar are of two different groups (1) Bandaria or Pahadia Kamar, and (b) Kachharia Kamar. *Pahadia Kamar* are different. During discussion one *Kachharia Kamar*, who lives in the plains, has opined "The Kamar lived in hills in the past, gradually they have come down from hill and began to live in plains, having their own deities.

Clan

The Kamar tribe is divided into a number of exogenous clans or gods. These gots are totemistic Dube (1951) mentioned that there are seven such clans found among them but their totemistic significance is gradually being lost.

Clan		Totem
Jagat		No totem (those who wandered about all over the world)
Netam		Tortoise
Markem		Tortoise
Sori	(a) Waghsori	Tiger
	(b) Nagsori	Gouha snake

Kunjam	Goat
Marai	No totem (those who do not eat any bird, fish, animal that has died a natural death).
Chedaiha	No totem (Those who are youngest)

Members of the Netam and Markam clans freely inter-marry and their unions are regarded as very appropriate. It is true that several clan names are indeed obviously of Gondi origin and occur among Gond tribe. Dube (1951) also expressed the same view. For instance, Netam would to be derived from the *Gondi* word *nei* for *dog*, and *Markam* from the *Gondi* term *Marka* for mango. Like the Netam of Gond tribe, the Netam clan of the Kamar observes the taboo on eating tortoise.

Kamar conception of *Murmati* or original earth has probably reference to the earlier settlement of the clans, from where they gradually migrated to the different parts of the present Kamar country. Dube (1951), mentioned, "Although the original earth which are attached with some of their ancestor spirits and, family gods, was left by their forefathers, they still maintain a sentimental tie with it. Dubey mentioned seven such places of their Murmati like *Od Pahar, Tori Bhui, Amamora, Sinhar hills, Dadaipani, Tuhameta, Dongarkhol.* Recent study (1997), reveals such 12 murmati (which is wrongly mentioned as sub clan in paper of the author) like- *Kotonia, Pandaria, Pondia, Bhat siuiya, Bammandebia, Jarandia, Dando yapalia, Toibhoinya, Kamaipuria, Amma-mouya, Bhundibasia, Amandeiya.* According to Dube, the Kamars knowledge of their murmati, today, is confused and does not play a significant part in their social and religion life. But their clan organisation an exogamous units is still important and occupies a very significant place in their social organisation.

Economy

The Kamars are traditionally shiffting cultivators, locally known as *Dahi* and *Beora,* and expert hunters. Collection of minor forest produce and basketry are their perennial economic activities. Agricultural labour, forest labour, fuel wood selling, charcoal selling are seasonal economic activities on which the Kamar subsist only for a part of the year. They have adopted settled cultivation to a great extent abandonning their age-old practice of shifting cultivation. Now hinting as a traditional occupation has little role in the Kamar economy. Now-a-days, hunting is merely a recreation for them. This is due to certain restrictions imposed by the government through the Land Revenue Act, New Forest Games Rules, and Forest Act etc. Urbanization, spread of education and communication network, various development schemes have helped them to take up new economic pursuits like government service, petty trades etc. Though in much smaller scale.

Life Cycle

(i) Birth

Life cycle of the kamar primarily centers round three stages, i.e. birth, marriage and death. Birth of a child is a fact of great socio-religious significance. After child birth, the umbilical cord is cut either with an arrow-head or with the knife by the suin, an experienced elderly women of their own community. The birth purificatory ceremony known as *Chhatti* is performed on the day on which the naval cord drops off. On this day, the father shaves his new born child after trimming the head-hair with a scissor. And then the mother and the child are given a pure bath. After this ceremony the child is cared and looked after by the family members and others. But the mother continues to be impure for two months, father the birth of a male child and for three moths after the birth of female child. On the last day of the pollution period a ceremony known as the *Handi Dharia* is performed and from this day the mother is allowed to cook or start house-hold work. On this day mother and the child are given pure bath. Dubey (1951), reported that there is no special ceremony for the naming of the child, although a few Kamars directly under the influence of caste Hindu, have begun to give it a little ceremonial colouring. It is their general belief that rebirth of some ancestors occurs in the form of the new born baby. On the very day to *Chhatti* one of the elders of t he family offers *hom-kuhara* (burning of Gum of Sal tree and incense) and some liquor to the family deities and may also sacrifice a chicken.

Marriage

The Kamar are endogamous tribe which indicates no marriages with outsiders are permitted. No marriage is also permissible between persons belonging to same clan. Among the Kamars marriage takes places in the month of *Fagun* (Fed-March), *Baisakh* (April-May). Marriage by negotiation or *Bihaw* is the general rule. Besides this, there are other following ways for acquiring a mate found among them.
a. Runaway marriage or *Odaria*.
b. *Paithu* or Marriage by intrusion.

c. Widow remarriage
d. Marriage by service or *Lamsena or Gharjawai*
e. Marriage by exchange or *gurawat*

The most commonest form of marriage is the *bihaw*, which is arranged by the consent of the parents of the bride and the groom. Marriage generally take place between adults. The average marital age of boys and girls are 17 years and 14 years respectively.

Marriage proposal are opened by the boy's side who sent their *Mahalia* (Middle man) to the house of the proposed bride. The *Mahalia* is either a brother, near relative or friend of the bride groom's father, who has the capacity for negotiating well when he goes to the girl's house with the proposal, he takes with him a bottle of liquor wrapped in a cloth. If the negotiations are successful and then the bride's party give their consent. Before the *Mahalia* i.e. engagement. It is also known as *faldan* or *mangni*.

A party of about ten people including the bride groom, *village Baiga* (priest), one or two elders and a few friends of the bridegroom goes to the brides' house. They take with them 3 bottle of liquor, about five to ten *Katha* of rice, and a few other sundries.

After an hour's rest in the girl's village the parties assemble in the courtyard of the house. The member of the both parties sit facing to each other. The boy and the girl are made to stand before the elders. Then after some convincial comments by the two parties liquor is spriknled over the couple. This is followed by the feast of rice and liquor brought by the boy's people. Before the bridegroom's party leaves for home, they fix the time for marriage.

After the engagement with the party of the bridegroom the girl goes to the house of her prospective husband for about a week. After this period the *Mahalia* bings her back to her father's place After *Faldan*, but before marriage it is the duty of boy's guardians to bring their prospective daughter in-law to their house on all important festivals like *Diwali, Deseara, Newakhai, Charchera* and *Hareli*.

As soon as the *barat* (marriage party) approaches near the *madwa* (marriage pandal) the bride's people welcome them after washing the feet of all the persons coming in the *barat*. The marriage party are offered tobacco and *bidi* for smoking. The boy's party brings with it about 1 *Khandi* of rice, 1 *tipa of liquor*(24 bottles), two *katha* (5kg) or pulse, other spices like oil, turmeric etc. two or three *lugra* (saree), *Fundra* (multi-coloured string for tying the hair), one pair of earnings. All these things are given to the bride's people accordingly to the agreement previously made.

By this time of welcoming the marriage party the bride's body is massaged with oil and turmeric. Then the bride and the bridegroom take seven rounds of the marriage post and are then seated near it. The marital rituals that follows in that of *tel-chadana* (rubbing of oil turmeric from the legs towards the head). The *suasin*, who are generally elder sister or friends of the bride, first rub oil mixed with turmeric on body of both bride and the bride groom.

The *mahalia* then takes the bride in his lap and the boy's elder brother takes the bride groom. They stand facing each other. Two person stand opposite to each other holding a piece of cloth between the *mahalia* and the boy's elder brother thus obstructing the bride and the bridegroom from seeing each other. Then the bride and bridegroom throw rice at each other.

The *mahalia* then goes up on the *madwa* and the bride and bridegroom are seated near the marriage post. The *mahalia* pours three of four *Handi* (mud vessel) of water over them. Consequently the group there become muddy. All then join together to sing and dance after consuming with liberal quantities of liquor.

Then they go with the new couple to the tank or the river for bathing. Here the new couple are required to play *panpudi-a* sort of hide and seek in water. When the bride and the bridegroom reach home after finishing their bath they find the *mahalia* sleeping under the *madwa*, and he is given a coconut and a bottle of liquor.

Every one then prepare for their ceremonies of *lagin Utana* and *tikan*. The man, either the village priest or one of the near relatives, is ready for lagin, observing a fast on that day. Near the marriage post a rectangular design with rice flour is made. The bride and bridegroom are seated on it, facing opposite to each other. The ends of their respective wears are brought together and made a knot keeping with rice grains and seven pieces of turmeric. Then the couple take seven rounds of the marriage post of *Madwa*. Then they sit for the *tikan* when friends and relatives offer them little presents. When the *tikan* is over, the man who has to see the *lagin* opens the knot.

Monogamy is the rule though polygamous marriage can also be

performed. They have no custom of paying bride price. But a fair list of articles is given by the bridegroom side to the bride's father. Dubey 1951, said "Bride price is neither asked for, nor it is ever offered. The Kamars do not hold in esteem the custom of "Selling away daughters", for a petty bride-price".

Death

To bury the deads is the traditional way of disposing of dead body among the Kamar. But it is also seems that reputed village priest or persons are dying in very old age, and those who are respectable, are cremated. The head of the copse is kept towards the north during cremation or burial. After the corpse has been buried a stone is erected above the head of the dead body and over the whole grave a heap of boulders small stones is placed. All the goods in the personal use of the deceased are kept near his grave.

When the funeral is over, all people participated in the funeral ceremony take their bath, wash their cloths and return to the village in file. The women sprinkle water mixed with cowdung in their houses and then take their bath and wash their cloths.

On the third day after death-a ceremony called as *Tijnahar* is performed for purification. The massage of the death is sent round to all relatives in the neighboring Kamar settlement. On this occasion all of them assemble i n the house of the deceased. It is necessary that all relatives should be present generally a member from each of them, Ceremonial hair-cutting takes place in the presence of all relatives by a member of other clan and then all take bath. After returning home they apply a little of turmeric mixed oil and with this they are supposed to have become clean. The women belonging to the deceased persons family throw away all the olden earthen post and cook a quantity or rice in a new earthen post or in washed pots (in case of aluminum or silver vessels) for those who have assembled. The funeral feast can be arranged within a year after the death it they are unable to arrange the same on the thirteenth day in case of unnatural death (accidental death) the Kamars do not perform any death rituals. In that case they go to the jungle along with the Baiga and sacrifice animal so that such mishappening is not repeated in the family.

Political Organisation

The elder member of the village 'Panchayat to take care of the social control in the community. Dube (1951) mentioned that there is no central authority common to the whole tribe. A group of settlement close to one another. Constitute their own panchayat which is supreme in the socio-religious matters of the members of the tribe living in the constituent settlements.

The panchyat have a *Kurha*, the chief of all the village *Sarpanch*, the presiding officer of the group panchayat and the *Chaprasi*- an official who is required to intimate to all concerned the date and place of the meeting of the Panchayat.

In the Panchayat, decisions are arrived at by a majority, Although votes of the people assembled are never taken, the elders present in the meeting freely express their opinions. The panchayat puniushes the offender by imposing a fine in cash and penal feast and expulsion of the member from the community. Adultery, incest between close relation, quarrels, social irregularities, are settled by Panchyat, Breach of any of the customary laws of the tribe are settled also by the panchayat.

Fair and festivals

There are several religious ceremonies observed by the Kamars. These are the following:

Hareli

This festival celebrated in the month of Sawan (July-August) is more important than others. On this day the Kamars do not go out on any economic pursuits. The Baiga-village priest takes his bath early in the morning and collects some branches of *neem tree* He keeps some of these branches in the shed of the *Mata* on the village boundary and fixes a few of these branches under roof of all the houses in the village.

The first thing which every family has to do in the morning is to offer a little quantity of salt to the cattle. All then go out to take their bath. All them assemble in the cooking room in the corner of which the platform of *Gata Dooma* is located. Women withdraw from the scene. Then the chief member of the family under whose roof the deities are lodged, keeps small quantities of rice on each of the five leaves kept in front of the platform of *Gata-Dooma*. The chicken intended for sacrifice is then brought in and left there. When they begin eating rice which signifies the acceptance of the worship by the *Gata Dhoma*.

The chicken is immediately sacrificed with a knife. Then *hom-kurha* is offered to the deities by burning some Sarai gum and they prey with some mantra (hymn). After worshipping the menfolks come out from the inner room. IN the Verandah they drink the liquor specially distilled for the occasion.

Nawakhali

Nawakhali is the new eating ceremony is another important festival of the Kamar. It is celebrated in any time in the month of Bhado or kuar (August-Sept-October) when a part of the new crop is ready. The data of celebration is fixed by consultation among the members of the village. On the day fixed for the festival, the Kamars reap some crops and bring it home. After the return of the menfolks the women go for bath. In this occasion, men from different families make a new wooden spoon (*Karchhul*). The women cook a little quantity new crops in a new earthen pot and offer the same before the platform of the *Gata Dooma*. They offer *hom-Kurha* by burning a little quantity of sarai gum along with chanting some mantras. Liquors adds to the festivity of the day. The whole day, in then passed in gossipping, occasionally in singing and dancing.

Pora or Pola

Pora or Pola is primarily observed by the Baiga - the village priest and the boys and girls of the village. The Baiga keeps a fast, the day previous to pora. On this day, he eats only once and it is necessary that the food which he eats should not be cooked or touched by a woman. On the day of Pora, he takes a bath early in the morning. Then unnoticed by any women he proceeds to the *Mata Kuriya* with six branches of Paddy, vermilion, five black bangles, one fundra (Strings for hair band) and two fowls and offers the same to the Mata. Returning to the village he distributes a little quantity of *gur* to all the families living in the settlement. The young girls are then given new baskets windowing fans, *chulha* (oven) specially made for their play. The boys play with earthen bulls bought from the Kumhar (potter).

Diwali

The Kamar observe *Diwali* with their neighboring Hindu village folk. Those who have cattle of their own give them a little *Khichadi* to eat. They offer *hom-kiuha* (gum of sarai tree) to the deities. They also participate in dance, performed by the village menfolks. In the evening all the villagers organize a drama made by local youth and other cultural functions.

Chherchera

The *Chherchera* festival which comes on the full moon day in the month of *Pus* (December - Jan) observe in a gaily mood. From the morning, the Kamar make their appearance funny by applying ashes to their bodies. Some put on marks made of dried gourd. Some are clad in wild bear's skin. Still others tie various jungle creepers to their bodies. They go in a team to every house door and collect small quantities of paddy and rice. When the collection is over, they return home, take their bath and cook and eat the rice in a great joy.

Fagun tihar

Fagun tihar is observed int he month of *Fagun* (Feb-March). They worship *Thakurdeo* in this day. This festival is performed in family-level. After taking their bath, the male members of the family assemble in the cooking room. *Homkurha* with *Sal gum* is offered. The head of the family takes some fresh half-blown *mohua* flowers, washes them with water and keeps in front of the *Gata-dooma* platform. On this great occasion meat or pork and mahua liquor is considered to be a necessity on this day.

Kamar deities

There are several distinct categories of deities worshipped by the Kamar. The family deities include Dharti Mata (Mother Earth), ancestral spirits, Bhudha-raja and Dulha Deo. All these are lodged in the inner room, on a special platform of the *Gata Dooma*. Outside the house, but within the tribal settlement, the Kamars worship different goddess like *Mai, Devi, Badi-Mata, Manjhli mata Sendurimata* and *Chhoti mata*. In the third category various deities connected with territorial cults and worships. The Kamars living around Bhatigarh hills near Manipur, worship the *Bhatigarh-mal* . Those around the *Bamhni hill* worship *Bamhnai mai*. The cult of *Kachna Dhurwa* is prevalent throughout the Bindranawagarh *Zamindari*.

"The goods and deities worshipped by the kamars are believed to safeguard jealously their legitimate rights and interests. Among the Kamars, the belief in *jiv*, which may in other words be described as the 'Soul substance' is universal. It is the *Jiv* which keeps a man living walking and talking. Death occurs when the *Jiv* levels the body permanently" Dube (1951).

REFERENCE

Dube, S.C. (1951): The Kamar, The Universal Publishers Ltd., Lucknow.

Khatua, N. (1998): Changing Trends Among the Kamar" in Vanyajati, Vol. XLVI, No.2

Khatua, N. (1998): "The Kamar Economy in Transition" in the Seminar Volume "Tribal Transformation and Development, by NIRSA, Hyderabad.

Mitra, M: (1996): 'Kamar' in Encyclopedic Profile of Indian Tribes Vol. II (Eds.) Sachchidanande & R.R. Prasad, Discovery Publishing House, New Delhi.

Mukherjee, B.M. and Nilanjan Khatua (1998): "Exchange and Reciprocity in Kamar Tribe" in Man in India vol. 78 No. 384, pp (349-364).

Russell, R.V. & Siralal, R.B. (1916): Tribes and Castes of Central Provinces of India. Vol. III, Cosmo Publishers, New Delhi.

Sheering, M.A. (1879): Hindu Tribes and Castes, Vol. V, Calcutta, Thacker Spink.

Photo Kamars Tribe

KINNAURI

Rajesh Khanna
and
Dr. A.K. Kapoor

INTRODUCTION

Kinnaur District, the north eastern frontier district of Himachal Pradesh and border district of India lies in the western Himalayas on both banks of river Sutlej. It is situated between 31°05'50" and 32°05' north latitude and between 77°45' and 79°35" east longitude. It is about 80 kilometers in length and nearly 65 kilometers in breadth.

Earlier, Kinnaur was the part of the princely state of Bushahr. The Bushahr merged with the territory of Himachal Pradesh after Independence, the Kinnaur region formed a tehsil of Mahasu district. it came into being as an independent district in 1960 along with some part of the former Rampur Tehsil of *Mahasu* district. After this forms the north eastern frontier district of Himachal pradesh along the international boundary with Tibet region of Republic of China.

Kinnaur is surrounded by the Lahaul Spiti in the north, Garhwal (UP) in the south and Shimla in the west. In the easterly direction Kinnaur has its boundary with Tiber and forms an international border. The Sutluj valley divides the district equally. The elevation of the peaks in mountain ranges very between 5,180 and 6,770 meters and therefore are covered with snow all the year around.

Area of the district is 5,553 square km. The entire population is classified as S.C. or S.T. The population of the district comprises of four distinct classes of *Kanets* (Rajputs), *Chamangs* (Kolis, preparing shoes, weaving, tailoring and musix drum beating) and *Domangs* {Lohar (Blacksmith) and Badhi (Carpentry), *Nagloo* (Basket makers)}.

Sutluj, the principal river of the district originates in the Himalayan and is perennial sources of water. The length of the Sutluj is about 130 kilometers in the district. Another river of the district is Spit of lee. The Baspa river, another feeder of the Sutluj, rises from Dhaula Dhar mountain of the Himalayan passes through valley bearing its name and meets Sutluj at a place called *Karchham* after a distance of 72 km.

Kinnaur, due to its geographically situation, has a long winter from October to May, the snowy season. Clouding is more heavy, persistent and prolonged in the long winter season. There are strong winds in the winter months and a short summer from June to September. From April to May is spring and from september to October is autumn.

The Hindustan Tibet road is only one important road led from Shimla and entered Kinnaur beyond Sarhan.

The geographically condition of the Kinnaur district have created barrier and hence the district is conveniently divided into three culturally barrier which are as follows.
(a) Lower region dominated by Hindu culture of the main land
(b) Middle region having a mixture it Tibetan and Hindu influence, and
(c) Upper region influenced by Tibetan culture.

The above mentioned cultural division correspond to the administrative division of the district into three sub division, namely *Pooh, Kalpa* and *Nichar.*

STATISTICAL PROFILE OF KINNAUR DISTRICT

S. No.	Particulars	Unit	Year	Kinnaur Dist.	Himachal Pradesh
1	Population	No.	1991	71,270	5,170,877
2	Geographical Area	Sq. Km	1991	6,401	55,673
3	Density of population	per sq. Km.	1991	11	92
4	Percentage of S.T. population to total population	%	1991	55.58	4.22
5	Percentage of S.C. population to total population	%	1991	26.87	25.34
6	Sex Ratio	No. of F/M	1991	856	976

Kinnauri

S. No.	Particulars	Unit	Year	Kinnaur Dist.	Himachal Pradesh
7	Literacy person Male Female	%	1991	8.36 72.04 42.04	63.86 75.36 52.13
8	No. of Household	No.	1991	16,333	969,018
9	No. of Village Total No. Inhabited Uninhabited	No.	1991	662 228 435	19,388 16,997 2,391
10	Cropped Area	'000 Hec.	1991	93.36	-
11	No. of Gram Panchayat	No.	1991	62	2,922
12	Allopathic Civil Hospital PHC CHC SC	No.	1991	1 17 3. 32	40 317 54 2,070

Census of India 1991, Statistical outline of Himachal Pradesh, Shimala.

ORIGIN AND HISTORY

The Kinnauri has strong association with Hindu mythology, Most of the ancient literature have referred to these people as 'Super Being' higher and different than the common man the Homo sapiens: and nearer to the order of God along with *Gandharva, Haksha, Kirat*, etc. According to the *Raj Tarangi Kinnauri* are said to have born from the shadow of Lord Brahma (Singh, 1969: 110)

Kalidas, the great Sanskrit scholar, has composed verses in praise of Kinnaur and has given them importance in his famous *Megadoota*. According to Chakravarti, Kinnauri might have their origin from *Sumerians*, branch of whom become famous by the name Simbiar and the consecutive distribution of Simbeari in the Himalayan area give rise to the people called *Kinnauri* (Kaushal, 1967). According to the Shashi (1971), the word Kinnar means half giant and on this basis they are also known as *Ashvamukha* (cf District Handbook, 1961).

The Kinnaur have been declared as Scheduled Area under the Fifth Schedule of the Constitution obey the President of India as per the Schedule Areas (HP) Order 1975 dated 21st November 1975. The inhabitant of the Kinnaur i.e. Kinnauri has been referred at several places in Sanskrit literature. There are many variants of Kinnauri such as *Koonauri, Kannaura, Koonawri, Kinnaur, Kinnauries, Kinauri,* and *Kinnauri*. The *Kinnauri* are divided into five ethnic groups i.e. *Kanet, Koli, Badhi, Lohar* and *Nagloo*. Mainly there are two division one of the *Kanet* and the other includes rest of the ethic groups are considered to be socially of low class and looked down upon by the *Kanet*.

On the basis of hierarchy, the *Kanet* are further divided into many groups based on the observance and closer touch with greater Hindu ways of life. The generic term *Kinnauri* also includes the low caste people commonly known as *Domang* and *Chamang*. The *Kanet* have treated them as their *serfs* having no status. These people mainly comprises of the artisan class and are considered untouchable whether they be *Koli* having the occupation of preparing shoes, weaving, tailoring and music drum beating, the *Badhi* having the carpentry, Lohar - Black smith and *Nagaloo* - Basket making. The language and the history or tradition of these people is not different and there is no marked difference in their religious and social customs and practices. They appear to be on continuum in this regards with the *Kanet* with some minor degree of variation in few cases.

The *Kinnauri* along the Tibetan border posses the *Mongoloid* and *Tatar* features and are of fair complexion and good looking with Persian features. *Homskad* is the *Kinnauri* dialect. It is the mother tongue of nearly seventy-five per cent of the population of Kinnaur.

LIFE PATTERN

Settlement Pattern and Housing

Commonly the houses in the Kinnaur are of double stories but the houses of nobles or landlords comprise of more than two stories. There is one living room on each story and ground floor is used for cattle shed, except where there is worship place as in case of ironsmiths. The first is always used for the living purpose. It has extends wooden balconies each story comprises only one room therefore there is no separate bathroom or kitchens. For the dual purpose of letting the smoke out and admitting the light, hole is provided in the room. The earth is set in the center of the room. The roof of the houses is mostly flat and are made of wooden planks covered with tree bark and overlaid with earth. Brass and Bronze utensils are in common use in the area. Aluminum utensils are beginning to find favor with the people especially during the travel. Earthen pots are also used besides women wooden articles. Vessels made of the metals are procured from the plains. Walls are decorated with picture of men women, trees, moon, stars, sheep goats and flowers drawn crudely with chalk like material.

Kinnauri wear woolen cloths throughout the year because of cold climate of the area. Men and women have a common head dress which is a woolen cap locally called *Thepang*. The dress of the men includes woolen shirts (*chamu-kurti*), long coat (*chhubha*), woollen *pyjams* (*chamu suttan*) mostly of gray colour. Some people put on *tapru-suttan*) embroided in various design and colours below the knees during the marriage and festival season. The dress of the women includes woolen *sari* (dhori) full-sleeved blouse (*choli*), *chhanli* or *shawl*. It is wrapped round the shoulders and its two ends are fasted together near breast by means of a silver hook called *digra*.

Ornaments are the most valuable possession of a Kinnauri women. They are normally made of silver and comprises of *mool trimani kantaie kandoch chalim shanglavang, digra, tomach, hung, lung, dhaglo*, etc. Men generally do not use ornaments except *Murki* for the ear and rings for the finger.

Kunnauri have three meals a days - in the morning in the noon and at night. Their staple food includes wheat, *ogla, phafra* and barely. Besides this *kangni* (kawing), *Cheema, maize (chhallia) koda (kodru) chollaie dhankher* and *bathu* are also used. Peas, black beans, mash and *masur* are the main pulses consumed. Cabbage, turnip, peas, beans, pumpkin, potato and tomato are the chief vegetables. Kinnauri relish meat. Smoking is widely common among the Kinnauri.

Religion

The traditional religion of Kinnaur is centered entirely on the principal village deity which is divinity, a doctor, magistrate, a judge, the chief executive, an astrologer, the village hero etc. Hinduism has introduced Rama, Krishan, the *Ramayana*, the *Mahabharata*, the *Gita*, the *Sukh Sagar*, the *Prem Sagar*, some of the *Puranas* and some of the relevant systems of worship over a period of time Later monastic *Buddhism* came to be established in the regions bordering Tibet. This led to the original form of animistic faith and worship is losing its traditional hold. The present situation is that village god and their retinues are still very strong and side by side there exist laministic *Buddhism* and local version of *Hinduism*. The religious rites of birth, marriage and death are performed in accordance with the local version of Hinduism as interpreted by the local priests who generally are the Lamas particularly in the upper and central part of region.

Family Structure

The joint family system prevails in Kinnaur. Under one roof not only father, sons, brothers but also uncles, nephews of the same decent live and sometimes even own property in common. The system is under serious strain due to the advent of modern civilization in the area. Inheritance of property is patrilineal. The division of the property among the polyandric group, the of *jethang* (primogeniture) is followed. In this rule the eldest has the first right to choose than the youngest. In practice a good field is inherited by the eldest brother and the ancestral house is inherited by the youngest. It is believed that the eldest can work hard on the field and get they yield desired and settle himself in life properly, the youngest son as a beginner should have at least shelter to begin with Girls have no legal right in the property.

Kinnauri are polyandrous people **"All brothers usually share one common wife"** that makes the polyandry of fraternal type. In the polyandrous family the relationship between son and fathers is not difficult to establish, Normally the practice is that the all the husbands are recognized as the fathers of each child. The eldest among the husbands is called *Teg Boda* (elder father) and others as *Jigich Boba or Goto* (Young Fathers). For day to day use the eldest among the living brothers is spoken of as the father of all the children born to a polyandrous wire. These days the institution of polyandry is gradually on its way out.

Economy

The chief occupation of the Kinnauri is agriculture. However, no single economy is sufficient enough to fulfil the requirements of the household because of the peculiar geo-ecological conditions of the area. Other economic activities include tending sheep and goatherds, domestication of some milk cattle, and undertake trading activities with the people of the adjoining areas and also work as laborers. Other ethnic groups may also have these as their economic pursuits. They are also some specialist of some particular occupations like carpentry, iron smith of making of shoe etc.

Political Organization

The political organization of the Kinnauri resoles around the village deity and panchyayat along with the modern system of administration. The village deity who commands great respect among the people and his words are respected by the villagers in order to avoid future curse of God. There is a Panchayat consisting of two or three noblemen of the village. The main function of the village Panchayat is to settle dispute among the people of the village. Members of the Panchayat include old and respectable persons of the village community, they known the facts of the dispute. Personal hearing are given to opposite parties to put forward their claims and counter claims. After hearing the parties, the Panchayat decides the dispute them and there to the satisfaction of all concerned. The old system of administration of justice generally and in personal matters particularly, still enjoys the confidence of the majority of the people in the region though the modern system of administration also exist in the area.

LIFE CYCLE

Birth Rituals

The Kinnauri do not consider pregnancy as an abnormal period Delivery usually takes place in a separate room. A midwife called *api* in the local dialect is respected by the baby like a mother throughout her lifetime. Mother is made to eat hot *ghee* immediately after the delivery. saturated hydraulic conductivity *Chuli khali* (hill fruit like apricot or peaches) is boiled in water and the mother and baby are bathed in it. During the first fortnight after the delivery, a daily massage with *chuli* oil is given to the mother and child followed by a hot water bath. During the fortnight after the delivery, the mother is usually served with a balanced diet consisting of the *ghee*, animal fat, *chuli oil* barley or *ogla status*, wheat *chapaties* with butter *halva*, coconut and rice. Chilies and sour or tart ingredients are avoided.

The mother and her family observe 'begnang' for the seven days in which they are not allowed to enter places of worship as they are considered unclean. The musical instruments and other vessels are kept in the temple and also not to be touched by them. On the seventh day the whole house is cleaned and *gomutra* (cow's urine) and *gangajal* (Ganga water) sprinkled everywhere.A smering coating) of the cow dung is done in the Kitchen. The mother is then brought out with the child in verandah Seven pebbles are placed over which mixture of saturated hydraulic conductivity *gomutra* and *gangajal* is sprinkled. The mother then goes round these pebbles seven times and ont he completion of each circle she throws away one of the pebbles. In certain cases a Lama also performs the *hawan* on seventh day. During this occasion close relatives and members of the clan (*biradari*) depute their representative to convey blessings to the newborn. They bring with them a few grams of *Ghee* or *chuli oil* and two kilograms of wheat or *ogla* four or *kanwni* rice as the present for the mother. A feast is arranged for these guests. The offering are received only from people of the same caste strictly on the basis of give and take.

Mundan

A mundan (shaving of the head) ceremony takes place when the child attains the age of 1 or 2 years. The day is fixed in consultation with Lama. This is done on the full moon day or during the bright half of the month. o.e. *shukla- paksha*. Each odd month is considered auspicious. The *Mundan* is performed by the maternal uncle or in his absence some other person whose mother and father are alive and hairs are buried.

In case a child happens to cut the upper tooth first then this is considered a bad oemn for the mother's paraents and brother. To ward off the evil effect, the mother or her husband would send a massage regarding this to the maternal uncle. Then the child's maternal uncle would bring a few cloths for the child. Before entering house, he would drop these clothes through *Dusrang* (outlet for the smoke). Mother would collect then and put them on the child immediately. The maternal uncle would then enter the house thorough the main door.

Marriage Rituals

Marriage is popularly known in Kinnaur as *Rehja* it is settled much earlier when boys and girls are very young. The marriage is settled by offering a piece of cloth (*khatak*) and bottle of liquor by the bridegroom. After some time the bridegroom father along with some other person goes to the prospective bride's house and agrees upon the day of marriage and decides how much money of bridegroom's side will give tot he bride's family. For the purchase the cloths and ornament for the bride, money is paid before the date of the marriage. If the wife leaves her husband and goes with another man, this money has to be returned. An offering to the family deity or village deity follows the acceptance of the proposal. A marriage date is than fixed in consultation with a *Lama* or the village priest. On the appointed date, the bridegroom goes to the bride's place and is accompanied by the small party of half a dozen or so along with the village band. The party stays there for two feasts held in the honour of the party at the bride's place.

The bridegroom returns home with bride after the Merrymaking during the night. The ladies belonging tot he bride's village but married in the groom's village go out to welcome the bride and take with them wine and other eatables for the guest. A *Puja* (worship) is performed to placate the evil spirits supposed to have come with the party than the party goes to the groom's house. The sister or mother or the groom welcomes the bride. The symbolic ritual called *oopage* is performed. In this Groom's maternal uncle wraps a turban around the head of groom and his brothers. Garland of *chilgoza, chulia* and walnuts are draped round their necks by the bride.

After the marriage is over, the groom's father sets asides some piece of land for the bride. This is confirmed in writing on a plain or stamped paper. The paper remains with the girl's father or maternal uncle in the presence of a Middleman. Similarly surety bond is given by the bride's father to the effect that said document should become inoperative in case of divorce. A list of weighed utensils is than prepared before they are given. In the event or divorce these utensils or cost there of has to be reimbursed by groom 's father.This custom is called *'bandobust'* ceremony. In the end a ceremony called *'borshimik'* takes place where the pride garlands all the members of a marriage party with the *chuli* of *chilgoza* embracing them and weeping bitterly, while bidding farewell.

Other forms of marriages are *dumtangshis* (Love Marriage), *dubdhub* (Marriage by capture) and *har* (enticing away someone wife).

Divorce

Divorce is permissible among all the group of Kinnaur. If the woman wants a divorce she usually does it through her parents. In the divorce proceeding, the parents of the women and her husband or husbands gather at a place on an appointment day and settle the accounts. The utensils, ornaments and cash given to the women at the time of marriage by the parents have to be returned by the husband or the husbands. Finally a twig is placed between the couple and they break this twig; this symbolized the breaking of the marriage.

Death Rituals

Earlier the Kinnauri used to keep the dead body on the hill top to be eaten by the animals and birds. But due to the impact of *Hinduism in kinnaur*, the dead body is cremated. Infants upto age of the two years who happen to die are buried. In case of Children above two years and below five years, the body is thrown into the river.

Panchratna (alloy of gold, silver, copper, brass and iron) is kept in the month before the death of the person. A *Lama* is often called to stand by and to recite some mantras and to pray for the eternal peace of the soul. The dead body is bathed in the warm water. *Brass lamp* is lit with *chuli* or mustered oil on the spot of the death. This continues to burn for seven-day continuously. A pot full of barley is also placed next to the lamp.

A band accompanies the funeral procession by plying sad tunes. The man leading the procession carries an urn with live coals. Barley is scattered at frequent intervals all along the last journey. One man from each household in the village accompanies the corpse for collecting wood and other material for the pyre. The son or nearest relative light the Pyre from the direction in which head is placed. The ashes are carried mostly to the *Ganga* or *Sutluj* . Close relatives shave their head in the respect to the dead. During this period the family members do not eat meat, oil, fried articles of food, onion, garlic or turmeric, nor do they season with *tudka* or *chhuk* (spices fried in heated oil) for the eight days. On the eight-day the family members purify themselves then the house is cleaned both actually and ritually. In the evening they get together and a feast is held in which no wood taboos are observed (called *kolyashinmg*). On the fifteenth day a general feast is held for the villagers in the temple. In this feast *chiltas* are distributed and these are taken home *Asting* is the last ritual after the death is known. It is performed on the thirteenth day following the day for death. A grand dinner is given to the relatives and villagers in whom *poltus* are distributed.

❑ ❑ ❑

REFERENCE

Census of India, (1961): District Census Hand Book, Kinnaur District.
Census of India (1991): Statistical outline of Himachal pradesh, Shimla.
Chakravarti, Chandra: Racial History of India.
Kaushal, R.K. (1965): Himachal Pradesh, A Survey of the History of the Land and its People, Delhi.
Shashi, S.S. (1971): Himachal's Nature's Peaceful Paradise, New Delhi.

❑ ❑ ❑

KORA

Rajesh Kumar Chaudhary

The word Kora is a corrupt form of *Koda* which is a *Mundari* word and it stands for cutting and digging soil. The occupation moral is also considered by them which is carried out by them since time immemorial is also considered by them as their primary and traditional occupation. Though there are some belief and evidence which corroborate the fact that once upon a time they worked ad *Kahar* or as career of *palkis* of Landlord and British Administrator.

The Koras in the state of Bihar are the inhabitants or *Dumka, Godda, Sahebganj. Deoghar, Pakur, Banka, Jamui, Mongher, Bckaro, Chaibasa, Katihar*, and *Dhanbad* district. The total population of kora tribe in the state of Bihar is 33,915. Out of which 17,790 (52.93 percent) are male and the female population is constituted by 47.07 per cent of the total Kora population and they are some 16,161 in number. The birth-rate of the tribe is 45.20 and the death-rate of the tribe is estimated to be 18.30. The annual growth-rate of the tribe is 8.92. The literacy-rate of the tribe is estimated to be just over 4.15 per thousand kora population. (1996 Census). The racial type of tribe is proto-australoid. The chief languages spoken by Kora tribe are - *Mundari, Sadani, Khorta, Patois, Dikuani* and *Hindi*.

Origin

This community, after Paharias may be considered as one of the early settlers or *Santhal* pargansas. Kora claim themselves to be *Nagawansi* i.e. one who descends from *Naga* or Cobra Snakes. They believed that once upon a time they used to live somewhere in Nagpur. But on the basis of oral history re-construction, I came to the conclusion that it was actually chottanagpur.

An interesting account of mythological story was recorded during investigation from one of the informant Sri Sushil Kora, about the origin and the nomenclature of this community, which help us understanding when, why and also how this community has been given the name kora. The story goes on to say that when lord Rama along with his army of monkeys were constructing the bridge in order to have control on Sri Lanka to get back sita from the clutch of devil king Ravana, Modi, a

Kora

Tribal community masquerading as monkey went there in benevolent mood to help lord Rama. They fought bravely and whole heatedly, by which the battle become less vigor and lastly it was won by the mighty and the unconguarable army of Lord Rama. After the battle was won, Rama became very happy with the assistance and help during the war by the Modi community. From there, Lord Rama gave the name *Kora* to this *Modi* community, because Sri Lanka was carried out by the *Modi* community. Thus since the days of Indo-Sri Lankan was this community is known by the name of *Kora*.

History

According to their old mythological stories and folk-songs one may come to the conclusion that they came to chottanagpur and settled there with *santhal, Munda* and *oraon* Tribal communities, after crossing the plains of Ganga, Jamuna Doab sometime during early days of Mughal in hills of *Rajmahal* and the adjoining districts of even West Bengal.

There are also evidence which can be taken as proof that during mughal invasion the koras have adopted the same strategy in connection with their migration, as adopted by the Santhals. It would be worth mentioning here that santhal came to settle in *Santhal Pargana* to clear the Jungles and to drive away the *Paharias*.

On the invitation of the then British Administration, during 1790 and 1810. It is said that during loden days Koras used to live with their powerful king (name unknown), who was then the ruler of a kingdom located somewhere in Nagpur (Chottanagpur). During Mughal invasion at the time, while Babur was the emperor, Kora king defeated and he fled to some unknown place, leaving the entire kora community in great distress. After that the Mughal army started plundering, looting and setting ablaze the villages that came in their ways. They also started converting the religion of the poor masses, who either had to adopt *Islam* or the death penalty. *Santhals* during those days were inhabiting those days deep inside the jungles. In order to save themselves from the wrath and vandalism or Mughal army kora community preferred to hide themselves inside the santhal village in the jungle.

Santhals wanted to help Koras and at the same time they were very much concerned about there own securities. Santhal the advancing Mughal army. They killed some pigs and it was left hanging on both the sides of the approaching village lane. This tactics of hiding and providing shelter to kora tribe worked as Mughal army did not enter the village because they thought that the village is inhabited by Santhals. And by that time Koras were already mixed with the Santhal population of the village. Later on both these communities came close to each other and decided to live together.

Social Division

The entire Kora community is sub-divided into 19 different clans which are locally known as *Custhi*. These are the totemic clan being associated with a definite group of individuals set in certain relation to an animal, a plant, an object animate of inanimate, after which they are named and in connection with which the view provide that the members of this group cannot establish material ties among them and that the object after which the group is named must be respected. Between clan members there are obligation for support in trouble, hospitality and recognition of kinship.

There subgroups of Kora tribe may include the local group of village community, which is a distinct social unit. It comprises a number of families, living in a common settlement, total or village, which perform certain ceremonies, functions for their common welfare. These subgroups among kora proves to be a bigger unit then the family itself. The sub-groups are the following:

1. Kach
2. Tamgaria
3. Kauri
4. Chiru
5. Porea
6. Merom
7. Kisarh
8. Sandwar
9. Chilrbail
10. Nagarhu
11. Basuki
12. Tirki
13. Toppo
14. Horo
15. Khuntah
16. Kadih
17. Hurduar
18. Sarh-sapu
19. Butkoi

Among all these clan *kach* is placed at the top and *Butkoi* is given the lowest rank in the clan hierarchy. Because the clansmen are of the opinion that kach (tortise) is a holi animal it never does any harm to anybody. Whereas *Butkoi* (pig) is considered dirty animal and is not clean therefore it is placed at the bottom. The rest all the clans or *Gusthi* may be placed intermediate between them.

Birth

When a child is born to a kora women the umbilical chord is cut with the help of an ordinary knife by the *kurasain* (Chemain). The placenta is buried in the floor inside the house. The baby is then given a bath which is not allowed for the mother for three days. Then after the third day *chatti* or *Narta* is celebrated. It may also comes on fifth or sixth day. Every member of the family have to cut their nail and hair by calling a

Thakur (Barber). The baby is the new cloth to put-on. Before this a mixture of mustered oil and turmeric is applied to the entire body of the baby. Then comes the *Shakhigorom* rituals, under which in the presence of the *Mahato* or the village chief, the parents give the name to the baby.

Marriage

Marriage among kora involve certain mutual obligation. The husband has exclusive right over the sexual favour of his wife. Marriage among same clan members are prohibited. Village and ogamy between members of different clan may be preferred. In the marriage the rules of generation is not strictly followed. Usually three generation from bride-groom side upto for-grandfather level and an identical generation by bride side is traced and given importance. The age of the marriage is also given importance. Early marriage after attaining puberty is generally given priority to them. Marriages are generally arranged with the help of *Agua* who does the job of a mediator.

Among kora arrange marriage or regular marriage is the main form or marriage. Before the marriage is solemnized it has to undergo a series of stages. These are the following

1. Selection of mate
2. Kanyanirikchan
3. Fixation of bride-price
4. De-a-hiri-ceremony
5. Marriage date
6. Exchange of articles
7. Sindur-dan
8. Dasaha
9. Kalsa-Badal
10. Tilkow
11. Sara-dhoti

Death

Among kora tribal whose traditional occupation is to dig and cut soil burial not the cremation is given importance. Relatives are informed. Oil and turmeric is applied on the dead body to preserve the body for 24 hours. Then it is carried to the *Marghatti* or the burial place on a *Charpai*. Than a graveyard of 6 feet by 2 feet is dug. The corpse is then placed inside it keeping the head in the south direction which is called *Dheri* is placed on it.

Then comes the *Hoy-ume* ceremony which comes on the fifth day after the death is occurred. All the relatives and the villages are called and given a head shave and bear and must act out. Then a feast is organised which is called *Bhoj-Locally made* rice bear of *haria* is also included in the feast.

Cultural Traits-Fair and Festivals

Almost all the village folks of the Kora village use to any their visit to the village weekly *Hatia* or the fair. Kora which has now becoming agricultural tribe and their economy also is in production-Consumption - Saving stage. The saving which chiefly includes paddy, wheat, vegetables, eggs, birds and the forest products viz; honey, wood, fruits, felspar of the sap soil are either exchanged by the article or goods or equal value or are sold on cash payment.

Festivals

The most important and popular festival observed by this community is *Karma* festival which comes in the month of *bhado* or August. There fore the annual calendar also start for then in *bhado*. Some delicious food like *pithak* is cocked which is offered to *cholosia bonga*, a friend of *karme*. On the eleventh day during *bhado* in the full moon a branch along with the leaf of *karma* tree is bought in the house by the dancing kora girls from the forest, and it is planted in the mid of the courtyard. This branch is then worship only by the female-folk.

Other festivals those are celebrated among them with equal religious fervor and deity are some of the Hindu festivals; mentioned may be made of *Durga Puja, Deepawali, Makar Sakranti, Holi, Kali puja*, etc.

Special Feature

When we see the history of this tribe we may recall that in order to save them from the wrath and vandalism and also the religion this tribe had to take shelter in the villages inhabited by Santhals. Living with them since past several centuries. *Kor* as are now sufereing from identity crisis. They have adopted many things from their neighbouring tribe including their clanship organisation has a great impact of Santhal community. But *kora* never uses their clan or total name in the family title, which santhal always does the same. Kora would also never mind using *Senthali* title mainly for getting government aid. One of the most notable special feature of this tribe is giving preference to burial over cremation of the dead body, becausee to their traditional occupation cutting and digging soil which prohibit them from the undue expenditure on fire-wood and other burning materials, for the cremation, and also partly because of the extreme poverty in which the tribes-men are living.

Political Organization

The tribes men or kora tribe are governed by the two types of *panchayats*: Institutional and traditional *panchayat*. The leader of the former is the government agent whose post is held after election, where as the leader of the traditional post is inherited. The chief of the traditional caste *panchayat* is called *Mahto*. To assist him in proper functioning *Gurait* and *charidar* are available to him as full time worker. It is also interesting to note that there is no *pahan* or the priest post found among them and this duty is also performed by the *mahto*.

The traditional word for the caste panchayat is *Kulhi shurup* or the caste panchayat is in session. Panchayat usually comes in session to resolve the minor disputes that arises between the two parties. These disputes include cheating, eve-teasing, land & property disputes quarrel etc.

❑ ❑ ❑

KORAGA

Dr. H.M. Maralusiddaiah Patel

In Karnataka, the Koraga is a Scheduled Tribe, distributed in Dakshina Kannada District. The Dakshina Kannada District lies between 12 degree, 27 minutes and 13 degree, 58 minutes north latitude and 74 degree, 35 minutes and 75 degree, 40 minutes east longitude. It is bounded by the Uttar Kannada district on the North, Shimoga, Chickmagalur, Hassan districts on the east, the Kasargod district of Kerala on the West. The district is characterised by the western ghats running in north-south direction. The district spreads over a geographical area of 8,441 sq.kms. of which 29 per cent is under forest. The area received heavy rainfall because of the high altitude and hilly nature of the timber, bamboo, cane and creepers. In Karnataka, the tribal population constitutes only 4.91 per cent of the total according to 1981 census. They are listed under the primitive tribes.

The Koraga are moderately built but strong, black skinned, thick lipped, broad and flat nosed. They have curly hair which is allowed to grow long and knotted at the back of the head. They use the cap for the head prepared from the arecanut leaf called *muttale*. Hair is scanty on face and body.

The Koragas are non vegetarians. Their non-vegetarian diet consist chiefly of beef and pork. Consumption of alcohol is common among them. Chewing betelnut, smoking beedi etc., are also common. The Koragas have their own dialect, **Koragara Bhashe**, which is a mixture of Kannada, Tulu and Malayalam languages. Within the same community there are some regional variations in their dialect. The Koragas are considered to be issue of a Brahmin woman by a Sudra (Luiz: 1962). They live in the outskirts of village and towns in *Koppus* (huts made of leaves). They are distributed in Karkala, Udupi, Kundapur, Mangalore and Puttur and Belthangadi taluks in Dakshina Kannada district.

According to Shering (Vol.III: 1974) "The Koraga's have three sub divisions viz. (i) Ande Koraga, (ii) Vastra Koraga, and (iii) Sappu Koraga these names are mostly based on the different kinds of dress patterns, on the basis of available literature on the community, it is seen that the following names have appeared as sub division; they are (i) Sappu

Koraga (ii) Vastra Koraga (iii) Kunte Koraga (iv) Kappada Koraga (v) Tippi Koraga (vi) Vanti Koraga (vii) Kaputus Koraga (viii) Bangaranna (ix) Kammavanna (x) Mangaranna (xi) Kumedennaya, and (xii) Manadore.

Clan

At present there are three divisions among the Koraga, they are (i) Sappu or Sappina Koraga (ii) Kapada Koraga, and (iii) Ande Koraga. All these sub divisions have a number of clans called *bali*.

Among the Sappu Koraga there are number of clans they are (i) Guttaru bali (ii) Kallaru bali (iii) Bijjagaru bali (iv) Hanthar bali (v) Konar bali (vi) Thadiyanna bali (viii) Taliyana bali (viii) Sirin bali (ix) Mokunnaya bali (x) Bangaranna bali (xi) Thirgathayana bali. The Koppada Koraga are mainly concentrated in Belva, Kuderu, Haladi, Koteswara, Gangalli of Kundapur taluk. Among the Kappda Koraga there are only two clans that are reported (i) Yakkas bali, and (ii) Maripidi bali.

The Ande Koraga are distributed in Uijjire, Guruvayanakere, Kuttuhur, Nethavathi, Kalmanja, Bellanja and Madantharu in Belthangadi taluks of Dakshina Kannada.

Marriage

The Koraga do not practice child marriage. The age at marriage for girls is about sixteen to eighteen years for boys it is twenty to twenty two years. Girls generally marry after puberty. As per the custom among the Koraga, cross cousin marriages is preferred. They cannot marry with the same clan (*bali*). Now a days Koragas have spouses among those belonging to sub divisions.

The initiative for arranging a marriage is usually taken by the boy's relatives. After the negotiations are successful concluded, a suitable day is fixed for the performance of betrothal ceremony. The marriage usually takes place during the month of April or May. They perform marriages on Sundays which is consider more auspicious. They worship the sun and other form of sun gods. For the initiation ceremony, the *gurikara* (head man), parents and the boy go to the girls house. They carry fruits, betel nuts and arecanut flower. Both the parties exchange fruits, betel leaves, betel nuts and arecanut flower. The girl puts on the arecanut flower on her hair when she appears before the gathering. This signifies that the girl hence forth belongs to the boy's family. There after, arecanut, betel leaves along with sugar is distributed to the gathering the end tea is offered to all those present on the occasion. This negotiation ceremony is known as *nisschaya* or *badda*. Then the marriage date will also be fixed. Then the feast is arranged all gathered.

A day or two before the actual marriage day, marriage booths are erected in front of the house of the bride as well as groom where the marriage rites are performed. Bamboo poles are tied to each other with rope and covered with mango leaves and coconut leaves. Early in the morning of the marriage day, the bride and the groom are smeared with turmeric paste and are given a ritual bath by their relations. After taking bath they put on new cloths. The bride also adorns her hair with *hingara* (arecanut flower) and jasmine flowers. The bridegroom puts on a headgear. The bridegrooms party leaves for the bride's place in a procession with the accompaniment of musicians belonging to their own community, and play on a *dollu (drum), chande* (a small drum with only one playing surface), *tala* (cymbals) and *vote* (flute). If the bride's house is near, they usually walk in a procession. If the distance is more, they hire vehicles. On reaching the bride's house, the groom's party is ceremonially welcomed by the bride's relations, and *gurikara*. They are next taken to a pendal erected for the occasion. There bride's parents sprinkle some rice on the marriage party which is supposed to herald good omen as well as signify the ceremonial reception of the marriage party.

The *gurikara* plays an important role and actually officiates during the marriage ceremony. During the marriage ceremony both the bride and the groom are seated besides each other on a mat; the bride being always seated to the left of the groom. Next, their palms are joined together and a coconut is kept. The father, mother and *gurikara* pour milk on the joined hands. During the time when these rites are performed, an earthen lamp is kept in front of the couple. Some *akshathe* are showered on the couple by *gurikara*, parents and relations. After the ceremony, the couple gets up and prostrate in front of their elders. In early days, there was no *tali tying*. Bride price of seven chakra (one chakra equal to one rupee and seventy five paise) along with new clothes, seven kilos of rice, betel nut, seven patti betel leaves (one *patti* equal to three leaves) are presented to the bride. The bride and groom walk up to *bhutasthana* deity place and pour some water. The couple are made to sit on a mat the bridegroom ties the *tali* around the neck of the bride. And the *tali* (pendant) is considered to be the marriage symbol.

Thereafter a feast is served to the guest. After that once again couple hold each other's hands and they start they journey towards grooms house. During this time she carries a mat, umbrella and a lamp. After reaching the bride-groom's house, the couple is ceremonially received and the relations shower rice on the couple. Then they enter the house, the couple is ceremonially received and the relations shower rice on the couple. Then they allowed to enter in the house.

Among the Koragas, remarriages are common affairs. Remarriage of a widow or widower is a simple affairs. It is attended only by parents, *gurikara* and some close associates. Thereafter a feast and *toddy* is served to all. Divorce and remarriage is allowed for both the sexes.

Birth

Puberty (*jevanthe*) rite for girls is observed on the 4th day of her first menarche, in some places it is observed on the 9th day. Upto 4th day of her first menarche, in some place and she is not allowed to do any work. After purificatory bath, she is allowed to come inside the house. For pregnant woman in the 7th month of her first pregnancy a ritual called *bayake* is observed in her natal house and *aarathi* is done. She is given cloth and sweets are given. The Koragas observe birth pollution on the 7th day and the mother is kept under controlled diet. Naming ceremony is observed on the 7th day and names are usually selected according to their birth day like Aitha (Sunday), Thoma (Monday), Angara (Tuesday), Budha (Wednesday), Guruva (Thursday), Thukra (Friday), Thaniya (Saturday) for male. The female is named Aithu, Thomu, Angaru, Gurubi, Thukni or Thaniyaru.

Religion

Koragas are Hindus with the practice of traditional tribal religion. The community has a head man *gunikara* or *budivantha*; he performs all rituals related to marriage, birth, death, etc. The property is inherited through the male line (*makkala santhana*). In earlier days it is through aliya santhananam (through mother's brother). The *bhuta* worship is more important in their day to day life. Worshipping *bhuta* and tree is common, they keep some stones under the tree to represent *buta* (spirits). They are basically worshippers of the sun and tree.

Economy

Their traditional occupations are basketry and drum beating and scavengery. Basket making is the major economic activity found among the Koragas. They prepare bamboo cylinders for stocking paddy, *kuttari* (safety of chicks), *batti* (basket), *thadpem* (for cleaning paddy, rice, etc.) The time taken to collect the materials required for basketry is indeed too long. It may just be a day or may go upto a week. In addition, the forest department has also brought in greater restrictions on collecting forest produces. Due to lack of demand for their products and difficulty in getting raw materials, this occupation does not enable them to meet their basic amenities of life. Most of them have shifted from their traditional occupation from scavengery to daily wage laborers. Basketry of different varieties and sizes are made from the raw material collected from the nearby forest. Earlier they used crude implements, but now-a-days the Government has supplied them with modern implements. Men and women belonging to different age groups are engaged in basket making. The percentage of the population engaged in baskettry goes on increasing with age. This being their traditional occupation, people belonging to the older generation is involved in basket making than the younger generation.

The Total persons belonging to basketry is 21.4 per cent. The total person belonging to basketry in the age group of 15-19 years is just 11.76 per cent and 20-24 years age group is 27.16 and 21.81 per cent for the middle aged persons. The maximum percentage is 25.00 per cent for the age group of 30-39 years age. Even in the aged group the total percentage is 18.64 per cent. A good many number of Koragas are working as sweepers and scavengers in the sanitary departments in towns and cities. Between the age group 15-19 years age the total percent of people involved in scavengery is 10.50 per cent. It is 8.64 per cent for the 25-29 years age group. In the age group of 40-49 years is of 14.58 per cent. The percentage of the above 60 years age groups is 11.86 per cent.

Demography

The total literacy among the Koraga according to 1981 Census is only 5.00 per cent (males 7.1 per cent and female 2.69 per cent). According to 1981 Census the total literacy per cent was increased to 20.81 per cent (males 28.92 per cent and female 12.63 per cent). During the recent studies it was 32.06 per cent.

❏ ❏ ❏

REFERENCES

1. Aiyappan A. (1948): Report on the Socio-economic conditions of the Aboriginal tribes of the province of Madras.
2. Fuchs S. (1981): At the bottom of Indian Society. Munshiram Manoharlal publication, Delhi.
3. Das S.T. (1989): Life Style - Indian Tribes, Vol. III, Gian Publication, Delhi.
4. D'Souza S.J.(1991):Koragas-a primitive tribe of S. India, Mangalore (unpublished).
5. Luiz A.A.D. (1962): Tribes of Kerala, Bharatiya Adimjati Sevak Sangh, Delhi.
6. Sherring M.A. (1974): Hindu Tribes and Castes, Vol.III, Cosmo Publication, Delhi.
7. Thurston E.(1909):The Castes &Tribes of Southern India, Vol.III (reprint 1975) Delhi.
8. Singh K.S. (1994): The people of India Vol. III, Oxford University Press, Delhi.
9. Maralusiddaiah H.M. (1996):. The Koraga, Encyclopedia of Dravidian Tribes, Vol. II ISDL, Thiruvananthapuram.
10. Maralusiddaiah H.M. (1995): The Koraga, Encyclopedia of Indian Tribes, Vol. III Discovery Publication New Delhi.
11. Maralusiddaiah H.M. (1998): The chancing Koraga, Social Welfare, Vol. 43, No. 1, New Delhi.
12. Maralusiddaiah H.M. (1998): The India Express, Karnataka Note Book, Bangolare.

352 *Ethnographic Atlas of Indian Tribes*

Photo of Koraga Tribe

MALE KUDIA

Dr. H.M. Maralusiddaiah Patel

In Karnataka State are concentrated in Chickamagalur and Dakshina Kannada districts. The Chickamagalur district lies between 12 degree, 54 minutes and 13 degrees, 55 minutes North and 75 degree, 5 minutes and 76 degree, 22 minutes east. It is bounded on the east by the Tumkur district, on the South by the Hassan district, on the north by the Shimoga district, on the climate and rainfall, the Western areas getting copious percipitation, while dry conditions prevail in the eastern portions. The western Ghats areas covered in the poeciloneuron facies (Pascal: 1988), but the forests in the Hassan and Chickmagalur districts are "greatly disturbed'. The area supports rich plantations of coffee. Towards the east, deciduous and xerophysic species take over; millets, maize, etc., are cultivated. The Male Kudia tribal population is found in the evergreen areas.

They are also known by Kudiya, Malaya gowda and Kudia. The other synonyms are Malaikudi and Malaya Kudi. The Male Kudia are prefer to live in the interior forests. Most of the houses are made out of bamboo wattle, and thatched with wild grass. They have aluminum vessels and earthen ware for utensils and storage. Men dress in a *Panche*, a cloth worn round the waist, and banyans and shirts. Women wear the sari, with one end taken over the breast from the left side, and knotted on the right.

The name Male Kudia implies that they are intimately connected with the hill. In Kannada *malai* or *male* means mountain and *kudi* means top. According to 1981 census the total population is 6,967. They also known by *Malayekandi*, which means hill dwellers or children of the hill.

Their traditional occupation was hunting and good gathering. They were to living in caves. Now they started living in the hill top in Western Ghates as coffee plantation laborers and agricultural laborers.

The male kudia are non-vegetarian with pork. Their staple food is double boiled rice. Consumption of alcohol is common among the male. Chewing tobacco with befel nut, betal leaves with lime is common among male and female. They are using a cap all *muttale* made out of arecanut palm.

Social Life

Social division exists among them. There are two groups (i) Oru Malai, and (ii) Nalu Malai. There are clans (*bali*) like saliyana, Moolya, Pergada, Bunnalu, Balaserna Bartheru etc. Marriage is allowed with different *bali*. The clan descent is traced through mother. Marriage with mother's brother's daughter and father's sister's daughter is allowed. Age at marriage is increase from 18-20 years for female and 20-22 years of male. Monogamy is the system followed strictly. At the time of marriage groom tie the tali to the neck of the bride at the *dhare*. Groom has to bring *tali*, toe-ring and nose stud along with the new clothes, *saree* to bride.

On attainment of puberty by a girl, she has to sit in a segregated hut for twelve days. The segregated hut is known as *muttumane* (polluted hut). On 12 day, they smearing turmeric paste to her body and giving a ritual bath and wear new clothes. Then she is allowed to do her normal work.

Birth

The Male kudia observe a pre-delivery ritual called bayake on the seventh month of her first pregency. From the husband family members has to bring some sweets, and eatables and new clothes, flower, betalnut, betalleaves and coconut. She has to sit on a chair and all are giving presentations. Before her departure for her natal house, she has to put her hands in flour liquid and keeps her hands on the wall at different places. At her natal place the newly born baby is given honey, both baby and mother are kept segregated in a separate hall. After removing the birth pollution she is allowed do the house work, then they visit any temple nearby. On the 16th day the child is named. They are prefer to call the child with their grand fathers and grand mothers name.

Death

The dead are kept out side the hut and body is given bath and carried to the graveyard or rear by place and cremated. On the 5th day, ashes and bones are collected and a heap is formed and a pendal is erected to make saturated hydraulic conductivity *pooja*. On 11th day rice balls are offered to dead. On the 16th day all the relatives and friends get feast.

The Male Kudias are Hindus and they believe in *bhuta* (spirits) and worship ancestors. They are very poor. A few collect minor forest produce, which they sell in the market. They are engaged in plantation as laborers and agricultural laborers. Only few of them are having few cents of land for cultivation and are having coconut plants. Traditional council exists.

headed by *gurikara* (head man). He look after religious, ritualistic activities of the community.

□ □ □

REFERENCES

Singh K.S., (1994): The Scheduled Tribes, People of India, OUP, New Delhi.

Iyear, L.K.A. (1930): The Mysore Tribes and Castes, Mysore University press, vol. III, Mysore.

Pascal, J.P. (1988): The Wet Evergreen Forests of the Western Ghats of India, French Institute Pondicherry. Pondicherry.

Ethnographic study of scheduled Tribes: Malekudiya and Yarava, Census of India, (1981) : Karnataka series IX, paper V.

D'souza, S.J. (1993): Male kudia. A primitive tribe of south India (unpublished) Mangalore.

Maralusiddaiah Patel, H.M. (1996) : The Male kudia Encyclopedic profile of Indian Tribes, Vol. II, Ed: Sachidananda, Discovery Publishing House, New Delhi.

Maralusiddaih Patel, H.M. (1996) : The Kudia, Encyclopedia of Dravidian Tribes, Ed: M. Menon ISDL, Thiruvananthapuram.

356 *Ethnographic Atlas of Indian Tribes*

Photo of male Kudia Tribe

SUDUGADU SIDDHA

Dr. H.M. Maralusiddaiah Patel

The Karnataka State, a region inhabited predominantly by Kannada speaking people, is situated in the west central part of peninsular India. It consists of a narrow elongated belt between the Arabian Sea and the Western Ghats with strikingly exquisite and enchanting coastline of about four hundred kilo-meters and the hilly track of Western Ghats with its magnificent ranges of scenic beauty and evergreen forests.

Karnataka State is situated between 11 degree, 31 minutes and 18 degree, 45 minutes north latitudes and 74 degree, 12 minutes and 78 degree, 40 minutes east longitude and lies in the west central part of peninsular India. It is bounded on the north by Maharashtra state on the north-west by Goa on the east by Tamil Nadu on the south west by Kerala state and on the west by the Arabian Sea. The Western Ghats rise in a series of terraces, but the general elevation is lower as compared to the stretch in the north. This fact has strong influence on the geography of the ordering territories, in the form of the forested hill country of the *Malnad*. It appears to be a haphazardly placed range of hills. The deeply dissected edge of the ghats edge with their deep gorges, water falls, and water sheds, interlaced with denser evergreen and semi-evergreen forests which constitute the core of the Malnad. Karnataka is known for the rich heritage of a varied wealth of flora and fauna. Some arts of the state have a variety of rich forests as in Chickmagalur, Uttar Kannada, Dakshina Kannada, Shimoga and Kodagu districts. Tribes and forests have a very good relationship in day to life. Most of the tribal people lives in the forest and depend mainly on the forest produce.

Dakshina Kannada district has a density of 282 persons per square kilo meter and happens to be the third most densely population district of the state. In sex ratio was 1,059 females for every thousand males. This sex ratio figure is very much higher than the state, this district has the highest sex ratio. Among the taluks of the districts, Kerala has the highest sex ratio of 1,152 per thousand males and in Sulya taluk there are only 964 females per thousand males. The total scheduled castes population in the state is 15.39 percent. The Sudugadu Siddha a scheduled tribe in Karnataka.

In Karnataka a large number of nomadic and semi nomadic groups of people are found. The Sudugadu Siddha is a nomadic community found in Chickamagalur, Shimoga, Hassan and Chitradurga districts of Karanataka. The term 'Sudugadu' means burrnal ground and 'Siddha' means one who acquired 'Siddi'. One who acquired mystic power in the cremation ground is known as Sudugadu Siddha. Tough the mother tongue of Sudugadu Siddha is Telugu, they communicate with the local people in Kannada. According to 1981 Census their total population was 7,669. They are non vegetarians. The Government has built houses for some of them. Others live in their own built houses which are little moderate.

The nomadic people obtain their livelihood through a variety of occupations like begging, selling herbal medicines, acrobats, jugglery, fortune-telling, trading hunting and gathering by migrating from one place to another. Still most of them pursue their traditional occupation. A small section of the Sudugadu Siddha own cultivable lands and involve in agriculture. The migration pattern of this community depends to a considerable extent on topography and season. The men war-saffron or white coloured shirt and dhoti and a head gear. They decorate their forehead, arms and chest with sacred ash (vibhuti) and vermilion. Rudrakshi beads and lingam adore their neck and carry a jolige (to collect the alms) and an umbrella. They walk in the street by making bell sound and alms are collected in their jolige after the service i.e. telling about the future of persons. They beg in the name of their deity *Siddappaji*. They also seek alms by standing on a nail footed bed in some busy places, fairs and festivals. During the harvest seasons they move from one place to another. During the harvest period children also accompany them and it is their duty to take care of the luggage's. They build their tents near temples or in the outskirts of village. There are no leaders among them.

The Sudugadu Siddha also called Adike Sidda, Pakanati Golla and Kadupapa. They recall their migration from Andhra Pradesh to Karnataka State.

Marriage
The Sudugadu Siddha one having exogamous surnames like Pattapari, Sali, Vibhuti, Pujari and Golladhari etc., Marriage with one's father's sister's daughter, mother's brother's daughter or elder sister's daughter is preferred. Junior sororate and junior levirate are permitted.

Adult marriages are practiced and the marriages are settled by negotiation and mutual constant. Monogamy and polygyny are the forms of marriage. Bride price of rupees one hundred one to there hundred one given at the time of marriage. During the time of marriage a tali is tied to neck of the bride.

Birth

Pre-delivery ritual *called Kubusa sastra madi ikkuvadu* is observed on the firth or seventh month of her first pregnancy. On that day she has to sit on a platform with new dresses borough from her natal house she allowed to back to natal house after this ritual.

Naming Ceremony

Naming ceremony is observed for the newly born child at the age of five month or ninth month. Tonsure is made for the male child before one year. Puberty ceremony *hosige* is observed at the onset of menstruation. She has to sit in a segregated room for seven days, on seventh day she is given a ritual bath and wear new dress and she is allowed to sit inside the house and wave *aarati* and sprinkling colored rice.

Death

The dead body are buried and ancestors are worshipped once a year. During the rainy season they stick to their villages; some of them who have small pieces of land, grow vegetables, horse gram, beans, ragi, etc. The Sudugadu Siddha strongly disapprove of those who do not practice their traditional way of life, they believe that the curse of their diety Siddappaji will be fall them, if they fails to practice the traditional way of life.

The nomadic communities of Karnataka, thus engage themselves in gain their livelihood through various sources. Some of the nomads are multi occupation list. Mere traditional occupation does not enable them to find sufficient income for a proper sustenance and hence they also do some other odd jobs. They have started Sudugadu Siddha Associations and co-operatives headed by the same community people for their socio-economic development. Government has started several schemes for the upliftment or this community people, and for the children the Government started free boarding hostels.

❏ ❏ ❏

REFERENCES

Ananthakrishna Iyer, L.K. : The Mysore Tribes and Castes, Vol. III PP-600-604, Mysore University Press, Mysore.

Thurston, E. (1909): Castes and Tribes of Southern India, Casmo Publication, Vol. VI, New Delhi.

Misra, P.K. (1971): Nomads in the Mysore city, Anthropological Survey of India, Calcutta.

Singh. K.S. (1993): The scheduled castes, People of India, Oxford University Press, New Delhi.

Sudugadu Siddha

Photo of Sudugadu Siddha Tribe

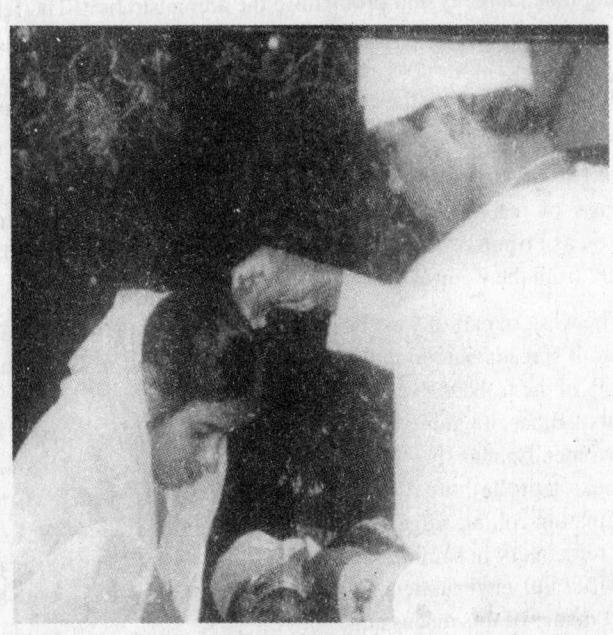

LODHA

Dr. P.K. Bhowmick

The Lodhas are considered as one of the Primitive Tribal Groups (PTG) of West Bengal since the revocation of the Criminal Tribes Act in 1952. Prior to that, they were treated as a criminal Tribe as they indulged in frequent crimes, and as such, were clamped by a set of rigid panal rules and regulations for maintenance of law and order by the Administration. This stigama of criminality has made them social isolates'. which has prevented them all along from margin with the societies around. Even they are not classed communities of the area though they share with them the same pattern of life of 'below-subsistence economy'. Thus, the Lodhas constitute a distinct neglected unit of population having hydraheaded problems of life including a great deal of psycho-somtional stress originating from these.

These together have resulted into occasional interethnic tensions and clashes in the past and broke down law and order altogether in this area causing much anxiety and problem to the administration. The feeling of antipathy and disturest prevailing against them among the other neighboring castes have created irreconcilable class hatred and antagonism. As a result, they are withdrawing themselves into a narrower shall and drifting away from the larger society aroung.

In 1957, however, the Lodhas were declared as 'scheduled Tribe' on the basis of recommendation by the Backward Classes Commission. Later on as Primitive Tribal Group (PTG), they are to get a special care, or grant from the Central Govt.

The western part of west Bengal is a continuous part of chottanagpur plateau, It spreads out along the western border of Midhnapur where the majority of the Lohdas live. Mayurbhanj district of Orissa and Singbhum district of Bihar run along the western border of the state of west Bengal were women Lohdas live. Here in the midst of groves of mango, *Mahua* (Madhuka latifolla), the dwarf *Sal* (shorea robusta), *Asan*, (Terminosoil of undulating rolling ridges, girdled by a chain of streams and rivulets which remain dry in summer and overflow their banks during the rains, - in this blissful environment of nature - live the Lodha - who are the subject matter of this discussion.

Lodha

It has been stated that the jungle-covered rugged terrain of Bengal-Bihar-Orissa border is now the homeland of the Lodhas. In spite of deforestation by felling of trees over the years which has affected their tribal economy, most of the Lodhas still cling to this ecology and environment.

In the *Jungle* area, the major ethnic group is the *Santals*, Along with them there are *Munda, Bhumij, Kora* and the *Mahato* - an aboriginal derivative and a few orissan castes like, *Karan* (Scribe), *Knandait* (warrior), *Raju* (cultivating casts), *Tili* (oil dealer) etc.

History

The term 'Lodha' is derived from 'Lubdhaka' - meaning *'trapper'* or *'fowler'*. There is a land-holding caste in Madhya Pradesh (Hiralal & Russel: 1916) named 'Lodha' or 'Ludhi'- immigrants from the United provinces (Uttar Pradesh) and originally belong to Ludhiana district of the Punjab. But, the present ethnographic data to do not support any relationship of the Lodhas of Bengal-Bihar-Orissa region and the Lodhas of Madhya Pradesh or Uttar Pradesh. They speak a corrupted Bengali i.e. Indo-Aryan Language group (Dasgupta: 1978) so long as the phonological and morphological structures of Lodha dialect are concerned. This clearly indicates that the group has been completely assimilated into the regional Bengali culture so far as their language is concerned.

Physical affinities of the Lodhas reveal (Bhowmick: 1956) that they belong to Veddid recial group having more affinity with the sild Kharia (Roy and Roy: 1937) of Dhalbhum, Malers (Sarkar: 1954) of Rajmahal and the *Chenchu* or *Krishna basin*.

Lodhas assert themselves as *"Savara"* - a generic forest dwelling community mentioned int he *puranas* and epic literature like the Ramayana. A good number of forest dwelling communities in India also feel proud in asserting them as 'Saveras'. According to the tradition of origin, the Lodha says that they are the descendants of king Vishwabasu - who once reigned over the jungle tract of the *Savara* country of *Nilachal* in *Orissa*.

From the legendary sources as well as from other evidences, it becomes very clear that this tribal group came in contact with the dominating Hindu castes from as early period. This prolonged inter-action has circumstantially made them to accept many regional Hindu traits - accelerating their Hinduization.

Demography

The Lodhas are distributed mainly in *Midnapur* and *Hooghly* districts of West Bengal, *Mayurbhanj* or *Orissa* and Singbhum or Bihar. The 1951 census records their total population as 8,346 in West Bengal of whom 6,040 live in Midnapur and 2,067 in Hooghly. But, in subsequent census reports separate enumeration of the tribe has been omitted. The authorities for the purpose of enumeration mixed up the Lodhas with the Kharia/Kheria since 1961. As a result, we get a total population of 45,096 in 1971 census.

Recording of less population of the Lodhas during 1951 census is due to the fact that some of them identified themselves as Savaras.

Table : 1
Approximate Lodha population in Midnapur District.

S.No.	Sub-division	Police Station	Population
1.	Jhargarm (Jungle areas)	Jhargram	7,000
		Jamboni	1,500
		Binpur	1,500
		Sankrail	1,500
		Gopiballavpur	1,500
		Nayagram	1,500
	Sub total		13,000
2.	Midnapur (Sadar)	Kesiari	4,000
		Naray angarh	6,000
		Dnatan	1,000
		Sabang	1,000
		Kharagpur	3,000
		Kotowali, Keshpur and Pingla	2,000
	Sub total		17,000
	Grand total		30,000

There are a few Lodha concentrated villages in the district. Most of them live along with other tribes and castes in the periphery of the villages. The total Lodha families studied by the author long age (1963) revealed that in 408 families, there are altogether 1,040 males and 967 females.

Education

Lodhas are neither interested not in a position to avail of the present educational facilities. As per report of the State Government (Das & Mukherjee: 1977), 3.3% of Lodhas are considered as literate. There is only four graduates and more than 50 persons who have passed Madhyamik (Secondary) Standard, a few of them are reading in a college. Since 1964 several Ashram Hostels meant for the education of the Lohas Children are attached to Basic Schools of which *Bidisa* hostels are considered as promising. Form Hostel there is provision for 20 seats but in one unit there are 30 seats. In Ashram the Lodha children get various facilities at the following rates as per present situation.

Table : 2
Items of Expenditure in Ashram Hostel

(in Rs.)

S. No.	Particulars	Expenses
1.	Meal Charge	Rs. 220/- Per head per month (Rs. 300/- from 1.4.98)
2.	Other charges (K. Oil, Soap, Oil, Hurricane, etc.)	Rs. 300/- per head per annum
3.	Sports & Games	Rs. 50/- per head per annum
4.	Medical facilities	Rs. 50/- per head per annum
5.	Garments	Rs. 80/- per head per annum
6.	Bedding (For every two years)	Rs. 100/- per head
7.	Remuneration for One Supdt.	Rs. 500/- per head per month
8.	Remuneration for one cook	Rs. 200/- per head per month
9.	Remuneration for one Helper	Rs. 100/- per head per month

The Lodha children are basically reluctant to attend the schools. This is due to less encouragement being given to them by their parents. The Lodha children roam in the *jungles* in search of wild fruits, small games, fishes and mollusca which they consume. Sometime a grown up boy is employed as cow boy by a caste people to look after his cattle at a nominal wage. Lodha children are reluctant to go to schools without any encouragement from outside. They being extremely backward require sympathetic encouragement and supervision of different nature along with non-formal or life centered type of education. These are ignored by the Dept. of tribal welfare who are entrusted to do this type of work among them and as such, in most of the Ashram Hostels, the authorities face tremendous difficulty to run the hostels. So, results are not satisfactory. Grants are released very irregularly and always in delay. The Dept. never sanctioned any amount for repairing or white-washing of the Ashram hostel building to create a good environment. Having political back ground some Hostel authorities get favour from the Zilla Parished for preparing of the building.

The Lodha children have many problems. A thorough psychoemotional adjustment is necessary to make then fit with the changed environment and special attention should be given to their uplift and socialization.

Economy

Occupation of the Lodhas varies from place-to-place. It has been stated earlier that the Lodhas are even now in a pre-agricultural stage of economy.

In the *Jungle* areas, they are engaged in collection of *Jungle* produces like -

i)   *Sal* leaves for preparing dining plates stitching by thorns.

ii) *Tendu* leaves for preparing *bidi* or country cigar.

iii) Edible roots and tubers for household consumption.

iv) Catching snake, lizard (Bengal monitor or *Godhi*). The hide is sold for cash money. Snake catching is a very favorite pastime of the Lodhas.

v)   Catching tortoise and fish from paddy fields and silted tanks. Most of these are sold in the locally and only a little is consumed by them.

vi) Some of them are engaged by the forest Dept. for constructing nursery beds.

vii) Earlier, most of the *jungle* Lodhas were engaged in *tusser* Cocoon rearing, but now-a-days they cannot do it due to prohibitory forest Laws.

viii) Some Lodhas collect firewood for fuel and sell these in the market.

In non-forest areas, Lodhas are found to be engaged in road construction and agricultural activities on wage basis but, very few of them have become successful cultivators, of course there are a good number of stolen property receivers, who encourage then in anti-social activities, Crime records in the police Deptt. also corroborate the involvement of the Lodhas in such anti-social activities. It has been observed that out of a total number of 1,600 active criminals of this district, the Lodhas constitute 1/3rd.

Land use

It has been stated that a good number of Lodhas are landless. Only a few have cultivable land. Those who have land are also not in a position to produce other crops or vegetables except paddy.

Now, Govt or India sanctions huge amount for the PTG (Primetive Tribal Groups) of which Lodha is one. This amount is being spent by the zilla Parishad.

SOCIAL ORGANISATION

Family is the smallest social unit among the Lodhas. A survey conducted among them revealed that out of 408 families, 278 (68.14%) are of simple or elementary type in which parents and unmarried children live together. Parents with old father of divorced daughter without children represented by 9 families i.e. 2.2%. Among the Lodhas conjugal infidelity is observed. parents with the children of previous marriage are found and they represent 18 families i.e. 4.41%. There are altogether 17 polygynous families in which two wives with their respective children live in a common house. Joint or extended type of families are 86 i.e. 21.08%. Here the old father with some of his married sons along with their children lives in a common house.

So far as family size is concerned, the 408 families surveyed are classified as follows:

Table - 3
Family size

S. No.	Partrculars	No.	Percentage
1.	Small sized families having 3 members or less	101	24.75
2.	Medium sized families having 4-6 members	228	55.88
3.	Large sized families having 7-9 members	63	5.44
4.	Very large sized families having 10 or more members	16	3.92
	Total	408	100

The society of the Lodhas is patriarchate. Due to prolonged integration with the local Hindus, they have been greatly influenced by the regional Hindu customs.

Sometimes the Lodhas proclaim their own identity. The Lodhas have a clan organization which is known *Gotra*. This is a patrilineal unit. A man born in a particular *gotra* will remain so till he dies. Girls after marriage change their clans and they are known by the clans of their husbands. After divorce a women again reverts to her father's clan till she remarriages. Table - 4 gives the details of clan characteristics as well as distribution of families by clans. Marriage in the same clan is strictly prohibited. There are a few taboos and restrictions in respect of food habit and other conventional observances in respect of some clans.

Table : 4
Distribution of clans

S. No.	Clan Name	Totamic objects	No. of families	Percen-tage
1.	Bhugta, Bhakta	Chirka, Alu, a kind of yam available in the jungle	120	29.41
2.	Mallik	Makar, a kind of mythological shark or sea-monster or salfish	78	19.11

S. No.	Clan Name	Totamic objects	No. of families	Percentage
3.	Kotal	Moon or grass hopper	68	16.66
4.	Layek, Laik, Nayak	Selfish (Ophicaphalua marulius)	67	16.41
5.	Digar	Propoise	21	5.14
6.	Paramanik	A kind of bird named Manik	20	4.95
7.	Dandapat or Bag	Bagh or tiger	10	2.45
8.	Ari or Ahari	Chanda-fish (Ambasisis range)	19	4.65
9.	Bhuiys or Bhunia	Salfish (Ophicaphalus marulius)	3	4.9

The totemic objects are respected and never consumed by the clan members, even it constitutes an unavoidable food item in Lodha society. But, a detailed analysis of Lodha clan names tells different story. Most of the Lodhas specially in acculaturated zones use their clan names as surnames, whereas the Lodhas in the jungle areas use *'Savar"* or *'sabbvar'* to express their personal identity without mentioning their clan names as surnames.

Marriage

Marriage by payment of bride-price is the general rule among the Lodhas. The bridegroom has to pay a sum of Rs. 7/- (seven only) at the time of marriage to the parents of the bride along with some clothes for the bride and her parents. When a girl is married in the 'teen age', a second marriage is termed as *sambar* generally no Brahman priest participates in Lodhas marriage ceremony. Mother earth (Basumata), the God of Righteousness (Dharam Devata) are also worshipped at the time of wedding. A wedding feast is given on the day of marriage to which all the traditional village officials including relatives are invited. Widow remarriage or marriage of a divorced woman is in vogue and this is known as *Sanga*, In such marriages no bride-price is paid. Only a sum of Rs. 1.25 paise is given to the guardian of the widow or the divorced woman by the prospective groom.

Political Organization

The Lodhas have their traditional tribal council which is known as *Panchayat or Desh*. The head or the council is called *Mukhia* who in all tribal affairs gives his verdict which everybody has to observe without demur. There is a village messenger known as *Atgharia* or *Dakua*. His main duty is to intimate the villagers about the particular decisions and directives of the pancyayet or village or community affairs. The religious head or the community is known as *Deheri* and the Assistant priest is known as *Talia*, who sacrifices the animal.

After the introduction of the panchayati Raj in the state, a good number of the Lodhas are being gradually associated with village administration. A few of them have affiliated themselves with some political parties of the locality and contested the last election in which the CPI (M) affiliated candidates won. Naturally this gave them the opportunity of mixing with other sections of the people, thus bridging up the hiatus so long prevailing among these communities.

Social Problems

The problems of the Lodhas are strikingly different from those of other tribes and castes. They are commonly stigmatised with the commission of crimes. It has been found that Lodha criminals constitute one-third or the active criminals in the Midnapur district. Even after the repeal of the criminal Tribes Act in 1952 and some welfare attempts on the part of the Government to improve their living condition, the lodhas have not responded adequately.

"The economic and territorial displacement under a new setting with the impact of scheming communities all around, affected very seriously their traditional patterns of economic life, and ultimately upset the aquilibrium of the whole society. Probably under such circumstances, pilfering, petty theft, lifting or articles from the houses of the neighbors and clandestine sale of jungle produce were first resorted individually, which in course of time developed into group habits, Amidst property, unsympathetic attitude of the neighbors, and stoic apathy of the than ruling Government, criminality cut a deep groge into their society in which the people had to roll down helplessly. (Bhowmick; 1963).

Mr. stemphen, the then Member of Law and order of British India introduced the Criminal Tribes Act in 1871. His remarks in this connection is very significant. He recorded: "The special feature of India is the caste system. As trade goes by caste, a family of carpenters will be carpenters, a century or five centuries, if they last so long. Keeping this in mind, the meaning of professional criminal is clear. It means that a tribe whose ancestors were criminals from times immemorial who are themselves destined by the usages of caste to commit crimes, and whose descendants will be offenders against law until the whole tribe is exterminated or accounted for the manner of the *Thugs*. When a man tells you that he is an offender against law, he has been so from the beginning, and will be so to the end, reform is impossible for it is his trade, his caste, I may almost say his religion is to commit crime."

The view was also shared by many Indians. Ultimately the Criminal Tribes Act was passed for suppression of such crimes and applied all over British India. As a result, more than 300 communities were declared as criminal Tribes.

Gradually the Lodhas faced many other social and economic problems with the march of time. They were affected very seriously.

These made them isolated and recoil into the shell of their old traditions. Also these developed in them coyness, timidity and imbued their mind with fear and distrust. Thus circumstanced, the Lodhas having no rudimentary education, no skill in crafts or arts, no land in their possession and no fixed employment - were compiled to live below the poverty line and indulged in spurts of anti-social activities wherever hunger provoked then to go against the society and the law of the land.

It is observed from the patterns of human living that every group of community has its own intrinsic problems. The problems vary from place-to-place and time-to-time on the basis of the nature of their exposure to the external situation and interactions.

Though attempts were made by the government along with a few voluntary organizations for the welfare of these communities for sometime past, yet from experience it can be said that these have either totally failed or have not produced satisfactory results. The basic problems of the Lodhas, according to close observation by the author are the following and have to be solved for their proper uplift:

1. Problem by People

Problem people having the common acute problems of living, they have a bunch of psycho-emotional problems. Chronic social neglect by the greater society has swarmed their mind and abilities. Laziness, reluctance to do any hard labour and restlessness have made them a typical parasitic stock. So due to this psychological freak, these problematic people should have to be treated very carefully. Otherwise they will become antagonistic and non-co-operative.

2. Problem by Neighbors

Their neighbors are also vary problematic. A good number of the people of the locality have forged clandestine economic deals with the them and buy from them the stolen articles at very cheap rates, as also employ them for agricultural work on minimum wages. To get their full co-operation, therefore, this false notion has to be dispelled and the rehabilitation schemes should have larger coverage.

3. Problem of Administration

The Administration sometimes creates more problems either by failing to understand the situation in reality or to implement the schemes meaningfully to cater their needs. Even in many cases the basic problems are not properly understood by the officials. Most of the welfare projects undertaken so far have failed due to such misunderstanding.

It is the duty of the Government, therefore, to make an endeabvour to bridge up the mutual gap between one ethnic group and another. "But the task or promotion of inter-ethnic harmony can never be accomplished by the Government alone. The wider society must be aware of the necessity of such harmony. The advanced ethnic groups must free themselves from the prejudices and angularities they have developed towards the backward communities. For this reason a scientific outlook must be developed, which would emerge from more intensive work of the applied anthropologists and action anthropologists among the tribal-folk in future. This, however, necessitates greater co-ordination between the planners and the action anthropologists and the follow-up measures to assess the working programmes. (Bhowmick: 1976).

❏ ❏ ❏

REFERENCE

Bhowmick P.K. (1963): The Lodhas of West Bengal, A socio-economic study, Calcutta.
Bhowmick P.K. (1968): Development Schemes as Factors of Social and Economic changes. *Journal of Social Research*. Ranchi.
Bhowmick P.K. (1970): Welfare programmes and Administration. *Tribe*. Udaipur.
Bhowmick P.K. (1970): Ex-criminal Tribes of India. *Indian Museum Bulletin*. Calcutta.
Bhowmick P.K. (1975): An Essential primary Considerations for Rehabilitation schemes. *Vanyalati*, Delhi.
Bose P.C. (1932-33): Racial Affinities of the Mundas. Bose Research Institute, Calcutta.
Daly F.C. (1916): Manual of criminal classes operating in Bengal, Calcutta.
Dasgupta, Dipakar (1978) : *Linguistic studies* Calcutta.
Rialay H. (1992) : *Tribes and castes of Bengal*, Vol. I & II.
Roy S.C.& Roy R.C. (1937) :*The Kharias* Vol. II & I.
Sarkar S.S (1954) : *The aborioinal Races of India*. Calcutta.

MEMBAS

D.K. Dutta

Arunachal Pradesh is a state on India situated on her North-East corner, bordering Tibet on the North, China and Burma in the East, Bhutan in the West, Assam and Nagaland in the South. West Siang District is located in the central part of Arunachal Pradesh, of all, the administrative headquarters of West Siang District, *Mechukha* stands at the highest altitude of 1,890 metres towards North-West corner of the District, Mochuk a sub-divisional as well as a Circle Headquarters, is inhabited by the Membas and the Ram's with a total population 7,050 persons as per the 1981 census.

ORIGIN AND MIGRATION

There are legends and migrational history of the Membas. In Tibet, *PHA-ZAMJU-SUMBO*, and ape like man, *MADA-SIMBO*, another kind of animal gave birth thousand of man in a day. This was the beginning of human beings. These men spreaded over Tibet in search of food and comfortable shelters. They were known as *Mubudungdu*, means a tribal community. There was no rules and regulations among them. But in-due course a person became the king to lead them in proper way. He was *Sugin Gombo* who framed laws for the community. The people obtained. The king and lived peacefully. They believed in animism. After a few decades, *Gyebo langdarang* became the king of the people. He was cruel and began to eat human flesh. At this, the people ran away from the kingdom and hid in the *jungle*.

In the means time, Lamas came into the area from China and began to control and converted the people into *Buddist Dahrme*. In Tibet, among the Lamas, it was come to light that the treasure of *Guru Pema Zongne* which is known a *Vheza Shingri* means hidden treasury would be found somewhere at the present valley of Machukh. *Lama Kardu Sange Rinzin* attempted to search the hidden treasure i.e. *Vheza shingiri*. He came towards India but did not find any suitable place for human being except dense forests and animals which made him disappointment. *Turden lordo gyamtcho* made a second attempt to visit Machukha. He proceeded through the dance forest to reach the valley. He had to return due to health ground and dies at Molounder the District *GAZA* in Tibet. He predicted that in his re-bi-rth he would explore the hidden treasure of *Guru Pema Zungne*. It was proved when seven years old *Cheeje Lingbo* told and proved that he was *Turden Lordo Gyamtoho*. When he attained adult-hood to reach the place of *Vheza Shingiri*, he accompanied many brave persons besides his disciples namely, *Tadung Gumbo Naksane Phogoiba Tashi; Romdo Awo nombe and lalung peam chom*. The accompanied persons were not only brave, but also know how to construct roads, how to arrange food and lodging at *jungles* and the art of protection. They were belong to seventeen different districts and gathered at saturated hydraulic conductivity *Pelung* in Tibet. Another expedition party under the leadership of *Lama Dukto thandang gyibo* followed the opposite direction of *Lama cheeje lingbo*'s starting point and promised to meet Lama Lingbo at the confluent of the river which flowed from *Tsampo in Tibet*. From *Pelung, Lama Cheeje lingbo* along with those persons started via *Lakhanya* at the border of India. Norbu Tanya is a place inside the Indian border where the expedition party lost most of their per animals. Even they crossed the *Kargong-La* and reached *nesang-Gong*. Where each of them felt that they were near their goal i.e. *Vheza shingiri*. At that time, a big tortoise appeared and prevented them for further movement. *Lama cheeje Lingbo* sat on meditation to face the situation. The tortoise turned into a tortorised shaped stone. The party then again moved slowly, but just after crossing a few kilo meters a bear with its two infants attempted to kill them. The *Lama* with his magical power turned them into stones. The party again faced an unusual scene-under a *Chandan tree Chandan-sandal wood*. family *Santalaceas Santalum Album Linn*, a tiger, a snake and an eagle remained one above the other. *Lama* and his party worried on it. *Lama* sat on meditation to see good or bed sign and determined if the unusual scene would vanish, they would proceed to *Vheza shingiri*. All of sudden, the scene vanished. This made him cheerful to move. They arrived at *Lumje*. The are was full of dense forest with huge trees. It was difficult to cut the jungle and make path to go ahead. *Lama Cheeje Lingbo* threw holi water on the *jungle* and waited for the consequence. At night, down pour started and eroded a portion of soil of the *jungle*. In the morning to their surprise, they found a path. They followed the path and reached a beautiful valley. *Lama Cheeje Lingbo* named it *Lhalung* which means place of God. The party constructed *Gompa*, temper named *samden Yancha* at the bank of a river called *Yargapchu* near *Lhalung*. They settled at the place of *Gampa* permanently and named it *Pimziling*. Some men of the party returned to

Tibet and spreaded the news of all about the area, returned to Tibet and spreaded the news of all about the area its beauty, fertility, availability of plant fruits and trees among the people of their own. Hearing the news of the land of *Vheza Shingiri* people of different clans namely *Onge, Naksang Vheza Hingiri* people of different clans namely *Onge, Naksang Mane, Chukla, Shiley, Sona, Ongbu, Rigar, Gyana, Sharjo Dorsum, Dolgormbu Bruru, Nyazong,* etc; started migrating to the valley, Later on Lama *Cheeje Longbo* selected some sites for habitation here and there on the northern bank of *Yargapchu.* He settled the people at *Darjiling, Galling, Singbar, Mechukh Karte and Kunseliagong.* When *Lama Cheeje Longbo* Located *Kunsella Gong,* a craw gave him a message that his other party who followed another route to reach *Vheza Shingiri* had returned from *Karte.* Them *Lama Cheeje* did not proceed further feeling the area upto *Kunsella-Gong* might be the end point of *Vheza Shingiri* and beyond this *Nyama Rirak* as *lama* Named.

SETTLEMENT

In Mechuha Circle, as per 1991 census total population is 3,112 in 30 villages. The new villages are settled with the consultation of *Lama* of the area. *Lama* finds out the auspicious date, time and place for habitation. A member posses a plot of land by purchase or by obtaining consent from the village elders. The owner of a plot of land on co-operative basis of the villagers collect household materials from the *jungle* first and construct the house. The houses have two-compartments with a *veranda.* There is only one door at the front side of the house where the *veranda* remains. The doors, windows, walls, roofs and floors are all made up of wood. The plinth area of course is made with stones and mud.

Food

The staple food of the Membas are maize, Sum, rice Day, millet Teri. These are cultivate yearly once at the cultivate beans. Besides potatoes, chillies etc are produced at the kitchen pumpkins, garden for consumption and sate the surplus ones, Verities of cucumber edible roots, herbs & shrubs are collected from *jungles* for consumption. Milk and milk products like butter ghee are favorite items of the Membas, Pigs, Cattle, Goats are rear in this houses. Fish are catches from time-to-time at the rivers, rivulets, springs, Dears, hares, bears, birds, monkeys, etc are hunted in the *jungles* for consumption and skins. Skins of some animals like monkeys, bears are utilized for making dresses, mates, etc. The traditional dresses are *Punum Chupa, Chuba, Khanjar, Dorma, Gichi* for men, *Phume-Chupa, Togye, Meo* for women.

Life Cycle

Marriage

In the Memba society the negotiation in marriage starts from boy's side. The parents of both boy and girl take help of a go between *Yamber* to negotiate any aspects of marriage. The go-between of the boy goes to the parents of the girl to have the consents of the parents and the girl. When both parties agree with the proposal of the marriage. The parents of both the boy and girl contact the village *Lamas* to find out the spacious date, time etc, to the girl, on the fixed day. The boy's father, brothers, a few relatives and go-between go to the house of the girl with two numbers of cows, silver coins; a basket fuel of butter say 40 kgs as an advance bride price, sufficient quantities or rice, meat and vegetables are also taken to the house of the bride for entertaining the invitee of the parents of the girl. In this function, both the parties set together and fix the date of marriage and the actual amount of bride-price. Then, the party return and arrange verities of items to threw a feast at the residence of the girl on the data of marriage. It is known *Lange tezang*. After completion of *Lange tezang*, the boy's party returns. Again the go-between and two-three persons to the girl's parent to being the bride in an auspicious day within a month. The parents brothers, relatives and a *Lama* along with the bride are received at the house of the bridegroom. *Lamas* of both the parties perform a worship at the entrance of the house of the bridegroom for prosperous life of the couple. The accompanied persons of the bride are entertained with a feast. Thus the negotiation marriage what is called *Chethpa Dacherong Namdi Chasa Gore* is completed.

Besides negotiation marriage, the Membas practice marriage by elopement marriage by exchange, Divorcee is approved by *Lama* apart from the village elders in the community.

Death

The Membas believe that man is mortal, it is an universal phenomenon but the way of dying is depended on the activities of the person concerned during the life-time from childhood to old age. A person dies with great pain if his or her activities is wrong during the lifetime. To pass on the stages from childhood to old age and ultimately dead, the membas carefully form certain norms so that he or she may dies peacefully. Mainly the aged person gets due respond from the young who may not be his or her sons or daughters. He or she is not treated as a burden of a family as he or she accumulates some earnings to his/her care takers as a customer rule. On the other hand, the healthy aged person does not sitting ideal, he or she does the light works of the households and the fields. The sicked person is look-after by the sons or daughters. When he or she dies, the dead body is covered with a cloth and placed a lamp near the body. Then, the co-village, relatives are informed about the death. A Lama of the village, relatives are informed who attends and reads out the holy book *Phona* to find out the reason of the death and also to selects the persons who would carry the body to the burial ground. It is also confirmed by the *Lama* that whether the corpse would be cremated, buried to disposed off by cutting into pieces for creatures. Before taken away the corpse, it is given a bath with warm water. The selected person carrier the corpse on his back to the burial ground. The burial ground is selected by Lama according to the holy book. It may be any sides or any directions or any distances from the deseased house. The body is buried in sitting position, in the grave. Rich persons offer *Thurbo*, big metallic pot where the corpse is placed in sitting position and covered with white cloth.Sometimes corpse is burnt as direction of the Lama. When an expectant mother dies, her body is cut open and the foetus is taken out. The foetus is buried, while the mother is cremated. As per another process of disposal of dead is by cutting the dead into pieced and throw them into river where the auatic creatures may consume. It seems that buried is the normal procedure of disposal of a corpse. Before burial dremition or making pieces the dead, the Lama recites the last rites. Then after three days after the death, *Shendey* worship is performed and the whole family assemble to hoist a flag *Dutheren*, at the burial or cremation ground. On the seventh day, a worship called *Dungi* is performed by four five Lamas at the deceased residence. On every seventh day, the *Dungi* is arranged and continued upto forty nine day, when another worship called *Geyo*, the members of the deseased family offer a shares, utensil, etc of the deceased are kept together near the five-place, and no-body enjoys by singing, deceased house. They do not use comb during the said period. This taboo breaks up only on Geyo. A year later, ritual called *Lengi* is performed.

The Membas always expect that the soul of the deceased person may complete peaceful tenure in the next world as they believe that after death, the soul of human beings goes either to heaven or hell where on completion of a long periods it again takes birth in this world.

Cultural Traits

The history of migration of the membas says that they converted into *Buddhism* from the faith of animism. The Membas were leaded from Tibet to Mechukha by the Lama *Cheeje Lingbo* who might be belongs to *Madayana Buddhims*. For which the membas, the follower of the *Lama* practice *Nyingma* sect of *Mohayana Buddhism*.

The sacred place of the community is known *Gompa, Temple* and the priest is the *Lama*. The history says that the *Samden Yanccha Gompa* near the bank of *Yargapchu* at primaziling is the oldest one. The *Gompa* was constructed under the supervision of *Lama Cheeje Lingbo*. The Lama with his disciples lived in the premises of the *Gompa* for many years. After his death the *Gompa* could not be maintained properly due to effect of flood of *Yargapchu*. No regular religious performance is done at the said *Gompa* at present.

The Membas worship at many sacred places located by *Lama Cheeje Lingbo* and his followers. A few places is mentioned below: There is a place where a cave and human sculptures formed by natural process near the headquarters of *Mechukha*. Both *Lord Shiva* and *Guru Nanak* were said to have meditated at the said site. It is also believed that *Guru nanak Premsubu* one of the incarnated Lamas sat on meditation at the place. However, it becomes the place of combined religions. The place is look-after by a Lama. Fair is organised on a day of *Markar-Sankranti* as per Hindu calendar. The people of the valley, Govt employees and *jawans* attend the fair. The *Jawans* took special care of arranging for stay, food, etc. on these days. The pilgrims offer (*'Prasad'*) to obtain blessing of their respective God/Goddess. The Membas offer 'So' it consists of *Neso* (Barlley), Paso (Kadu), Deso (Rice), *Tagjom* (Roti), *Sur* (Surpy), Asempuch (Bread of maize). *Targa* (Walnut), *Lobu* (Raddish), *Tem* (Soya-bean), etc.

They write hymns of Lord Buddha on pieces of papers and hang at the branches of trees or posts in many places at the road-sides of the temple.

Most of the pilgrims go ahead to the cave temple *Nesarma* which is at a distances of two hours food march. This is the place of meditation of *Gurus*. A lama is deputed on the day of worship at *Guru Nanak Premsubu* to perform similar worship at *Nesarma*.

There is a cave at a distance of about four kilometer from the headquarters *Mechukha* known *Yougyen Dubu*. The cave is like a channel formed at a side of hillock. The inside of it is dark. There is place in the cave where once a Lama sat on meditation for a long period. The Dubu means place of meditation. Now, just at the entrance, a house is constructed for the devotees. Regular worship is carried by *Lama Thelly Norbu* in the house. He sits on meditation in the cave from time-to-time. In the day of Holi and Mag-Purnima as per Hindu calendar, the pilgrims of the valley and other places came and set up camp near the *Yougyen Dubu* to worship *Makhandu, Mata Chekar Bumje*.

Phup-Khana is another cave like *Youghyen Dubu*. The Membas offer worship there, ont he auspicious day.

Karte - when *Lama Cheeje Lingebo* set on meditation on a big stone at *Karte* water started to accumulate on the stone. Since then, the water acts as medicine. The Lamas perform worship at *Karte* for prosperous life of the Membas. The pilgrims use to visit the place to have some water. It is said that the Lamas start first worship for New year in the month of *Dawa Tangba* (January-February) at *Karte* then at the other pilgrimage centres of the valley.

Besides this, the Membas have two big Gompas near the *Mechukha* township. The Lama and other care takers stay there. The Lamas perform worship for the Membas as and when required for blessing of God apart from the scheduled worship.

There are both individual as well as community festivals among them. The major festivals of the Membas are *Losar, Lha Soeba, Pemasuba, Pemajaling, Dosipai, Kart Holain, Towadrupa*, etc. The losar festival perform twice in a year. At the beginning of New Year i.e. in the month of *Dawa Tangba* (January-February) and at the last part of the year, i.e. *Dewa Chungipah* (December-January). The purpose of the former is to ensure the welfare and a happy and peaceful life in this New year and the later to express their gratefulness to the Gods for keeping them happy and prosperous is in the outgoing year.

The Membas arrange dances, Songs or plays and the traditional games like arrow shooting, fighting, etc. for entertainment in the festivals, in marriage in house making ceremony, etc.

Bardo pantomine is famous among the Membas. It is said to be part of the Bardo festival which is celebrated during November-December.

The Pantomine bring the feeling to the spectators that a person leaders a pious life in this world goes to heaven after death. While a person leading a sinful life goes to hell after death. The story of the Pantomine goes like-Dikchung was laymen who had to hunt and fish to maintain himself and his family. At his death, his soul was brought before *Choijegopu* who was a God. He recorded than activities of human and from the recorded activities of each person, he judges whether the person was sinner or pious man. *Dikchung* kneeled down in front of *Choijegepu* and told him that he had to do fishing and hunting to maintain his family during his life time. The good and bad activities of *Dikohung* were also examined. And then it was taken away for punishment in hell. On the other hand, *Gomohen* was also a layman who passed his life in religious activities. He was also brought before *Choijegepu* who told that he had his worldly life performing religious activities. *Gomchen* was examined from record of *Choijegepu* and declared that he was a pious man. So, he was taken away to heaven.

The whole story is expressed by the dancers having different masks and dresses. Musical instruments like cymbals, drum, etc. are played in the dance from time-to-time. To witness the colourful Bordo pantomine at the Gompa, visitors from all the corner of the valley and fur distance place use to come to Machukha. In these days, people are found to be in festive mood at the small township of Mechukha.

Political Organization

The days when a head known Deva was selected to represent some villages on the basis of capacity to collect taxes and control the villages. Deva had been empowered to punish the quality person. There was physical as well as fine system. No body could go against the decision of *Deva*. He was the supreme authority of law and order of his jurisdiction. There were numbers of subordinate staff to assist Deva in the council. They were selected from different villages by the Deva. The were some persons known *Go-Wa*, The Tibetans set up the organization with a view to collecting the Taxes in the form of kinds. Horse were also used to carry the lodges. *Deva* and others were very strict in collection of Taxes. The defaulters were punished even by torture and sometimes chase the properties. The defaulters or accuses had to knelt down position on sharp stones laid on ground to give statement before *Deva*. The reason behind of such arrangement was not to speak unwanted lengthy version and false statement.

When the system of Tibetan was abolished, the *Devas* were given to the status of political Interpreters (P.I) and the *Seems* were offered as *Gams*. The main function of P.I.S. are to make the local people aware of the function of the administration. They represent the administration in the village councils and help in the decision of any problem of the villages councils. The P.I.S. act as quite and accompany the Govt. officials/officers on tour in his area and act as interpreter as they know the local dialect and mostly Hindi. *Gam* means 'Goan Burah'. There are two-three game is a village. In such case one of them is defected as *Head Gams* are given woolen red coats to distinguish them from others. *Gams* look-after the petty civil and criminal accesses of their respective villages. They serve as a link between the administration and the village or villagers. It is the duty of the *Gams* to arrange right from accommodation to meals for Govt/official officer when they visit the village particularly where no inspection bungalows.

For the development of the village, *Anchal Semities* are formed in each block of every district. There is *anchal* is the development works like sanitation health, public works, education, agriculture, etc. The elected members of the Anchal Samit guide the villagers to perform the works.

The village council where the *Gams, Anchal Samiti* members and knowledgeable persons included to take decision land. Where the cases are not settled at the village level, the village elders or village council forward the case to the court of law. Where the cases are settled as per IPC. In 1961 (Indian) panal coda IPC. was introduced in Arunachal Pradesh.

❑ ❑ ❑

Membas

Photo of Membas Tribe

NAIKAS

Dr. Md. Azeez Mohidden

Gujarat state has 29 tribes, out of which, some are minor ones and some are major ones in terms of their numbers. About 72% of the population is concentrated around the eastern border of the state extending across districts from north of south, beginning from Sabarkantha to Panch Mahal, Vadodrara, Bharuch, Surat, Valsad and Dangs. According to 1981 Census, the Naikas/Naikas/Naikda (280,230) is the fifth largest tribe.

The Naika inhabit throughout the state, barring Kutch and Saurashtra region. They are mainly found in the plains of Ahmedabad, Gandhinagar, hills and plains of Valsad, Dangs, Surat and Panch Mahal districts. Almost three fourth (72%) of them live in villages located in the plains, Chiefly concentrated in the districts of Valsad and Surat which include Scheduled Tribe Areas and Plains Areas as well as the Union Territories of Dadra-Nagar Haveli, Daman and Diu whereas Dangs district is wholly a Scheduled Tribe Area.

ORIGIN

The Naika myths, legends and folk-tales tell that the Naikas were originally Bhils, that they were actually heads of different bands among the Bhils, that as band heads they went by the designation, Naikas united into a distinct class and that the Naikas as a class separated from the Bhils and in course of time became the progenitors of the tribe of Naikas.

The Naikas represent a class of people with qualities of leadership. The word '*Naika*' means a leader, a chief, a governor. It was used as a title of authority or from of address.

HISTORY

The Naikas were nomads and has contacts with several tribal and not-tribal populations before they were settled in the present habitat. They were hunters, gatherers, fishermen, as well as plough cultivators. Between the thirteenth and sixteenth century AD, when the Naika territory remained under the control of a few Koli/Warli chiefs, Bhil

Rajas and Naikas, the Naikas cleared the forests and tilled the land. They became land owners by virtue of their earliest occupancy. In course of time, other tribes like *Dhodias, Dubals, Koknas* and *Dhankas* as well as non-tribals infiltrated into the Naikla habitat where they were given shelter. These developments resulted to culture contacts on a sufficiently wide scale. Although they shared the same habitat, spoke the same version of Gujarati as link language, grow similar crops, use same agricultural implements, have same type of dwellings, domesticating animals etc, yet there were variations in inter-tribal relations. Only *Dhodias* and *Naikas* were freely intermingling at feasts and ceremonies with some instances of inter-marriages. The *Naika* Priests of Local deities functioned at many *Dhodia* tribe. Other migrant tribes like *Dublas, Koknas, Dhankas* as well as *Dhodas* also considered the *Naikas* their social superiors.

In the eighteenth century AD, the Naika territory passed though a period of political turmoil. Agricultural tribal societies including that of the Naika became completely disorganized in consequence of the Maratha's revenue system. There were further levies by robbers like *Pindiaris, Mewasis, Bhils* and other criminal tribes who threatened the peaceful life of their periodical depredations. The *Naika* society underwent several changes when the *Naika* came under the British rule in 1891 A.D. British opened rail roads, constructed a network of all weather motorable roads and introduced a new revenue system of taxation. As a result, *Sindhis, Banias, Bohras, Parsis, Pathans,* etc., traders like Lohanas and agricultural castes like *Anavil Brahmins, Kunbi Patidar*, the *Patels* started settled in different villages in the Naika region. By the beginning of twentieth century, the original inhabitant tribal population gradually lose their properieotory rights over land to influx of non-tribal population gradually lose their properieotory rights over land to influx of non-tribal population and became marginal farmers. With these developments, the villages of *Pardi, Vapi* and *Valsad* in the *naika* area grow into towns. Much of the alienated land continued to be at the hands of non tribals even after 'Land to Tillers Act' in 1957 by the Govt. Of India, Legislation in 1961 followed by Amendment Act of 1973 by the Govt. Of Gujarat.The money economy introduced by the non-tribals made disastrous impact on their system of agriculture, in which produce was drown from their own consumption. The new polity in terms of Statutory village panchayat also exploited the ignorance of tribals.

SOCIAL DIVISIONS

The Naikas have several sub-tribes, the *Mota Naikas*, the *Nana Naikas*, the *Naikdas*, the *Kapadia Naikas* and the *Choliwala Naikas*. The *Mota Naikas* are distributed in the Chikli taluk of Valsad district and southern taluks of Surat district. The Naikda are found distributed among the Panch Mahal and Vadodara district in central Gujarat. Now a days, these two divisions are by no means exclusive as well as once existed old differences showing the superiority of *Kapadia Naikas* to the *Choliwala Naikas* does no longer exist. Despite sub-tribe feeling does exist consciously and strongly among the *Naikas*. The nucleus of social organization is the 'parivar' (Family). The average size of the Naika family is 4-5 and large and very large families also do occur. The other principal units are lineages, clan and kindred.

The Naikas reckon descent along the male line. They are patrilineal exogamous body of kin based on demonstrated descent and formed across three or four generations whose members are able to trace their genealogical ties to their ancestor. There are no specific names for lineages. A lineage is not only a group or recognition, but also a group of co-operation.

Each Naika subtribe has several patrilineal exogamous clan called '*Kud or atak*' which includes several lineages. The members of a clan believe that they are the descendants of a particular ancestor, but they cannot actually demonstrate their genealogical links to their ancestor. It is difficult to trace the origin of the clan with totemic objects although some clans are named after object of animal.

The Naikas also have two types of ego-oriented aggregates of relatives called *Sagae Sambhandhi*. One type of kindred is a category kin subjected to constant change through the life cycle. The other is a quasi group consists of those relatives of an individual who have identical right and obligations with regard to the individual Kindred of both types overlap in their memberships. That, each individual will belong to several different kindreds.

Life Cycle

Birth

Accompanied by two female matrons, the '*Bhabhi*' (elder brother's wife) presents a new saree, one coconut and some sweets before taking the seventh month pregnant woman to her natal home for first delivery. Delivery usually takes place at home attended by local experienced '*Dai*' (midwife). Depending upon the sex of the child borned, the coconut is broken on fifth or sixth day followed by putting the child into a cradle, Purificatory rite is performed ont he eleventh day. *Fui* (father's sister) gives a name to the child after the day of the week (like Soma bhai/Somi ben for male and female child respectively). In urban settlements, she selects a name as per the suggestion of a *Brahmin* priest on the basis of the birth star of the infant.

Marriage

The Naikas usually acquire a mate within the same village or neighboring. villages through an intermediary a go-between (Vastadio). The boy's people initiate the talk of marriage. After getting the formal consent of the boy and the girl, match is finalized by handling over three sarees, a coconut and some quantity of grain to the brides party and assembled relatives and friends enjoy hot drink called 'chotitoddy'. A date is fixed from paying bride price (Amount varies from village to village), transacting marriage expenses, present some connotate of paddy, Kidney beans (wal) and silver anklet to the bride and enjoy a drink called '*Motitoddy*' in the presence of *Panch* (Council of elders) in the ceremony called '*Sagai*' (Betrothal).

Marriage is solemnized within six months to one year. Two days or a day before, both parties erect a marriage pendal. The maternal uncle presents new clothes and some gifts to his nephew or niece on the day of marriage known as '*Masala lane*' Lead by '*Andwaria*' (elder sister's husband), the groom party goes in procession to the bride's house wherein they are received by bhabhi (elder brother's wife), two elder members and two matrons. The bride is asked to stand in front of the groom and the horn-blower (*Turwala*) ties the clothes of the bride and groom. By persuasion or force, the groom opens the closed right fist (consisting of grains) of the bride. After receiving '*Mangalsutra*' from bride's brother's wife, the groom ties it around the neck of the bride followed by some presentations by the assembled relatives and friends. The *turwale* unities the clothes of the bride and groom before a warm send off to the bride is given. The newly wedded couple enter the groom's house after undergoing procession and some rituals. Generally the *Naikas* are monogamous. Divorce is allowed on genuine grounds. After one year of death, generally all young widows practice junior levirate in order to make sure that she does not bear the deceased husband's child in her womb. No elaborate rites are performed in the remarriage of widow/divorcee.

Death

Except children below twelve years, men and women who die of an epidemic or women who die during pregnancy, all the Naikas are cremated. Pollution is observed for eight or nine days. On twelfth day, the little obsequies (*Chota karma*) is performed by '*Shaman*' (*buva*) who brings the departed soul into his body by magic in order to know its last wishes /desires, allow it to take farewell from one and all of the family members. Final obsequies (*bada din*) is performed on an auspicious day during the period from December to February, in which the *Shahman sings* to the accompaniment of a musical instrument (*dolki*) all through the chosen night to almost eight o'clock in the next morning Some Naikas also perform first anniversary.

CULTURAL TRAITS

The Naikas believe that every being including man, plant and animals have soul called '*Jiv*'. In their belief the supreme god is '*Bhagwan*'. They also believe in a number of spirits. They have numerous divinities like *Baramdev, Narayandev, Brahminidevi, Bhavanimatha,* etc. These have numerous divinities like *Baramdev, Narayandev, Brahminidevi, Bhavanimatha,* etc. These deities seems to have been originated from Hindu deities, but worship is guided by tribal way. These deities are worshipped to ward off the evil effects of black magic, to have better crops and to detect the whereabouts of missing animals and persons. There are neither shrines not fixed idols. The head of the family worship the household god/deity by seeking the services of *Shaman* who sacrifices follows of goats. The *Naikas* also adopted several Hindu Gods and started worshipping them in Hindu fashion. A few Naikas also worship *Bhavanimatha* or even *Pirs*' (Muslim saints) by offering coconut, some money for the fulfillment of their desires/wishes. They generally celebrate Holi, Diwali and Diwas. Now-a-days started celebrating other Hindu festivals like *Nagpanchmi, Dussehra, Rakshabandhan,* etc. as per Hindu calendar and tradition.

SPECIFIC FEATURES

Tribal Sub plan, the Integrated Child Development Scheme and the Small Farmers Development Agency are functioning for the development of tribes all over Gujarat including the Naikas. A vast majority of the Naikas were able to construct brick walled houses with tiled roofs under the Housing Improvement Scheme. Establishment of primary and secondary schools in a number of Naika settlements, appointment of teachers from tribals, free supply of books and other materials for children, grant of scholarships to all tribal children and night schools under the Adult Literacy Programmes have helped the Naikas in acquiring more literacy and encouraging education among their female children.

The Atul Rural Development Trust and the Atic Rural Development Fund setup in the year 1978 and 1979 respectively have been co-ordinating the efforts of the Government and non-Government agencies in order to make the Naikas reap maximum benefits in about 40 villages located in Chikli, Valsad, Dharmpur and Pardi taluks of Valsad district.

An association called *Naika Mitra Mandal* and now '*Naika Samaj Sudharan*' formed in October 1969 at Vasiyar village in Valsad district had several achievements with reference to reformation and unity among the Naikas. The organization was able to wean the Naikas from spending huge amount of money lenders, make of liquor at the cost of basic needs and also from the clutches of money lenders, make conscious of their rights for benefits guaranteed by the Constitution. It has propagated the idea that unless the Naikas too acquire economic prosperity, educational benefits, political awareness and appropriate representation in political bodies, the Naikas cannot dream of their socio-economic betterment. It has also encouraged the unity of the tribe and the adoption of the language, food habits, ritualism and social customs of local dominant agricultural castes, especially the *Patels*. Some of them have been trying to initiate the way of the life of the *Patels*. Very few started adding the caste title 'Patel' after their names. All these had helped the Naikas to build a better social image than their earlier stance vis-a-vis other tribes.

Political Organization

Traditionally, the Naikas had a political system in the past which is different from the present one. Almost three generations ago, the Naika settlements closed to one another had their own *Panch* or *Panchayat* which was supreme in the legal and socio-religious matters of the members of the tribe living in the constituent settlements. Depending upon the size of settlements, two or three Panchayats had a common hereditary local chief called *'Karbhari'*.

The advent of the British administrative and judicial system dealt the severe blow to the powers and status of these tribal *Panchayats*. The new administration appointed to *Pate* (village headman) and his assistant (police patel) for keeping the land record, collection of taxes, giving hospitality to the visiting government servant. These hriditory officers became salaried employees of the government with the introduction of statutory officers became Panchayats in the year 1952. Owing to multi-tribal habitat, the Naikas have very few representatives in comparison to numerically more and better off *Dhodias* in the local village Panchayats.

Even today, there is the *Zila Panch* or *Zila Panchayat* at the district level. It has members from all the local tribal groups. The *Zila Panch* takes into account the traditions and customs of the tribes before pronouncing the Judgement. It has the powers,divorce, love intrigues, witchcraft and offenses of adultery. Even the law courts in the district are seeking the opinion of the *Zila Panch* for settling divorce cases.

❏ ❏ ❏

REFERENCES

1. Administrative report of the Dharampur State (1940-41): Gazetteer Bombay presidency, vol. VI B, Revakantha, Cambay and Surat Agency, 1927, pp. 69-79 Bombay; The Government press.
2. Census of India (1981): Gujarat Primary Abstract of Scheduled Castes and Scheduled Tribes, series 4; paper 3 of 1981, New Delhi: Controller of publications, 1983.
3. Enthoven, R.E,, (1975): The tribes and castes of Bombay, vol. II & III (reprint), Delhi: Cosmo publications.
4. Lal, R.B. (1982): Modern industry and the Tribals: A study of the effects of industrialization on the tribals in South Gujarat, Ahmedabad: Tribals Research and Training Institute, Gujarat Vidyapeeth.
5. Mohidden, Azeez Md. (1986): Some aspects of religion among the Naikas of Gujarat, VANYAJATI, vol. XXXIV, No. 3.
6. Padmanabham, P.B.S.V & Md. Azeez Mohidden (1984): Tribes in contemporary India-Naikas of Gujarat (unpublished report).
7. Shah, P.G. (1964): Tribal life of Gujarat, Bombay, Gujarat Research Society.
8. Sherring M.A. (1974): Hindu Tribes and Castes, Delhi, Cosmo publications, vol. I (reprint).
9. Trivedi, Harshad. R. (1993): Tribal Land Systems, Land Reform Measures and Development of Tribes, New Delhi, Concept Publishing Company.

SAHARIA

*Pramod Misra
and
Dr. A.K. Kapoor*

The Saharias, a Scheduled Tribe of Rajasthan predominatly inhabit in Shahabad and Kishanganj Tehsils of Baran District. They are the most Primitive and backward of all the tribal communities of the State. According to 1991 Census, the total population of Saharias in Baran District is 47,822. Before independence, the Saharias were bought and sold like chattels and were treated as slaves. unaware of settled life, they practiced *dahi* or shifting cultivation, Living in isolated dense forests, they became extremely shy by nature. The used to run away on seeing a man of the civilized world. It is said that the Saharias feared the so-called civilized man more than the dangerous animals. Previously it was in Kota district, but split of district in two parts Baran and Kota. Thus the premitive tribal group transferred in Baran district.

HISTORY

The world Saharia appears to have been derived from the Persian World, "Sehi" meaning jungle. The Muslim rulers reckoned Saharias as Inhabitants of forest. The Census monograph 'SANWARA' gives a different view. According to in the word Saharia is derived from Persian word 'Seher' meaning desert. The occupation of the region, along the river Indus, by foreign rules seems to have compelled them to quit the area. These are possible conjunctures and need historical support.

Even in the absence of genuine historical account it may be stated that the Saharias have been one of the first settlers of Rajasthan. James Tod (1839 has mentioned them along with Minas, Bhils and Gujjars as the primitive dwellers of the region who "are still but little removed from Savage life." Now a days Saharias is the only primitive tribal group of the state.

DISTRIBUTION

The Saharia belt in Baran District lies beyond the parbati river in its eastern part. This part of the District is surrounded by Saharia occupied

Districts of Madhya Pradesh on three sides. To the north by Morena and Gwaliar, to the east by Shivapuri and to the west by Guna which forms a major portion of the Saharia tracts.

The Saharias of Rajasthan are concentrated in two Tehsils of Sahabad and Kishanganj which also coincide with Panchayat samitis.

The Shahabad Tehsil can be divided into two district divisions (I) upreti a plateau or the uplands formed of the villages from Kelwads in the west to the Samarania, Mundiyar, Mamoni, Kaloni, Baint, Sahahapur, etc. In the east upto Sahahabad. (2) Taleti formed of the low level villages beginning from Shahabad to Deori, Bamagaon, Faredua Taleti and Kasba Thana. The are is Characterized by parallel drainage and all slopes are westward. Lohai, Andheri, Sukhan, Dunbraj, Bilas, Bomi, Kul, Charoli are all ephemeral rivers. The Kunu is a perenial river. If flows from south to north and drains the Taleti part of the area into the river.

The Kishanganj Tehsil forming the Western part of the Shahabad Panchayat Samiti' does have some portion of the upreti but the rest of the area in the Tehsil is plain, with deep soil depth and higher water table.

CLANS

Saharia is an endogamous tribe divided into number of clans, each clan named after some ancestor or a place to which they originally belong. The following clans are found among Saharias:

Bedgor, Bareliya, Bhilodiya, Chackrya, Chowdarya, Dediya, Devaria, Debariya, Dareliya, Garwar, Gogaya, Haleriya, Jarkoliya, Jajwar, Khagania, Kuhar, Kanachfriya, Kheti, Khanwar, Kheliay, Kundawar, Khadeliya, Kareaniya, Khadiya, Karuriya, Kanwal, Lagayahi, Mogriya, Navtriya, Navriya, Parenatia, Pateja, Parondiya, Rajouriya, Rewar, Raichohan, Ragpita Chohan, Rathwar, Sanoriji, Silwar, Sopariya, Solvia and Solanki.

From above list it appears that except Bhilodia which can be directly linked with Bhils, there are at least four clans which appear to bear the names of Rajput clans like *Rai Chauhan, Solanki, Devaria, Ragpita* Chauhan.

HAMLET PATTERN

Saharias do not have disperse pattern of living as found among the Bhils of Southern Rajasthan. They not have even separate and scattered hamlets. However, the hamlets are slightly for off from the main villages. Each village has a cluster of Saharia families in a separate hamlet known as *Saharana'*. In the Saharana no other caste people live. In the centre of each Saharana they construct Umbrella type' shelter house which is called *Panchayati Bungalow* where all Saharias sit together to discuss, gossip and settle their disputes. Shoes are not allowed in the Panchayati *Banglow*. Women are also forbidden from entering the hall. It is believed that as women come from other villages, Secrecy cannot be expected from them.

MARRIAGE AND FAMILY

Saharia is an endogamous tribe but each clan in it is exogamous. They believe in totem and taboos and observe them during rituals and ceremonies of marriage. Marital alliance between the mates of same gotra is prohibited because by virtue of their affiliation to a common totem. The members of the clan would be reckoned as brothers and sisters. Exogamy based on clan is strong among the Saharias.

The tradition of getting married inside Saharia tribe has remained very rigid among them. Inter-Tribe or Inter-Caste marriage was a punishable crime upto a few years ago. If a Saharia women married a non-Saharia person, he was compelled to pay penalty to Sahariya Panchayat and to eat and drink with Saharias, otherwise the woman used to be out from the caste.

With changing times, the restrictions on getting married outside the tribe have also started reducing. However the cases where Saharia women got married to persons of other caste were rare.

In the past child marriage was prevalent among the Saharias. Now Saharias donot favour early marriage particularly child marriage. The average age at which a girl is married varies between 15 to 18 years. For boys the age varies between 16 to 20 years.

Widow marriage of remarriage called *'Nata'* is permissible among the Saharias. A widow can be married only to a widower or to a divorced person. Even an unmarried person can marry a widow and vice-varsa, but such a union is not much favoured by the society. When a widow gets remarried or a married woman falls in love with other man and wants to live with him, the new husband has to pay *Jhangads* (an amount against marital expenses) to the previous husband or his family. A man may have more than one wife at a time (Polygaymy), but a woman can never have more than one husband.

The family of Saharias is a nuclear family with the youngest son staying with the parents and the elder sons moving out with their families or procreation into separate homes. The daughter on marriage is given only movable property as clothes, ornaments, etc. The inheritance or immovable property is patrilineal.

LIFE CYCLE

Marriage Rituals

Sagai or Lagan

In Saharias, the initiative for setting a marriage is generally taken by parents of the bridegroom. Decisions regarding selection of the partner are always taken by the parents. There is no system of seeing the bride. The performance of betrothal is very simple. In two donas (leaf bowls). they put grass, rice and turmeric and a copper coin. Then the *Panchas* touch the bowls and give their blessings. After this the bridegroom's sister-in-law and patel exchange the bowls seven times and then each go to their village with the bowl in their hands. The guests are farewelled by putting turmeric tilak on their forehead. The girl's father presents a turban to the bridegroom's father or elder brother and greets him by saying 'Ram Ram'. The bowl is taken inside the house with songs. Until the arrangement for music is made, the bowl is placed in a house in the neighborhood. This is called 'Lagan'.

The day of marriage is decided by *panchas* at the time of engagement without consulting the priest.

Bindayak

On the day of *'bindayak'* the boy applies on his body a paste prepared by mixing turmeric, floor, oil and water. His aunt and sister-in-law put *mehandi* (henna) on his hands. Then the bride-groom worships *Ganeshji*. Afterwards the aunt and sister-in-law tie *Moli*' thread on his right wrist for which he pays some money in the form of *neg* to them. From this day singing or songs starts which continues till the day of procession. Everyday the bride-groom worships *Ganeshji*.

Tel Bithana

The bride-groom is seated on a wooden slab on the day of *'tel bithana'*. Then both aunt and sister-in-law touch his body, beginning from feet to head with hands dipped in oil. This is repeated, but the direction of applying oil is reverse i.e., from head to feet. This is called *'tel utarana'*.

Mandap

A mandap is built in the girl's house where the actual marriage takes place. Four poles are driven in the ground and bamboo staves are placed diagnolly on them. These are covered with leaves and twigs to from a shed. The four poles are from *Jamun* trees. On both sides of the entrance of the house, four-pitchers, one above the other are placed. These are tied with red cloth or *Moli* Thread. it is called *Chavari bandhana*' on this day, the bride-groom's father gives a feast to the whole community in which *jawar* on *bajra-ki-roti* and *curry* prepared from the same floor are served. After the feast the procession (barat) starts for the house. Women and children also join it.

Padat

The *barat* reaches the bride's house on the day prior to the marriage. This day is called *Padat Ka Din*'. The bridegroom goes to bride's house in a palaki (palanquin) if one can afford it. Use of a bullock-cart is more common for this purpose. During the procession, instead for employing a band people beat thalis (copper plates) which makes a sing-song noise. But now, use of a band to some extent has also started amongst the Saharias. Most of their customs have a resemblance to Hindus. However, a significant deviation from Hindus can be seen during the ceremonial touching of the *toran*. The Saharia bride-groom is not mounted on horse-back, but is simply lifted up by his *Sawasa* i.e. sister's husband.

Phere Pandna

For performance of pheras (Seven rounds around the fire) neither a priest nor a nuptial fire is lightened. This ritual has important difference from Hindus amongst whom presence of a priest and nuptial fire are important for phereas. The bride's sister-in-law ties the *gatha- joda* of the bride and bride-groom and bring then in the mandap. The bride sister near a pole of mandap and bride-groom makes six circles round the pole.The seventh circle is taken by the bride. The *Patel* of the village assists in the process of promises taken both by bride. The *Patel* of the village assists in the process of promises taken both by bride and bridegroom and this completes a Saharia marriage. Then, the bride and bridegroom go to *Janwasa*' (place where the barat stays) where the bride-groom's father gives his blessings to them. After this, the bride and the bride-groom worship their god and goddess and seek their blessings.

Barat Vidai

When the marriage party departs on the second day, a tilak is put on the forehead of the each of its members.

Gona

After marriage the bride stays in the in-laws' house for about a week and then comes back. She again goes to her in-laws' house after one year. At this time, a ceremony is performed which is called *'gona'*. A large number of guests from both sides gather at the bride's place for the farewell of the bride. Women of the bride's sing vulgar songs and make jokes. The bride-groom pays *neg* to the women for their songs. The bride wears new clothes at the time of her farewell.

Birth Rituals

Customs related to birth are the same for both male and female children. Mostly the sweepress conducts the delivery. Just after the birth of a child, a messenger is sent to girl's parents with sweets. On the third or fifth day after the delivery the mother and child are given a bath and taken out of the house for ritual purification. It is called *'bahar nikalana'*.

After delivery, the mother is given *jaggery* and *Mahua water* to clean internal organs and impurities form the body if any. During the inaternity period, the mother is fed on *dalia* prepared from *jaggery* and *jawar* or wheat flour. All oily foods, meat and spices are taboored. The collective pollution involving family members is observed for three days during which contact with outsiders is forbidden after which the house is sacralised with cow dung. An elderly woman ties an *amulet* round the waist of the new child and conducts the simple name giving ceremony. Sweet balls are distributed. In this day the girl's parents bring clothes. They are served with meals. It is called *'pachalana'*. The Saharia women to take care of the house, the Saharia woman starts performing domestic chores immediately after this ceremony.

Mundan

The cutting down of the hair for the first time has ritualistic importance in Indian Societies, specially of a male child. This ritual is known as *'mundan sanskar'*. The Saharias also perform it for male as well as female children. A barber is called for this purpose who uses a pair of scissors for it. He charges Rs. 20 to 25 depending upon the economic condition of the family. *'mundan sanskar'*. The Saharias also perform it for male as well as female children.

Death Rituals

The Saharias cremate their dead. For thirteen days the close relatives of the deceased stay and eat at his house. On thirteenth day, a feast is given to whole community. On the third day also, a feast is arranged for relatives only. Either on the third day's feast or on thirteenth day's feast all male family members of the deceased have off their hair. Offering hair to the soul of decease is an important ritual connected with death ceremonies among most of the societies in India. The ashes of the deceased are put into *Kapildhara* (a pious river of the Saharia tract) or *Sitabari* (a religious place in Kelwara which has water ponds of historical origin).

Cultural Affinities

Religion

Besides following *Animism* (belief in spiritual being), the Saharias also profess Hinduism and with the same devotion they worship, *Ram* and *Hanuman* and have high respect for "*Ramayana*". They are true devotee of goddess *Kali* and during *'Navratras'* they worship *Bijasan Mata, Amba Mata, Balaji* and *Bheruji* and *Tejaji* as deities. They have faith is supernatural powers. The rituals observed by them are akin to the Hindu rituals.

Fairs and Festivals

Saharias celebrate all those festivals which are celebrated by Hindus. The festivals generally celebrated by them include *Makar Sankranti, Mai Saptami* (Navratra Pujan), *Holi, Savani Amavas, Janmasthami, Raksha Bandhan, Deepawali* and *Teja Dashmi*, etc.

Dresses

In the past, Saharias used to cover only the lower portion of their body. But, gradually due to contact with civilized people, they started wearing more clothes in order to cover the whole body. Saharia males wear dhoti, tied upto knee and a shirt called *'Saluka'* to cover the torso. The head is covered by a turban (*safa*). Only a few Saharia wear shoes. Small children generally remain naked. Even during the oldest days of winter many of them can be seen naked. Saharia woman generally like coloured dresses. Girls start wearing *Ghagra, Saluka* (blouse) and *Orhni* after the age of seven years. A Saharia women can rarely be seen in *Sari*.

Ornaments

Saharia women are very fond of ornaments. Because of poverty, they wear ornaments made form *gillet, aluminium* or *brass*. Women in rich families have, however, silver ornaments. On the forehead, they put *bore* and around the neck *hanshi* and *chain* . In the nose they *long* or *murki* (cloves) made of silver and in the ears *kanphool*. On their elbows they wear *bara*, and on this wrists metallic bangles locally known as *mangli*. Around the legs they wear an aluminium anklet called *Kada* and *Nevari*. The *Navari* is a loose fit and has a hinge-joint so that it can be easily put on or taken off. The *Kada* rests on it Below it, they wear *tora*. In toes they put *bichhia*. Unmarried girls are prohibited from using this jewellary they are also not allowed to put on *mehandi* (henna) or to wear the brassiere - like *jacket,* called *reja*. Traditionally, a girl wears the *reja* for the first time gifted by her in-laws at the time of her marriage. The widows, however, are permitted to wear all ornaments except *bichhia*.

Male Saharias do not use jewellery. However, a few well-to-do Saharias can be seen putting on *long* or *murki* clove in their ears, a *tabij* or *chain* around the neck and silver buttons in their shirts.

Economy

In the past the economy of Saharias was forest-based. The collection of forest produce and hunting were their main occupations. Agriculture was of secondary importance and was practiced by few Saharias only. During state times, they were forced to work as bonded labourer by both *Zagirdars* and rulers. No Saharia could ever think of escaping it. They were forced to do all types of labour in the form of *beggar*. This included work's in the fields, cutting of fuelwood, etc. For their subsistence, the Saharias were provided with one kilogram wheat or any other grain every day. After independence due to various measures taken by the government for the upliftment of Saharias, their economy has undergone considerable change. They were provided with land and other subsidies. Now labour and agricultural are their main occupations. Not only in the past but even now the forests are an important additional source of income of Saharias. Saharia's are engaged in various forestry development works and forecasting operations concerning of timber, firewood and other minor forest produce like *Tendu Patta*' (Diospyros melanoxylon) Bidi leaves, *gum, honey* and front of *Amla, Achar* (Bachanania Latifolia), *Mahua* (Basis latifolia), etc. also forms an important source of income for livelihood.

Political Organisation

Sahariya Panchayat is concerned generally with the control and regulation of relations between different members of society and to maintain tribal traditions, administration and rules. It can use physical force, punish a person and can impose fines. It consists of a headman or *Patel* who is assisted by a council of elders. The number of members of a headman or *Patel* as locally known, takes decision to call a meeting. He conveys his decision to *Pradhan* who passes on it to *Barai*. It is the duty of *Barai* to inform whole community about the place and time of the meeting. The *Panchayat* is reached to a decision either through consensus or majority verdict and the headman has no power to overrule the majority verdict.

The headmen of many village join themselves into a group which constitutes the main panchayat body or council. On major disputes all headmen collect to take the decision.

Photo of Saharia Tribe

SANTAL

Dr. Atul Chandra Bhowmick

Santal is a corruption of *Saontar* and this name was derived either from *Saont*, an obscure village in Midnapore where they ruled for two hundred years (Skrefsurd) or from a small tribe of *Saonts* in Sarguja and Keonjhar in Orissa (Dalton). The origin of Santals is traced back to a wild goose (*hasdak*) coming from the great ocean at *Ahiri Pipri* laid two eggs. From these eggs *Pilchu Haram* and *Pilchu Budhi* were produced, the parents of Santals. Their earliest abode was *Ahiri pipri santals'* progenitors migrated to *Khoj-kaman*, successively to *Hara, Sasangbera, Jarpa, Kendi, Champa, Saont,* all conjectural. Santals are considered as autochthons of santal parganas. Now they are concentrated in *Hazaribagh, Bhagalpur, Singhbhum, Manbhum, Midnapore, Bankura, Purulia, Mayurbhanj, Balasore and Keonjhar.*

They call themselves *Hor* (Man) *Hopen* (Son), sons of Man. They are study, simple hearted and subsist on traditional agriculture. Others work as day-labourers in colliery, industry, tea plantation and government services. Racially they belong to Proto-Austroloid stock and linguistically to Austric group.

History

The land-lords exploited them miserably. Ultimately the revolted against them in June 1855 under the leadership of *Sidu, Kanhu, Chand and Bhairab*. But they were ruthlessly suppressed by the British.

Social Division

Santals have the following twelve exogamous totemic clans (Paris). The procreation of the first seven clans were *Pilchu Haram* and *Pilchu Budhi*. The next five were added later.

Each clan is sub-divided into sub-clans (khunt/khul), whose function primarily for family deities worship. The sub-clans of *Hasdak/Hansda* (wild goose) are Barwar, (Eagle-slayer). Jihu (Babbler, a kind of bird), Kerwar, Manjhi-khil (worship at *Manjhithan*). Naeke-Naiki-Niaki-khil, Nij (oneself), Roh-Lutur (Ear-pierced) and *Sada* (Apply no vermilion at *Puja*).

Murmu (Nilgai) - *Bital* (outcasted), Boor (Fish), *Chopear*/Coopier (Hind quarters small as bullock), *Ganr* (Fort) *Handi* (Earthen vessel). *Muro, Nij, Sada* Sanda, Sikiya (chain), Tikka (Mark on forehead and Lahar (Cut); *Kisku* - Abar, Ah, Kachua (Tortoise), *Lat* (Baked in leaf-platter), Nag (Cobra), Nij, Loh-Lutur, Sada and Somal (Deer); *Hambrom/Hemorom* (Betel-nut) - *Dantela* (pigs with large tusks for sacrifice), Gua (Areca-nut), Johur, Kumar, Laher, Naika-khil, Nij, Loh-Lutur and Uh; *Marndi/Mandi (Grass)* - *Buru-birit/beret (of the hills), (Crab), Laher, Manjhi-khil, Naiki-Khil, Nij, Roht/Roeth (Panjaun tree). Sada, Khenda Weapon or Sari* and *Rupa* (Silver); *Saren/Soren* (Constellation of pleiades (sorenko) - Barchi/Barchir (Spearman), Hat, Sada, Jogi (*puja* by begging, Lat, Mal, Mundu/Badar (Dense Jungle), Nij, Sankh/Sak (Couch-Shell), Sidup/Siduk Bundle or straw), Turku, Ok (Suffocation with smoke), Jihu, Bitol and Khanda (Buffalo worshipper).

Tudu - Agaria (Charcoal-burner), *Chigi/Chiki (Impale), Dantela, Lat, Manjhi-khil, Naiki-khil, Nij, Loh-Lutur, Sada* and *Sung; Baske/Baski* (Breakfast) - Nij, *Sada*, sure (Cooked along with rice and Mundu; *Besra/Besera* (Hawk) - Bundra, Kahu (Crow), Kara guza (Buffalo. There are two bling brother, from their names this sub-clan begins), Nij, Sada, Sibela (Cultivated fibre yielding plant- *Crotalaria juncea* D.C.), Son, Sing and Loat (Creeper).

Pauria (Pegion), *Chero* (Lizard) and *Bedea* (Sheep)? have no sub-clans.

Earlier all clans enjoyed equal social status. But now Besra and Chero are considered inferior to other clans. Beded is deemed more lower as they could not say who was their ancestral father and is now extinct.

Nuclear and rarely Extended families are their family structure. Santals are patriarchal, Patrilocal and patrilineal in descent.

Birth Ritual

When a *Santal* woman becomes pregnant, the couple observe certain taboos. The husband does not kill animals, nor participate in funeral ceremonies and touch dead bodies. The wife rarely comes out of house in the evening, noon or during eclipse, cross streamlets, nor weep over death or sit on verandah with loose hair.

In each child birth parents observe five days impurity. Specially prepared gruel in liberated to *Sing bonga* and served to all family members. No religious ceremonies are performed in that family before performing *Janam chatiyar* rite. The wetpnurse cuts umbilical cord (*bukaw*) by an arrow-head. The cut out placenta, then buried into a pit, dug by a needle near *doorsil*. Metallic plate is rung to test the new-born's hearing ability and inform neighbours. *Janam chatiyar* is per formed on fifth day and third day for boy and girl birth respectively by sprinkling turmeric, mustard oil and water taken from naeke house over new-born head. *Naeke* scatters *pituli* (Mixture of *atap chal* (Sunned rice powder with water) on feet of the male and female persons standing in rows and distributes bitter - rice to them. Then they dance and *janam chatiyar dah* for identifying whose child he is. Male child attains social right and privilege at the age of four to twelve years by performing *chacho chatiyar*, the initiation ceremony in drinking home-brewn rice-beer handia/hanriya and declared purified and attains manhood for *Jan Baha* Collection of bones). Marriage is not permitted before performing *Chacho chatiyar* nor even cremated his corpse, only buries.

> A *janam chatiyar dah* in their dialect
>
> *Ta kayah racha re dah bunbhukah kan*
>
> Dah bunbhukah kan mana chaole
>
> Buhelen.
>
> Kishuyah racha re dah bunbhukah kan
>
> Dah bunbhukah kan mana choole
>
> Buhelen.
>
> (Whose courtyard is over flown with spring water. The water over-flows the rice).

Naming Ceremony

The male or female child is named after the grand-father or grand mother respectively, if they are alive. If expired, the great grand father or great grand-mother name is assigned or when more issues. First rice giving ceremony is held in even month six or odd month seven for male or female respectively. Maternal uncle first gives rice to the child. Child is allowed to select a coin, earth lump, paddy, pen and doll, indicating its future.

Death Ritual

Santals cremate dead bodies on riven banks. Children and pregnant women only buried. The dead, wrapped in a shroud, is carried by kismen and co-villagers and scatters parched rice and cotton seeds to avoid malignant ghosts. The corpse lays on pyre. Eldest son or in his absence, his brother puts a grass between lips and coin in his hands prior to setting it fire. Son puts a burning wood in the corpse's mouth and others kindle then the pyre. After burning charred skull piece is preserved in an urn to thrown as relic into the Damodar river. A hen is nailed at corner after taken round the pyre thrice. Participants take bath and drink *handia* purchased out of deceased money. On return to the village a sheaf of leaves is hung at doorway of the dead. Participants assemble in the deceased's house to shave and bathe on sixth day in *tel nahan* (oil bath) ceremony and offer earth, oil cake, oil and *sal/sarhul/sarjam* (Shorea robusta Gaertn.) twig to *Marang Budu, pitchu, Haram, Pilchu Budhi*, departed soul and his parents. The village mourns for six days and no religious rite, marriage is performed by the deceased's family. Woman who died without tattooing is considered impure and punished by Jomraja.

In the last ceremony-chandan, a he-goat is sacrificed in the room where death occurred. *Atap chals* are smeared with ozzes blood of a slain goat and are taken by all family members. A ceremonial feast is given signalling resumption of their normal life.

Cultural Trait

Festival (*parav*) is intimately connected with *Sautal's* life and each has two aspects - (1) *Magico-religious* covering sacrifice and offerings to deities for appeasement, and (2) *Recreational* through drinking, dancing and singing. They propitiate invisible supernatural beings through exorcims, magic and religious rites.

Their chief festival is *Sohrae/Sohrai/Goreya/Bandana*, the harvest and cattle-caressing festival, observed in last five days of *pous* (December-January), after crop harvest. Most merriest, *Jog-manjhi* entertains all, cattle are anointed with oil, daubed with vermilion and *handia* to drink. On second day each family head offers sacrifice to *Marang Budu, Orak bonga* and *Abge bonga*. All unmarried persons may indulge in promiscuous intercourse, if commiteted, is punishable less that at other times. Next important is *Baha*, the spring festival and *Sarhul*, both are celebrated in *Falgoon* (February-March) when sal trees blossom, indicating renewal of life. It marks the end of agricultural year, ushering in a new hope, celebrated by chorus, dancing and music. They consume freely any quantity of *handia* and *mahua*. Neake, on behalf of community offers first fruit of *mahua/matkom* (Butter tree-*Bassia latifolia* Roxb). *sal, palas* (parrot tree/Flame of forest-*Butea frondosa* Roxb). Flowers and fowls to benevolent *bongas* at *Jaherthan* and supplicates to protect village. Men and women throw water at each other for washing their malice, hatred and enmity, as purificatory ceremony. Village adverse situation promted public sacrifice of fowls in reverence to tutelary secret *bongas* (Abge bongas), viz., *Bahara, Duarseri, Dharasore, Kethomkudra, Champa-denagarh, Garsinka, Lilachandi, Kudrachandi, Dhanghara, Kudraj, Gosain Era (youngest sister of Moreka/Mareko). Achali, Deswali Pahardana Cando bonga* (the moon). But in *Ashar* (June-July) or in *Agrahayan* (November, December) they worship the benevolent secret household godlings (*Erok/Aerak/Orak bongas*), viz., *Baspahar, Deswali, Sas, Goraya, Sarenawdi/Sarchawdi* and *Thuntatursa*, redeemers of *Santals*. Household head only knows their names. He discloses their names to the eldest son in his death bed. Their supreme god has many appellations - *Thakur/Jau/Jiu Sin/Sing bonga*, the sun god, their creator and preserver. He is invoked reverentially during famine and drought with white fowl sacrifice. Every third year, family head offers goat to Him hoping prosperity. Six chief *bonngas* in *Santal* pantheon are (1) *pargana bonga*, god illness and chief of all *bongas*, (2) *Marang/Maran (Great) Budu* (Mountain), (3) Moreko, the fire god, (4) *Jaher/Jair Era*, a sister of *Moreko*, (5) *Gosain/Gosea Era*, worshipped against sores with white fowl sacrifice, and (6) *Manjhi bonga/Manjhi Haram* spirit of the first founder and village headman and acts as adviser to present headman for village welfare. He is offered rice-beer and two pigeons. *Gosain Era, pargana bong and Manjhi bonga* have supervisory activity over all godlings and restrain from harming men and worshipped in public. *jaherthan*, sacred groove of four harming men and worshipped in public. *Jaherthan*, sacred groove of four *sal* and one *mahua* trees and abode of first five *gongas*, except *manjhi bonga*, who resides at *Manjhithan*. Under each tree a stone represents a deity. Three of the four *sals* must be in row for malignant *Jaher Era*, lady of the groove, *marang Budu* and *Moreko*. Out-rowed fourth *sal* for *pargana bonga. Gosain Era* resides in *mahua* tree. *Manjhi* bonga. Sankrant Sakrat parav is ancestral worship in pous. Home made cakes (Pitha). flattened rice (chira) and molasses (gur) are offered to *Hapramko bongas*, ancestors spirits and to *Marang Budu*. Erok sim is first agricultural festival with winter paddy (erok) sowing in *Ashar*. Fowls are offered to *Marang Budu Jaher Era, Moreko, Turuiko, pargana bonga,*

Gosain Era, Manjhi sima bonga and *Bhare bonga* during winter paddy sowing. *Hariar sim.* offering festival for sprouting seedlings is in *Bhadra* (August-September). *Naeka* offers fowls to *Bapu Thakur* at *jaherthan* for seedlings growth. *Iri-gundhi nawai/nauai,* offering festival of first fruits of *iri(pancicum miliaceum* Linn.) and *gundhi* (Millet-Panicum frumentaceum Roxb). in *Bhadra. Naeke,* on behalf of community, offers ears of millet and fowls to *bongas* at *Jaherthan* with libation of milk praying soil fertility and rain. Then starts *Janthar,* first winter paddy harvest in *Agrahayan. Magh sim* is invoked in *Magh* (January-February) near water and cuts grass indicating end of Santal year when dissolves village organization. After ten days *manjhi* convenes a general meeting and is re-elected as *Manjhi* with other village officials, offering rice-beer to all. Virtually their succession is hereditary, succeeding from father to eldest son. If one desires to resign, he puts rolled sal leaf at the ear of his choice one. *Sima bonga,* boundary god is propitiated twice a year with fowl sacrifice for his appeasement. *Jom sim* and *marang Budu,* each is offered a goat. Every Santal has to perform this sacrifice once in his life on full-moon day in *Falgoon* or *Baisakh* (April-May). In *Mak-more* (cut five) puja three goats and fowls are sacrificed to *Moreko* (has five brothers) to prevent crop failure, epidemic outbreak and calamities. *Karam* festival is celebrated in *Aswin* (September-October), wishing wealth, more progeny and to avert evil spirits, *Moi muri,* for blessing crops and *Basumata,* for land fertility. *Kisan bonga, Naihar bonga* and *Thapna bonga* are exorcised in illness. Hostile curins, *rikas* and bhuts (*Berha pat, Manger pat Budha pahar, pauri pat, Dwarsani pat* and *Baghphut*) are exorcised by magic and offerings. *chata-Pata* and *Jatra-parav* take *Kudam naeke,* religious functionaries propitiate benevolent bongas for blessing and malevolent bongas to avert their calamities and misforture. *Sohrae, Baha. magh sim* (fowl), *Hariar sim, Iri-gundhi nawai* and *Mak-more* are religious festivals. *Santals live* in sylvan surrounding, so their festivals rest heavily on seasonal manifestations.

Special Feature

Santals are aware of their common genesis, distinctive political organization, heritage, traditional socio-cultural traits and language.

They have a close blood tie against operation by *dikus* (outsiders) for security. They have a common feeling during building *bandh* (dyke), elephant expelling form agricultural fields, annual hunting and public festivals.

Political Organization

Santals have orthodox three political organizations (Daman-i-koh).

(1) *Village organization* functions for village disputes, and comprises of the following executives:

(i) *Manjhi* - Village headman, sole guardian and respected spokesman. No public function is done without his consent. In consultation with village elders he fixes dates of festivals and instructs *Godet/Gorait* to inform all. When a new bride is brought into the village he gets one rupee from bride's father as fee for her village membership. In annual hunt he receives the best part of *slains*. Family disputes are reconciled by himself, if fails, convenes village council.

(ii) *Paranik/Paramanik* - Assistant headman, adviser to **Manjhi** and presides over meetings in absence of *Manjhi*.

(iii) *Neake/Naeki* - Village priest to propitiate the gods for village community welfare.

(iv) *Kudam- naeke-* Assistant village priest, worships hills and jungles bad spirits. He propitiates spirits with rice and blood, taken out by scratching his arms.

(v) *Joga/Jag-manjhi* - Guarding moral of the youths, arranges communal feast, carries orders of *Manjhi*, watches the conduct of young boys and girls in *akhra* (Dancing ground) and expels any one for misconduct. If any spinster becomes pregnant in his jurisdiction she is responsible for that offense.

(vi) *Jog-/Jag-paranik* - Assistant to *Paranik*.

(vii) *Godet* - Village messenger.

These officials settle village disputes, crimes and breach of customary social codified laws, and punish the offender with fines at *man jhikhar*. The officials are chosen at the time of village foundation, thereafter re-elected to serve the successive terms follow. They enjoy rent-free lands as remuneration of their services. All villagers are members of the village organization.

(2) *Bungalow* - Several villages collectively form a large federal unit-*bungalow*. It's headman is *parganit* and his assistant, *Desh-manjhi*. They are elected by and from the headmen of the constituent villages. *Bungalow* has two councils:

(i) *Panchayat* - Upper council for critical affairs, and

(ii) Kulidrup - Lower council for petty disputes.

Bungalow deals with inter-village disputes.

(3) *Lo Bir Baisi* - Highest council- the Supreme court sits once in a year in the last night of the annual hunting *(Disom sendra)*, held in *Chaitra* (April) for *sola-anna* (whole) judgement *(pargana bichar)*, presided by *Dehri* (Leader of annual hunt) for re-trial of the unjust and malafide decision taken in the village council or *bungalow*. All participants of the hunt take part and have equal status irrespective of social and economic position. The highest punishment is *bit lah* (Social excommunication) for violating clan exogamy and incest. This is a temporary punishment and can be withdrawn by performing *Jom jati* with fines. But violator of tribal endogamy is not pardoned and is spelled permanently from the community.

❏ ❏ ❏

REFERENCES

Biswas, P.C., (1956): Santals of the Santal Parganas, Bharatiya Adimjati Sevak Sangh, Kingsway, Delhi.

Dalton, Edward Tuite, (1973): *Descriptive Ethnology of Bengal*, (Reprinted), Cosmo Publications, Library Road, Delhi.

Hembrom, Dr. T., (1996): The Santals- Anthropological - Teological Reflections on Santali & Biblical Creation Tradition, Punthi Pustak, Calcutta.

Ray, Ujjwal Kanti, Amal Kumar Das & Sunil Kumar Basu, (1982): *To be with Santals*, Cultural Research Institute, Schedules Castes and Tribes Welfare Department, government of West Bengal, Calcutta.

Risley, H.H., (1981): *The Tribes and Castes of Bengal*, Voll.11, (Reprint) Firma Mukhopadhyay, Calcutta.

❏ ❏ ❏